This book charts the aspirations of women towards priesthood and the resistance that they have encountered. It brings together, in one place for the first time, a record of the documents and debates on this issue over the last two hundred years in the English Methodist Church, the Church of England, and the Roman Catholic Church. In a lively, yet sensitive, overview the author interprets these debates at a number of levels, and draws on sociology, history, biblical studies, theology and psychoanalysis. The patriarchalisation of ecclesial structures, and its subsequent theological and christological legitimation, emerges as a recurring pattern in her presentation. Dr Field-Bibb therefore offers a feminist analysis of the resistance to the ordination of women in an attempt to break down what she sees as a false consciousness propagated by subversive symbols.

WOMEN TOWARDS PRIESTHOOD

WOMEN TOWARDS PRIESTHOOD

MINISTERIAL POLITICS AND FEMINIST PRAXIS

Jacqueline Field-Bibb

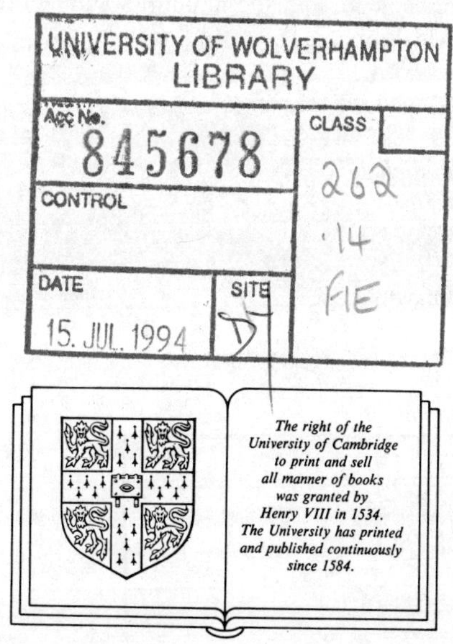

CAMBRIDGE UNIVERSITY PRESS
Cambridge
New York Port Chester
Melbourne Sydney

Published by the Press Syndicate of the University of Cambridge
The Pitt Building, Trumpington Street, Cambridge CB2 1RP
40 West 20th Street, New York, NY 10011, USA
10 Stamford Road, Oakleigh, Melbourne 3166, Australia

First published 1991

Printed in Great Britain at the University Press, Cambridge

British Library cataloguing in publication data

Field-Bibb, Jacqueline
Women towards priesthood: ministerial politics and feminist praxis.
1. Christian church. Women's ministry
I. Title
262.14

Library of Congress cataloguing in publication data

Field-Bibb, Jacqueline
Women towards priesthood: ministerial politics and feminist praxis/Jacqueline Field-Bibb.
p. cm.
Includes bibliographical references.
ISBN 0–521–39783–7
1. Ordination of women. I. Title
BV676.F54 1991
262′.14–dc20 90–34002 CIP

ISBN 0 521 39283 7 hardback

CE

CONTENTS

ABBREVIATIONS

ACC	Anglican Consultative Council
ACC	*Anglican Consultative Council: Report of Proceedings*
ACCM	Advisory Council for the Church's Ministry
ARCIC	Anglican–Roman Catholic International Commission
CA	*Church Assembly: Report of Proceedings*
C.A.	*Conference Agenda*
CC(C)/(Y)	*Chronicle of Convocation (Canterbury)/(York)*
CWMC	Council for Women's Ministry in the Church
GS	*General Synod: Report of Proceedings*
ICEL	International Commission on English in the Liturgy
IJPA	*International Journal of Psycho-Analysis*
LC	*Lambeth Conference: Report of Proceedings*
MOW19	*The Ministry of Women* (1919)
MOW35	*The Ministry of Women* (1935)
MR	*Methodist Recorder*
NPC	National Pastoral Congress
OR	*L'Osservatore Romano*
OWP	*The Ordination of Women to the Priesthood* (1972, GS 104), also known as the 'Howard Report'
OWP(S)	*The Ordination of Women: A Supplement to the Consultative Document GS 104* (1978, GS Misc. 88)
PECUSA	Protestant Episcopal Church in the USA
PFL	*Pelican Freud Library*
SE	*Standard Edition of the Complete Psychological Works of Sigmund Freud*
WCC	World Council of Churches
WHO	*Women and Holy Orders* (1966)

Numbers in brackets in the text normally indicate page references to the document currently under discussion. Freudian references are to *PFL*.

Lower case is normally preferred throughout. The principal decision-making bodies of churches are capitalised, as are committees sometimes identified by their initials. A few words appear capitalised and in lower case according to context and emphasis. Quotations and the spelling of names normally follow the document currently under discussion.

Summaries of longer reports and of other items are indented in case the reader should wish to by-pass them on a particular reading.

ACKNOWLEDGEMENTS

I gratefully acknowledge a number of most useful and encouraging meetings with Joseph Laishley of Heythrop College from the earliest stages of this project until it reached its present form.

I appreciated David Martin's help as external PhD advisor and, following his departure for the USA, the sociological advice of Betty Scharf. I am grateful to Gregory van der Kleij for reading the psychoanalytic sections and for his encouragement throughout.

I am also grateful to Oliver Beckerlegge for putting me on the track of the early Methodist material and to William Leary for checking some of those references; to Pauline Webb for lending me some crucial personal notes; to Jean Robinson and Kenneth Greet for making available material at Central Hall; to David Samways of the *Methodist Recorder* for undertaking large amounts of photocopying; to Daphne Frazer and Mary Tanner for arranging access to material at Church House and to Brenda Hough for her help in the archives there; to Ann Scott for her courses on psychoanalysis and female identity; to the Riminis for a spell on their computer; and to others who have been of help, some of whom are mentioned in the reference material.

INTRODUCTION

'Woman, believe me, the hour is coming when neither on this mountain nor in Jerusalem will you worship' are significant among the words recorded as part of an exchange between the woman of Samaria and the Johannine Jesus. In them religion and its liturgical celebration are delocalised and deinstitutionalised. As women have sought subsequently to harmonise with the life and praxis of Jesus and his community of disciples, the 'how' to implement this praxis has often led towards the Christian institutions which have emerged and thence towards institutionalised roles which have appeared and developed and claimed to provide the focus and locus of this praxis. Yet the history of this movement on the part of women is a history of recurring rebuttals ranging from the early Christian expansion to contemporary times. In the period covered by this book, which begins with the female itinerant preachers of seceded Methodist connexions, an ideological factor emerged which, on one level at least, aided this impetus of women. As the concept of 'equality' jostled for a place in eighteenth-century thought patterns, the idea of its application to women and ministry had a greater chance of success than hitherto. This was because of the relationship between ecclesial institution and state whereby dominant ideologies tend to be internalised by Christian institutions.

Yet the tension between the words of Jesus in John 4 and institutionalised Christianity remains. This book traces the movement of women towards ministry under the banner of equality, whether consciously held or not. It looks at the storms which have raged around the issue and asks 'Why the resistance?' and 'Why this direction of women's impetus in the light of the Johannine exchange?'

The quest for answers to both these questions leads first to the primary sources: the official documents of selected churches. It is within these official records that institutional resistance together with its result are recorded. Part One consists of summaries of all the relevant documentation in each church so that the momentum of the issue is allowed to emerge from within. The advantages of this approach outweigh the disadvantages (for example the non-inclusion of proposers' arguments in the non-democratic churches) as the documents portray the vicissitudes of institutional thinking and policy. Likewise, I have not edited out the repetitious strategies of committees – for example in the Methodist material of the 1920s – in order to give the reader the full flavour of the frustrating procedural manoeuvring aimed at subverting the moves of women towards ministry.

I chose the Church of England as the axis for this presentation partly because of its position as the Established Church of this country, and mainly because of the wealth of theological documentation produced by its governing bodies. The arguments and positions of two wings within this church – the Liberal Protestant and the Anglo-Catholic – are to some extent institutionalised in the positions of the Methodist and Roman Catholic Churches respectively. I therefore placed their documentation on either side of the Church of England to illustrate how institutional decisions are affected by each position when its opposite is not operative to any appreciable extent. The churches appear in the order in which the issue emerged: first the Methodist Church, then the Church of England, followed by the Roman Catholic Church. This order is also historically (and hence ecumenically) appropriate as the Methodist Church seceded from the Church of England and the Church of England from the Roman Catholic Church. The focus is on England throughout. However, the reader may be glad to know that this has not essentially restricted the interpretation as similar patterns seem to emerge in other countries and churches. Some other (predominantly American) material can be found in Appendix A.

Part Two is about the power relations in which the aspiration and resistance discovered in Part One are grounded. In Section One the social undercurrents of the three periods into which the documentation falls are examined for clues to elucidate the ebb and flow of argument, movement and resistance. Social (marriage-related) and ecumenical (union-related) considerations are of particular interest. Section Two uncovers the procedural strategies aimed at frustrating the movement of women towards ministry. The third section follows the movement of biblical interpretation towards the traditional and the symbolic, which is particularly oppressive to women, and then returns to the social dimension in the exemplary model of critical feminist theology selected to stand against the churches' interpretation. This throws light on the social pressures and choices leading to the patriarchalisation of the early Christian movement, but not on the sustained resistance nor the recurring process whereby the impetus of women is assimilated and defused by the dominant power structures when it can no longer simply be repressed. Finally I consider the unconscious forces at work which give rise to such aspirations, reactions and associated symbols. I suggest 'answers' lie in the unconscious politics which forge a 'false' relationship between self identity, sexuality and institution.

PART ONE

DOCUMENTATION

SECTION ONE

THE METHODIST CHURCH IN ENGLAND

It was never John Wesley's intention that his 'conversion' on 24 May 1738 should lead to a secession from the Established Church. His aim was its revitalisation. In Bristol in 1742 the members of the nascent organisation decided to divide themselves into classes of about twelve and to appoint leaders to be responsible for oversight and to receive class money.[1] This pattern was adopted generally and evolved into a closely knit organisation with strong central government. A year after the Bristol meeting, Conference met – originally as a consultative but soon as a governmental body. In 1746 circuits coordinated neighbourhood meetings, and eventually quarterly and district meetings emerged. Discipline was deeply rooted. In Newcastle in 1743 Wesley read the rules, and excluded sixty-four members for a variety of offences.[2]

Within Wesleyanism from the first it was accepted that women could testify. Many were appointed as class-leaders. Wesley gave vague approval to short exhortations by women, but only slowly came to endorse their preaching[3] 'in extraordinary cases'. Their help in covering the districts reminded him of deaconesses of early Christianity.[4] At his death there were a number of women local preachers, but the Conference resolutions of 1803, and particularly of 1835, discouraged the practice, which eventually disappeared.

Wesley remained a Tory, and it was always his intention to remain within the Church of England. Yet because his ministry reached out to the growing industrial population, which was largely outside the influence of Anglican clergy and had few dealings with them, it is not surprising that the movement eventually became a separate denomination. In America his followers organised as a church in 1784, but in England Wesley prevented a formal separation. After his death in 1791 the rift with the Church of England gradually widened. The most decisive separation occurred in 1795.

Meanwhile the discipline within Wesleyanism ensured the relative worldly success of many of its adherents, and, as Wesleyanism became more established, secessions occurred, mainly to recapture the spirit of early Methodism, and drawing inspiration from the Friends. The catalysts were the vexed issues of women preachers and non-clerical leadership – although Wesley trained preachers and class-leaders he refused to give them a place in constitutional government and one may note that as late as the 1970s it was the ministerial session that had legally to take the final decision on women ministers. The Methodist New Connexion was the first to secede in 1797. The Camp Meeting Methodists led by Hugh Bourne joined with the Clowesites to form the Primitive Methodists in 1811; William O'Bryan's Bible Christians emerged in 1815. The Protestant Methodists (1827) joined the Wesleyan Methodist Association (1836), who in turn united with the main body of Wesleyan Reformers (1850) as the United Methodist Free Churches (1857). Then the Methodist New Connexion, the United Methodist Free Churches, and the Bible Christians came together as the United Methodist Church (1907), and this church in turn reunited with the Wesleyan Methodists and the Primitive Methodists to form the Methodist Church (1932). In the early years the question of female ministry appears in the Conference documentation of the Wesleyan Methodists, the Bible Christians and the Primitive Methodists.

The meetings of the seceded connexions took place initially in houses and barns until chapels could be built. The Bible Christians evolved from a gathering at Lake Farmhouse in Devon (the home of the Thorne family) on 9 October 1815. Twenty-two people enrolled in a class proposed by William O'Bryan. This movement was to spread from North Devon to Canada, Prince Edward Island, Australia, New Zealand and China.[5] The first quarterly meeting was held in January 1816 and already a membership of 237 was recorded, and the following year the number had risen to 920,[6] and the first chapel was built. The first annual Conference was held at Baddash, Launceston, in 1819, under the presidency of William O'Bryan.

Bible Christian records give the most detailed information on women preachers, and at this first Conference the subject of female preachers was on the agenda. Women were listed as female itinerants. They were never stationed with men under their authority, having the status, rather, of helpers. Their names were not advertised prior to a meeting, but simply the information that 'a female' was to preach.[7] Nevertheless, it was women, namely Mary Ann Werrey, Mary Toms and Catherine Reed, who pioneered the movement in the Scilly Islands, in the Isle of Wight, in Guernsey and Jersey, in Northumberland and in London. During Mary Ann Werrey's mission to Northumberland she came into conflict with William Mason, her superintendent, and the words recorded in 1825, 'Mary Ann Werrey is desisted',[8] are possibly an indication of the imbalance of power between women and men in the organisation.

At this same Conference problems concerning leadership began to emerge. A form of deed for enrolling chapels was drawn up, according O'Bryan the sole authority for appointing preachers. 'Some of the Brethren considered for one man to be invested with such unlimited authority was not according to scriptural order, and consequently became dissatisfied.' The following year an amended deed was sought as discontent had grown:

> The expression of these sentiments was not agreeable to the views of the Founder of the Connexion, who intended in this respect to copy the example of Mr. Wesley, in regard to the Methodist Connexion. As may be naturally supposed, discussions on this subject became exceedingly painful. Mr. O'Bryan candidly expressed his intention of managing the affairs of the Connexion on the principle that, if all the Conference were opposed to his views, his single vote was to determine every case.

Neither did he wish the 'Lay brethren' to vote at Conference, but agreed when it was put to him that it was futile for them to travel long distances to be present if they were not allowed to vote. At the 1827 Conference O'Bryan asked his critics to draw up a paper showing how they wished connexional affairs to be managed. The six-point document vested authority in the Conference, with O'Bryan as president, 'no moral obstacle prevent', and allowing him choice of circuit. This was signed 'by all present – twenty Itinerant Brethren, and three Representatives'. The same year a proposal to drop the word 'Arminian' in the connexion's name was not voted on when O'Bryan expressed his opposition. At the tenth Conference, 'The agitation respecting the authority claimed by Mr. O'Bryan was greater than it had hitherto been, and matters occurred which induced him to relinquish the Presidential chair for this Conference.' Over these difficulties, James Thorne draws a decent veil, but during this Conference the word 'Arminian' was dropped. In 1829 O'Bryan left the connexion temporarily and the Conference permanently, the leadership position being taken eventually by Thorne.[9]

The tension between authoritarian and democratic tendencies was never fully resolved in the seceded connexions. This perhaps was not surprising at a time when the concept of 'equality' was struggling for a place in contemporary thought patterns. Women were inspired to take their place among the itinerant preachers, yet within the structures the pursuit of equality was effectively about power-sharing among the brethren. Paradoxically, it was the authoritarian stance of Wesley and of O'Bryan in their respective connexions that facilitated the ministry of women. When the influence of each was no longer effective, although the women fought a rearguard action their acceptance as preachers and the numbers of female itinerant preachers respectively declined.

I THE FIRST PERIOD: THREE NINETEENTH-CENTURY CONNEXIONS WITH FEMALE PREACHERS: TOWARDS INSTITUTIONALISATION

1.1 Wesleyan Methodism from 1744: 'an extraordinary call'

The first Wesleyan Conference took place in 1744, but John Wesley's personal influence with the connexion remained dominant. Consequently, during the second half of the eighteenth century, his changing attitude towards women's preaching continued to be of particular importance.

This can be traced through his correspondence.[10] On 14 February 1761 in a letter to Sarah Crosby he wrote concerning her preaching:

> Hitherto I think you have not gone too far; you could not well do less I apprehend, all you can do more is when you meet again, to tell them simply 'you lay me under a great difficulty; the Methodists do not allow of women Preachers; neither do I take upon me any such character, but I just nakedly tell you what is in my heart.' This will in great a measure obviate the grand objection, and prepare for John Hampson's coming.[11]

Then Mary Bosanquet wrote to him in 1771 asking for 'advice and direction' in connection with objections levelled against her ministry arising mainly out of 1 Timothy 2: 12 and 1 Corinthians 14: 34, the final one being: 'But all these were extraordinary calls; surely you will not say, yours is an extraordinary call? Answer. If I did not believe so, I would not act in an extraordinary manner.'[12] Wesley replied on 13 June:

I THINK the strength of the cause rests there, in your having *an extraordinary* call; so I am persuaded has every one of our lay-preachers; otherwise I could not countenance his preaching at all. It is plain to me that the work of God termed Methodism, is an *extraordinary* dispensation of HIS providence. Therefore I do not wonder, if several things occur therein, which do not fall under the ordinary rules of discipline. St Paul's ordinary rule was, *'I permit not a woman to speak in the congregation,'* yet in *extraordinary* cases, he made a few exceptions; at Corinth in particular.[13]

Then on 2 December 1777 he wrote to Sarah Crosby: 'The difference between us and the Quakers in this respect is manifest. They flatly deny the rule itself, although it stands clear in the Bible. We allow the rule; only we believe it admits of some exceptions. At present I know of those, and no more, in the whole Methodist Connexion.'[14] However, the extraordinary seemingly was becoming too ordinary, and on 25 March 1780 Wesley sent a message to John Peacock: 'I desire Mr. Peacock to put a final stop to the preaching of women in his circuit. If it were suffered, it would grow, and we know not where it would end.'[15]

Wesley was instrumental in giving official endorsement to the 'extraordinary' call of Sarah Mallet, who noted:

But the voice of the people was not the voice of some preachers. But Mr. Wesley soon made this easy by sending me a note from the Conference, by Mr. Joseph Harper, who was that year appointed for Norwich. The note was as follows: *'We give the right hand of fellowship to Sarah Mallet, and have no objection to her being a preacher in our connexion, so long as she preaches the Methodist doctrines, and attends to our discipline.'* This was by order of Mr. Wesley and the Conference of 1787 (Manchester.) From that day to this I have been but little opposed by preachers.[16]

Wesley commented on 15 December 1788, 'IT gives me pleasure to hear, that prejudice dies away, and our Preachers behave in a friendly manner.'[17]

Not all preachers' ideas developed in the wake of Wesley's, and opinion remained divided. Mary Bosanquet relates how, at one Leeds Conference . . . several preachers talked to Mr. Wesley against women's preaching, (as there were then several female preachers in the connexion,) some however spoke in favour of it. Mr. Wesley spoke in favour of it in particular cases. *Thomas Mitchell*, a venerable man, got up and said to those that opposed, *'I know not what you would do with[out] the good women, for all the fish they catch, they put it into our net.'*[18]

The women made varying concessions. Sarah Crosby never went into the pulpit, but always spoke from the steps; Ann Lutton preached to women only; in Mary Bosanquet's journal appears:

Again, they say, why do you not give out, I am to preach? Why call it a meeting? I answer, because that suits my design best. First, it is less ostentatious; Secondly, it leaves me at liberty to speak more or less as I feel myself led; Thirdly, it gives less offence to those who watch for it. Others object, 'Why yours is a Quakers' call? why then, do you not join them at once? I answer, though I believe the Quakers have still a good deal of God among them, yet, I think the spirit of the Lord is more at work among the Methodists; and while I see this, though they were to toss me about as a foot-ball, I would stick to them as a leech. Besides, *I do nothing but what Mr. Wesley approves.*[19]

After Wesley's death opposition to women's preaching hardened. His successor, Jabez Bunting, was an uncompromising opponent, describing an 'extraordinary call' as 'every fanatic's plea'. As editor of the *Methodist Magazine* he omitted references to preaching in the published lives of women, the biographical notice on Dinah Thomas in 1821 being a case in point.[20] Moreover, an account of the life of Elizabeth Collett, written by a minister and submitted by her son, was returned by the editor unpublished 'lest it should be a precedent to young females in the Connexion, who are ready to step into the work'.[21] A letter from her did appear in June 1794, but was accredited to 'Mr' rather than 'Mrs E. C.'[22]

As a counter-move, in 1825 and 1828 Zechariah Taft published in two volumes his *Biographical Sketches of the Lives and Public Ministry of Various Holy Women*. In a preface to these seventy-eight lives he wrote that great efforts had been made to preserve the memory of male preachers,

while many *females*, whose praise was in all the churches while they lived, have been suffered to drop into oblivion, and their preeminent labours, and success in the conversion of souls to remain as destitute of any public record, as though they had never existed; or if any account of their exemplary piety is preserved, their public labours are either suppressed, or passed over in silence. It is very easy to account for this, the great majority of Biographers and Editors of Magazines, are enemies to female preaching, so that we have very little concerning their labours, except what is found among the *Friends*, or people called Quakers (1: i).

To open the contemporary case for women preaching he cited Wesley, who had argued that anyone instrumental in the conversion of sinners was an instrument of God, even though he were a layman. This rule, argued Taft, should apply to women too, and he quoted Wesley's own retort on this score: 'Because ... God owns them in the conversion of sinners, and who am I that I should withstand God' (1: iii). The argument about women addressing mixed congregations amounted 'to nothing in a country where they always mix in society, and where females are allowed to address companies of men and women in the public theatres, markets, fields, and shops; ... surely, they may be allowed to address them, upon the subjects which regard the soul, and eternity' (1: iii–iv). Mr Wesley, he pointed out, did not so much as hint that it was improper for women to address men in his notes on 1 Corinthians 14: 34–35, and Taft drew attention to the development of Wesley's views between the notes of 1753 and his subsequent letters to women preachers. Mrs Fletcher (previously Mary Bosanquet), who asserted that she did nothing but what Mr Wesley approved, 'did [not] confine her ministry to her own sex, ... *nay* she was a *minister to ministers*; for several Clergymen attended her ministry, in the Vicarage barn, at Madeley, on Monday evenings' (1: v).

But the women in the Methodist Connexion 'have not had that encouragement which they ought to have had, and which they would have had if Mr. Wesley had still been living' (1: v). 'Many, very many, have suffered a *martyrdom* of conflicting passions, arising from a *sense of their duty to God* on the one hand, *and of opposition from men* on the other' (1: v).[23] Some had left to join other connexions. Taft returned to this theme again in the preface to volume 2:

And when it is remembered that no female preaches for hire; but that they have to enter into this field of labour, through much opposition from the counter-workings of their own mind, and the unchristian insinuations, and discountenance of hostile spirits; it is not to be wondered at that many, perhaps most of those that have not had the above mentioned overwhelming convictions have shrunk from the cross and buried the talent which God gave them for public usefulness (2: ix–x).

But elsewhere he added a rider:

I believe the ordinary call of God to the ministry is to men, and the extraordinary call to females. But in this extraordinary call I do not consider *any* female strictly and fully called to the *pastoral office*; or to be the regular pastor of the Church of Christ, but I do believe that the Lord calls some females to be fellow-labourers with the *pastors*, or *helpers*, or as we should call them *Local Preachers*, and I think we should *help*, or encourage those women, who thus help us in the Gospel (I: vi).

Taft had married one such woman, Mary Barritt, in 1802, and she had been the catalyst for the controversy culminating in the Wesleyan Conference resolution of 1803:

Q. 19. Should women be permitted to preach among us?
A. We are of opinion that, in general, they ought not.
1. Because a vast majority of our people are opposed to it.
2. Because their preaching does not at all seem necessary, there being a sufficiency of Preachers, whom God has accredited, to supply all the places in our connexion with regular preaching. But if any woman among us thinks she has an extraordinary call from God to speak in public, (and we are sure it must be an *extraordinary* call that can authorise it,) we are of opinion she should, in general, address her *own sex*, and *those only*. And, upon this condition alone, should any woman be permitted to preach in any part of our connexion; and, when so permitted, it should be under the following regulations: 1. They shall not preach in the Circuit where they reside, until they have obtained the approbation of the Superintendent and a Quarterly-Meeting. 2. Before they go into any other Circuit to preach, they shall have a *written* invitation from the Superintendent of such Circuit, and a recommendatory note from the Superintendent of their own circuit.[24]

This was revised in 1910 but was never repealed. It remained the official Wesleyan Methodist position until the Methodist union of 1932.

Following this resolution many women defied the law, although their names never appeared in official listings. Mary Barritt preached where an asterisk was marked on her husband's preaching plan, and this caused a complaint to be made to the 1833 Conference. Bunting alluded with scorn to the device, but John Pawson supported her preaching and recommended her employment for special services.[25] In 1835 Conference expressed its strong disapproval of female preaching.[26]

1.2 The Bible Christians and the Primitive Methodists: 'our female preachers'

Meanwhile, the orientation of Wesleyan Methodism under Jabez Bunting proved incompatible with the ministry of William O'Bryan in Cornwall and Hugh Bourne in Staffordshire, both of whom, simultaneously and independently, decided to employ women preachers in their seceded connexions.

Hugh Bourne's interest in the subject can be traced to his contacts with the Quakers.[27] He read their books in 1799, and met the Quaker Methodists of Warrington at the first camp meeting at Mow Cop in May 1807. Later in the same year he attended their annual meeting at Macclesfield and accepted an invitation to preach in their societies at Warrington and Risley.[28] At their second annual meeting the matter of female preaching was discussed, and Bourne was asked to prepare answers to certain questions that had arisen. The result was a pamphlet, *Notes on the Ministry of Women*, published in 1808,[29] the same year that he was expelled from the Wesleyan Methodist Connexion.

Bourne prefaced this basically scriptural pamphlet by pointing out that he had not hitherto greatly reflected on the controversy because he and his associates did not think it their duty to hinder those whose preaching had proved effective. 'Instead of stopping to reason about various things, we find it best to be pressing on.'[30] As indeed he did, enlisting the help of Mrs Dunnell, who, though not a Primitive Methodist, was the first woman itinerant to work under his supervision.

Thirteen years later in the *Primitive Methodist Magazine* for 1821 an account 'On the Rise of Female Preachers in the Connexion which originated in Cornwall' appeared. Referring to the prophecy of Joel 2: 28–9 as applied to Acts 2: 17–18 Bourne wrote:

> a remarkable coincidence has taken place in our connexion, and in the connexion which arose in Cornwall. It is really surprizing, that the two connexions, without any knowledge of each other, should each, nearly at the same time, be led in the same way, as it respects the ministry of women. Both connexions employed women as exhorters, and as local and travelling preachers.
>
> When the two connexions became acquainted with each other, and found so striking a similarity in their proceedings with regard to Female Preachers, it became a matter of desire to know by what steps each connexion had been led into the measure. (162)

There follows a letter from William O'Bryan of the Bible Christians to Hugh and James Bourne. In the *Minutes* of the 1821 Primitive Methodist Conference the book committee were put at liberty 'to receive matter from W. O'Bryan, and to insert in the magazine, from time to time, such of it as they may think proper',[31] and this letter was part of this correspondence between the two connexions.

In it William O'Bryan referred to a letter from Hugh Bourne, who had 'desired me to give some account of the rise of our Female Preachers' (162). He described how, in 1801, when he had begun to speak in public, his decision to remain single had been reversed because of certain ministerial difficulties which had driven him to look for 'a wife like-minded with myself' (163). In the event, Catherine O'Bryan became 'our first Woman Preacher' (167). Then,

> In October, 1810, a separation took place between me and my old friends, the Methodists. I was again left nearly alone, and under far more trying circumstances than at my first out-set; for then, from the preachers I had no opposition, but rather a little help; but now they opposed me, might and main, and got some of the local preachers to join herein also. (164)

But his preaching invitations had multiplied, his wife also being very active, and then in 1815 he came across 'a young woman among the Methodists, ... Elizabeth Dart, [who] attended the preaching, and soon all the society where she belonged, joining with me, she felt drawn out to speak for God in public, and has been well received and rendered useful' (165). Soon after he had heard that a Johannah Brooks had spoken 'and the clergyman had her put out of church'. 'I tolerably well knew, what encouragement she was likely to have from dissenting churches; as well as from what is called the Church of England.' When he made contact with her, she joined him. He concluded his letter: 'I could not well give you a view of the subject, or state the rise of our Female Preachers among us, in a less compass, and for the sake of brevity have omitted much, worthy of remark, which may come forward another time' (166).

1.2.1 The Bible Christians

In the *Minutes* of the first Conference of the Bible Christians,[32] four replies to questions on the subject of female ministry are recorded. The first stressed that a woman could be called to *'Speak to edification, and exhortation, and comfort'*. This was based on the prophecy of Joel 2: 28–9 and applied to Acts 2: 17–18:

We believe, we ought to praise God, that the kingdom of darkness is shaken, and the kingdom of the Redeemer is enlarged, *whoever* be the instruments God is pleased to use; and that we dare not be so insolent, as to dictate to HIM, who HE shall employ, to accomplish HIS gracious purposes.

The next three questions dealt with objections to women's preaching:

we are sorry on the part of the gainsayers, that they have so far committed themselves, as to oppose it without ever producing an argument, (worth being called an argument) against it. We have seen a *little* tract or hand bill, printed at Helston, and sold by a Mr. H-e; signed *Methodious* [*sic*] most probably his own compiling; which is *every way* so *little*, that we thought it beneath our notice, to answer it in any other way, than by silent contempt; as the common sense of the reader should be a sufficient reply.[33]

Next, 1 Corinthians 14: 34,35 was considered as an objection first to women preaching, then to 'giving pious instruction'. The former was dismissed,

For in all the Churches that we have any knowledge of, they allow their Women, either to sing, or pray, or instruct the Church; yea in some places they permit them to exercise in ALL these, and yet say, *Women ought to keep silence in the Churches!!!* What a heap of inconsistences!!!

and the latter was equally swiftly demolished: 'Paul was too *pious*, to oppose *piety*, and too *wise*, to *oppose himself*; which he must have done, if he had opposed pious Women speaking on pious subjects, to the edification of others.'

In these 1819 *Minutes* Elizabeth Dart headed a list of 14 female itinerants, as opposed to 16 males. The number of women listed annually rose steadily to 27 (possibly 28 – see Appendix B) in 1825–7. Some figures noted by Thorne[34] over this first decade are of interest. In 1820 there were 6 men in full connexion with 19 on trial and 19 women, with the 44 spread over 17 stations. In 1821 there were 27 men and 18 women, both spread over 18 stations. In that year an Itinerant Preachers' Annuitant Society was established, which by Conference of 1864 had paid out to widows and superannuated preachers the sum of £3,853.7s.6d. In 1822 there were 32 men and 18 women, the 50 covering 21 stations. In 1823 numbers were 35 men and 21 women, with an overall total of 5,050 'in Church-fellowship'. In 1824 there were 47 men and 21 women who together covered 30 stations, with 6,200 'in Church-fellowship'. In

1825 numbers were 51 men and 27 women; due to some imperfect returns membership was only estimated to be 6,369. In 1826 there were 56 men and 27 women with membership recorded at 6,433. In 1827 62 men and 27 women itinerant preachers were recorded, with 8,054 in church-fellowship. In 1828 there were 59 men and 22 women with a recorded membership of 7,845.

After the 1825–7 peak, the number of female itinerants gradually decreased, reaching single figures in 1842 (6 with 1 on trial). Subsequently only 10 new names appeared, mainly in 2 small clusters, following 2 single new recruits. Martha Hutchings was listed once in 1846. In 1851 Susanna Hobbs was recorded as having travelled for one year because, although recommended by the Faversham quarterly meeting and the London district meeting, it had been feared 'her health was not equal to the work' and in fact she appeared for the last time in 1853; Mary Jullif put in a brief appearance on trial in 1855. Then in 1861 Elizabeth Dymond and Elizabeth Jollow joined Sarah Hutchings, who had been listed the two previous years, and after Elizabeth Dymond's last appearance in 1869, no female itinerant was listed in active work for over twenty years. Finally, the last four women appeared between 1890 and 1907, 1894 being the year of the final cluster of entries.

A total of seventy-five female preachers appeared between 1819 and 1907. Catherine Harris travelled the longest (1825–53), and remained in the *Minutes* until 1873 when her name was dropped from the list, possibly 'because there was no other "female preacher" and there seemed to be no point in listing an elderly lady who had long been a supernumerary'.[35] Eighteen were listed for ten or more years: Elizabeth Dart, Patience Bickle, Ann Cory and Susan Baulch from among the (first) 1819 entries, and Lillie Edwards from among the (final) 1894 entries. Thirty-one were noted in the *Minutes* for three years or less, thirteen being listed once only.[36] The names of all Bible Christian female itinerants, together with their travelling dates, are listed in Appendix B.

The hard conditions the preachers encountered were reflected in the *Minutes*, and must account to some extent for the high drop-out rate. Concern about the preachers' health is revealing. 1820: 'Let all, both male and female; take care of their health; beware of taking too long journies, and of remaining with wet clothes on; and also, beware of going out after preaching at night; and of sleeping in damp beds,* *it being so very injurious to health*', with the note: '*Our friends who lodge the preachers, are earnestly requested to pay particular attention to this, especially in winter, as otherwise it may possibly cost the preacher his life!' (13). After a question concerning '*worn out preachers*', the issue was raised of the sisters, 'should they be unable to travel, through indisposition of body', to which was given the reply: 'We agree that when any of them shall be so disabled, they shall (if needed) be entituled to receive the same support, as when they travelled; so long as they continue to maintain a becoming character, and remain single; or if married to a travelling preacher' (7). 1823: *'It is desired to be remembered, that our Sisters are not expected to preach any more than* TWICE ON *Sundays'* (7). 1825: women preachers were admitted as members to the preachers' fund (to which they had to subscribe ten shillings annually, at Conference). 1839: The hardships had curbed the progress of Margaret Pinwill, who remained on trial a fourth year 'on account of the delicate state of her health' (6). 1851: Health was also a problem for Susan(na) Hobbs, as noted above. Obituaries occurred in the *Minutes* for three women who died in active service: Margaret Adams (1819–22); Ann Potter (1825–35); and Jane Gardiner (1838–41).[37]

An eye was kept on the general conduct of itinerants. In 1820 appeared:

> Our sisters who travel as helpers, should keep their own place, be watchful, always neat, plain, and clean, discreet, humble, grave as mothers in Israel; diligent according to their sex, as well as our brethren, being as much as they can, their own servants, and helps to the families where they go: and when they leave their room in the morning, leave everything in its proper place. (12)

Seemingly some failed to take due note, because Pyke (1941) notes that in 1825 appeared: 'Q. Are our preaching women so plain in dress as formerly? A. Some of them are not. Q. What can be done to prevent this evil? A. Let them be admonished, and if they will not reform, let them travel no longer' (30). In 1820 there was a word of advice, 'to be very careful in choosing partners' in marriage. 'We recommend to our Itinerant brethren, who intend to marry, to choose their partners from among our sisters, who have dedicated themselves to the service of God, by coming forward as travelling preachers: and we do agree that those preachers who so marry, shall be entituled to the first support from the connexion'(7).

In 1820 single female itinerants were allocated £1.10s. a quarter as opposed to £3 for a single man, although in 1830 and 1831 there was the expectation that women should 'give up ten shillings of their salaries the ensuing year', to improve the finances of the connexion. The women's allocation was raised in 1837 to £1.15s. a quarter, and it was decided that all single preachers should 'bear their own expenses for medicine and medical attendance except in cases where the Doctor's bills exceed the sum of ten shillings per year'.[38]

In the peak year of 1827 concern was expressed that some had been sent out too early to travel, and the reply was given: 'In the case of taking out females, let the Assistant preacher converse with them closely, on the nature and importance of the work, and let them also be proposed at a quarterly meeting, and let none be sent out without the sanction of the Quarterly meeting' (11). The following year a trial period of three years was set.[39] The women were never stationed so that male preachers were under their authority but some, such as Elizabeth Gay in 1819 and in later years Eliza Giles and Lillie Edwards, were stationed alone yet with the instruction 'to labour under the direction of the Superintendent of the District'.[40] The regulations governing entry were substantially unchanged in 1892 but by 1894 and 1896 conditions noted in the *Digest of Rules* (1897–1907) were more demanding. At the end of a course of study an examination by the superintendent of the district was required, and 'she must have had a certificate from the Quarterly Meeting of each Station on which she has laboured during her probation, as to her Christian character, acceptability as a speaker, and general fitness for the work, and produce a medical certificate as to health' (50–1). There followed the stipulation that 10s. per quarter had to be paid into a fund. Finally there was a note that female preachers 'are expected to attend the District Meetings and take part in the business, without the power of voting'.

In 1894 (the year the regulations were revised) occurs the final cluster of four women preachers in the general Conference records. That year Eliza Giles (1890–8) was already in full connexion; Lilly L. Oram resigned after one year, and Annie E. Carkeek became a connexional evangelist. It is the fourth, Lillie Edwards, who is of particular interest, as the union between the Bible Christians, the United Methodist Free Churches and the Methodist New Connexion terminated her ministry as an itinerant preacher in 1907. An extract from the report of the examining committee reads:

xxvi. – We adopt the following report of the Committee re. Miss Edwards, and endorse the arrangement made:- In view of the anomalous position that Miss Edwards would occupy in the United Church, the Sub-Committee has entered into an agreement with her that she retire from the ministry, and that she be paid the sum of £135 as a full and satisfactory discharge of all our Connexional liabilities to her, and that henceforth she shall have no further claim upon the Female Preachers' Fund. We recommend the Conference to appoint Miss Edwards to the Hastings Mission as a special agent for the ensuing year. We desire to place on record our appreciation of the services of Miss Edwards in our ministry during the past thirteen years. In the discharge of her various duties she has exercised conspicuous ability and has done good work for the Denomination. We hope that she may continue to serve the Church of Christ for many years, believing her to be specially fitted for the duties of preaching and organising Christian work. (6)

Lillie Edwards appeared as a 'female special agent' in the first Conference *Minutes* of the United Methodist church.

1.2.2 The Primitive Methodists

The Primitive Methodists, on the other hand, did not have such a long record of female itinerant preachers as the Bible Christians, although in the early years their respective founders gave women a great deal of support. Between Bourne's enlisting the help of Mrs Dunnell and the *Primitive Methodist Magazine* article quoting O'Bryan's letter, he encouraged Elizabeth Austin of Mill Dale, Mirah Slack of Codnor, Anne Milward of Alstonefield, and Hannah Parrot. Sarah Kirkland was twenty when she began to preach in 1814, and two years later she was engaged by Bourne as the first woman itinerant preacher in the connexion, he himself paying her two guineas per quarter. Her work in the Derby circuit was so well received that the quarter day meeting insisted on the right to pay her salary.[41]

After the first general Meeting which began on 10 August 1819 – exactly seven days before that of the Bible Christians – another group of female itinerant preachers made their appearance: Sarah Spittle, who was a pioneer in Shrewsbury; Mary Allen; Jane Brown, who gave the sermon at the opening of Canaan Street chapel in Nottingham; Jane Ansdale, who went as a missionary to Weardale and who married the rector of an episcopal church in Philadelphia, and Ruth Watkins, who together with William Knowles founded the Primitive Methodist Mission in New York in 1829.[42] But the female preachers in Primitive Methodist listings were often difficult to identify as Christian names are not always given and reference must be made to varying outside sources. For example, between 1841 and 1847 initials appear in 1841–3 and 1846, while the *Minutes* of 1844, 1845 and 1847 list only men.

Yet if 1844 appears to signal an end to female admissions, Elizabeth Bultitude was still at work within the connexion. She was the last of their women preachers. Born in Norfolk in 1809 of Wesleyan Methodist parents, she was converted at the Primitive Methodist camp meeting in 1826 when she was seventeen, and on 22 July 1832 she began work as an itinerant preacher in the Norwich circuit. She travelled for thirty years, and was superannuated in 1862. She died on 14 August 1890 at the age of eighty-one. Seemingly the low pay was a source of some difficulty because 'What money I had would not allow me to dress smart enough for the people', she remarked at one point, but she nevertheless could boast.

> Here ends thirty years' labour. In all the thirty years I only missed two appointments, one, when there was a flooding rain, and the other a heavy thunderstorm; and being planned out of doors, I did not think it wise to go. I have walked thousands upon thousands of miles during the thirty years. I have visited from ten to forty families in a day, and prayed with them. I have preached five and six times in the week, and three, and sometimes five times on the Sabbath.[43]

The general Meeting *Minutes* laid down guidelines for dress and conduct. In 1819 appeared: '17 Q. In what dress shall our Travelling Preachers appear in public? A. In a plain one . . .; and that our Female Preachers, be patterns of plainness in all their dress'' (5) – perhaps a reflection of Quaker influence on Bourne – and there is no record of the women having erred in this connexion. In *Various Regulations* (1832) was recorded:

> No preacher, travelling or local, shall be allowed to take any female alone with him, nor to suffer any female to accompany him, (his own wife excepted) in going to or returning from any of his appointments, or do or suffer any such matter as may cause scandal, on pain of being admonished for the first offence, and put out of office for the second. And the female preachers shall be under the same regulation. But this rule is not to be made a subterfuge for any travelling preacher; for such, if convicted of using undue freedoms, in any such case, must be forthwith laid aside . . .

Also, no married female shall be allowed to labour permanently in any Circuit, except that in which her husband resides, special cases excepted. (5)

There are more details about allowances than in the case of the Bible Christians. In 1819 the salary of a female travelling preacher was fixed at £2 per quarter, as opposed to £4 for a single man, and was raised in 1823 to £2.2s. with board and lodging, and in 1831 to £2.10. a quarter after two years with a maximum allowance of £2.10s. for board and lodging, this was ratified as late as 1849. In addition, the 1820 *Minutes* laid down that any profits from books 'shall be divided equally amongst all the travelling preachers both male and female in the circuit in which the books were sold' (9). Some help was given in the case of illness and in 1823 Anna Stanna received £5 for 33 weeks illness. In 1829 it was decided in case of sickness to allow a female preacher six shillings a week out of the contingent fund, and that same year Mary Allen of the Lincoln circuit received £1.4s for 1–29 November, and £1 towards her doctor's bill.

The women were allowed to join the Primitive Methodist Itinerant Preachers' Fund, and Ruth Watkins and Elizabeth Allen were admitted in 1829. The following year the annual meeting of the fund resolved 'That females pay half in every respect of that is paid by the men, and be entitled to half of the annuity in all similar cases, only that £3 be allowed for each funeral. But in the case of her marrying she shall have no further claim from the fund'. But in 1836 it was decided 'that the fund be no longer open for the admission of females', and this was ratified in the new regulations brought into operation in 1841: 'No female travelling preacher shall be admitted as a member of the Society.'[44] The lack of security imposed by the closing of the fund, together with the regulation passed four years earlier that meant effectively that women had to travel alone, must have been of considerable discouragement to prospective female itinerant preachers.

The year 1890 was a landmark for the three connexions which had minuted female preaching: Elizabeth Bultitude, the last Primitive Methodist female itinerant, died; Eliza Giles headed the final cluster of entries among the Bible Christians; and within Wesleyan Methodism of the Wesley Deaconess Order was founded. The year marked the cross-over of two eras, because the evangelistic fervour which facilitated the itinerant ministry of women gave way to more structured and more firmly established churches.

2 THE ENTRY OF WOMEN AS MINISTERS INTO TWENTIETH-CENTURY INSTITUTIONALISED METHODISM[45]

2.1 The second period

2.1.1 The Wesley Deaconess Order

In Wesleyan Methodism, then, the deaconess order itself, and hence women representatives at Conference and the question of women preaching, all came to the fore. Four years after the founding of the order, Conference noted the presence of a women representative, and while business continued as usual, it was resolved 'that in future no Chairman of any Synod shall receive the nomination of a woman Representative until the Conference shall have determined, by legislative action, to admit women as Representatives, and until such new legislation has been submitted for approval to the District Synods'.[46] In 1895 the committee's report was received, but its recommendations rejected. A resolution proposed by a second committee was adopted: 'The Conference, learning that a responsible Council has been formed for the management of the Wesley Deaconess Institute, recommends the Institute to the confidence and sympathy of the Connexion.'[47]

In 1901 a statement, and in 1907 a report, both concerning the Wesley Deaconess Institute, were laid before the respective Conferences'.[48] In them the history of the institute was sketched from its founding in 1890 when a sister-in-charge with 4 student probationers moved into a house in London. In 1901 there had been 54 fully accredited deaconesses and 13 probationers, and by the time of the report in 1907 the numbers had increased to 98 consecrated or fully accredited deaconesses and 56 probationers and 19 accepted candidates. The aim of the institute was 'to supply to the Connexion at large women for women's work. Further, the Institute gives the Circuits this additional advantage – that changes, when necessary, can be effected without needless friction, without embarrassment to the Circuit on the one hand or to the Deaconesses on the other' (500). Any suggestion of a possible clash between the authorities of the circuit and the superintendent minister or his committee were dismissed in the report as groundless.

Recognition as a connexional institution was requested and granted in 1901 when a general committee was appointed. This fuller recognition was required in order to secure connexional confidence; in order to attract 'the best class of such workers'; and in order that the 'necessary discipline and control would be also more easy and more effective' (a point made twice over). The protestant nature of the work was also stressed: 'An agency of this kind is necessary to counteract the efforts of communities desiring to use their influence in favour of Romanism avowed or concealed' (502). The two concerns of control and of Roman influence re-emerge in the Church of England debates on the sisterhoods.

Not surprisingly, the related issues of women representatives and of women's preaching resurfaced. In 1909 Conference provisionally resolved that 'the time has come when duly qualified and elected women shall be eligible as Lay Representatives to the Conference', and this was resolved after having been submitted to the districts.[49] The same year the 1803 legislation on the preaching of women was reviewed, and in 1910 was revised. The wording was more gracious and the words restricting the preaching of women to their own sex were omitted, but otherwise the provisos remained unaltered, and a note was added: 'So far as possible the preaching of women shall be restricted to neighbourhoods in which there is no special opposition to such preaching'.[50] Effectively new ground was opened up to deaconesses in particular. In 1920 a resolution was confirmed granting permission to local preachers' meetings, in the case of Wesley deaconesses and other women who had already been preaching under the sanction of the regulations of the Conference of 1910, 'to receive them upon Full Plan without further examination', and a resolution was sent to the ministers in the districts, that Wesley deaconesses should 'be members of the Leaders' Meetings of the Society and Quarterly Meetings of the Circuits to which they are appointed'.[51]

2.1.2 The first impetus: the superintendent of the order raises the issue of women ministers

At the 1922 Conference the Reverend Dr W. Russell Maltby, superintendent of the Wesley Deaconess Order, agreed to convene a committee 'to consider the whole question of the admission of women to the Ordained Ministry, to the work of a Deaconess and kindred forms of service, having regard not only to the conditions of our organisation, but also to the interests of the work of God amongst us'.[52] The committee made an interim report to the 1923

Conference, and were reappointed together with representatives from the representative session. Their unanimous report,[53] presented in 1924 and incorporating much of the 1923 report, began:

> The widespread changes in the work and status of women have created a new situation which demands fresh consideration on the part of the whole Church. In times past, Methodism was a pioneer in entrusting responsibility and offering opportunities of service to women, but in recent times the changes in this respect have, for good or evil, been greater and more striking outside the Churches than within.

That these widespread changes in job opportunities, suffrage, education, and in social conventions would undoubtedly 'have immense consequences in subsequent history', and that already the change was 're-acting powerfully on the minds of the younger generation', was noted by the committee. They were 'not aware of any function of the Ordained Ministry for which a woman is in principle disqualified merely on the ground of her sex'. But the committee did believe themselves aware of serious practical obstacles to the admission of women to the itinerant ministry:

> A Conference declaration, for instance, that women might be accepted as candidates for the Ministry on the same terms as men, would solve nothing at all. No one contends that in such a Ministry as ours, men and women are simply interchangeable, and that it is immaterial in any given appointment whether the Minister appointed is a man or a woman.

That some changes were necessary the committee were not in doubt. Although the church could accommodate women dedicated to it, it still withheld from them 'their full share in the direction of their own work', and thus 'the freedom and scope' enjoyed by men, a state of affairs unacceptable to educated women in particular. The committee believed:

> that women, as well as men, may be called to devote themselves entirely to the work of the Church, and that whatever the ultimate goal may be, the immediate way forward is in the development of a Ministry of Women parallel to the Ministry of Men, under as definite a sense of vocation, equally recognised by the Church, held in the same honour, trusted with *adequate* authority, and united by the same bond of fellowship [italics added].

As an interim policy it was recommended that certain women should be 'formally ordained to such a Ministry', and that women missionaries and deaconesses 'should have the full recognition as of colleagues with the ordained Ministers'.

Dr Maltby, in proposing adoption of the report,[54] said that the church was facing a revolution in terms of the relationship between the sexes. In secular regions the subordination of women was going or had gone, but they had made no corresponding advance within the church. Large numbers of young, educated women would be glad to give their best services to the church if they could find an adequate sphere. Yet 'Nobody who looked at the question thought they could simply accept women candidates for the ministry, and then allow them to be put into any circuit where they might happen to be wanted.' Men and women, he said, were not interchangeable, but there was a wide area of Christian work for which men and women were both fitted. Mrs Bolton, seconding, said she had been abroad and had seen the openings for women in other lands. No Conference could turn back the tide – it was desirable, rather, to harness the movement, which was of Christian origin, and to 'Let the women have their full and proper share in helping to set up the Kingdom of Heaven on earth.'

The report was adopted by the representative session, but only received and given general approval by the pastoral session. In view of 'the many difficult questions involved', the report was remitted by Conference for consideration by an expanded committee.[55] This committee[56] pinpointed such questions as revolving in particular around the statements concerning the development of a parallel ministry, and concerning formal ordination to such a ministry on an interim basis. They offered detailed recommendations in so far as they would differ from those applicable to men whereby women could be accepted for the ministry. Differences of note were: 'As by marriage a woman accepts another vocation involving responsibilities that do not admit of her fulfilment of the duties of a Wesleyan Minister, the marriage of a Woman Minister shall be regarded as equivalent to resignation'; and with regard to proposed lists of appointments of women ministers, 'No appointment previously held by a Minister who is a man, shall be included in this list, unless the consent of the Conference has first been expressly obtained.'

Dr Ryder Smith presented the report in the absence of the convenor, the Reverend Dr Robert Bond.[57] He said that the clause, 'The Committee is not aware of any function of the Ordained Ministry for which a woman is in principle disqualified merely on the ground of sex', was pivotal to the whole scheme, while the second part of the report was a thought-out scheme to admit women to the ministry which could be abandoned if it proved a failure. He moved the adoption of the first part. There was interest outside the Conference, he continued, and to those outside its ways were puzzling. 'Last year the Representative Session accepted a report without question. This year the Representative Session was not allowed to discuss it. Last year the Pastoral Session made a move in this direction. This year – if Mr Cartwright's amendment were carried – they would seem to be going back once more.'

The Reverend J. H. Cartwright then moved his amendment, that in view of the issues involved and the many difficulties arising from the report, the whole question be remitted for fuller consideration to a larger and fully representative committee. This, he said, was required by the size of the question; he went back to New Testament principles, and he thought of apostolic practice. He 'objected to ill-considered and hasty legislation, which was the prolific mother of irremediable mischief'. The Reverend C. Ensor Walters, seconding the amendment, said that it was no dishonour to the women of the church to say that on the lines of the deaconess order they could find their proper sphere. The setting apart of women by ordination was an innovation without precedent in the Christian church. Dr Harold Morton thought the proposals were a break with the whole apostolic order, and that the report did not enquire into the practice of the New Testament such as 'St Paul who "permitted no woman to teach or hold authority over the man"'. He asked that the committee be required to prepare a biblical statement so that scripturally he could be convinced it was right. Dr J. Scott Lidgett agreed that a statement of scriptural principles should be given, but reminded them that apostolic precedent did not settle apostolic principles. He added that social conditions of New Testament times were not necessarily a guide for all times, and he, too, made appeal to Paul: 'In Christ there is neither male nor female'. Dr Maltby urged that some step forward be made, such that any suggestion of impeding what the representative session had already approved should be removed. They should act according to their own principles rather than looking 'so much to the Anglo-Catholic section of the English Church, with which they had no affinity at all'. Nevertheless Mr Cartwright's amendment was carried by 175 votes to 142.

As the amendment became the substantive motion, Dr Maltby

said he did not wish to press the report against the wishes of the Conference, but thought it desirable that the pastoral session, having lifted the discussion from the representative session, should at least approve the first part of the report before recommitting the whole matter to a committee. His motion was passed by 202 votes to 105.

Two final points were agreed. First, that the committee should be asked to prepare a statement showing the biblical grounds on which such a departure was based. Second, a suggestion that there was a discrepancy between the agreed statement that her sex did not disqualify a woman and the statement that marriage would debar her from continuing in the ministry led to a rewording of the statement, which according to the *Methodist Recorder* now read: 'A woman is not disqualified from the ministry merely on the ground of sex.'

Prior to the 1926 Conference the committee had been specially enlarged to deal with the admission of women to the ministry. They declared themselves convinced 'that a certain number of women with special gifts do indeed believe themselves called to the Ministry and any tests that would be applied in the case of men go to confirm that conviction'. The report[58] they produced stated:

> Believing that there is Apostolic authority for regarding Women as on a spiritual equality with men in the Christian Church, and that the limitations of the Ministry of women in Apostolic and subsequent times were due to the conditions of those times, and are not binding in face of the situation that now prevails, the sub-Committee recommends that women should be eligible for the ministry of the Wesleyan Methodist Church, as far as possible on the same conditions as men. (71–2)

However, the concern remained, 'As by marriage a woman accepts another vocation involving responsibilities that do not admit of the fulfilment of all the duties of a Wesleyan Minister it is necessary to determine what in that event the position of a Woman Minister is to be.' Alternatives would be to regard either marriage as equivalent to resignation, or a married woman as a minister without pastoral charge. The pastoral session report recommended, and the representative session strongly recommended, the former, it being already the rule in the case of deaconesses. The report sent to the pastoral session included a biblical statement based on the distinction between apostolic principle and apostolic precedent, and

Pauline writings on the state, on slavery, and on women were considered in this light. In the case of the women, 1 Corinthians 14: 34 and 1 Timothy 2: 12 were contrasted with Galatians 3: 28: 'The former texts imply that there are conditions of society in which the public ministry of women would do more harm than good. This is so everywhere as long as the public estimation of womanhood emphasises sex rather than personality.' Current welcome changes were 'ultimately due to the influence of the Christian principle of the value of personality, alike in men and women'. This concept underlay many Christian doctrines. The statement concluded: 'There is nothing in the New Testament that requires the permanent exclusion of half the human race from the Christian Ministry.'

In moving adoption of the report,[59] Dr Ryder Smith said the part on the admission of women to the ministry followed in the wake of a resolution passed already that sex was no barrier. In the case of the one difficulty, marriage, the committee had recommended resignation. If, therefore, this claim on the part of womanhood were just, they could not turn back the whole scheme. In reply to a question he added that Methodist union was not a reason to begin to hold back all sorts of questions, and that, on the contrary, some experience on the part of one of the churches would be an advantage.

Mr Walters moved an amendment which referred the matter back to the committee, refusing to adopt the report, and recommending the development along the lines of the deaconess order. He believed that the first part of the report destroyed the second, arguing that it was impossible for men to enter into some walks of life. He objected to the proposals because they lacked scriptural, catholic authority, even though the pastoral session had received a little scriptural homily. Such a thing had never been done in the whole history of the catholic church. He would listen if the Methodist Church were called to an ecumenical conference on the matter. Returning to the report he asked why, if a woman was not to be debarred from the ministry by the fact that God had made her a woman, was she to retire if she married. Why did not he, himself, retire from the ministry when he married? (Which was met with laughter and cries of 'Why?')

Dr Scott Lidgett replied that they had been asked to remember that for two thousand years the catholic church had never recognised nor permitted the full ministry of women, but asked whether the Catholic Church, as commonly understood, had recognised the ordination of Wesleyan ministers. Mr Walters had said there were limitations imposed by God which they could not overcome, but he wanted to know where, exactly, God had imposed the limit. Speaking in favour of the amendment, the Reverend Dr J. E. Rattenbury complained that the scheme was one which admitted only unmarried women; he argued that it was not an attack on women's ministry, but upon the assumption that this particular type of ministry was the best or the highest for women. In reply Dr Ryder Smith pointed out that in the Wesley Deaconess Order marriage also meant resignation.

Two women spoke against the amendment. Miss S. Pugh Jones said she had striven in vain to find any opposition points to refute other than that from tradition, which had already been dealt with. Rather than being regarded as a fight for sex equality – which savoured too much of the political platform – she asked that it be seen as an issue of spiritual equality depending upon the spiritual quality of the person. She dissociated this from 'those sentimentalists' who arged that women had more spiritual influence than men, pointing out that people who so argued were generally reactionary on this particular issue. Lady Newbald Kay went further. She said the ministry of the Wesleyan Church might delay God's purposes, but they could never stop them. There had always been difficulties in the way of women's service in the ministry. She quoted the incident when Florence Nightingale had been spoken of on the floor of the House of Commons as 'that indecent hussy'. She wondered how Conference dared to hinder women in their calling.

Although this delaying amendment was rejected (173:187) and the report should have been adopted, the two sessions of Conference adopted conflicting resolutions which were subsequently returned, unconfirmed, by the legal conference to the respective sessions. The basis of the conflict concerned a wide difference of opinion in the representative session, and although this session did in fact provisionally adopt the report, the pastoral session gave this difference of opinion in the representative session as its own reason for rejecting it.[60]

This position of the pastoral session was seen by Dr Ryder Smith as a delaying power possibly quite within its right,[61] but he urged adoption of the report. He did not think that the pastoral session was disposed to veto things which had passed after a 'wide divergence' of opinion in the representative session, and although that session had referred to 'obstacles', he said that difficulties came with any great change and had to be faced with patience and courage – the two listed 'difficulties' had been met with proposals. The whole question ought not to be indefinitely postponed; the ministry was about the only sphere still closed to women and for the Christian ministry to be the last preserve of man alone was surely somewhat cynical.

Mr Cartwright moved an amendment based on the difference of opinion and on 'the serious practical obstacles', urging further consideration by a committee to secure further opportunities for consecrated women, and the recognition of a diaconate of women in the church. This, he said, would enable them to recognise the work of their gifted sisters in a real ministry of the church, though not in the ordained and itinerant ministry. He referred at length to the difficulties raised by marriage, suggesting that when a minister married he was 'twice as well fitted for the ministry as before', while a woman who felt 'the call of nature and God' had to then say 'good-bye to the sense of any life vocation to the ordained and itinerant ministry'. Further, there was no demand in the church for women ministers. In the Church of Scotland and the United Free Church it had been determined that it was not the will of the church that women should be ordained, and whereas the Bible Christian Church had thrown its ministry open to women there was currently not a single woman minister in it.[62] He asked whether any successful experiment was ever dropped.

Dr Lofthouse said that women were turned away from the church because of the bar, and found avenues of service outside Methodism. But Mrs Norman Sargant claimed she voiced the feelings of the rank-and-file of the women of Methodism who did not want the matter brought forward; she was in favour of women as local preachers only. Miss Hunter returned to the 'personality' argument, saying the logical deduction was that women should come to the ministry as well as men. In this she was supported by the ex-president, Dr Maltby, who said they had to decide whether the church was living on principle or starving on precedents. He quoted a deaconess who had described Mr Cartwright's amendment as 'insulting', and asked whether they thought they would 'take any harm by receiving the Sacrament at the hand of a woman' – not that he thought they would receive many such applications, but such women could not be kept in a subordinate position. Dr Rattenbury protested that the opposition was not ultimate, but practical, and suggested a redrafting of the amendment to incorporate development of the diaconate of women in order to meet Dr Maltby's criticism, and this was accepted by its proposer. Replying, Dr Ryder Smith said Mr Cartwright's proposal put the movement back several years; in a decision between organisation and principle a Christian assembly should surely stand by the latter and alter the former. However, the voting for the amendment, after a re-count by scrutineers, was 239:209, so it was then put as a substantive motion and carried.

Reporting[63] in 1928 the committee acknowledged the 'incalculable value' of the work of deaconesses but added that though improvements could be made in training and other matters, they did not consider this would meet the situation they were appointed to consider under the mandate of 1923. They were satisfied

> that there are women in Methodism endowed with special gifts and called of God for service in His Church, of wider scope and sometimes of a different character from that for which Deaconesses have been trained. Some modification of our organisation is required to enable the Church to give ungrudging endorsement to such a call and provide an adequate sphere for its full exercise.

They recommended that a woman should be able to offer for the ministry under the same regulations as applied to men, although among the listed regulations were that marriage should be regarded as 'equivalent to resignation'.

Dr Maltby, opening the debate,[64] said it was seven years since the question had first been put. A revolution was proceeding all over the world that affected the question; doors everywhere were opening to women, and the Conference should look beyond its own denominational walls, particularly as they had already decided that co-partnership was Christian in origin. The order of deaconesses could not answer the aspirations of the women of whom they were thinking – indeed, the deaconesses themselves in their convocation[65] had passed a resolution that would automatically exclude themselves from the ministry which they nevertheless desired for others. Neither let Conference stress the itineracy of the Methodist ministry as inapplicable to women; they had already found it possible to make exceptions to a rigid itineracy, and any necessary modifications might be made, and he moved that general approval be given to the part of the report preceding the various regulations. Mr Cartwright, seconding, said it was a more workable plan than hitherto. He did not think it went as far as Dr Maltby's speech, as the final decision as to the status of the gifted women was left to be decided later, and in some cases it might be decided by marriage. It was a question of securing opportunities rather than status for these women, and for this reason he thought the amendment to be proposed was a delaying one. He thought the time had come to send the question down to the synods so they could examine and criticise the scheme. He had been an opposer in past years, but this scheme was one he could support.

Mr Walters moved an amendment referring the whole matter back to the committee with instructions to consider forming a diaconate for women. He said he was in favour of the creation of a ministry parallel to that of men, but not for a few women to enter the itinerant ministry which he saw as a subordination of women. His main objection to the scheme was the regulation concerning marriage – a call to the ministry was a call for life, and the elemental fact of the difference between the sexes remained. The Primitive Methodist Church had permitted women candidates, but had none, nor were any in view. He wanted a real ministry of women. The trouble with the committee was that it was faced with a certain loud demand – not from religious circles but from without, from feminist circles, and it could not set itself against it. The Reverend Thomas Tiplady added that they were proposing to put someone higher than the deaconess; he wished women would cease to imitate men and dare to be themselves.

The Reverend R. Newton Flew replied: Mr Walters' objection to marriage being equivalent to resignation was an argument to delete that provision, not an argument against the proposal to admit women; Mr Tiplady's comment about lowering the status of deaconesses should be referred to the deaconesses; and as regards imitating men, he asked whether anyone supposed they would. The ministry, he said, was changing under their eyes and a greater specialisation of function was evolving. Developing this last point, Dr Maltby reminded them that the Conference was an assembly of men; the only way to get a parallel ministry was to admit women into the ranks of the ministry and then to allow them to specialise as they might feel led. He said that the argument that they should be permanently excluded from the ministry because they might marry and so resign applied equally to a parallel ministry. In fact, they had long been face to face with the question when they sent women to posts of loneliness abroad[66] and accepted their sense of vocation and their life intention – equally so with the deaconesses. When put to the vote the amendment was lost (114:184).

Dr Maltby then proposed that Conference approve the beginning of the report, subject to the rights of the pastoral session (which in the event approved the first sentence and gave general approval to the remaining clauses),[67] and approve in general the various regulations, but before endorsing the report as provisional legislation the committee should elucidate certain of the recommendations. An amendment to give general approval to the whole scheme having been lost, Dr Maltby's resolution was put and carried.

Dr Maltby presented a revised report[68] to the 1929 Conference – notable in it was an addendum to the regulation that marriage should be regarded as equivalent to resignation, 'unless on special application the Conference shall otherwise determine'.[69] He said that some movement had taken place over the previous six or so years and that the church should at that point show continuity of policy. Even were Conference to move then, there could be no candidate until 1931, and no woman ordained until 1938. The women who three or four years previously had been ready to offer, and who would have passed any possible test with the greatest ease, were not available because of the passage of time. He begged the Conference not to delay any longer in opening the way for those who were called of God to the work. Seconding, Dr Scott Lidgett said that the New Testament offered sufficient guidance in terms of principle and precedent. The church had often too long delayed in taking advantage or account of changes in economic or social conditions, and he urged them not to make the same mistake about recognising the work and position of women. Forthcoming union should not be an excuse for delay; on the contrary, it was of the essence of leadership that they should show they had the courage to face up to these issues and decide them.

Dr Eric S. Waterhouse moved an amendment, accepting the principle but, in view of the 'difficulties' of the itinerant system, the lack of demand, and forthcoming union, urging the suspension of legislation until the new church was constituted. He said he sincerely believed in the New Testament principle that women should be received into the ministry on an equal status with men, but he wanted to know how far they were going to face the very serious practical difficulties for the sake of vindicating a principle. He referred particularly to Methodist union, and the past and current history of the Primitive Methodist and United Methodist Churches in this respect; he thought it would be a disadvantage to carry women ministers into the united church. Although Dr Maltby replied that he had received assurances on this issue, the amendment was carried by four votes (177:173).

Dr Ryder Smith then moved an amendment to the substantive proposition that the other Methodist Conferences be invited to join in appointing a joint committee to consider the subject, and to report to the three Conferences – in this way, he said, only one year would be lost. Dr Waterhouse withdrew his amendment and Dr Ryder Smith's amendment was carried. It was subsequently agreed that the number of committee members elected by Conference should be twenty, with ten from each of the other Conferences.[70]

The joint committee duly reported to Conference in 1931.[71] Interestingly they took clauses from the 1923 report – notably that there was no function of the ordained ministry from which a woman was in principle disqualified merely on the ground of sex, which avoided the 1925 redrafting of the statement – and from the 1928 report – notably that which had received formal approval that year. In presenting the report[72] Dr Maltby said that it was eight years since the question had been raised and the committee appointed, and it had been reappointed, changed, enlarged and diminished on various occasions and had gone on presenting reports. Two years previously it had presented a similar report, and a resolution had then called for the appointment of a joint committee in view of Methodist union. This committee had now reported to the other Conferences: that of the Primitive Methodists had accepted the report unanimously, and that of the United Methodist Church by an overwhelming majority. He thought there was thus no further need of delay, particularly in the light of having voted to call in the other churches. In merely commercial circles such an invitation would make the ensuring suggestions binding. He referred to the changed status of women over the previous twenty or thirty years, its Christian origin, and their previous agreement on the principle of the ordination of women, and then to the remark of an ex-president of Conference who did not object to defending the principle providing deductions were not made. It was impossible, he argued, to go on dividing and postponing while there were really women who felt called of God to the ministry. The report did not dispose of every conceivable difficulty, and even if those already raised were removed, others would be found by the opponents. He begged Conference to go forward, and concluded with a definition of inertia: 'A tendency of a body to remain at rest or to continue in the same line of motion.'

Then Mr Walters moved his amendment to the effect that the final decision should be taken by the united Conference, that in its interim considerations the joint committee should look at the relation 'of the already well constituted ministry of women' to the proposed scheme, and that Conference should reaffirm the 1925 (rather than 1923) statement that the Conference was 'not aware of any function in the ordained ministry for which a woman is disqualified merely on the ground of her sex'. Mrs Andrews remarked that a principle was involved because for years women had been kept on the doorstep of the church. Then Dr Maltby, replying, referred to Mr Walters' part in committee as that of Casabianca standing on the burning deck when everyone else had fled. He asked what would happen to the report, as it would stand neither approved nor condemned, and this would be out of line with the other two Conferences which had taken up a position. He would remind Mr Walters that the worst obstruction was that which was in the deep, subliminal parts of the mind. The voting on the amendment was 114:107, but the result of a re-count was 96:98, to which Mr Walters objected, and after some discussion it was agreed to adjourn. It was eventually resolved to adopt the report, subject to confirmation by the 1933 Conference, remitting to the committee for further consideration questions concerning training, allowances and marriage. It was further resolved to request the deaconess committee, in conjunction with the committee concerning women and the ministry, to consider the whole question of the status of the deaconesses and their position under the constitution of the united church.[73]

The committee duly followed these instructions, but found that the final suggestion seemed to open up more difficulties without removing the older ones.[74] Their report was remitted by the Wesleyan Conference of June 1932 to the uniting Conference, which was to meet the following September.[75]

2.1.3 Dwindling momentum following union in 1932

The uniting Conference received the report and referred it back to the committee. When it was presented to the 1933 Methodist Conference[76] it had been substantially revised. After acknowledging the work of the Wesley Deaconess Order and of women missionaries overseas, their union into a new Order of a Women's Ministry (*sic*) was proposed. To this order a woman who believed herself called to the ordained ministry would have initially to apply.

The report having been proposed for adoption, Mr Walters said he had been a member of the committee and had no desire to obstruct.[77] The Wesleyan and United Methodist Conferences had voted on the principle, it was true, but the question had never been raised in this form by the Primitive Methodists. They had had freedom from the first, but there were no longer women on their stations; meanwhile the Wesleyans were divided. They had already in the church a definite order and ministry of women, and there were no functions which a woman might not carry out because of her sex. In the United Methodist Church deaconesses could administer the chalice, and under the new constitution a 'person' might do so. They could not allow women to enter the ministry and then treat them differently, for example as regarded marriage. He was unmoved by the statement that few women would offer – that was not the way a branch of the holy catholic church should settle a thing of such moment.

In the same spirit Dr Waterhouse moved his amendment to the effect that the committee should formulate a scheme for the constitution of the proposed women's ministry that clearly indicated 'its character as a distinct ministry'. He saw difficulties in that it was not clear whether members would be responsible to that order or to Conference. There were moreover great difficulties in putting women into ordinary itinerant work – for example young women would be popular but it would be increasingly difficult to employ them as they reached middle age.

A number of speakers saw the issues in a different light. Mrs Elizabeth Absolom asked that there be more women on the committee; currently there were only six among the forty members. The Reverend Richard Pyke said he could recollect women ministers in the little Primitive Methodist Church to which he had belonged as a youth. He expressed some surprise that their ministry, which had been frankly and generously recognised by their church, had not developed. Looking further back to the Bible Christians, no one could overestimate the great work done by women, who in 1815 had formed half its ministry, yet after a few years even in this church women's ministry had subsided. But it would be a false deduction to say that history condemned or even discredited the recognition of women as ministers. The present day was dissimilar both in opportunities of education for women, and in conception of their place in the work of the world. Again, the conditions under which they had asked women to enter the ministry were created by men, for men. Surely if they expected women to enter the ministry it was reasonable to expect conditions to be changed. He hoped the Methodist Church would lead in a way that other churches would desire to follow. Dr Dorothy Farrar said it was not easy for a woman to sit through some of the discussion; surely, once it was established that a woman was called of God she should be welcomed. Attempting to describe the call to a woman, she said she knew what it was to preach and to take up Christian service; it was something that came near to the call of motherhood, a call to bring new souls into the kingdom of God and to nurture them in every possible way, something that could only be told to a sympathetic hearer. She supported the resolution with a good deal of hope because of the new personnel brought into Conference as a result of union. It was contrary to the spirit of the Methodist Church to pause for practical difficulties; did Mr Walters waver when faced with the practical difficulties in evangelisation? She knew the country roads were dark, but women in Burma and China were not afraid of country roads at night. If they took the responsibility of sending women to the foreign field, why not send them to work at home, she asked. The spirit of adventure under the guidance of the spirit of God should be sufficient to remove the difficulties. This sentiment was echoed by Dr Ryder Smith, who said that no new enterprise could be undertaken with any faith if every detail of procedure had to be known first. Had that been John Wesley's attitude, the Conference would not be meeting.

Rising to meet some queries, Dr Maltby said that the paragraph about the union of ministries which had been put in to meet what Mr Walters and others had sought, was bound to be indeterminate until the other authorities had met together. He said he had been on committees on this issue for ten years, and all sorts of dilatory resolutions had been carried, and they could not perpetually go round in circles. Dr Waterhouse's amendment might just as well be definitely hostile. He wanted to know what the supporters of the amendment wished to withhold from women. It was difficult to get suitable candidates for the deaconess order because they were not granted the same opportunity accorded to men doing the same work; he and his friends wished to remove a humiliating wrong. The amendment having been put and lost, the motion was carried by a large majority.

As the next stage was to send the adopted report to the synods as provisional legislation, Conference, referring it also to the Methodist Missionary Society and the Wesley Deaconess Order, requested them each to appoint five representatives to meet with the current committee to receive the synod reports and report to Conference.[78] The following classifications were made of the results[79] in the representative and pastoral sessions respectively: approval of principle and scheme, 11, 8; approval of principle but desiring another scheme, 7, 5; referred back for further consideration to committee 6, 6, or to quarterly meetings, 3, 2; approval of new order but not itinerant ministry, 9, 9; rejection of resolutions, 10, 10. While the proposed unification of the deaconesses and the missionaries had not been approved by either body and Conference was recommended not to proceed, the committee considered that though the synod resolutions were indecisive, they clearly indicated that a large number of synods were unwilling to give a negative answer. Judging these two parts to be separable, the committee attached further proposals for the admission of women to the itinerant ministry 'following the existing procedure' with the usual modifications.

The Reverend G. E. Hickman Johnson moved the adoption of the report.[80] He admitted that the scheme sent to synods had been a compromise which had pleased no one. Nevertheless, Conference should decide whether or not it wished to receive women at home and abroad into the itinerant ministry. The Wesleyan Church, he said, was gradually becoming accustomed to the idea. Dr Maltby, seconding, again spoke of the part women were playing outside the church. Over the previous six years he had not heard a single new objection to the admission of women to the ministry, and he felt humiliated at some of the synod discussions. He suggested that some people took their ideas of women from the novels of Jane Austen.

The idea had been advanced that the work of the ministry was physically beyond the power of a woman, yet they sent women missionaries to labour single-handed in lonely tropical stations a hundred miles from their nearest neighbours; another objector had said it would be unsuitable for a woman to preside over a trustees' meeting.

Dr Rattenbury believed the itinerant ministry was unsuitable for women, and proposed an amendment to the effect that, as lack of support did not justify procedure into the main project, the committee should be dissolved and a new committee appointed to consider the development of the existing ministries for women. Dr Waterhouse, seconding, believed the Methodist Church already gave more opportunity to women than any other church, adding that the experiment of women ministers had failed where it had been tried. Later, Mr J. Duckworth thought the Congregational example of Miss Maude Royden[81] was not applicable to the Methodist ministry. The Reverend R. H. B. Shapland warned that a step forward would alter the character of a call to the ministry by setting the ministry against marriage.[82]

There were a number of speakers against the amendment. Among them Mrs Duncan Leith said the only thing the church could give women was the right to enter the ministry. Mr Pyke said he would like to discuss Dr Rattenbury's argument that the system was unsuitable for women. That seemed to suggest that they regarded their system as final and inflexible, but he asked if any of them, looking out on their world of the day, supposed for a moment that the Methodist Church or ministry had adapted itself adequately to all the needs of the age. It was obvious to him that methods would have to change, and every gift invoked.

The voting on the part of the amendment calling for the dissolution of the committee was 189 to 159. After this the discussion became somewhat heated. There was considerable interruption and the putting of numerous 'points of order', and the vice-president announced that he would not take his seat until the Conference was quieter. Eventually the part of the amendment calling for a new committee was carried. Immediately Dr Maltby pointed out that so far they had not discussed that part of the amendment, yet now the Conference wanted another committee. He said he had spent hundreds of hours on the matter and he was not prepared to go on wasting time preparing futile schemes when they could not get an adequate and rational discussion of a great subject in the Conference. At this point Mr Hickman Johnson appealed to Dr Rattenbury to consider whether he could not drop his second paragraph. He pointed out that he had achieved his end; he had killed the committee and stopped the movement, so asked if he could not leave things as they were. But Dr Rattenbury would not (but see below).

Three days later Miss Hilda Roseveare proposed a resolution with regard to the composition and procedure of the new committee, which Dr Maltby thought would mean excluding anyone who knew anything about deaconess work. He moved an amendment to the affect that the appointment of the committee set up on Saturday night should be suspended for twelve months, and this was seconded by Dr Waterhouse. It was finally decided to invite the Reverend J. W. Sawyer to move the resolution of which he had given notice, that, in accordance with rule 13 of Conference rules of debate, the second part of Dr Rattenbury's motion be rescinded, and Conference postpone the appointment of the commitee until the Conference of 1935. After considerable further discussion, the resolution to rescind was adopted, and it was ruled that Miss Roseveare's proposal could not therefore be adopted. The *Minutes* of the ministerial session show concurrence with the decision and an addendum somewhat ironically expressing the desire to 'respond worthily' to the changing situation by making 'such adjustments in our organisation as will give to women called of God full scope for the exercise of their ministry'.[83]

In fact it was in 1937 that the committee was appointed[84] and they reported to Conference the following year.[85] As required by Dr Rattenbury's amendment, they had considered the existing ministries of women: deaconesses (currently totalling 385) were ordained with the imposition of hands, but unlike male candidates for the ministry did not need to prove an ability to preach; women missionaries had no order or ordination, although a few were set apart for a specifically pastoral teaching service and the ministry of the word. The committee continued:

> Both at home and overseas there are women called of God to the ministry of the Word and Sacraments, who in full-time service have proved their gifts and fitness. By ordination the Church would acknowledge the call, and such ordinations, even if few, would be an earnest of the Church's desire to allow no impediment in the way of women called of God to this ministry, and would open the way for further developments in the light of experience.

Conference gave general approval to the report, and referred it back for further consideration.[86] The committee returned it to the 1939 Conference in a slightly expanded form and including the proviso 'That over a period of years, she has made proof of her gifts and fitness in the full-time service of the Church'.[87] Notably in these two reports there was no mention of marriage implying resignation.

In moving adoption of this 1939 report,[88] The Reverend W. Russell Shearer said that Methodists held no theory of apostolic succession, but they represented traditions of church life whereby men from the humblest and most unprivileged circumstances could offer for the ministry, and that Conference ought to be very careful concerning its right to refuse women with a sense of call. He was supported by Mrs Hickman Johnson, who pointed out there were few professions into which girls could not enter on equal terms with their brothers, and that the time had come when the church should offer its daughters what it offered its sons. By way of example, she referred to a young woman who, unable to offer for the ministry, had become the youngest woman don at Oxford.

Dr Rattenbury wanted an assurance that the report proposed an experiment in exceptional circumstances, and did not imply a general acceptance of young women candidates. Young women, he thought, could only give a qualified offer as a candidate for the ministry, and the idea of a life vocation would be broken down by marriage. The president replied that in his opinion the way would be opened for the entrance of women, but Mr Hickman Johnson pointed out that the phrase 'that over a period of years, she has made proof of her gifts and fitness in the full-time service of the Church' had been a limitation in the minds of the committee.

Three amendments were then proposed. Dr Bond moved 'That women shall be eligible as candidates for the ministry on the same conditions as men', on the basis that this was the only honourable way of recognising the equality of women, but his amendment was defeated. Next, the Reverend William Watson did not like the sound of private negotiations behind the scenes and proposed that instead the candidate went immediately before the quarterly meeting and the synod, but this was also defeated. Then the Reverend C. Edgar Stephenson moved that the phrase, 'that over a period of years, she has made proof of her gifts and fitness in the full-time service of the Church', should be deleted, but without success.

When the motion to adopt the report came to the vote it was

defeated (221:237), and the report was received only. A committee was appointed by the ministerial session to report on the ministerial implications of the current scheme and to make proposals for 'such adjustments in our organisation as will give to women called of God full scope for the exercise of their ministry'.[89]

Possibly due to the war, it was not until 1944 that the report came again before a session of Conference.[90] The committee said that the work of women abroad, where there was a shortage of ministerial staff, would be rendered more effective by the training and status of the ordained ministry. At home too there were openings for women: the committee was convinced that there was 'scope for the services of women in the ranks of the ordained ministers of the Methodist Church', and that this was in addition to the primarily pastoral work of deaconesses. The report was received by the ministerial session, and the committee was reappointed to meet with a committee appointed by the representative session,[91] the joint committee to present a report to the following Conference.[92]

This committee did not believe the church could be 'content with the announcement of a principle on which no action has been taken after the lapse of twelve years'. A beginning had to be made by 'the extension to women of the full Ministry of the Word and Sacraments, and that Ministry must then prove its value by what it brings to the service of the Church'. The committee thought acceptance of the proposals would be the beginning of an experimental period, 'the opening of a door which indeed the Conference has declared to be open but through which no one has yet been permitted to pass'. There followed seven proposals closely resembling those of the 1944 report:

1. That the Conference declare its readiness to receive, for Ordination to the Ministry of the Word and Sacraments, women who believe themselves to be called of God to this work, and who, on offering themselves as candidates and through the period of their training and probation, prove themselves to have the fitness and the gifts required for this Ministry.
2. That men and women in the Ministry shall have equal status and shall receive allowances on the same scale.
3. That the marriage of a woman Minister shall involve her retirement from the active ministry, unless in special cases and on the application of the person concerned, the Conference shall determine otherwise.

4. That until the Conference is able to judge to what extent it is possible for the Church as a whole to make use of women ministers, only those women candidates shall be received whose maintenance is undertaken by a Connexional Committee or Department which desires their service. The Committee or Department shall recommend to the Stationing Committee the sphere of the appointment.
5. That the Conference appoint a Committee consisting of three representatives each (of whom one shall be a woman) of the Ministerial Training Committee, the Deaconess Committee, the Overseas Missions Committee and the Home Mission Committee, to consider matters concerning the presentation and examination of women candidates for the Ministry, and the training and probation of women Ministers; the Committee to be allowed to co-opt not more than six other members.
6. That for a woman missionary in a District Overseas who desires to offer for the Ministry, the procedure shall be the same as that for laymen missionary candidates, the recommendation of the District Synod being regarded as the equivalent of that of a Quarterly meeting in the Church at home. Any such candidate recommended by an overseas Synod must return to this country to be examined by a Synod and the July Committee.
7. Women nationals in Districts overseas which are ready to accept women ministers, shall be examined according to the procedure arranged for men candidates. Their training shall be under the direction of the District or Provincial Synod (where the latter exists) and their allowances in accordance with the Synod's arrangements.

The report was duly brought before the 1945 Conference and the Reverend Walter H. Armstrong moved its adoption.[93] However, the Reverend Harold G. Fiddick moved an amendment that the report should be sent to the overseas missions, home missions and youth departments for comment as to the need and demand within each department's sphere for a new and superior order of the ministry of women. He believed the various orders of ministry had been given by God in answer to a need, and he wanted to know what the current need was.

Others spoke in favour of the motion. Dr Farrar, replying to Mr Fiddick, pointed out that deaconesses had no power to enter the ministerial session and had no privileges such as the minister possessed. She asked what harm could be done by allowing them to enter the ministry, and how it could help some women to hold others back. Miss Hilda Marris said she had been in complete charge of a church, under the direction of the superintendent minister, and at a time when women were fulfilling so many of the functions of the ministry the church had no right to bar the way to acceptance in the ministry. Miss Roseveare did, however, point out that the committee's recommendations held little security for women.

Mr Fiddick's amendment having been lost, the motion was adopted and the report sent down to the synods. Meanwhile the ministerial session adopted clauses 1 (the voting was 190:138), 2, 3 (having substituted 'resignation' for 'retirement'), 5 (having added 'and sphere of service' immediately following 'the training and probation'), 6, 7, and rejected 4.[94] However, some confusion arose later as the words 'provisional legislation' did not appear in the *Daily Record* in connection with the directive of the representative session to the synods,[95] so some treated the matter as sent for consideration and comment, as the 1946 report[96] shows.

The committee analysed the synod returns of representative and ministerial sessions respectively for the first five clauses as follows: (1) unqualified acceptance 29, 30; qualified acceptance 3, 3; (2) acceptance 30, 30; (3) acceptance 10, 10; 'resignation' instead of 'retirement' 22, 20; (4) acceptance 14, 14; rejection 15, 16 (others gave no judgement/qualified acceptance/wanted further consideration); (5) acceptance 17, 16; added 'sphere of service' 10, 11. It was pointed out that two-thirds of the synods had voted favourably on the principle, and that only ten had rejected it outright. The committee recommended that the 1945 report together with ministerial amendments should be returned to it and that its recommendations should be brought before the 1947 Conference.

During this 1946 debate,[97] Mr Hickman Johnson pointed out that for the first time the question had been remitted to the overseas synods and that they had been unanimously in favour with the exception of one small sub-synod in the West Indies. An amendment by the Reverend Kingsley Lloyd to halt the process due to insufficient support was lost (168:190), as was an amendment by Mr Tiplady recommending that the deaconesses and women missionaries should be made members of the ministerial session on the same terms as ministers. The successful amendment was moved by the Reverend Dr W. F. Howard:

> The Conference directs the Committee to consider the enlargement of the sphere of service of members of the Wesley Deaconess Order and of Women Missionaries Overseas, so that those who attain a standard equivalent to that of Candidates for Ordination, should receive Presbyters' orders to administer the Sacrament as well as preach the Word of God. These Women Ministers, if Deaconesses, would be subject to the discipline and direction of the Department of Women's Ministry, now known as the Wesley Deaconess Order, and if Women Missionaries to the discipline and direction of the Overseas Missions Committee.[98]

After being passed by a large majority, it was, together with the scheme as adopted by the representative session in 1945 and the variations proposed by the ministerial session, referred to an enlarged committee for presentation at Conference in 1947.

In fact, it was 1948 when the next report[99] was presented. The committee had consulted both the deaconess convocation and the women missionaries in overseas work and both bodies had accepted the 1945–6 recommendations, and both had rejected decisively and with virtual unanimity the proposal for a parallel ministry together with the suggestion that candidates should be accepted only from among their members. Therefore the committee had not thought it profitable to consider the alternatives further, and they had addressed their considerations to the 1946 proposals. The committee pointed out that were the principle to be not only reaffirmed but also implemented, consequent difficulties could then be resolved. There followed nine proposals, the first three corresponding with those of 1946 but with the substitution of 'resignation', the fourth required from a woman candidate the recommendation of her quarterly meetings and the last five brought the procedure for women into line with that for men. The committee added a footnote pointing out that their voting ratio was 11:3 more or less throughout.

The report[100] was presented by the Reverend W. J. Noble, who said the issue was to bring an agreed principle into effect. Proposals for a parallel ministry had been rejected by the deaconess order and the women missionaries, and both had urged that the door of the ministry should be opened, not only to the deaconesses and missionaries, but to any woman who received the call of God. He was seconded by the Reverend A. E. Binks, who said that if a woman were accepted, she would be accepted on the same terms as men from candidature to stationing, but with the exception that, if she married, this would be regarded as resignation or retirement.

Dr Howard said he interpreted the issue in a different light. In his view the current situation had arisen out of the first post-war Conference, where there had been a backlog of business. There, a series of resolutions had been carried, and the matter sent to the synods. This had led to bewilderment two years previously at the London Conference. In view of this, together with considerable opposition to the general principle, he had decided to move an amendment to institute a 'complementary' order of women ministers. Such could in the fullest way represent all the functions that women could perform in the church. He said he had had difficulty in getting the committee to concentrate on the issue of a complementary order of women ministers. He added that in the case of marriage, men enriched their ministry, whereas in the case of women, marriage would mean leaving that ministry. Mrs Elsie Harrison, commenting, referred to the ministry as a 'brotherhood' into which no woman could enter; should she do so, she would be nothing more than a non-union member in a closed shop.

Also against the motion was the Reverend Daniel T. Niles of Ceylon, who referred to equality in creation, but added that God used men and women differently. In the Bible, he said, the succession to which the ministry belonged was a male succession; God could have chosen, but did not choose, women. What was at stake was not ordaining women into the Methodist ministry, but into the church of Christ. He appealed for them to wait for a judgement from the church as a whole in the light of the formation of the World Council of Churches. Turning to the question of marriage, he described this as a natural rather than a practical difficulty. Wifehood and motherhood, he said, were more inclusive than husbandhood and fatherhood, and currently the former had been made more difficult by wars that had devastated populations.

A number spoke in favour of the motion. Dr Farrar disagreed with Mr Niles, and thought the Conference ought to look, as the Lambeth Conference was looking, further East. She referred to an Anglican document (which had been quoted in the press) by an Eastern province on the subject of the ordination of women to the priesthood which said: 'We understand that other provinces of the Anglican communion are afraid that our action may prejudice relations between our communion and some other Christian sects, e.g., the Romans.' Were they, she asked, to wait for the Church of England, while the Church of England waited for Rome. Mr Hickman Johnson said the question had been first raised ten years before union when he himself had nominated a woman candidate for the ministry and his quarterly meeting had accepted her. His chairman, Dr Dinsdale T. Young, had ruled her out of order, saying that there never had been a woman candidate and it was to be presumed that there never would be. He (Mr Hickman Johnson) had consulted Dr Ryder Smith, who had said, 'You must ask the Quarterly Meeting to send a memorial to Conference, and the Conference will appoint a committee which will meet for twenty years.' If they took into account the delays of the war and Methodist union, Dr Ryder Smith had been right. The committee had been meeting for twenty-five years – and in that time they had asserted the principle that women were spiritually equal, indeed their consciences had forced them to say it. He was supported by Dr Maltby, who said that the church, in claiming that the movement to treat women equally originated within it, could be told by cynics that it was only too ready to claim credit where it was not due. It was an act of honesty either to act accordingly to their belief, or to have it expunged from their books and say it was not true.

An amendment to affirm the principle but to wait until negotiations with the Church of England had progressed having been defeated, the vote was taken to accept the committee's recommendations. The result was 185 for the motion with 256 against. Consequently the report was received only, and Conference declined 'to declare its willingness to receive for Ordination to the Ministry of Word and Sacraments, women who believe themselves to be called of God to this work'.[101]

There the matter rested for eleven years.

2.2 The third period

2.2.1 Pauline Webb reopens the issue

The issue was reopened when Miss Pauline Webb raised a point of order at the 1959 Conference:[102]

I still fail to understand in what way this motion would be rescinding the Conference's decision to reject the memorial of the Sheffield North Quarterly Meeting given on p. 541 on the *Agenda*. That memorial asked us to reconsider the status of Wesley deaconesses with the particular end in view of giving deaconesses permission to give the Sacrament. We are asking for something entirely different: a Commission to examine the place and work of the Order in Methodism – and according to the OED place and status are quite different things – and the admission of women to the ministry which has nothing to do with giving deaconesses permission to give the Sacrament. In fact if you insist on regarding our motion as a notice to rescind it would mean that if our motion were carried, its effect would be surely to accept the memorial which is not at all what we are asking for.

She pointed out that the Methodist Churches in New Zealand and South East Asia were ordaining women ministers and the Church of Sweden had reached a decision to accept women candidates, while in the Lutheran Church conversations were taking place. Yet the only reference to be found in the Methodist ordination report was a very vague acknowledgement of the anomalies existing within the Wesley Deaconess Order, and a brief reference to a decision taken eleven years previously. Not that it was her intention to argue at that point the case for the acceptance of woman ministers:

Indeed, I must confess I personally would be far more interested in hearing the arguments of those who oppose the idea, for I cannot imagine what reasons theological, psychological or even plain logical they could produce in defence of their position. But this Commission would give them an opportunity to tell us.

It would also, she added, give them an opportunity to remove some of the very shameful anomalies existing in the Wesley Deaconess Order. She had been assured that a certain deaconess, who was fulfilling all the functions of a minister, could not have permanent recognition for reasons she (Pauline Webb) found very difficult to understand.

I'm told that to admit women to the Ministry would raise all kinds of practical difficulties. I can only wonder then why in the case of our deaconess we simply add considerably to her practical difficulties by expecting her to do the work of a man but paying her less money and giving her no manse. Such discrimination would, I submit, not be tolerated now in any other profession than the Christian ministry.

Then summing up:

I ask this Conference to set up this Commission so that the matter might be examined, not in the light of what was happening a generation ago, but of what is happening now. I would like to see on that Commission representatives of the Faith and Order Committee, of the Wesley Deaconess Order, of the itinerant ministers, and of lay men and women who together might give real time and prayer to the topic that they might decide what Methodism shall say on this issue in the Councils of the Churches, what she will say to these women who, as even the 1948 minute frankly admits, may feel themselves called to what you, Mr President, have called the most glorious of all privileges, ministry in the Methodist Church, but who at present, if they remain within Methodism, face all the heartbreak of being unable to answer that call.

As a direct result of this intervention a committee was appointed to consider the status of deaconesses and the admission of women to the ministry. They took as referent for their report[103] the question 'How can the Methodist Church best make use of the devoted service that women can offer their Lord?'

The summarised report is indented in case the reader wishes to pick up the historical thread a few pages on.

> First the ministry of women was considered historically. 'Jesus Christ restored woman to that status of equality with man before God which was part of God's original intention for her as the Old Testament describes it.' Whereas she had been created in God's image (Gen 1: 26–8; 2: 18–23), as a result of sin she was objectified and became the property first of her father and then of her husband. But Jesus spoke in the same way to both sexes (Jn 4: 7–27), offering to women friendship, help and forgiveness as he did to men (Lk 7: 36–50; 10: 38–42). Some of the women who had been healed accompanied Jesus and his disciples on some of their journeys (Lk 8: 2), and some were among the witnesses of the resurrection. No theological conclusion could be drawn from the absence of women among the twelve or among the seventy (Lk 10: 1) since the social conditions would have precluded their inclusion. Their restored status was recognised by the apostolic church. Several were leaders of the churches (Acts 16: 13; 1 Cor 1: 11), others 'laboured in the Gospel' (Rom 16: 12; Phil 4: 3), and Prisca took a leading part in instructing Apollos (Acts 18: 26). Some fulfilled regular ministries. Philip's four unmarried daughters were prophetesses (Acts 21: 9); Paul took it for granted that women should prophesy (1 Cor 11: 5); Phoebe was a 'deacon-

ess' [*sic*] of the church at Cenchreae (Rom 16: 1); and the author of 1 Timothy 3: 11 was held by some to refer to women as included in the order of deacons. Some women formed an order of widows (1 Timothy 5: 3–16).

Two passages appeared not to tally with the overall picture. 1 Corinthians 14: 33b–5, which in some older manuscripts appeared after verse 40, was considered an interpolation by some scholars, but not by the committee. They preferred the interpretation that some women were interrupting the prophets, so Paul forbade them to speak when a service was in progress. 1 Timothy 2: 12 was assumed to be post-Pauline, and evidence that the post-apostolic age wished to curtail the freedom of expression that Christian women, in their new-found liberation from social bondage, were claiming. This passage linked with a debate concerning presbyter-bishops. Some considered that as women were not included among the latter, women therefore did not take part in the superintendence of churches or in the celebration of the Lord's Supper in New Testament times, while others would translate 1 Timothy 5: 2 as 'female presbyters'. The committee thought the second position did not fit the context of 'an Epistle which everywhere so definitely forbids women to exercise any authority over men or to be teachers (II: 12)'.

Three 'beliefs' of the early church concerning women were discerned, namely, that the difference between the sexes had been transcended (Gal 3: 28), that the 'charismata' of the Spirit were given to both sexes – but 'we are not . . . told . . . that women are the recipients of *all* the "charismata" ', and that the subjection of Genesis 2: 21–2 was operative (e.g. 1 Cor 11: 3; Eph 5: 22–4; 1 Tim 2: 13–14). The committee were of the opinion that it was on the basis of the third that women were excluded from among the presbyter-bishops, and thus from administering the Lord's Supper:

> It is held by others that the reason was that, since it is a priest who administers the Lord's Supper, and a priest represents Christ Himself, and only a man can represent Christ, women are incapable of administering the Sacrament. But the notion of the minister who administers the Lord's Supper as a priest representing Christ is wholly alien to the New Testament, which never refers to an individual as a priest at all. The doctrine of the 'priesthood of all

> believers' means that we are all taken up by faith into the priesthood of Christ, and are identified with Him in His complete self-offering as we offer ourselves completely to God

and this applied equally to women. The committee concluded that of these three beliefs, the first two were concerned with 'the great matters of faith' and remained forever valid, whereas the third was bound up with the conditions of the age and therefore had no such binding validity.

After New Testament times, as the emphasis on priesthood increased, so the likelihood of the ordination of women decreased, because it was linked with the idea of representation of Christ, added to which there was a reaction against 'priestess'-associated religions. Seemingly no question of ordination arose until well after the Reformation.

Women did exercise the ministry of deaconess. There is a probable allusion in Pliny's letter to Trajan about the Christian church in Bithynia (AD 112), but the first post-New Testament Christian reference to them as an institution dates from the beginning of the fourth century. The way in which Clement of Alexandria and Origen referred to the New Testament deaconesses seemed to the committee 'to imply that the order had lapsed in their time' (late second and early third centuries), but the fourth-century writers spoke as if the order were well established in their own time, 'and we may take it that it was revived in the course of the third century'. There was evidence for its continued existence until the eleventh century; it began in the East, spreading to Gaul and then to Rome. By the late Middle Ages it has disappeared both in East and West, in the West at least the functions of deaconesses being taken over by abbesses and nuns.

After ordination by the bishop with the laying on of hands, the deaconess' functions included acting as an intermediary between the bishop and women who wished to consult him, assisting at the baptism of women (but not actually baptising them), taking and administering the consecrated elements of bread and wine to the sick, teaching the faith to women and children, and keeping the doors by which women entered the church. Many writers and some Councils during this time pointed out what women were not allowed to do, such as baptise, or preach, or pray or sing aloud in church, approach the altar, or bless, thus implying that they had actually done these things. The lower age-limit for deaconesses varied from forty upwards and they were always either virgins or widows.

In the West, where the monastic orders proved more attractive to women, the abbesses received far greater powers than any woman had previously held in the church. Within their own nunneries they conducted all the services of the church except the eucharist. They held virtually supreme control over those under their authority, including the male inmates of the double monasteries. 'The principle of the subjection of women certainly did not operate in their case.'

The Reformation critique of monastic life and of the illicit influence of women in high ecclesiastical places meant that the whole position of women had to be rethought by Protestants. This resulted in a great emphasis on family life, and 'on the spiritual influence of mothers on their children', while the part unmarried women could play in church life was obscured. It was not until the nineteenth century that the order of deaconesses was established in any church of the Reformation. It was begun by Pastor Fliedner in Kaiserswerth on the Rhine to care for the old and the ill, and spread rapidly among Protestant churches on the continent, including the Methodist ones. The first Anglican deaconess was ordained as such by the bishop of London in 1862.

The admission of women to the ministry had been considered by most churches except the Roman Catholic and Orthodox during the current century. The Church of England and the Church of Scotland had taken no positive steps, but the General Assembly of the latter had voted in 1960 for their admission to the lay eldership. Several of the Lutheran Churches admitted women to the full ordained ministry, and in Germany there was in all such churches an order of vikarinnen, trained in the same way as men ordinands, in some churches 'ordained' and in others 'consecrated', and whose functions varied. The Congregational Churches, the Disciples of Christ, the Baptist Churches of Great Britain, and the Northern Baptist Churches of the United States admitted women to the ordained ministry on equal terms with men. The Presbyterian Church of England, having earlier asserted the principle, had one ordained minister. Where the Methodist

Church had united with other churches to form the United Church of Canada, and the United Church of Christ in Japan, each accepted women on the same terms as men. In the Methodist Church of the United States women had been admitted as 'supply pastors' and 'ordained local preachers' more than thirty years previously but without a vote at Conference, guaranteed appointment or retirement benefits; it was in 1956 that they gained 'full clergy rights'. This ruling also covered those European Methodist Churches which were under the jurisdiction of the Methodist Church of America. The Methodist Church of New Zealand had three ordained women ministers.[104]

In the second part of the report the history and functions of the Wesley Deaconess Order was examined. The Wesleyan order had been founded in 1890 by Dr T. B. Stephenson with the three guiding principles that there should be vocation but no vow, discipline without servility, and association without excluding freedom. From 1902 the order was based at Ilkley, and in 1928 the course was extended from one year to two. When the order was recognised as a department of the church in 1907 there were 175 deaconesses, including 14 overseas and 19 in college. In the Free Methodist Church an order existed (founded in 1891 by the Reverend T. J. Cope and based at Bowron House, Wandsworth), and deaconesses, but no organised order, in the Primitive Methodist Church (the Reverend J. Flannigan began to train sisters who later came under the home missions department). Following union, 25 deaconesses from the Primitive Methodists, 57 from the United Methodists, and 290 from the Wesleyan Methodists merged at Ilkley in 1935.

The 1936 Book of Offices included a service for 'The Ordination of Deaconesses', where 'ordination' replaced 'consecration', following the wording used in the Church of England and the United Methodist Church. In 1942 Conference adopted various resolutions, including 'Ordained Deaconesses are not to be regarded, any more than Ministers, as employees. The only right relationship is an honourable colleagueship, in which no gifts of leadership and insight need be denied their exercise, and a Deaconess will have scope and freedom to do the work for which she has been trained and ordained.' Among the various regulations adopted were that candidates should intend life service, ordinands should be personally presented at Conference and admitted to full membership of the order by a resolution of Conference, continuity of service should be assured, stations printed in the *Minutes*, and ordained deaconesses in active work should be members of the representative session of synod. In 1943 Conference resolved in the light of the openings for women in society that it was 'deeply concerned lest the Church should show itself timid and unadventurous in entrusting women with responsibility and opportunities of leadership'. To this the convocation of the order replied in 1947 by approving (200: 5, 4 neutral) the resolution of the Conference committee that women should be admitted to the ministry with the same status as men save that marriage should normally imply resignation. By a similar majority the convocation disapproved of the alternative suggestion of the Conference committee concerning a parallel ministry of the word and sacraments designed only for women [see above, p. 47].

In the absence of a welfare state, originally deaconess work was philanthropic, with a spiritual impetus. Over the decades there was an increasing demand for deaconesses to preach, and at the time of the report there were about 60 who had pastoral charge of societies, and 38 who had dispensation to give the sacrament. Others served in industry, moral welfare, and youth work. The caravan campaigns had continued since 1934, and the chaplains' assistants had been serving since 1940 when the first woman appointed to a chaplaincy in the armed forces was a Wesley deaconess. Need rather than policy had effected these changes. 'Financial consideration and manpower shortage have also played their part in bringing about the present situation in which the Church is increasingly using Deaconesses to fill what would otherwise be ministerial appointments in the Circuits.'

In order that deaconesses should be given the status that was their due, which in turn would render their work more effective, the committee made a number of recommendations. First, that the confusion with regard to status should be clarified. In many circuits a deaconess was recognised as a member of ministerial staff, but in others her name appeared only in the list of local preachers or class-leaders. 'Honourable colleagueship' (1942) should mean that a deaconess was a member of the circuit staff meeting, and was responsible, like the ministers, directly to the superintendent. On the circuit her name should appear following the list of ministers. Secondly, whereas ministerial appointments had to have the sanction of synod and Conference, a deaconess' appointment was subject only to a vote at quarterly meeting. A committee was working on this, but the committee recorded 'our belief that this somewhat casual method of opening and closing Deaconess appointments diminishes their status, and lessens their security'. Thirdly, another committee was considering pay, which in the judgement of the committee was too low: 'Circuits should not be encouraged in the belief that cheap ministerial labour is available by securing a Deaconess.' Fourthly, although scope for gifts of leadership had been extended since 1942, the committee recommended continuity of policy until a decision was reached concerning the ministry. Continuity of policy with regard to dispensations between one deaconess and her successor was also recommended. Fifthly, although thirty-eight deaconesses were authorised to administer the sacrament the committee did not recommend an extension to all as this 'would be tantamount to ordaining Deaconesses to the Ministry of the Word and Sacraments, and so forming a parallel ministry to that of the men'. Finally, it was recommended that training at Ilkley be extended to three years.

The third part of the report addressed the issue of women and the ministry. Following a historical summary of the movement (which surprisingly omitted the years 1920–32, during which Dr Maltby initiated the movement prior to union [above, pp. 25–37]), the committee considered various practical considerations. The scholarship and intellectual ability of women were beyond question, and their sympathetic understanding equipped them for pastoral duties. While it was queried whether a man would take his problems to a woman, it was pointed out that a man minister like a deaconess often built up a predominantly female church. It was suggested that women faced problems emotionally and personally and thus would be subject to nervous strain which would have to be faced normally without the support of a married partner.

However, were these difficulties decisive, it would be concluded that a call to the ministry was delusory and the traditional exclusion determinative, and indeed it was sometimes argued that the call was experienced by few, and few had the required qualifications. But numbers were not crucial in matters of the spirit, the committee pointed out, adding, 'Where the Church declines to admit women it is not to be expected that women will think of the Ministry as God's way for them.'

Were women to be admitted to the ministry it should be on the same terms as men, and the minister free to hold any office. No vow of celibacy could be required, but a married woman minister should not 'be encouraged to neglect her home to serve the Church',[105] and so she should either resign or be without pastoral charge. If the latter, she should remain a minister, answerable to the ministerial session of her synod, and 'There are circumstances ... such as early widowhood, in which it might be possible for her to resume her ministry'. A 'fundamental difficulty' remained in either case, namely, the primacy of the ministry as a lifelong service and thus the question of whether marriage annulled the ministerial call.

Finally the committee agreed that the ecumenical aspect should be taken into account when making such a change in church order, particularly with regard to churches with whom they were engaged currently in conversations.

In conclusion:

> We are not able to bring to Conference a recommendation on the Admission of Women to the Ministry that would command the support of all the members of the committee, and we have good reason to believe that the division among us accurately reflects the corresponding division among the Methodist people.

They again drew attention to the practical considerations, some of which had 'no facile solution', and were of the opinion that an immediate decision would not be in the best interests of the church. They recommended full consideration of the issue at district and circuit level.

Among the resolutions concerning deaconesses attached to the report were:

(a) That a Deaconess be recognised by the whole Church as called of God, and trained and ordained for the service of the Church.

(b) That she be recognised as one whose service is primarily evangelistic and pastoral, and that she be not denied opportunity to exercise gifts of preaching, initiative and leadership.
(c) That she be recognised as colleague on the staff of the Circuit to which she is appointed, responsible to the Superintendent, and thus sharing in the policy-making of the Circuit.
(d) That her name be printed on the Circuit Plan following those of the Ministers.

Presenting the report to the 1961 Conference,[106] the convenor said that deaconesses had been used in situations for which they had not originally been intended, and as they were now working in the ordinary work of the church the question of their status had naturally arisen – they should not be regarded as a pool of cheap, trained labour. Conference later approved a resolution moved by the Reverend Harold Key that deaconesses who retired from active work should 'remain members of the representative session of the Synod in the District in which they reside', with the addendum suggested by the Reverend Leslie Davison: 'and retired by pastors on the official Home Mission lists'. The resolutions concerning deaconesses were passed.

As far as women and the ministry were concerned, the convenor pointed out the problems were complex and should be considered by the whole church.[107] Mr David Foot Nash moved an amendment to the effect that the part of the report on women and the ministry should be sent to those engaged in conversations with the Church of England, 'with the indication that no outcome of the conversations will be acceptable to Conference which does not preserve its future liberty of action and freedom of judgement on this issue'. He said the Church of England should also be presented with a picture of Methodism five years hence, adding that in the years to come the answer to manpower might be womanpower. Replying, Dr Harold Roberts said they had no mandate to conduct negotiations, and he trusted that if they were able to come closer together they would not agree to withhold the liberty of judgement they stood for. The amendment was defeated, and the report accepted with slight modifications. The words 'and we have good reason to believe that the division among us accurately reflects the corresponding division among the Methodist people' were deleted, and after 'facile solution' was added 'Nevertheless, having stated the practical problems, it is recognised that the issue facing the Church is whether it is God who is calling women to the Methodist ministry. A consideration of practical difficulties is part of our task in seeking God's will, but what He wills is always possible.' It was agreed to send the report to the synods and quarterly meetings, and that the committee should confer with the overseas districts.[108]

The committee presented their analysis of the replies of the synods and quarterly meetings to the 1963 Conference.[109] Of the 28 synods that replied, 4 rejected the proposals, 11 were non-committal, and 13 gave general approval while in most cases asking for further consideration of the theological and practical issues raised. The wide variation in resolutions received from the 140 (out of 920) quarterly meetings defied analysis in a brief report, but roughly two-thirds approved in principle, with many asking for clarification or for a detailed scheme, while one-sixth were non-committal and the remaining one-sixth opposed. The committee added that publication of the report on the conversations with the Church of England had made the ecumenical aspect of primary importance, and the conversations had proceeded on the assumption that in both churches only men were ordained. It was thought unilateral action 'would stultify the discussions by altering a basic factor', and would 'confuse both issues'. The committee did recommend exploration of the theological, practical and ecumenical aspects,[110] and were reappointed so to do.

2.2.2 Ecumenical delays and discussions

In 1964[111] and 1965[112] the committee recommended no action, and requested reappointment. In 1966 they presented a slightly fuller report with a brief historical survey of the years 1948–63, but reiterating the belief that a decisive resolution would impede conversational progress.[113] An Anglican commission considering the subject and due to report[114] in the autumn had been invited to a joint meeting, but without effect. The committee recommended the appointment of a joint Anglican–Methodist committee, and asked not to be reappointed.

Presenting the report, the Reverend A. Kingsley Turner said like Jacob the committee had served for seven years, but had no 'reverend Rachel' to present to Conference.[115] This he saw as part of the cost of ecumenism. In its earlier days it had had a mandate to bring recommendations to Conference, but had been brought up sharply 'by the information it received about the ecumenical situation, especially with regard to Anglican–Methodist relations'. No joint meetings with the Anglican commission had materialised. The official Anglican–Methodist negotiating committee had not been asked to consider the question because it was felt that its agenda was already so full that a decision on women in the ministry could not be reached by 1968 and 'we did not want to hold up its deliberations with this particular problem'.

Seconding, the Reverend Rupert E. Davies said he was committed to both courses, namely, the ministry of women and ecumenism. He referred to Conference's reaffirmation in 1961 of the declaration made in 1933 that no function of the ordained ministry could be found from which women were disqualified by reason of sex, and said he believed that there were theological reasons for accepting women into the ministry in the new creation which was the work of Christ. Moreover, the psychological reasons urged against were not compelling; women had psychological capacities which were complementary to those of men, which could lead to a more effective ministry of partnership. But nevertheless he added that a vote in favour would complicate the ecumenical situation.

Miss Webb, the ex-vice-president, moved the following amendment to precede the words of the committee's resolution:

> This Conference affirms its conviction that women may properly be ordained to the ministry of the Word and Sacraments. Recognising that it would not be wise to take unilateral action at the present time, it desires to discuss with representatives of the Church of England the implications of this principle for the ministry of both our Churches and for our recognition of the validity of the orders of women so ordained in other branches of the Christian Church.

She said the committee's proposal took back to square one a discussion which had been going on for at least seven years. She agreed that immediate unilateral action would not be wise, but the cause of unity would not be furthered by their refusing to have any convictions of their own. The issue should be seen in a wider ecumenical context: at least forty members of the WCC ordained women, some of them were churches within their own denomination, and others were churches that were moving into closer union with Methodism. She indicated three courses open to Conference: to declare their conviction that women should be ordained and then discuss with Anglicans what this meant for their own ministry, and what might happen to any woman they might choose to ordain before stage two of the union; they could say that women should not be ordained, and in that case thy must face up to their relationship to women already ordained in other churches; or they could do what the committee suggested, which really meant doing nothing at all. She concluded: 'I for one do believe that God is calling women to the ministry of the Church . . . and I devoutly believe that Methodism will have the wisdom to recognise this fact and even to rejoice in it and, please God, soon make it possible for women to be obedient to that call.'

A number of speakers supported Miss Webb's amendment. Dr Maldwyn L. Edwards said that many in the Anglican Church were sympathetic to the ordination of women, and that by admitting women to the ministry they would strengthen their hands, as well as those of sister churches. It was not desirable to be so careful over tactics that convictions would be obscured. The president of the United Church of Zambia, the Reverend Colin M. Morris, supporting the amendment, said, 'It will be a great help to those of us who have responsibility in the autonomous Churches and who are facing a similar dilemma'. He added that if it were argued that there might not be room on the agenda, his answer would be that any agenda which could include the question of fermented or unfermented wine and omit women in the ministry was an unbalanced agenda. Miss Eileen Tresidder remarked, 'The Methodist Church has a great tradition of declaring where it stands, and I hope we will not enter into these negotiations without doing so.'

The amended resolution was passed by an overwhelming majority.

In 1967 the ministerial session of Conference instructed the Faith and Order Committee to explore the meaning of being in communion with another church, and in 1968, having adopted the report, asked for another on the meaning to be attached to the nature and extent of communion between churches. In May of the same year the report of the Anglican–Methodist commission, *Women and the Ordained Ministry: Report of an Anglican-Methodist Commission on Women and Holy Orders*, was published.[116] In point of fact, the Anglican–Methodist scheme did not receive a sufficient majority in the Convocations of the Church of England, although at the Methodist Conference held on 8 July 1969 the scheme received a vote in favour of 77.4 per cent, 75 per cent having been required.

2.2.3 Towards ordination

In 1970 the Faith and Order Committee presented to Conference the report requested in 1968.[117] This included endorsement of the section in *Women and the Ordained Ministry* about the Methodist Church ordaining women under stage one to the effect that although neither church should criticise the other, an irritant though not necessarily an insurmountable barrier to stage one would have been introduced. A suggested solution was for an agreement such as the one operating in the Church of South India, whereby women Methodist ministers would not perform (the committee understood 'would not claim the right to perform') in the Church of England those acts in Anglican practice reserved to the priest. Stage two would be more problematic.

The committee asked Conference to adopt these observations on stages one and two and to agree attached standing orders for the admission of women to the ministry. The first three were:

(i) Women who offer themselves for the ministry shall do so under the same conditions as men, in relation to candidature, training, probation, ordination, status, stationing, allowances and retirement, except as provided below or elsewhere in Standing Orders.

(ii) Married ordained women ministers shall, if they so request, be exempt from the normal stationing by the Conference. At any subsequent Conference they may ask for appointment to a Station. In the case of such exemption their names shall be printed in the Circuit in which they reside, and they shall be expected to give such help to the Circuit as they are able, and in appropriate cases shall be entitled to receive remuneration by the decision of the Circuit Quarterly Meeting.

(iii) Married probationer women ministers who are not able to be stationed annually by the Conference shall withdraw from the ministry. If subsequently they apply for reinstatement by the Conference, regard shall be had to the training they have received and the years they had travelled when they withdrew.

These three were followed by two taking into account the previous training and experience of deaconesses requesting candidature, and a final one on pensions. The committee added a note on consequential standing orders.

The Reverend A. Raymond George, presenting the report,[118] spoke first about the observations on *Women and the Ordained Ministry*. They had preferred 'would not claim the right to perform' because if the Methodists ordained women and stage one was implemented with full exchange of clergy, the Church of England might then say that until they had women in the Anglican ministry, they could not let women ministers perform functions that women in the Anglican Communion could not. Under their preferred phrasing, if a Methodist woman minister were invited by a local Anglican church, she would not refuse. Turning next to the decisions concerning the admission of women to the ministry, he said that according to counsel's opinion such were proper to the ministerial session. Accordingly the latter had resolved that it asked the representative session 'to state its judgement about the proposal that women may offer as candidates for the ministry in accordance with the Standing Orders provisionally prepared for the purpose'. The standing orders which were accepted provisionally by the ministerial session would only become effective should Conference finally by the vote of the ministerial session in 1971 confirm that it had agreed to accept women as candidates for the ministry. Finally Mr George pointed out that in the standing orders the important phrase was 'under the same conditions as men' – although some special provisions had been made, that was the overriding principle.

There was some debate on the legality of the proposed process. The Reverend Douglas A. Wollen did not think they ought to take lying down a ruling by some solicitor to the effect that the ministerial session alone could make the decision. A delay, he said, was a serious matter to those women who felt themselves called to the ministry, and moved that the representative session should accept for immediate implementation the standing orders concerning the ordination of women that had been submitted to the Conference. The Reverend Irvonwy Morgan thought Mr Wollen's proposed action would wreck any possible form of union with the Anglicans. He said that the catholic and conservative evangelical wings of the Anglican Church had united, and together constituted a powerful force, the former totalling 1,000 priests and the latter 3,000; the total number of priests was 9,800. Together the two wings would use the weapon of the ordination of women to destroy any scheme of union. He urged Conference to delay the issue until they saw whether the Anglican Church achieved its 75 per cent majority for the scheme of union. The Reverend Douglas W. Thompson disagreed, saying he had every sympathy with Mr Wollen's position but he did not think his proposal was viable. In reply to Mr Morgan he did not think their proposed legislation was out of tune with the minds of many Anglicans. He said the whole world trend was toward an equal partnership of women and men, that church life was enriched in the places where the ministry of women was accepted, and in this he thought the Methodist Conference was required to take the lead. However, after further legal argument Mr Wollen withdrew his proposal, adding 'But I feel it is really intolerable that the opinion of one, or two possibly, legal men should be produced to restrict the powers of the representative session of the Church'.

Then the Reverend David H. Tripp proposed the motion, 'That the representative session of the Conference reiterates its theological approval of the admission of women to the ordained ministry, and adjudges such admission to be both practicable and desirable.' He gave examples of churches that already admitted women to the ministry: several German churches, several Dutch evangelical churches, the Congregational Church in Britain, and the Church of Sweden. 'I get the impression that the most healthy thing in ecumenical relations is to do what you think is right', he added. In support, Mr Cecil Sharp said that in favour as he was of Anglican-Methodist union, fundamental beliefs were more important than schemes of union. One of those beliefs was equality between the sexes. On the other hand, Miss Lillian F. Todd spoke against the motion as it seemed to her confirmation of the trend in which the number of women in the church increased, while the number of men decreased. Mr Tripp, having accepted an amendment to his resolution such that the last four words read 'practicable, desirable and timely', it was carried by a large majority. It was further agreed that the observations and resolutions approved by both sessions should be sent to the synods in their representative sessions for discussion and report to the ministerial session of the Conference of 1971.[119]

Twenty-nine synods reported their acceptance, with one adding the sentence 'That, should full Church Union with the Church of England be accomplished the Methodist Church make every effort to ensure that women ministers be on the same footing as men ministers in all matters pertaining to the Ministry'.[120] Therefore Conference in its ministerial session resolved to accept women into the ministry of the Methodist Church on the conditions outlined by the Faith and Order Committee at the Conference of 1970. Next, the standing orders were sent to the ministerial session of the district synods, and any practical problems associated with the entry of women into the ministry were referred to a working party of the general purposes committee, to report to the 1972 Conference.[121] Its report and resolutions were accepted by the ministerial session of the 1972 Conference.[122] The final decision to admit women as ministers was taken by Conference in 1973, and seventeen women were ordained in 1974.

Meanwhile the future of the Wesley Deaconess Order was in debate. In 1971 their convocation discussed whether a woman ordained to the ministry could remain a deaconess.[123] In 1972 it became clear that deaconesses accepted into the ministry would be reluctant to sever their links with the order, and a resolution was passed in the light of the proposed admission of women to the ministry asking the Faith and Order Committee 'to examine the meaning of both presbyteral and diaconal ministries'.[124] The following year the warden, the Reverend Brian J. N. Galliers, remarked that he did not envisage the end of the order even though twenty-three members were candidating for the ministry,[125] but finally the 1978 Conference resolved that recruitment to the order was to cease, that a committee should consider the present and future role of the order, together with the possibility of a new order of lay service within the church.[126] At this stage there were 287 Wesley deaconesses, of whom 90 were in church appointments, 24 in other appointments, 37 without appointment because of marriage (30), home claims or studies, and 136 were retired.

By the end of the 1978 Conference, 89 women (including 32 from the Wesley Deaconess Order) had been accepted for training for the ministry: of these, 51 had been ordained to the ministry, 13 were probationers in circuit appointments and 25 were in college.[127]

SECTION TWO

THE CHURCH OF ENGLAND

After the dissolution of monasteries, there followed three centuries during which women had no officially recognised part in the structures of the newly Established Church. In 1845 the Anglican Sisters of Mercy, based on European deaconess houses, were founded and by 1860 there were approximately twenty-five such sisterhoods, working among the poor and sick. In the recently restored Convocation of 1858, notice was placed of a proposal for reviving the order of deaconesses in the Church of England. In 1861 Elizabeth Ferard, who in 1858 had been at the continental foundation of Kaiserswerth, offered to introduce the deaconess order in England, and founded the religious community of St Andrew in London. The seeds had been sown for a debate, contained in official church documentation, which was to last over a hundred years.

I THE SECOND PERIOD: THE ISSUE EMERGES IN THE CHURCH OF ENGLAND

1.1 Sisterhoods and deaconesses: 1861–1919

On 9 July 1861 at the Convocation of Canterbury the Reverend R. Seymour proposed that the upper house be asked to 'deliberate and agree on certain rules by which women ... may be associated together on terms and conditions distinctly known as those which the Church of England has sanctioned and prescribed'[1] (828). He recalled that

> the very mention of such an object immediately excites fears and suspicions lest the leaven of some old error should be at the bottom of it: it is surmised that some undue merit is attached to a single life as compared with married life; and that we want to lay the foundations of the old monastic and conventual life which was abolished in England at the time of the Reformation. (830)

He illustrated the groundlessness of such fears with a historical survey of the work of such women, adding, 'if the Church allows women thus to form themselves into Sisterhoods to do her work (for her work it is) amongst the ignorant, the fallen, and the afflicted, she is bound to give them the protection and the comfort of her open sanction' (838). Otherwise, those who both from 'natural weakness' and 'the nature of the work' deserved 'the tenderest consideration and care', were exposed to 'continual uncertainty as to . . . their position in the Church'. He added that discrepancies were occurring between dioceses and between successive bishops, and legislation was required to cover minimum age, designation, parental versus ecclesiastical authority, mode of reception and rule of life, dress, and the question of vows.

The following February a more generally worded amendment was moved asking simply for 'sanction and guidance' as the time was 'not yet ripe for any such express and formal enactments'.[2] Whereas it had been reported that the bishop of London was ready to accept the term 'deaconess', the Reverend H. Mackenzie objected 'to committing the Church of England to the recognition of Orders as conferred upon Deaconesses in the same sense as that in which they are conferred upon Deacons' (916) because if interpreted as 'ordination', it would be contrary to the scriptural passage, 'I suffer not the woman to teach, neither usurp authority over the man.' He added, 'I hope it will be clearly and distinctly understood that we do not regard the commission given by our Lord to His Apostles as in any strict sense applying to those women who are proposed to be organised into societies.'

Disquiet was expressed lest the sisterhoods 'interfered' with the parochial system, and concern about the forms of devotion (that they should be 'in harmony with our Prayer Book'), and the making of vows. Often voiced was the need of 'ecclesiastical supervision and control' to curb 'indiscretions'. Moreover, 'any extravagances into which they have fallen are owing to the fact that they have been left to themselves; . . . that they have been unable to look up to the Church to father their institutions' (912). Were this to be rectified, it was believed 'these females would give themselves wholly to the work, and would only be too thankful to be guided and directed by the clergy' (916).

Mr Seymour accepted the amendment because he had meanwhile received letters from sisterhoods and from those engaged in reviving the order of deaconesses, expressing apprehension at the direction the house was taking. They thought it would be wiser simply to declare the church's sanction and to abstain from uniformly laying down definite and distinct regulations.

Two days later on 14 February the upper house concurred with these sentiments. In the words of the president, it would 'injure the cause we desire to promote if we were to interfere with the exercise of their free judgement and discretion' (964). A motion was passed offering encouragement, and placing the onus of guidance on parochial clergy. Thus the way was clear for the bishop of London, Dr A. C. Tait, to ordain Elizabeth Ferard deaconess in July 1862.

Thirteen years later the lower house appointed a committee to consider 'the rise, progress and present position of Sisterhoods and Deaconess Institutes in the Church of England',[3] and the report was presented in 1878.[4] Historically, the committee noted the 'very grievous corruptions' that had found their way into the conventual life and although these had been countered by stricter rules, not more than six additional institutions had been founded in England during the 180 years immediately preceding the dissolution of the monasteries. The committee acknowledged the good work done by active communities subject to Rome, and 'similar bodies in Eastern Churches, especially in Russia', while the value of that done by the Church of England sisterhoods since their revival could scarcely be overstated. Yet this gladness was alloyed with anxiety:

> We fear for those communities which fail to seek and obtain recognition from the rulers and fathers of our Church, and consequently are subject to no regulating authority to which they would feel it their duty to submit, when contrary to their own opinion or taste. There seems to us real reason to fear that (where there is no such regulating authority) practices and principles may be admitted that are really alien from the Church of England. (5)

The report was based on four larger and ten smaller independent communities, the former numbering not less than 460 and the latter (who had replied) not less than 200, and thus a large number of women was involved, 'and . . . their influence must be powerful and widely extended' (6). It was necessary therefore to secure them in a loyal and faithful attachment to the church; 'above all things, . . . they should receive a friendly recognition from the rulers and fathers, and from the synods of the Church, and . . . the sisters themselves should thereupon show a readiness to submit to episcopal authority' (7). It was suggested that the affiliation of smaller communities to one of the larger ones already under episcopal authority would be advantageous (presumably to the clergy) and would be 'an additional security against the introduction of forms, practices, or principles open to objection in themselves, or likely to give offence' (9), while the subordination of younger women to older ones would be 'a wholesome guide to enthusiasm'.

On the other hand, the number of deaconesses was limited, but they had obtained a distinct recognition from the archbishops, and from the majority of bishops. 'The submission of the deaconesses to existing authorities is absolute' (7). Their mission (and its withdrawal) was from the bishop. The committee had no anxiety about them and wished they were more numerous.

The lower house debated a series of resolutions.[5] First, that there was 'great reason for thankfulness' for the work already done in the Church of England 'by Sisterhoods, Brotherhoods, and Deaconesses, work which could scarcely have been otherwise accomplished'. Interest was expressed that sisterhoods were more popular than deaconess houses and it was pointed out that sisterhoods worked independently of the bishop. Archdeacon Emery remarked, 'I think the time has come when our Fathers in God should take Sisterhoods in hand'; 'woman's nature really requires direction' (243). Secondly, the house expressed its thankfulness for the 'Episcopal recognition already accorded to these institutions in several dioceses' (247). It was felt there was less likelihood of the 'great evils existing in the religious houses at the time of the Reformation' being repeated if the sisterhoods were under the supervision of a bishop. The third motion gave rise to a long debate on the subject of vows, the limits of obedience, and the use of the prayer book. In its amended form it read: 'In view of the great danger which may arise without the safeguard of Church authority, it is desirable that certain principles should be laid down for their regulation', with the rider, 'and that no such institution shall receive such sanction as Convocation can give, unless it is willing to acknowledge the binding character of such general principles as shall accordingly be laid down' (263). The final resolution requested their lordships to direct their attention to the recognition and regulation of those institutes by the synods of the church. The appointment of a joint committee was proposed.

In 1883 the upper house debated whether the organisation and rules of sisterhoods should be brought directly under episcopal supervision.[6] There was widespread feeling in the house that the sisterhoods were too independent. The bishop of Chichester had wished to use an institution in an auxiliary way, but on enquiry, had found 'they were under a very strict rule, and that they were determined to admit of no interference whatever which should disturb their practices' (136). Deaconesses, on the other hand, were viewed in a more favourable light as they were under the immediate direction of the bishop. The house decided to appoint a committee to consider how sisterhoods should be brought under the authority of the church.[7]

On 8 July 1885 the joint committee reported[8] that it had considered sisterhoods in relation to 'the work which, by the constitution of human nature, woman is fitted to do, and to the character impressed on her sex', which was towards the sick, children, and the needy. 'These employments stand to her in the place of the public duties, or physical toils, which occupy men' (274). They recommended that the establishment of branch houses should require the assent of the bishop, and external work that of the parish priest, while within the communities vows should only be made in so far as release could be granted by the bishop. On the other hand, the deaconess acted and worked under the parish priest and the bishop. The committee recommended that deaconesses should be admitted by the bishop with the laying on of hands, that there should be adequate probation, that episcopal release from the office should be required, that there should be no unlimited promise of celibacy, that licence should be from the bishop, that dress should be simple but distinctive, and that a move between dioceses should require episcopal permission.

During debate, the bishop of St David's pointed to the ambiguity of the deaconess' position, a position analogous to that of the deacon. 'A deacon was a member of a recognised order in the Church of England; the deaconess was not, and they could not make her a member of a recognised order' (278). The bishop of Winchester referred to the bishop of Durham, 'who had most distinctly expressed himself to the effect that the orders of the Church were imperfect so long as they lacked deaconesses'. He agreed with the bishop of St David's that they had no legal power to revive the order of deaconesses, but what they could not do in law, at least they could do in practice, and possibly at last as part of the constitution of the church and realm. The committee was asked to submit resolutions based on the report.

A series of resolutions was duly put before the upper house on 7 and 9 May 1890.[9] The work of the sisterhoods and deaconesses was recognised, but there was a move to guide, direct, and even check the work of the sisterhoods. According to the bishop of Winchester, 'Sisterhoods are always asserting their authority over Deaconesses, and Deaconesses are strongly tempted to become Sisters and quit their position as Deaconesses because they are pretended to be an inferior body' (175). However, the bishop of Oxford thought the paper was going too far in recognising the deaconess as a distinct order. He said he would agree to the laying on of hands provided 'it is not to be understood as conferring the character of an order', but, rather, appointment and benediction (176). When the finally agreed resolutions were brought before the house on 4 February 1891,[10] the bishop of Ely pointed out that 'benediction' implied 'whatever sanction it is in our power to give'.

The revival of the office of deaconess received the recognition of the Lambeth Conference[11] of 1897, as did the revival of the sisterhoods. A committee appointed to consider the relation of religious communities to the church and to the episcopate stated that 'No full statistical information is at present available as to the progress that has been made, or as to the variety of usage in different branches of our Communion'. The committee cautioned against too general an application of the term 'deaconess' to women engaged in 'good works' in the light of the revival of the office, and recommended careful training for deaconesses.[12] At the Lambeth Conference of 1908 the committee confessed to 'some disappointment' in recommending a further postponement of formal or authoritative corporate action throughout the church. The deaconess network, seemingly, was developing too slowly.[13]

Nine years later and in the light of the forthcoming Lambeth Conference an archbishop's committee was appointed to consider 'the sanctions and restrictions that govern women in the life of the Church, and the status and work of deaconesses'. In 1919 it presented its historical report, *The Ministry of Women*.

Summaries of this and other more substantial reports in the Church of England are indented in case the reader wishes directly to pick up the historical thread a few pages on.

The committee noted that whereas in Judea and the Roman Empire generally women were socially, educationally, and influentially inferior, they appeared frequently and prominently in the gospels where Jesus gave no endorsement to their lower status. They followed him, stood by him at the cross, and were the first to whom he manifested himself. On the other hand, the twelve and seventy were men, the Lord's Supper was instituted in the presence of the apostles only, the apostolic commission was delivered to men (Jn 20: 19–23), as was the evangelistic charge (Matt 28: 16–20). 'These facts taken together are proof that there were functions and responsibilities which at the first our Lord assigned to men and did not assign to women' (2). Consequently church government and responsibility for the ministry of word and sacraments has always been entrusted to men. This position is confirmed by a number of passages, notably in Acts, which bear on the place and work of women. At Pentecost women prophesied, yet the apostle did not sanction teaching in public by women (1 Cor 14: 34–40; 1 Tim 2: 12). Privately they served. Phoebe is referred to as 'deaconess' [*sic*] (Rom 16: 1), and this is later recognised as a class of church officials (1 Tim 3: 11), together with widows (1 Tim 5: 10) and virgins (1 Cor 7: 7). While Galatians may sweep away distinctions in Christ, 'these mundane differences are indelible: and each variety has its opportunity of special service' (4). The committee concluded that the restriction of the priesthood to men from apostolic times might have been due to the exclusion of women from public posts of official administration, or to the influence of Jewish usage in Temple and synagogue, or 'it may have been due to the recognition of fundamental differences in function and calling inherent in the natural variety of sex' (4–5).

Between the New Testament and the *Apostolic Constitutions* the only reference of importance to a deaconess is in Pliny's letter to Trajan (about AD 112) in which he refers to *ancillae quae vocantur ministrae* (*Ep.Lib.* x, xcvi). There are references to apostolic times in Clement of Alexandria (*Strom.* iii. 6, ed. Potter 1, p. 536) and Origen (*Ep. ad Rom.*, Book x: 17). Yet in the writings of the leading Greek writers of the fourth and fifth centuries there is no hint of any lapse and subsequent revival of the order. From the early part of the fourth century down to the eleventh, or even later, there is continuous evidence for the existence of deaconesses. There are patristic references in the days of SS Basil and John Chrysostom; the Councils of Nicaea (AD 325) and Chalcedon (AD 451) legislated for them, and when in exile John Chrysostom wrote letters to Olympias and a body of forty deaconesses attached to the Church of Constantinople. St Epiphanius describes their duties in Cyprus, and Gregory of Nyssa and Theodoret refer to them as being at the head of a body of virgins. We have here the beginnings of an identification of deaconess and abbess which becomes more clearly defined later in the West. From the sixth century onwards they are found in the West, although not in Rome until the eighth century, and as late as the eleventh century three popes gave the local bishops the right of ordaining them. Their functions included servant of the bishop, assistant at the baptism of women, bearer of the eucharist to the sick, teacher, and keeper of the doors at churches.

They continued in the separated Eastern churches, but in the Orthodox East they have remained in abeyance since the Middle Ages. In the West traces remain in the consecrated nun. The contemporary Roman Pontifical contained a rubric directing the bishop to hand the breviary to the newly consecrated nun with 'the faculty of beginning the canonical hours in place of the diaconate of women' (7). A Carthusian nun was vested in stole and maniple, and sang the liturgical gospel at Matins. It would seem, the committee remarked, that the deaconess first became monastic and then disappeared, leaving some scanty traces of what she once was.

As regards ordination, the earliest evidence of the laying on of hands is in the *Apostolic Constitutions*. Χειροτονία and χειροθεσία were used, as of other orders. Nicaea contains an obscure reference to ex-Paulianist deaconesses, who were to be regarded as unordained. Chalcedon speaks of ordination with imposition of hands. Justinian's *Novels* uses χειροθεσία, and the same forms of address were applied to deaconesses as to other clergy, while their rank seems to have been with deacons and before sub-deacons. In the consecration of a Carthusian nun the stole and maniple are delivered with the same words as are used in the ordination of a deacon.

The evidence of the *Apostolic Constitutions* and older Greek Euchologia justifies the assumption that the diaconate conferred was as real a diaconate as that conferred upon men. In the *Apostolic Constitutions* the bishop lays his hands on the deaconess, using *εἰς διακονίαν* as for a deacon. In the Greek Euchology, the prayer which accompanies the laying on of hands admits her to the rank of ministers, *λειτουργοί*. Any restriction of function due to sex or circumstances was not a defect or absence of order.

Among the Nestorians deaconesses in the absence of deacons could give both the bread and the wine of communion to women in the churches. They read the scriptures to assemblies of women, and in the absence of the clergy took care of the altar, the lamps and the communicants' roll. Among the Monophysites in the sixth century, abbesses were deaconesses, and in the absence of ordinary ministers had power to enter the sanctuary and say public prayers, and to give communion to their own religious in their churches. Deaconesses presided at assemblies of women and read the scriptures to them. The bishop could permit them to pour water and wine into the chalice but not to take part in the service at the altar, since they were, according to St James of Edessa, deaconesses not of the altar but of sick women (12).

Tertullian says that it is not permitted to women to speak in church, nor to baptise, nor to offer, nor perform the duties that belong to men (*De Vel. Virg.* 9), and he is indignant that women teach and baptise, contrary to the command of the apostle (*De Bapt.* 17). The *Apostolic Constitutions*, the Gallican Statutes, and the *Older Didascalia* forbid women to baptise too, but St Isidore of Seville says that those baptised by women are not to be rebaptised (Augusti, *Denk.*, p. 115). The *Apostolic Constitutions* says that women cannot bless (viii, 28), and abbesses are forbidden by Charles the Great to bless, or to lay hands on anyone, and in AD 825 a Council at Paris forbade an abbess to consecrate nuns (14–15). The *Apostolic Constitutions* and the *Testamentum Domini* forbid widows-president to speak in church, and in the *Older Didascalia* women are not to teach at all. Gelasius, as proof of the popular contempt for religion, complains that 'women are appointed to minister at the sacred altars'. Moreover, the Isidorian Decretals attribute to Pope Soter a law forbidding women to touch the sacred vessels or consecrated pallia, or to carry incense around the altars.

When the deaconess had become absorbed into the nun, we find no ministrations of women outside the religious orders. Here they carried out the full choir services of the church, carried out the majority of processions themselves, and admitted and clothed novices, and even read the whole of the burial service.[14]

The committee concluded that from the earliest days two tendencies were at work, 'the one recognising the deaconess and giving to her and other women definite parts in the administration of the sacraments and services of the Church, and the other ignoring the deaconess or curtailing her position, and limiting to the minimum the share of women in church services' (20).

1.2 Deaconesses and priesthood: 1920–48

The day *MOW19* was presented, a motion to allow women to speak and pray in consecrated buildings was put before the upper house, and in 1920 the lower house, and in each it was overcast by the shadow of priesthood. In the upper house the bishop of Oxford proposed an additional clause formally and canonically restoring the diaconate of women, adding, 'there was no doubt that the Church had, both in East and West, asserted in the extremest form the principle that women were not admissible to the priesthood' as a matter of theory rather than of legislation.[15] The debate in the lower house followed a similar pattern. Dr Sparrow Simpson was not in agreement with a critical interpretation of 1 Corinthians, arguing for 'the principle of the subordination of women in the order of creation and the order of grace'. The office of preacher was refused to women in the New Testament, while the priesthood was not explicitly barred. He argued that the supporters of the feminist movement would say, 'If you base your objections to our priesthood on the ground of tradition, and if, in spite of tradition, you are prepared to admit us to your pulpits, you are accepting the principle of tradition in the one case, and you are cancelling it in the other'.[16] In conclusion, the upper house appointed a joint committee to consider the principles which should bind a bishop when sanctioning women's ministrations; the lower house resolved that it was 'not desirable' to grant the proposal.

The matter of the formal and canonical restoration of the order of deaconesses was referred by the upper house to the Lambeth Conference.[17] This body, meeting in 1920, passed as resolution 47 that the diaconate of women should be formally and canonically restored. In resolutions 48–52 it was added that the 'Order of Deaconesses is for women the one and only Order of the Ministry which has the stamp of Apostolic approval, and is for women the only Order of the Ministry which we can recommend that our Branch of the Catholic Church should recognize and use'. It was to be primarily a ministry of succour following primitive patterns rather than that of the modern diaconate of men. A uniform pattern of 'Form and Manner of Making Deaconesses' was to be adopted destined for *The Book of Common Prayer*; this ceremony to include the laying on of hands by the bishop, the giving of the authority of office, and the delivery of the New Testament. The functions of a deaconess were detailed as: to prepare for baptism and confirmation; to assist at baptism and to administer in case of necessity; to pray with and to give counsel to women; and, with 'the approval of the Bishop and of the Parish Priest', in church 'to read Morning and Evening Prayer and the Litany, except such portions as are assigned to the Priest only', and in church to lead in prayer, to instruct and exhort the congregation.

These recommendations were contained in the committee report no. 5 on the position of women, inspired by *MOW19*. Other recommendations which did not find their way into the conference resolutions were:

> In our judgement the ordination of a Deaconess confers on her Holy Orders. In ordination she receives the 'character' of a Deaconess in the Church of God; and, therefore, the status of a woman ordained to the Diaconate has the permanence which belongs to Holy Orders. She dedicates herself to a lifelong service (102)

and, as regards functions, 'to render assistance at the administration of Holy Communion to sick persons' (104).

At the first meeting of the upper house following the Lambeth Conference, the bishop of Ely, as chairman of the committee that had drawn up the conference resolutions, proposed a motion to approve resolution 47, and to appoint a committee to approve resolutions 48–52.[18] During the debate that followed, the bishop of London drew attention to the unrest that had arisen following the resolution, and which had been formulated by Professor Turner in the *Church Times*. In his letter he had argued that no woman ever 'undertook a public function' in a mixed congregation, and that no order of women ministers 'was ever universal, and an order of limited currency' could not and had never been regarded 'as on a level with the orders universal in the Church. In other words, Deaconesses were not in Holy Orders.' He had noted 'with thankfulness' the Conference decision not to ratify the committee's judgement that a deaconess was in holy orders, and had ended his letter with the suggestion that misunderstanding might have been avoided if *διακονία* and *λειτουργία* had not both been translated by 'ministry' (14). The bishop said that he had received a deputation not opposed to the revival or recognition of deaconesses, but which had echoed Professor Turner's sentiments. He pointed out, moreover, that a very large minority in the Lambeth Conference itself had opposed the words 'in Church also to lead in prayer and under licence of the Bishop to instruct and exhort the congregation'. At this point the bishop of Exeter suggested that the chancel be veiled off, and women permitted to address congregations in the nave.

The bishop of Truro replied that the world of the day, and the place of women in it, was very different from that in which Professor Turner had conducted his researches. He (the bishop) believed that the spirit of God was leading them, and it was their business so to equip the church as to bring it into the twentieth rather than the fourth century. There might be occasions when they could quite definitely depart from ancient traditions, though not traditions which had the absolute authority of the Master. He concluded that the bishop of London had set before the house the anxieties of a large number of people who took a certain view, but he thought it was as well to remember that there were a large number on the other side who were equally anxious. The resolution was carried.

In 1923 the Convocation of Canterbury passed a series of resolutions, based on those passed at the Lambeth Conference, formally restoring the office of deaconess. In 1925 the Convocation of York followed suit, with the reservation of the permission to speak in consecrated buildings. In 1924 the upper houses of both Convocations agreed on the service for making deaconesses, which included the laying on of hands, and the delivery of the New Testament.[19]

The Lambeth Conference of 1930 reiterated that the order of deaconess was 'for women the one and only Order of the ministry', but the phrase 'which has the stamp of Apostolic approval' was dropped both in the resolution and in the report of the committee on the ministry of the church. At the same time the deaconess' functions were slightly extended to include baptising in church and officiating at the churching of women, and also instructing and preaching, 'except in the service of Holy Communion' – thus repeating the pattern noted historically in *MOW19* of diminution of status alongside extension of function. The committee frankly admitted that 'the hopes underlying [the] action of 1920 have been but meagrely fulfilled' (177), and set out to give new content, purpose and clarification to the 1920 Lambeth resolutions. Conjured up is 'a vision of a great Order of ministry for women, distinct from and complementary to the historic Orders of the Church':

> We desire ... to affirm that the order of Deaconess is an Order *sui generis*: the only Order of ministry open to women, but an Order which both from the solemnity of its ordination and the importance of its functions can satisfy the fullest desires of women to share in the official work of the Church,

wrote the committee, adding that historical precedent did not need 'entirely restrict us in our endeavour to enlist the great gifts and special contribution of women to the varied and immense needs of the Church to-day' (178). They wished to universalise the form and making of deaconesses in England, which they perceived as a real ordination, but the delivery of the New Testament by the bishop was no longer advised as 'we are informed that such a modification will make for unity ... and will also tend to remove a cause of confusion between the Deacon and the Deaconess' (179).

This change in direction from that in which Lambeth 1920 had been pointing may be seen in the context of a movement, formally expressed in a memorandum, *Women and Priesthood*,[20] which had been sent to the archbishop of Canterbury, as president of the Lambeth Conference, from a group of clerical and lay members of the Church of England, who could not see any objection in principle to the ordination of women to the priesthood. A majority of the committee could, but seemingly the strength of the case offered led them to conclude that a fuller answer was needed on the theological side than had been given in 1920. Consequently, an archbishops' commission was appointed 'to examine any theological or other relevant principles which have governed or ought to govern the

Church in the development of the Ministry of women'. Their report, again called *The Ministry of Women*, was presented in 1935.

> Whereas *MOW19* was historical, the emphasis of *MOW35* was theological. The commission noted that with the possible exception of occasional references in the first four or five centuries outside the Greek Church, the assumption that women could be priests had not been challenged. Thomas Aquinas had simply provided a rational framework for what was then regarded as indubitably right. Some felt that what had been rarely discussed in the past needed further reconsideration and justification, and in particular Aquinas' view of women's subjection was questioned in the light of Galatians 3: 28. Others felt that the constant practice of the church being rooted in the historical development of the church's ministry was a weightier argument, and would say that the Pauline passage did not imply identity of function.
>
> No single argument was considered by the commission to be sufficient ground for the exclusion of women. Two arguments were brought by witnesses. The first noted the usage of the masculine in reference to God and that the incarnation took place in the male sex, arguing that although 'our Lord in His manhood transcended sex ... those who carried on His mediatorial work should do so on behalf of both sexes while being men as He was man' (28). To this it was countered that the claim that the sex of the priest had to be the same as that of Christ and that only then was the element of sex transcended was precisely the claim that was questioned. The second argument concerned the relationship of the persons within the godhead as involving an equality combined with subordination. But this argument from analogy, while showing that subordination did not involve spiritual inequality, did not prove that the same sort of relation ought to obtain between man and woman in the sphere of the Christian ministry. Another witness laid special emphasis upon the teaching of the Bible and the church, which he argued pointed to the conclusion that the admission of women to the ministry would be contrary to the will of the Spirit.
>
> The commission differed with regard to the weight to be given to the respective arguments.

While the Commission as a whole would not give their positive assent to the view that a woman is inherently incapable of receiving the grace of Order, and consequently of admission to any of the three Orders, we believe that the general mind of the Church is still in accord with the continuous tradition of a male priesthood. It is our conviction that this consensus of tradition and opinion is based upon the will of God and is, for the Church of to-day, a sufficient witness to the guidance of the Holy Spirit. (29)

They also thought that to admit women under article 34 would 'raise a doubt in the minds of many, or confirm the opinion of those who deny that the Church of England is part of the Catholic Church of Christ' (30).

With regard to deaconesses, the commission saw the principal issue as the significance of their ordination. Deaconesses had been alarmed by the apparent regression between the 1920 and 1930 Lambeth Conferences. In the upper house on 3 July 1931 the archbishop of Canterbury had said that the status of women 'who are in Orders' should be decided and that any hesitation, as at Lambeth 1920, to use the phrase 'in Holy Orders', was largely due to the legal position which the phrase 'a person in Holy Orders' involved. The women should be regarded 'as being an Order within the Church to which they are solemnly ordained'. The commission saw it as an advance to have affirmed in 1930 that the deaconess was not simply the female equivalent of the deacon and thought a new 'great Order of ministry' could channel the unused gifts and capabilities of women. They also agreed with Lambeth 1920 that ordination conferred on her a 'character', that she was dedicated to a lifelong service, and that her status had the permanence of holy orders – although not parallel to any of the three orders, she should rank among the clergy. The commission concluded: 'The Order of Deaconesses . . . is a Holy Order and the one Holy Order at present open to women in the Church' (48).

Two additional contributions to *MOW35* are of interest. Although the dean of St Paul's agreed with the commission that it would be inexpedient to ordain women at that time, he differed otherwise with their conclusions. Policy and expediency should be distinguished from principle, he argued, and the tradition was not irrevocable if the possibility of the

'Christian Church as a whole' taking an alternative decision was envisaged. The Christian ministry was a ministry of the word and sacraments, and to develop a ministry of women which excluded the possibility of eucharistic celebration carried an implied inferiority. He saw no grounds of principle against the ordination of women.

He considered two theological objections: that there was something in the nature of women that rendered them incapable of becoming priests; and that the question had been settled by some authority. The first, involving the Romish notion of 'character', had not been submitted to the commission, but 'I may say that I should regard the conception of the grace of orders which this theory implies as erroneous and approaching dangerously near a magical view' (75). In a less extreme form it was expressed as some psychological or physiological disability which was ultimately an argument based on expediency. The dean suggested that it would be conducive to clearer thinking if the opponents were to ask themselves if they would regard a woman's ordination to the priesthood as valid though irregular, or entirely invalid. The second, namely appeals to some authority, pointed to the choice and actions of Jesus – to which the dean countered that thus only Jews could be admitted; to Pauline observations – which the dean saw as irrelevant; and to the authority of the church – which he thought was a more formidable position. Nevertheless, he was of the opinion that the principle could be decided by one part of the church, and that reunion, not an immediate prospect in any case, should be considered with caution by any Reformed church: 'many drastic changes were made at the Reformation, such as the repudiation of Papal authority and the abolition of the celibacy of the clergy, which are hardly less determinative of the life of the Church than would be the opening of the full ministry to women'. By accepting this objection they ceded their right and duty to advance more quickly than other churches. He agreed with the signatories that the Spirit guided the church, but took a different view 'of the manner in which this guidance should be recognised'. He concluded that not only was there no case against the ordination of women, but that the theological principle of personality should lead to the opposite conclusion.

In Jesus Christ there was neither male nor female, and the ministry and institutions of the church should be judged, and if necessary reformed, in the light of this principle.

Also attached to the report were psychological and physiological considerations outlined by Professor L. W. Grensted. He argued that the strong feelings on both sides together with 'a wide variety of rational explanations' pointed to 'powerful and widespread subconscious motive', which he attributed to 'infantile fixation', which differed between individuals:

> it is clear that the general acceptance of male dominance, and still more of feminine inferiority, resting upon sub-conscious ideas of woman as 'man manqué,' has its background in infantile conceptions of this type. These commonly, and even usually, survive in the adult, despite their irrationality, and betray their presence, below the level of conscious thought, by the strength of the emotions to which they give rise. It is strongly in support of this view that the admission of women to Holy Orders, and especially to the ministry of the sanctuary, is so commonly regarded as something shameful. This sense of shame cannot be regarded in any other light than as a non-rational sex-taboo. (81)

Historically, in the Old Testament and elsewhere, evidence could be found for the strength of these unconscious forces. A sacrificing priesthood was typically a male priesthood, although there was a secondary principle by which in some pagan cults the sacrificial act was performed by older women. This rested directly on the radical significance of sex-function and was typical of nature religions. Although priestesses occurred they had distinctive functions. The correlation of the eucharist with pagan and Old Testament ideas of sacrifice which took place in the second and third centuries was undoubtedly a factor in restricting thc priesthood to men, thus confirming the operation of these unconscious motives which were operative in Christianity as strongly as elsewhere. In periods of free expression when women had wished to move into male roles they had met with powerful forces of resistance. Were these established arrangements to be upset, the professor suggested the loss could well be greater than the gain. On the other hand, the Christian priesthood rested not on subconscious emotional factors, but on the institution of Christ. 'So far as psychology is concerned there is no theoretical reason why this Christian priesthood should not be exercised by women as well as by men and in exactly the same sense. The difficulties which the psychologist foresees are emotional and practical only' (83).

The professor did perceive a difficulty in the theory of the sexlessness of the [male] priest. 'Psychologically sex is never irrelevant where personal relationships are concerned, and the Christian priesthood cannot be conceived apart from the system of personal relationships, pastoral as well as official, within which it is exercised'. It did not explain why it should be confined to one sex. The theory of the priest as sexless did not 'prevent the play of the unconscious psychological forces with which we are concerned. It is equally true that the play of these forces would not cease with the admission of women to the priesthood' (83).

In January 1939 both houses of the Convocation of Canterbury agreed to regulations on the status and function of deaconesses, and the York regulations were brought into line with them in 1941. It was affirmed that the 'Order of Deaconesses is the one existing ordained ministry for women, in the sense of being the only Order of Ministry in the Anglican Communion to which women are admitted by episcopal imposition of hands'. With regard to status, no mention was made of 'Holy Order', as in *MOW35*; with regard to function, although Lambeth Conferences had recommended that the deaconess be allowed to administer baptism, officiate at the churching of women, 'read Morning and Evening Prayer and the Litany' and to preach 'except in the Service of Holy Communion', these Convocation resolutions only permitted her these functions '*in case of need*'. From 1947 deaconesses were governed by canons D1–3, which were amended over the years, with major changes in 1969 and the substitution of a new canon D1 in 1973.[21] The Deacons (Ordination of Women) Measure of 1987 finally closed the order of deaconesses to new recruits.

In May 1945 the presidents of both Convocations reported to the upper houses that a letter had been prepared by the archbishop of Canterbury William Temple[22] in answer to the bishop of Hong Kong on the matter of the latter's purporting to have ordained a deaconess to the priesthood.[23] The letter was sent, although the archbishop died before signing. The relevant passage reads:

I cannot think that in any circumstances whatever an individual bishop has the right to take such a step, which is most certainly contrary to all the laws and precedents of the Church, and I therefore feel obliged to tell you that I do profoundly deplore the action you took and have to regard it as *ultra vires*.[24]

After the war, the diocese of South China had proposed to its province a new canon to provide that, for an experimental period of twenty years, a deaconess might be ordained to the priesthood. No action was taken, but a question was sent to the 1948 Lambeth Conference as to whether such a liberty to experiment would be in accordance with Anglican tradition and order, since such was based on the autonomy of national churches. The Conference replied 'that in its opinion such an experiment would be against that tradition and order and would gravely affect the internal and external relations of the Anglican Communion' (*LC1948*, res. 113). The committee report made it clear that the reply did not result from a discussion of the principles upon which the tradition and order rested. It was thought that the time was not yet ripe for further discussion (quoting *MOW35*), and that the order of deaconesses should 'satisfy the highest aspirations' (*LC1930*, res. 67).

2 THE THIRD PERIOD

2.1 *Gender and Ministry*: the issue of 'ministry' raised

The report of the Central Advisory Council for the Ministry (CACTM), *Gender and Ministry*, was presented to the Church Assembly[25] in 1962. The working party had considered the role of women within the 'priestly body' of the church in the wider context of the rapidly changing sexual relations in English society. They thought note should be made of the vast gulf between the social context of the early church fathers and the relationship between the sexes in twentieth-century England. However, they perceived the real question to be not of the relative status of men and women but the 'question of the nature of ministry'. They asked in what sense a priest's calling to be 'in Christ' was different from the lay Christian's; what was meant by 'indelible seal' as other vocations also required a lifelong commitment; and expressed their bafflement that the recognition of holy orders was given to only one out of the many ministries. They added that many people would be encouraged 'if the too-prevalent attitude towards the clergy as the recipients of some semi-magical status could be clearly and forcibly disclaimed, discouraged and discarded' (11).

The working party pointed out that while the role of women depended on clarification of the role of the laity, there was ambiguity surrounding *laos*, which meant *whole* people of God, but which had come to mean the non-clergy. According to the New Testament, the whole church was priestly. There was a priesthood of the laity just as there was a laity of the priesthood in so far as priests remained part of the *laos* while receiving a 'representative priesthood'. The Church of England had not evolved a truly representative ministry for women. There was confusion surrounding the status and function of deaconesses, and they were convinced 'that the Church needs without delay a representative ministry of women just as it needs a representative priesthood of men' (17):

> We have only to say this however to become conscious of the fear, strongly felt by some, that an extension of the ministry of women as a lay vocation within the total Ministry of the Church will be 'the thin end of the wedge' leading to the demand for the ordination of women to the priesthood. (19)

They suggested that though women were not ordained priests, did not 'celebrate the Eucharist', and did not 'give the Father's blessing to the congregation', this did not mean 'that *functionally* they could not perform these acts as members of the priestly Body which is the Church'. It was simply that the Church of England did not 'call its women members to minister thus *sacramentally*'. It was recommended 'that the various reasons for this withholding of the ordained and representative priesthood from women, reasons theological, traditional, instinctive, anthropological, social, emotional, should be much more thoroughly examined'.

On 7 November the bishop of Lincoln, moving that the report be received by the Church Assembly,[26] pointed out that the primary concern had been to ensure that the ministry of women be discussed theologically, in line with or against the changed status of women. They had deliberately avoided the more particular, and in many ways the more limited, issue of the ordination of women to the priesthood, as the issue would be divisive, but they could certainly accept the recommendation that the reasons for withholding the ordained and representative priesthood from women should be thoroughly examined by a competent group or commission of theologians. Seconding, the dean of Westminster pointed out that although it was nowhere proposed that women should be admitted to holy orders, 'CACTM would not dare to say that never, *never*, in the future history of Christendom as a whole could women enter upon Holy Orders'. Above all, they had been at great pains 'to set the ministry of women within the priestliness ... of the whole body of the Church' (685).

Predictably, a number of voices were raised in protest. Mr O. W. H. Clark was concerned about the recommendation that qualified lay women as well as lay men should be permitted to take statutory services and give addresses at them. He thought that the report failed to come to grips with the ways in which the 'dignity and ministry of women' could be expressed in a positive way, and that by implementing this proposal they would be 'just aping the men', which would also be to depart from the general tradition of church order. Such a move would not reassure catholic Christendom. He looked on the report as the 'thin end of the wedge' towards the ordination of women (687–90). Canon R. L. Hussey 'revolted from the idea of a mixed ministry', suggesting that to raise the subject of the ordination of women was 'nibbling away at the foundations of the Catholic Church'. He wanted emphasised 'this counterbalance between priest and layman, just as there was between man and woman'. He drew the attention of those who thought the ministry of women was undervalued to 'the Blessed Virgin Mary', adding that the church, in holding her up as a model, was responsible for the emancipation of women (690–1).

The Reverend F. P. Coleman argued that the church, though influenced by society, was not the product of society, but the gift of God, as was her ministry. The argument that because of social changes the church had to reorder her ministry was a dangerous line to take. It was for them to find God's will for what he had given; it was not a question of 'some think', 'some say'; they were a body within a tradition, with a common mind (693–4).

The Reverend (from 1969 Prebendary) Henry Cooper returned to the 'imitation of men' theme. He found the phrase 'priesthood of the laity' wholly untheological, suggesting it was 'borrowed from the Free Church phrase, "the priesthood of all believers", a vain thing fondly invented by those who had no true priesthood'. He pointed to the existence of a doctrinal reason against the ordination of women, 'in the theology of creation and not in the findings of Church

Councils, which had never so far pronounced on these things because there had been no need' (705–6).

Taking an opposite position, the bishop of Woolwich argued that the report was right in stressing that the theological question was not whether women should be priests, but how the priestly ministry of the whole body was to be given in a community where six out of ten of its confirmed members were women. He did not think that the report should be allowed to get away with the sentence, 'We are convinced that the Church needs without delay a representative ministry of women just as it needs a representative priesthood of men.' He believed that it needed a representative ministerial priesthood in which male and female were as irrelevant theologically, if not socially, as black and white. This would come, but meanwhile they should pursue the full ministry of the laity, such that lay men and lay women had the same openings. He did not think that the skeleton of the priesthood of women could be put in the cupboard as neatly as some speakers had suggested. The report referred to

> the fear ... that an extension of the ministry of women as a lay vocation within the total Ministry of the Church will be 'the thin end of the wedge' leading to the demand for the ordination of women to the priesthood. This fear has again and again inhibited the dispassionate consideration of women's work in the Church.

This the bishop thought was true, but so was the fact that it was not open for women. It was simply an issue of responsibility, not of theology – and the refusal to face it was having a sterilising effect on all efforts on behalf of women. A deaconess could not do all that any man under the new canons could do; she was in orders, but not in holy orders. There was double-think on this subject. The report was right in suggesting that the kind of mentality engendered by this sort of clericalism should be clearly and forcibly disclaimed (699–701).

Miss (from 1986 Dame) Christian Howard said that this was a question of intellectual honesty, and the question should be discussed on its merits. She called for an enquiry into the theological and other reasons for the refusal of the admission of women to the priesthood (703–5).

The bishop of Lincoln, replying to a point raised by the chairman, remarked on the depth of the prejudice against the ministry of women revealed in the earlier speeches. He pointed out that the report had not stated categorically that there was no doctrinal reason against the ordination of women. The real issue was indeed one of responsibility; to see how the priestly body of the church functioned through men and women. The priesthood of all believers was a fundamental biblical concept, *pace* Mr Cooper. To suggest that because it was wished that the service of men and women in the church should reflect their changed relationship in the world it meant that women should ape men or be imitation men was not only offensive but also a hundred years out of date. Women were asking, rather, that the particular gifts of their own sexuality be brought to bear and used in the total service of the ministry of the church (707–9).

Finally, a motion was carried asking the archbishops to appoint a committee 'to make a thorough examination of the various reasons for the withholding of the ordained and representative priesthood from women' (713). The resulting report of this archbishops' commission, *Women and Holy Orders*, was presented to the Assembly in 1966.

2.2 *Women and Holy Orders*: the issue of 'priesthood' considered

Factors leading to the reopening of the question were the emancipation of women (considered a minor argument), new insights awakened by the spirit of the times, the failure of the church to provide an adequate ministry for women, and the shortage of clergy. The commission had responded with a unanimous report, based on written and oral evidence, as the cost of a sociological and statistical analysis to indicate the mind of the church would have been prohibitive.

The New Testament gave no clear answer to the question. Checks to female freedom were prescribed in 1 Corinthians 11: 3–16; 1 Corinthians 14: 34–5; 1 Timothy 2: 12; in connection with which it was a reasonable though not necessary deduction to conclude that the second was an interpolation in the spirit of the third. A suggested background to the third was Gnostic asceticism. It was not clear if the subordination implied here and in Ephesians 5: 22–33 of wives to their husbands was applicable apart from the marriage relation, whether it had permanent validity, and whether this principle of male supremacy was necessarily and in all circumstances a bar to the conferring of valid orders upon women. There was substance to the notion that Paul expected the role of women under Judaism to continue. On the other hand the church had fostered a more individualistic estimate of the personality, and this tendency 'could have become radically disruptive if there had been any major change then in the accepted understanding of the rôle of women' (14).

Although some church fathers stressed the sanctity some women had attained, the majority saw them as frail emotional creatures, subordinate to men on account of the fall and perhaps even by the original creation. From the late fifth century onwards there was a succession of prohibitions against women assisting in the sanctuary at the eucharist, on the ground that their presence was a threat to the chastity of the clergy. The only authority cited was scripture, especially the Pauline epistles. The reinforcing of the Pauline doctrine on the basis of Genesis 2–3 by the Aristotelian doctrine that the female was a defective male provided the possibility of a more developed statement such as appeared in Aquinas' *Summa Theologica* III suppl., 39. There he met three objections to the tradition with the argument that since woman was in a state of subjection she could not receive the sacrament of order. Again, in *ST* II–II, 177, 2, he explained that women were not allowed to teach publicly in church because of the subjection imposed by Genesis 3: 16; because men might be tempted to lust; and because normally women were not fitted for public teaching.

At the Reformation the radical sects such as the Anabaptists accepted women ministers, and female ministry became associated with social revolution and dissidence. Some Lutheran theologians classified women's preaching as 'things indifferent' and in modern times Lutheran Churches had accepted women as ministers, though not without some controversy. But the more traditional bodies in communion with Rome, Constantinople and Canterbury had not hitherto made an official and recognised move in this direction.

Next, the commission posed four questions to draw on empirical data from psychology, biology and sociology. The first concerned demonstrable psychological differences significant to a priest's tasks. Here, not only had general trends to be distinguished from individual performance, but no mental aptitude or personality characteristic was confined to men, and no biological or psychological qualities prevented women from performing these tasks. The second asked whether these differences were universal and unalterable. The reply was that though to some extent some psychological differences were innately determined, learning by experience had greater weight. Male/female roles differed between cultures; 'Theological statements about the "nature" of man and woman, or of masculine and feminine "principles", often involve assumptions about the desirability of particular sexual rôles and need to be considered in the light of the genetic and sociological evidence' (18). The third question concerned the symbolism of the priest and the possible effects of a change in the traditional sexual symbolism. It was replied that such was 'as yet imperfectly understood' but that the ordination of women would have profound psychological consequences. Finally, the existence of 'powerful irrational motives' were noted, and the difficulty in predicting and controlling behaviour prompted by them was stressed.

Ecumenically of theological interest were the questions of ministry and of relationship between the sexes. Difficulties surrounding variety of practice and discussion were illustrated in the WCC document, *Concerning the Ordination of Women* (Geneva, 1964). Out of the 168 member churches of the WCC in 1958, 48 admitted women to 'the full ministry', 9 admitted women to 'partial or occasional ministry', 90 did not admit women at all, while 21 did not reply. In Sweden ordination had produced division and bitterness. Some pressure had been put on the Church Assembly by the government, and the first ordinations had taken place in 1960. By 1965 eleven women priests had been ordained, and a greater number of ordinands and men priests had withdrawn. In England the Convocations had at once acted to exclude women ordained in Sweden from celebrating in their churches. Prior to the event, the archbishop of Canterbury had written to the archbishop of Uppsala, warning that the ordination of women would introduce 'a cause of embarrassment and dispute between the two Churches'.

In the Roman Catholic Church ordination was explicitly restricted to men. Theological speculation, however, was more open than canonical prescription, and ranged from perceiving women as inherently incapable of receiving holy orders, to according such ordination validity should the church so decide. The attitude to the practice of non-Roman churches was that it 'would be regrettable, and a set-back to unity, if a major historical Church were to act unilaterally in admitting women to the ministry'. However, the question of the ordination of women, even to the diaconate, was seen as of very little importance; more important was the function of lay ministry in the church as complementary to that of the clergy. The idea was utterly alien to the tradition and ministerial theology of Orthodoxy. Moreover, a firm distinction was 'drawn between the office of the deaconess (while it survived) and that of the deacon; he is a member of the sacred hierarchy; she was not'.

In England the Congregational Union admitted women to 'full ministry of Word and Sacraments' in 1917, and currently had thirty-four full-time woman ministers in service, almost exclusively in the smaller churches. The Baptist Union followed soon after but had only a small number of women on the ministerial list, an alternative ministry being offered by the deaconess group. The Methodist Conference had approved the principle between 1933 and 1945 but had received divided support from the synods. In 1948 Conference reversed the position, but in 1960 it was stated that there was no reason for excluding women on account of their sex. Still, the committee set up by Conference was divided: there was no theological impediment, yet there was little evidence of a desire for women ministers, quite apart from the difficulty in placing them. Currently, a report from this committee was under consideration at district and circuit level. It was noted in the light of the current Methodist/Church of England conversations, that the practice and its significance of giving dispensations to deaconesses (thirty-eight in 1962) in respect of pastoral charge to 'give the sacrament' might well have to be considered by those charged with negotiations.

Within the Anglican Communion there had been divisive feelings on two occasions. The first was the 1944 Hong Kong ordination, and the second the expressed intention of Bishop Pike of California in 1965 to ordain a deaconess a deacon in the light of his interpretation of the amendment to a canon made the previous year. Following domestic protests and a warning from the Vatican Secretariat that this would be an 'insurmountable obstacle' to unity, the bishop had referred the matter to the house of bishops. The house had resolved against, and declared expressly that deaconesses should not be permitted to administer the bread and wine of communion.[27]

Conclusions drawn from this ecumenical survey were: first, although division on the question no longer corresponded to episcopal and non-episcopal churches, nevertheless, resistance coincided with a high doctrine of the church, the ministry and the sacraments; it would be divisive in the Church of England. Secondly, such a step would strain relations with the Roman Catholic, and particularly with the Orthodox, Churches. Thirdly, the growing awareness of the nature of the church and its ministry as a theological question, and the subsequent sharpening of consciousness on doctrinal issues, would make the introduction of women ministers more difficult and divisive than it had been a generation or so previously.

The case against the ordination of women was put. First, it was argued that it would be contrary to the tradition of the church. It could not be validly maintained either that the apostles had failed to implement Christ's intention or that he had erred in failing to declare it. Secondly, Christ and the apostles had deliberately included women with men in the wider priesthood of the *laos*, and if the ministerial priesthood was composed only of males, this was in the divine ordinance as much as was the existence of the church itself. Allied to this was the contention that the maleness of the Christian priesthood must have had deeper grounds than mere conservatism or a 'poor estimate of the feminine nature' in the light of the esteem and value accorded otherwise to women in Christianity. Fourthly, all theistic religions had male priesthoods whereas female priesthoods belonged to pantheistic or monistic nature religions. The Christian church, rooted in the biblical view of God, had without question adopted the former. The introduction of a female priesthood would alter the essential character of the church and affect the human psyche at those deep levels at which it responded to religious symbolism. It 'could be more disruptive of the Christian Church than any heresy or moral deviation'.

Fifthly, the assertion that the ordination of women was the logical outcome of a steadily growing recognition of woman's full humanity was fallacious. 'A philosophy of social evolution making for this kind of equivalence of women with men has no backing in historical, philosophical, biological or religious theory.' Sixthly, there had been an enlargement of masculine aptitudes in Western civilisation 'and the feminist movement, by bringing women into the characteristically masculine way of handling life, has aggravated the disease'. The refusal to recognise complementarity and polarity tended towards further and more deep-seated restlessness.[28] Seventhly, the view that sex was irrelevant to the question was based on a no longer tenable belief in a sexless human nature underlying sex differences. 'There is in fact a masculine and feminine human nature with some complication from the shadow of the opposite sex in each.' The complementariness of the sexes required a representative priesthood, and 'a male priest represents both sexes in a way which a woman does not in organised society and in the Church'. Eighthly, there was an overwhelming probability based on 'the example of Our Lord, the teaching of the New Testament and the universal practice of the Church' that women could not receive 'Holy Orders'. Only an ecumenical council should dare assume the responsibility for ordaining them. Ninthly, practical difficulties were involved in being both a priest and a married woman but celibacy could not be imposed on women only. Tenthly, congregations were indifferent to the question. Finally, it was no deprivation to withhold the priesthood, as woman had 'their own kind of ministry' and much of the value of the 'specific gifts of the feminine sex' would be lost if women were drawn into the ordained priesthood.

The case in favour of the ordination of women was then presented. This was based on the need for renewal and for adapting the ministry of the church to the requirements of the day. It was not based on a basic identity underlying masculinity and femininity, nor on keeping abreast with the secular employment context. 'It is however argued that the differences between males and females do not correspond precisely to the differences which are said to make men capable of ordination and women incapable.' Indeed, a woman 'would bring to the priesthood particular gifts and insights which would enlarge its scope, enrich its witness and render it truly representative'. Opponents' arguments based on temperament, intelligence, tenacity of purpose or spiritual insight were to be rejected, as were those based on inferiority, deficiency or Pauline restrictions. Those derived from parental or nuptial imagery were to be treated with reserve. The image of divine Father, Christ, and Ephesians 5, should be balanced with Isaiah 49: 15; 66: 13, and Galatians 4: 19. It was not known why male dominance had persisted for so long. Social conditions had imposed restrictions on women, precluded them from positions of authority, and encouraged a male dominated paternalistic order. The Church of England had often been unready to accept change in the past, but now should reflect the partnership that had replaced paternalism in society. The concept of priesthood had moved from authority to service, and women were equally eligible to serve.

The commission then presented 'a third view', namely, that although there were no theological reasons against the ordination of women, there were powerful reasons why they should not be ordained. These were: that unilateral action would be unwise; that it departed from Anglican tradition; that needless controversy would be caused; and that it diverted the church from more urgent questions such as the ministry of the whole church. 'It may be that the Holy Spirit is leading the Church to such changes', but greater unanimity should be awaited between the churches and within the Church of England.

Finally, the commission turned their attention to the vicissitudes of the order of deaconesses. The confusion surrounding the order dated from its revival in 1861. The Tractarian revival had stimulated 'a new quality of devotion to the Person of Our Lord', whereby religious women following the example of those in the New Testament expressed their following of Jesus through a revival of the religious life complete with vows and celibacy. Yet contemporary Convocation debates revealed suspicion of 'these ladies', and they had to stay on the fringes of the church for a long time. When Elizabeth Ferard received 'dedication' at the hands of Bishop Tait, two sorts of 'order' were fused in the Deaconess Order of St Andrew, so many churchmen had difficulty in appreciating that what had been revived was an order of ministry.

The most serious source of confusion was the uncertainty of official pronouncements, particularly the discrepancies between the 1920 and 1930 Lambeth Conferences. New canons on the order of deaconesses, the 1924 Form and Manner of Making Deaconesses, and the 1939–41 resolution of Convocations further complicated the issue. In the latter it was stated that the order of deaconesses was 'the one existing ordained ministry for women'; they are admitted by episcopal laying on of hands and thereby declared to receive the blessing of the Spirit for the work of a deaconess. They were given a 'distinctive and permanent status in the Church' and were 'dedicated to life-long service'. They had to produce the same documents before ordination as a man had to produce before being made a deacon, and the 'Form and Order bear close resemblance to that used for the making of a deacon'. The words of ordination were precisely the same as those used for a man, with the substitution of the word 'deaconess' for 'deacon'. This in the commission's opinion showed a careless use of words. A deaconess is 'ordained'. She receives a 'character'. She is dedicated to a 'life-long service'. She is a member of an ordained ministry. She is in 'a Holy Order'. But she is not in 'Holy Orders'.

Historically, minor orders and holy orders were both 'ordained', but at the Reformation offices from the sub-diaconate downwards were cut away, and the word 'ordained' reserved for deacons and priests. So although there were historical precedents for applying the word 'ordained' to a deaconess, 'What did *not* follow and what no ecclesiastical lawyer could allow to follow, was that the deaconess was thereby admitted into Holy Orders as that term was known to the law, and known to comprise bishops, priests and deacons, and these alone.' From here arose the *sui generis* phrase. Yet just as the social conditions occasioning the service of deaconesses in the early church passed, and religious orders offered openings for women, so too the contemporary church might decide that the social conditions occasioning the nineteenth-century revival of deaconesses had passed, and had been replaced by professions offering status and other forms of service to women: 'to prolong it [the order] as an anachronism might be to discredit it'. An alternative was the reform of the order of deacon, making it a holy order of service to which men and women could be admitted on equal terms.

The commission recommended that the next Lambeth Conference should clarify the status of a deaconess; that her functions should be of general application; that her duties under canon D1 clause 2 be extended to apply to the whole congregation;[29] that it should be decided whether she could administer the chalice and read the epistle; and that the restriction in canon D1 clause 3a, 'in case of need', should be removed.

On 15 February 1967 the Church Assembly debated the motion that *Women and Holy Orders* be received.[30] The bishop of Chester said that the commission had not been required to judge the issue and had produced a report presenting 'a fair and accurate setting out of the issues for and against', to which were appended six essays exploring aspects of the subject, and representing the opinion of the authors. This statement was later challenged by Miss F. H. R. Williams, who argued that a committee had been requested to 'make a thorough examination of the various reasons for the withholding of the ordained and representative priesthood from women', whereas the commission formed by the archbishops were required to 'examine the question of women and Holy Orders'. The Assembly had asked for an answer, but the archbishops had not (213). That the commission was composed of two women and seven men did not escape the notice of Mrs E. D. Moffet (206).

The bishop underlined several issues arising from the report, including ecumenical considerations. The Church of England was 'in a particularly delicate position, poised as it is between the Catholic and Reformed traditions and belonging to both'. He remarked on how comparatively small an impact had been made by women ministers in the churches which ordained women, noting that there was currently only one Presbyterian minister in England (a point echoed by Prebendary G. B. Timms, who said that this was not the most compelling means of proclaiming the parity of men and women (211)), while on the other hand unexpected murmurings were coming from the Catholic Church, although 'the sharp reaction by Fr. Charles Boyer of the Vatican Secretariat for Christian Unity to Bishop Pike's intention to ordain a deaconess a deacon' did not suggest a pending change of heart. 'Serious divisions' had been caused in Sweden by the ordination of women, but 'it may be that this is less marked among the laity than among the clergy'. He drew attention to the 1966 Methodist Conference, held since the report was prepared, which had passed a resolution affirming its conviction that women might be ordained, and desiring discussion on the subject with the Church of England. The bishop concluded that basic issues underlying much of the thinking on the problem were prejudice, the meaning attached to the word 'representative', and the realm of the symbolic. In his opinion the most important sentence in the report was 'What a priest symbolises is perhaps even more important than his actual capacities' (*WHO* 46). Running through the report were questions surrounding the respective symbolism of the sexes, symbolism as yet little explored or understood (190–7).

A glance at church documentation suggests that Miss Howard was right in her belief that the debate could not have occurred four years earlier. She detailed her reservations about the report. First, the compilers had tried to consider the question in isolation from the whole current debate on the ministry, both ordained and lay. There were a number of highly questionable definitions of women; there was no definition of what was meant by holy orders. Secondly, she did not see how the proposed lay diaconate could work within the current paid professional ministry. Thirdly, she did not find satisfactory the statement that women could enter other professions. Fourthly, in the Swedish Church Assembly delegates opposed to the ordination of women had voted in favour because they could not accept the arguments raised against. Fifthly, although some people said that women did not want to be ordained, it was hard to offer oneself for something one's church did not offer. She concluded by pointing out that the Church of England would have to get its ministry right, and that she wanted the matter to remain open (198–200).

A number of other points were raised. Mr G. E. Duffield agreed with a remark of Miss Howard's that some who were not at the time in favour of the ordination of women ministers would prefer to see reasons expressed other than those of Canon Demant (200–1), who indeed was also criticised by Canon R. S. D. Stevens (208), and his arguments refuted in some detail by the Reverend Professor G. W. H. Lampe (214–18). Canon J. P. Hickinbothom and Prebendary Timms referred to the unsatisfactory treatment of women in full-time church service, and the former noted the broad hint in the report that the deaconesses were out of date and should be wound up (201–2); and was effectively supported by Deaconess L. B. Kidsdale who mentioned the reluctance of the church to create an effective ministry for them. Prebendary Timms picked up the point in Mrs Kay M. Baxter's essay concerning the confusion surrounding the term 'ordination', which he proceeded to clarify, saying that the term 'must not be confined to that act of the Church which admits a person to the Order of Presbyter or Priest'. He said that the plenitude of ministerial authority in the church was conferred by our Lord upon the twelve, and later this inhered in the episcopate, which is where discussion should begin. He referred to the Orthodox position, where the bishop was the representative of Christ, the bridegroom, and suggested that it was because of this symbolism that hesitations arose illogically, but not less validly (210–12). From an opposing theological viewpoint, Mrs M. B. Ridley thought that the need for more ministers of word and sacrament could be ignored by the church at its peril; it was very lightly touched on in the report. She referred to the plight of mission countries, and also recalled the example of Hong Kong. She believed the key point was the recognition of women as persons, and cited the note by the dean of St Paul's in *MOW35* (202–5). Finally, the Assembly received the report and passed it to the church for consideration.

On 3 July 1967 the debate was resumed[31] on a motion moved by Professor Lampe. He proposed, in the light of inconclusive theological objections on the one hand and the unwisdom of unilateral action on the other, further consideration by the working party set up by ACCM and CWMC, and by the joint Methodist–Church of England committee, in consultation with other interested churches.

The Reverend Professor D. E. Nineham pointed out that the motion was in response to an invitation from the Methodists. It was important first to clear the issue of principle, and then to move to the practice (in contrast to the amendment later to be proposed by the bishop of Chester). *The Times* had described the motion as 'phrased in the most cautious terms'. He said it was only a very small minority that held the view that 'there is something about women as such which makes it for ever contrary to the will of God that a woman should be ordained to the priesthood', and their spokesman in the report had been Canon (The Reverend Professor V. A.) Demant. He refuted a number of points that had been raised by him and underlined his limited view of history (279–82).

The bishop of Chester moved an amendment to omit the first part of Professor Lampe's motion as he thought it premature to decide on the principle that day. With this the professor disagreed, arguing that it would be useless to have conversations with the Methodists and others on the ordination of women if it was not clear whether this was theologically acceptable; it would be useless for ACCM and CWMC to consider priesthood in its enquiry into the ministry of women if it were unclear whether priesthood in this context was or was not a theological possibility. He added that to accept the principle of the ordination of women because it was right but to delay the implementation was the respectable way to keep in step with the Orthodox and Roman Catholic Churches (294–7).

During this long debate a number of speakers spoke against the ordination of women, taking varying perspectives. Prebendary J. H. B. Andrews said that the church had 'no such custom'. He referred to a breaching of the custom in 1815, when the Bible Christians had women preachers, later called ministers, equal to men. These people went out from their places of origin in North Devon to other parts of the country in need of evangelisation. In the second generation of that body the number of women gradually diminished, until in 1907, when the Bible Christians joined with other bodies to form the United Methodist Church, there was only one woman minister (Lillie Edwards) left. The failure of this breach with custom, he thought, had not been properly studied (301–3). Also starting from a text, the Reverend J. W. Wenham wanted a return to the male priesthood based on Genesis 1–3 as 'the foundation of the biblical doctrine of man'. He linked 'intuition' with tradition as a combined and powerful witness to his position (292–3). The Reverend (from 1968 Prebendary) Harold Riley made a number of points: referring to the motion, he said there were no conclusive theological reasons for any Christian doctrine whatsoever; he particularly objected to the use of the 'representative' argument which had been spelt out in the document sent to members by the Anglican Group for the Ordination of Women, arguing that it was equally non-representative in not including children. He concluded by quoting the statement of the 1935 commission that the consensus of tradition was a sufficient witness to the guidance of the Spirit (286–9).

Other speakers took a more moderate position. Mrs. P. V. Lloyd suggested that reasons other than theological should be considered, notably better recognition of the current service of women. She underlined the prejudices breaking through in the debate: 'Some people would call these theological reasons. To me they are necessarily prejudices and fears, particularly on the part of the clergy.' She wanted further consideration of one priestly function, namely, the pastoral need for deaconesses to be given the power of absolution (283–6). Mrs B. E. Haworth referred to a remark by Canon C. D. Smith, who had said that 'presiding at the holy mysteries' was 'probably one of the specific functions' which should be reserved to men priests (Miss P. M. C. Evans later drew attention to this resistance to a woman 'being allowed to celebrate the Eucharist' (306)). She said the crux of the matter was what was understood by priestly function. The continuing activity of the body of Christ was a corporate activity, comprising male and female. She linked this with Professor Lampe's opening remarks in the previous session where he had said he hoped that they would remember they were talking about people rather than members of a particular sex (291–2). From a different viewpoint, the bishop of Bristol stressed the need for an understanding of Christian ministry together with a Christian understanding of sexuality, and mentioned the lively discussions among Roman Catholic theologians into the kinds of ways in which the changed situation of women in contemporary culture had to be theologically interpreted (303–5). Meanwhile, Mrs J. M. Mayland believed 'that Professor Lampe's motion is the only motion which holds in balance the longing desire of those who believe they are called, together with a concern for the equally sincere feelings on the other side'. She remarked that Paul must groan whenever he was called upon to support the opponents of the ordination of women on the grounds of something he wrote so long ago, miles ahead as he was of other thinkers of his time; he would surely have expected them to have progressed a little in 2,000 years (289–90).

The bishop of Chester's amendment was carried in the house of clergy (87:85), but not in the houses of bishops (4:14) and laity (83:112). Another amendment was moved by Canon Smith, to replace the first part of Professor Lampe's motion that there were no conclusive theological reasons against by a phrase recognising the weight of church tradition against, which again was carried in the house of clergy (100:64) but not in the houses of bishops (5:14) and laity (91:106). When the motion was put, it was carried in the houses of bishops (12:4) and laity (115:81) but not in the house of clergy (70:96). Finally Miss V. J. Pitt moved that women be considered on the same basis as men as candidates for holy orders, and following a request by Miss Howard to count abstentions, this was lost in all three houses of bishops (1:8, abs. 8), clergy (14:96, abs. 20) and laity (45:103, abs. 32).

Motions on deaconesses arising out of *WHO* were not debated, but were remitted to a working party on women's ministry set up by CWMC and the ministry committee of ACCM in 1967, and their report, *Women in Ministry: A Study*, was published in 1968. They had examined the proper role of women within the accredited ministry of the church and signalled an important factor to be the Anglican–Methodist unity scheme, particularly at stage two, when the uniting churches would need to decide how to unite their somewhat differing patterns of women's ministry. Not only Methodist Conference resolutions and the Wesley Deaconess Order would have to be taken into account, but also the dispensation granted to some lay people including thirty-six deaconesses to administer communion. The working party noted that the Anglican–Methodist Committee had recommended that following entry into stage one, no further dispensations should be granted, and those authorised should be reviewed after three years 'in the hope that the conditions which have made dispensations necessary may soon be removed' (38). They added that until the priesthood issue was resolved, it would be 'almost impossible to make any clear definition of women's part in ministry'. The church could either stop ordaining candidates for the presbyterate to the diaconate and admit to the latter accredited ministers and those who accepted a lifelong commitment to the order, or as a sounder course abandon altogether the idea of a permanent diaconate, and admit those called to a permanent ministry of word and sacrament to the priesthood, leaving diaconal functions to a wide variety of accredited lay ministries. The working party concluded by endorsing the recommendation in *WHO* that Lambeth Conference should clarify the status of a deaconess, and the *sui generis* phrase in relation to it.

The report was available to the 1968 Lambeth Conference

committee which considered the ordination of women to the priesthood. The Conference as a whole passed resolutions[32] that current theological argument on the subject was inconclusive (thus reflecting the lack of unanimity among bishops); that national and regional churches or provinces should study the subject and report to the ACC; that the ACC should initiate discussion with churches which did and did not have women ministers and report; that before any national or regional church or province made a final positive decision the advice of the ACC should 'be sought and carefully considered'; and that meanwhile canonical provision should be made by all for qualified women 'to share in the conduct of liturgical worship, to preach, to baptize, to read the epistle and gospel at the Holy Communion, and to help in the distribution of the elements'. In the Conference 'Reports of Sessions',[33] the 1920 Lambeth Conference committee statement was reaffirmed, and it was concluded that deaconesses should be regarded as being in the order of deacons and that canonical provision should be made for this. Furthermore 'no conclusive theological reasons for withholding ordination to the priesthood from women as such' were found, and it was noted that while scripture was divided, tradition reflected unacceptable biological assumptions such that 'the appeal to tradition is virtually reduced to the observation that there happens to be no precedent for ordaining women to be priests. The New Testament does not encourage Christians to think that nothing should be done for the first time' (106).[34]

In May 1968 *Women and the Ordained Ministry: Report of an Anglican–Methodist Commission on Women and Holy Orders* was published. The commission had been set up by the archbishops and by the Methodist Conference to discuss the matter in the light of the 1961 (and following) Methodist reports and of *WHO*, for mutual information and forecast, and to suggest a procedure should one church make a unilateral decision on the issue. It was thought possible that the Church of England would declare that there were no conclusive theological objections within five years, but that the declaration would not be implemented for many years more, whereas it was thought safe to assume that the Methodist Church desired to go ahead and ordain women into its ministry. Should the Methodist Church go ahead during stage one, the commission stated that it would not be proper for its action to be criticised, and though an irritant, it would not be necessarily an insurmountable barrier during stage one. A proposed model of accommodation was an agreement such as in the Church of South India whereby women Methodist ministers would not perform in the Church of England those acts which in Anglican practice were reserved to the priest (celebration of communion, laying on of hands at ordination, pronouncing of absolution, and blessing). The full consequences of unilateral action would become apparent at, and might hinder, stage two.

In fact, although the Anglican–Methodist scheme received a 77.4 per cent majority (75 per cent required) in favour at the Methodist Conference held in Birmingham on 8 July 1969, that same day the voting in the Convocations failed to achieve the required majority, the figures in Canterbury being 27:2 (93 per cent majority) in the upper and 154:77 (67 per cent majority) in the lower houses, and in York 11:3 (78 per cent majority) in the upper and 71:34 (68 per cent majority) in the lower houses. Some who voted against said they were not against unity, but only against the current scheme. When General Synod replaced the Church Assembly, the issue was raised again, and placed under articles 7 and 8. Final approval stage was on 3 May 1972, but the voting results in the houses of bishops (34:6, abs. 0. 85 per cent), clergy (152:80, abs. 1. 65.52 per cent) and laity (147:87, abs. 1. 62.81 per cent) meant that the motion failed again, and eventually the scheme petered out.[35]

On 5 November 1969 the Church Assembly debated *Women in Ministry: A Study* (1968).[36] The bishop of Portsmouth, moving that the report be received, pointed out that the committee had been hampered by the uncertainty concerning women and priesthood, and by the ambiguity over the status and function of deaconesses. It had, however, gathered together facts about women in ministry. He drew attention to the instance, currently being looked into by the canon law standing commission, whereby the deaconess was debarred by canon law from preaching at a communion service while a parish worker or reader (of either sex) might do so. Professor Lampe thought the whole discussion should be shifted away from the sphere of status (deacon versus deaconess; clerical versus lay) and concentrated on trying to work out the proper functions of different people within the body of the church, and the question of status left to follow upon the definition of function. Even the question of accrediting was not easy. 'Those are the questions – who needs to be accredited to the lay sphere and the sphere of the ministry and sacraments? Towards the asking of those questions, perhaps in a rather clearer way than hitherto, I believe this Report makes some contribution' (561). Mrs Moffet thought the discussion on the diaconate was an excuse for putting off the question of the priesthood. The report was received, and referred to the dioceses for study and action.

Meanwhile, work on the revision of canon D1, 'Of the Order of Deaconesses', continued and it was presented for royal assent in 1972. The restrictive phrase 'especially over women' was removed from the paragraph relating to pastoral care, and now a deaconess could preach, distribute 'the holy sacrament of the Lord's Supper' and read the epistle and gospel (see also p. 84 above).

2.3 The ACC and *OWP*

The ACC held its first meeting at Limuru in Kenya in February–March 1971,[37] and a divisive issue was the ordination of women. Lambeth Conference 1968 had asked the churches to study the question: eight had done so, but had not sent in reports. Postponement of discussion was not possible because the bishop of Hong Kong (presumably following *LC* 1968, res. 37) had asked for guidance on what course to follow as his diocesan synod had approved in principle the ordination of women to the priesthood. The council was aware that provinces were still studying the question but, as member after member made clear in the debate, it would be improper to postpone whatever decision lay within the power of council. So they passed the celebrated resolution 28 asking the churches of the Anglican Communion to consider the subject and report before the ACC met in 1973; replying to the bishop of Hong Kong that if with the approval of the appropriate bodies he ordained women to the priesthood his action would 'be acceptable' and that they (the ACC) would use their good offices to encourage all provinces to remain in communion; and asking the secretary general to request metropolitans and primates to consult with other churches in their area on the subject prior to the following ACC meeting.

On 3 July the standing committee of the General Synod referred this Limuru resolution to ACCM and CWMC, asking them to pass to Synod any recommendations by 1 September 1972. At its final meeting in November 1971 CWMC noted the strong differences that had existed in the past among its members on this issue, but on this occasion passed a resolution stating that a 'very large majority' of them had come 'to believe that the Church of England should now take steps to enable women to be admitted to the Order of Priesthood. The Council hopes that this expression of opinion will encourage the Church to find a common mind in the matter.' Both councils decided to invite Miss Howard to produce a survey of the current state of opinion on the ordination of women. The result was a consultative document, presented by ACCM in 1972, *The Ordination of Women to the Priesthood.*

> It was made clear that at issue was what would further the gospel rather than what was good for women. Within the church there were divergent positions arising from differing views of the nature of biblical authority. Although there was acceptance that the Bible should be interpreted in its historical perspective and related to the circumstances of its composition and its meaning and purpose for its first readers and authors, some held that in the last analysis the canonical books were entirely trustworthy and the Bible was God's self-authenticating word challenging us to either faith or unbelief. Others using insights gained from historical and critical scholarship would acknowledge the Bible as a common reference point unique in its claim to record the message of God to the world, yet would not hold the words of the Bible to be authoritative as they stand written, and would wish to consider how far the Bible is authoritative for Christian thought and action.
>
> Attitudes to tradition ranged from the Eastern Orthodox Church, where tradition was the church in its continuous life, through the Roman Catholic Church, where tradition was generally perceived as divine truth not expressed in scripture alone but orally transmitted (the Council of Trent laid down that tradition and scripture were to be received as of equal authority), to the Protestant appeal to scripture alone. Ecumenical study over the previous fifteen years had reached a consensus that tradition was the handing over of the gospel contained in scripture, the transmission of a living reality through the Spirit. The Anglican position was that the faith and doctrine of Christianity are handed down in the wider context of a living communion which is the church universal, of which the Anglican Communion forms a part and that con-

sequently interpretation should be made against the wider background and with regard to historical sources.

Priesthood is one facet of ministry: 'For the Son of Man also came not to be served but to serve (diakonésai) and to give his life as a ransom for many' (Mk 10: 45). This ministry is inherited by the church, which has the nature of both servant and priest, such that all Christians share in the priesthood of Christ by their baptism. According to *LC* 1968, some, 'recognised by the Church as its representatives', were called and empowered to be 'priests of the priestly people', and were 'set apart by God for their special ministry' by ordination. Such ordination was received 'through a bishop, the representative of Christ and the universal Church and a symbol of its unity'. The ACCM ministry committee in *Ordained Ministry Today* was of the opinion that the ordained priesthood enabled the priesthood of the church to be exercised, that in addition to baptism, holy orders conferred a distinctive character or nature, and that such priesthood was disclosed through acts such as communicating the faith, pastoral care, the exercise of leadership and presidency, 'especially in worship and sacrament'. Yet Miss Howard pointed out that the 'accepted background and tradition of ministry is now being challenged in almost every Church as a result of the study of the New Testament and of early Church history, as well as by changes in the patterns of society and by new ecumenical experience'. Opposing interpretations were 'office in the community', versus 'state of life in the Church' linked with specific functions. 'A continuous re-assessment of the meaning of ministry and of ordination' was needed.

Moreover, anthropological research had undermined rigid sex-role assignation and it was preferable to envisage a sexual spectrum 'with wide normal variations and among which occasionally occur intermediate forms which are difficult to classify as either male or female'. Factors such as these had brought into question the absolute and unchanging nature of sexual identity; Dr Robert F. Hobson had written in *WHO* (56) 'Throughout the centuries debates have continued about whether the differences between men and women are due to nature or to nurture.'

Next Miss Howard considered the biblical evidence. The

position of women in the first century in Greece was hinted at by Demosthenes: 'We keep *hetaerae* for the sake of pleasure, concubines for the daily requirements of the body, wives to bear us legitimate children and to be the faithful guardians of our households' (*Against Neaera*, par. 122), while Plato and Aristotle held that the sexes were equal, and inherently inferior, respectively. In Roman culture a woman was completely subject to her husband even to death. She, together with slaves and minors, was not a *persona* in law, and thus the church caused scandal both by allowing a woman to marry a slave and by refusing to accept the sweeping powers of the paterfamilias. Jewish culture too appears to have been restrictive although the gospels reveal a more open Judaism than that which emerges from legal regulations and rabbinic comment on them. Women were legally inferior, having no right to bear witness, since Genesis 18: 15 indicated that they were liars. The worship of God was a man's responsibility primarily; a woman could not enter the covenant relationship through circumcision, and was restricted to a separate court in the Temple which she could not enter during monthly periods or after childbirth. All the prohibitions of the Torah applied to her, but 'the observance of all the positive ordinances that depend on the time of year is incumbent on men but not on women'.

In the gospels women ministered (*diēkonoun*) to Jesus (Lk 8: 1–3; Mk 15: 40–1). They were concerned with his burial (Mk 15: 47–16: 1; Matt 27: 61; Lk 23: 55–6), were the first to discover the empty tomb (Mk 16: 1–3; Matt 28: 1–6; Lk 24: 1–3; Jn 20: 1), encountered the risen Lord and his angels and brought the news to his disciples (Mk 16: 5–7; Matt 28: 7–10; Lk 24: 4–11; Jn 20: 2,11–18). Jesus' relationships with women were in contrast to the contemporary Jewish attitudes. The woman of Samaria (and the disciples) was astonished that Jesus talked with her (Jn 4: 9,27), and she consequently acted as witness and evangelist (Jn 4: 29,30,39–42). The Syro-Phoenician woman whose daughter Jesus healed was a gentile (Mk 7: 24–30). The woman with an issue of blood was ritually unclean and was breaking the law both by being in the crowd and by touching Jesus, yet he healed her (Mk 5: 25–34). The woman taken in adultery (Jn 8: 1–11) and the woman who was a 'sinner' (Lk 7: 37–50) are neither of them women with whom a rabbi would associate. Even where 'respectable' Jewish women were concerned, Jesus' attitude was unusual: he commended Mary, rather than Martha the traditional housewife (Lk 10: 38–42), and he talked about the Torah with them (Jn 11: 20–32). He praised the woman of Bethany who anointed him and promised that her action would be remembered wherever the gospel is preached (Matt 26: 6–13). It is also significant that although motherhood was considered a woman's highest task (she might hope one day to bear the Messiah), when Mary's motherhood was extolled in biological terms, Jesus replied, 'Blessed rather are those who hear the word of God and keep it' (Lk 11: 27,28; cf. Mk 3: 31–5). Moreover, though marriage is not for the age to come (Mk 12: 25), Jesus restored marriage to God's original purpose (Mk 10: 2–10 *et al.*).

Acts and the epistles are considered next. The three basic divisions within the Jewish religion, symbolised by the arrangement of the Temple courts, of Jews from gentiles, men from women, and priests from people, were overcome in Christianity (Gal 3: 27–9). Since entry to the church was by baptism rather than circumcision women attained fundamental, spiritual equality with men. Their participation in the 'royal priesthood' is not denied (1 Pet 2: 9). Women played an active part in the spread of the gospel and in the establishment of local churches. In Romans 16: 1–3 Phoebe is referred to by Paul as 'our sister' and a *diakonos* (common gender) of the church at Cenchreae; he commends her to the church at Rome as 'helper (*prostatis*) of many and of myself as well'. He refers to his 'fellow workers', e.g. Priscilla and other women mentioned in Rom 16. Priscilla shared with her husband in the instruction of Apollos (Acts 18: 26). The four unmarried daughters of Philip the evangelist prophesied (Acts 21: 9), while Acts 2: 18 (quoting Joel 2: 28) and 1 Corinthians 11: 5 assume women will prophesy.

Three passages in the epistles call for closer examination. The first is 1 Corinthians 11: 3–16, where prior to forbidding a woman to pray or prophesy with her head unveiled Paul writes: 'the head of every man is Christ, the head of a woman is her husband, and the head of Christ is God'. He appears to base his argument on the grounds that man is the image and glory of God but woman is the glory of man, that it is disgraceful for a woman to pray uncovered, and that 'we recognise no other practices, nor do the churches of God'. The second passage is 1 Corinthians 14: 34–6: 'The women should keep silence in the churches. For they are not permitted to speak (*lalein*), but should be subordinate (*hupotassesthósan*) as even the law says. If there is anything they desire to know, let them ask their husbands at home. For it is shameful for a woman to speak in church. What! Did the word of God originate with you, or are you the only ones it has reached?' (One group of manuscripts places verses 34 and 35 after 40.) The third passage, 1 Timothy 2: 11–15, is part of a code of social relationships: 'Let a woman learn in silence with all submissiveness (*hupotagê*). I permit no woman to teach (*didaskein*) nor to have authority over men; she is to keep silent. For Adam was formed first, then Eve: and Adam was not deceived, but the woman was deceived and became a transgressor. Yet woman will be saved through bearing children if she continues in faith and love and holiness, with modesty.' Problems arising from these passages are Paul's use of Genesis, the contradiction between what is permitted in 1 Corinthians 11 and forbidden in the other two passages, and the significance and meaning of headship. Sharp differences of interpretation arise.

Conservatives point out that Galatians 3: 28 is concerned with baptism, and that the 'royal priesthood' is irrelevant to the ordination issue. They argue that the New Testament provides no evidence that women exercised a missionary or teaching office, and that Acts 18: 26 refers to private instruction. They add that public teaching and preaching were specifically excluded in 1 Corinthians 11; 1 Corinthians 14 and 1 Timothy 2, and that prophecy was an individual gift and had no direct connection with preaching. They argue that this prohibition would naturally extend to responsibility for sacramental rites; that the only quasi-official position in which a woman is found is that of *diakonos*, which would tally with the function performed by women who accompanied Jesus.

They explain the disagreements in the Pauline passages by saying that 1 Corinthians 11 referred to the Christian community and the other two to public worship; that because Paul used the example of a woman praying with an uncovered head as self-evidently scandalous did not imply permission to pray or prophesy. They posit a possible Gnostic background whereby sexual differences disappeared because masculine and feminine belong to the *sarx* while in the *pneuma* all natural and created distinctions are abolished. They insist that these historical injunctions relate to a permanent principle, namely, the subordination of women, which is found in other parts of the Bible. The principle is indicated in the representation of God as father; the description of women as the weaker sex (1 Pet 3: 7); the household codes which require wives to be subject to their husbands (Eph 5: 21–4; Col 3: 18; Titus 2: 5; 1 Pet 3: 1–6) – this subordination is also of women to men (e.g. 1 Cor 11: 3).

Conservatives consider that the principle should be expressed today in varying ways. Some Lutherans argue that the command to silence is still binding, while others contend that different practices could express the same principle. Some Anglicans might argue that while a woman might lead in prayer, she should not assume an office where she did so normally. Other Anglicans, while not objecting to women's ordination, would think it wrong for a woman to be in sole charge of a parish, let alone of a diocese. Some would deny that the principle applied outside marriage and the Christian congregation, Lydia possibly being an example of a Christian woman with secular authority [Acts 16: 14–15].

There are alternative interpretations of these passages. Although under Jewish law women could not bear witness, each gospel depicts women as the primary witnesses of the resurrection. While there was no woman among the twelve or among the seventy, the 'New Testament does not encourage Christians to think that nothing should be done for the first time' (*LC* 1968, 106). Thus Jesus chose no gentiles, yet after the resurrection such were admitted without first becoming proselytes (Acts 10), an innovation Peter justifies by pointing not to the actions of Jesus but to the present act of God (Acts 11: 5–17); there was no programme for the abolition of slavery. Above all, there is no evidence that Jesus treated women as subordinates, and the evangelists' treatment of the subject might be taken as endorsement in some of the earliest church teaching of his attitude.

Passages in the Acts and epistles are open to a variety of interpretations. The word *prostatis* applied to Phoebe does not occur otherwise in the New Testament or other Greek books of the Bible, while elsewhere it has the sense of protectress, and cognate words in the New Testament are used for ruling and directing (cf. 1 Thess 5: 12; 1 Tim 3: 4,5,12; 5: 17). Moreover, the contradictions noted above have led some commentators to postulate 1 Corinthians 14: [33b–35] as an interpolation in the style of 1 Timothy 2: [12] which they would regard as non-Pauline, a suggestion slightly supported by the placing of these verses after verse 40 in some manuscripts.

The subordination required in the social codes seems to be a matter of practical adjustment rather than ethical principle, although Paul develops it theologically and finds the unity of husband and wife a symbol of the unity of Christ and the church. But as Genesis 3: 16 – on which he appears to base the principle of female subordination – applies to the fall rather than creation, it might be concluded that such was not part of the creator's original intention. It is questionable how far we are bound by an exegesis which the original passages did not require. It would seem that Paul's original purpose was to protect the infant church from accusations of dishonouring marriage and tolerating sexual confusion rather than to assert a principle, and other customs might now be required for the furtherance of the gospel such as the current practice of deaconesses, lay workers and women readers leading worship and preaching.

The question as to whether women can validly celebrate the eucharist today is anachronistic in so far as there was no 'eucharist' in Paul's day, but a fellowship meal during which one of the *episkopoi-presbuteroi* took bread and broke it. Equally anachronistic are the terms 'apostolic ministry' and 'apostolic order'. The New Testament evidence leads to the conclusion that the church developed its 'ministries' in response to the needs of the day; that 'there is no divinely appointed, unchanging "church order" valid for all ages and places'.

Turning next to tradition, Miss Howard examines patristic and scholastic writings on women. Most comments by the fathers are on Genesis 1–3 or 1 Corinthians. For example both Chrysostom and Ambrose warn against pressing too far the parallels between God/Christ, men/women; Irenaeus notes that Paul 'spoke accurately of the gifts of prophecy, and recognised men *and women* as prophesying in the Church'; both Clement of Alexandria and Chrysostom regarded subjection as due to abuse of privilege rather than inherent 'weakness'; and Augustine saw women's servitude as a direct result of sin. Spiritually women were perceived as equal because made in the divine image (Gregory of Nyssa), and equal in 'excellence of character' and 'philosophising' (Clement of Alexandria), or martyrdom (Athanasius). Most of the early patristic writings are concerned with marriage and virginity with a tendency to eulogise the latter, and with reflections on Mary.

References to women and priesthood occur in writings concerning heretical sects which had female presbyters. Tertullian says, 'it is not permitted to women to speak in church, or to teach, or to baptise or to offer, or to lay claim to a man's function or to the priestly office'; Irenaeus criticises Magus Marcus, who 'led astray silly women', encouraging them to prophesy and 'make their own thank-offering in his presence'; Chrysostom writes, 'let the whole female sex retreat from such an office ... and similarly the majority of men'; and Epiphanius, 'Never anywhere has any woman, not even Eve, acted as priest from the beginning of the world', adding that if Christ had intended to confer the priesthood on the female sex he would have ordained the virgin Mary. In the *Apostolic Constitutions* women are debarred from teaching and priestly functions although deaconesses have special tasks.

The scholastics and later theologians considered the question as part of a theological system, and towards the end of the Middle Ages one detects a hardening of position. They argued that for reasons of natural or divine law a woman's sex rendered her *incapable* of receiving orders; the signification required in sacramentality would not be met by woman's state of subjection. Added to this were other arguments, such as that women were lacking in reason, showed fickleness of mind, might entice men to lust. The Reformers (with the exception of George Fox, the Anabaptists and the early Independents) did not challenge this tradition. Martin Luther (except in an emergency) and John Calvin declared against a female ministry.

Some would distinguish between the accumulated deposit of doctrine and the customs of church life, and would argue that the second can be changed according to article 34. It is here that they would site the issue of women and priesthood, arguing that if the underlying scriptural authority is subjected to new interpretation then the tradition itself comes under scrutiny. It has to be debated whether change should come through an ecumenical council or through general consensus in the Anglican Communion.

Theological arguments are then considered, such as how far the relation between the sexes belongs to the order of creation and how it relates to redemption. Some would argue that though woman's basic position is modified, the duty of obedience still applies. Professor von Allmen says, 'they are what they are at the level of their vocation at the very depths of their being ... Not to respect the ontological character of manhood and womanhood is to put oneself at odds with the doctrine of creation, and also with biblical anthropology.' Others would say that redemption has removed any sex inequality by transcending it.

Natural law has appeared in the debate. Orthodox Archimandrite Georges Khodre wrote about the 'mystery of womanhood' in terms of complementarity in the WCC publication *Concerning the Ordination of Women*, 61–2; Professor Demant speaks of male and female aptitudes, adding that women are constitutionally unsuited to certain kinds of impersonal role (*WHO* 105–7); Prebendary Henry Cooper in a letter to the *Church Times* (31.12.71) writes of initiative resting with the male, even though often elicited by the female, and asks, 'do we want *ab*normal women in the ministry?'; Professor Eric L. Mascall (1958) writes of the different involvement of the two sexes in the incarnation (26). It has been suggested that the nature of priesthood is connected with 'the psychological nature of man'. Reasons given are that the subordination of women makes it more appropriate; that male and female functions are complementary and those male are consonant with priesthood; that sex occupies a more central place in feminine human nature and the appearance of women as leaders of worship and ministrants of the sacraments would destroy the sexless tone; that sacramental priesthood belongs to the dominant sex.

This reading of the evidence has been questioned. Dr Sherwin Bailey has written, 'In Christ ... sex is neither abolished nor transcended but sexual division and antagonism are done away [with], and with them traditional notions of headship and subjection.' The true structure of sexual relation is one of partnership (*Theology*, September 1954). Moreover, recent Anglican experience of women leading worship would not lend support to the idea that women are more 'sexual' than men. Mrs Kay M. Baxter questions that the issue of sex-relationship should enter into the ordination debate at all, for priesthood is not a role of domination, but rather a role of ministering (*WHO* 121).

Another theological issue is of the consecration of women to the episcopate, to which some would accord priority. Those opposed would argue that a woman cannot represent a male Christ; that a bishop is a symbol of unity and whereas a man can represent both sexes a woman can only represent her own; that the bishop is the father of his diocese and no woman can be a father; that it would be inexpedient for male clergy; that if someone held that a woman could not be ordained there would be worry about the validity of a female bishop's ordinations. Proponents would argue that a bishop is an agent and that Christ can be represented only by the whole church; that representation is of the cosmic and ascended Christ, of his humanity rather than his manhood (the use of 'man' is confusing and can lead to the conclusion that women are the variant, based on outdated anthropology); that expediency cannot determine a theological question; that women hold posts of authority and if this is at the cost of personal distortion the same is true for men.

A further area of theological argument concerns symbolism and priesthood. On the one hand it is pointed out that father language in connection with God is analogous, suggesting the initiatory aspect of creativity, reflected in man/woman, Christ/church, priest/people relationships, to which it is replied that if God is all perfection one would find there all good characteristics, both male and female. Some would argue that symbolism connected with preaching and leadership in the New Testament is masculine, and that with listening, female, and that women as priests would destroy the male symbolism of the liturgy which has grown up through the centuries. Proponents argue that to be fully inclusive female symbolism is also required, particularly if the priest is thought of as representing the risen Christ. They would add that the symbolism of presidency at a meal is modelled on the paterfamilias.

A contemporary question that is addressed is whether it is women's sexuality that is experienced as the real bar to priesthood:

> The symbolism which accompanies womanhood is often gentle and humble, but it is also sometimes demonic: the witch is usually represented as a female. Does this represent a deep unconscious fear of woman, and above all, of her sexuality? Is this fear intensified by the very nature of Holy Communion which is not only cerebral but also involves physical contact: there is giving, receiving, taking and eating real bread and real wine. (48)

Images and roles of women are not easily altered.

The Anglican Communion and other churches are considered. Since the ACC meeting in 1971 some action had occurred within the former. On Advent Sunday 1971 Bishop Baker of Hong Kong ordained Jane Hwang and Joyce Bennett[38] to the priesthood. In January 1972 the Synod of the Church of Burma accepted the ordination of women in principle and its introduction when circumstances should require it. The Synod of the Church of the Province of New Zealand approved the ordination of women in principle, but refused a second reading of a bill to implement it. The South Pacific Anglican Council decided against women priests. The 1970 General Convention of the Protestant Episcopal Church in the USA defeated (in the clerical order) a resolution to endorse the principle. The house of bishops received the resolution and referred it to the special meeting in October 1971, meanwhile requesting 'an in-depth study'. The doctrinal commission of the Church in Wales had discussed the issue and their report was to be presented to the bishops in the autumn of 1972. In April 1972 the Provincial Synod of Central Africa passed a resolution that each bishop should commission a paper from a member of his diocese on the subject and that any resulting resolutions should be passed to the episcopal synod.

Ecumenical statistics issued by the WCC in 1970 showed that 72 member churches ordained women or had accepted the principle and 143 did not. Wholly opposed were the Eastern Orthodox, Oriental Orthodox, and Old Catholic. In communions in which some churches did ordain women, the highest proportion was in the Western world; Eastern Europe occupied a middle position, and the lowest proportion was in Asia, Africa and Latin America.

In Great Britain the Baptist Union had admitted women to the ministry since 1918. The Congregational Union of England and Wales admitted women to the ministry in 1917, and that of Scotland in 1929. The Presbyterian Church of England accepted the principle in 1921; its first woman minister had been ordained twenty years prior to the writing of the report, and the first woman to follow the ordinary course of training was ordained in 1965, and there were currently four women ministers. The Church of Scotland agreed to ordain women in 1968 and the first woman was ordained the following year. The United Free Church of Scotland admitted women to its ministry in 1929 and in 1960 the moderator of the General Assembly was a woman. The Methodist Conference had passed a resolution in 1970 reiterating its theological approval, and the first women were currently being accepted for ordination.

The Church of Sweden was of interest. In 1925 women were allowed by law to hold all state offices, but church offices were exempted. In 1957 the Church Assembly rejected a government bill to remove the exemption and in the following year the bill was passed by a newly elected Church Assembly amid bitter controversy. The first ordination took place in 1960, and there were currently 80 women priests. During this period all the bishops appointed had been in favour of the ordination of women, save in two cases where the names submitted to the church minister by the diocese were all opposed. Many parishes were served by group ministries, which had facilitated the adjustment. There appears to have been a majority of the laity in favour from the start, and the majority of priests were probably currently in favour.

The Orthodox Church holds that women cannot receive the sacrament of ordination because it is prohibited both in scripture and in subsequent rulings of the church. Deaconesses were only blessed. The bishop is seen as the representative of Christ; the church is the bride of Christ; the bishop carries out the functions of bridegroom towards the church, and it is therefore normal that he should be a man. Moreover, customs surrounding menstruation would be a serious practical and psychological barrier. Were the Church of England to ordain women a certain amount of recognition of Anglicanism would be ended. However, one Orthodox representative pointed out that the determining factor was what was right, not what was expedient, and he himself could see no theological impediment. Within Roman Catholicism the question had become one of theological speculation and of some practical agitation among Roman Catholics, particularly in the radical fringe in Holland, Belgium and Germany.

Of the nearly 1,000 women engaged in ministry as deaconesses, licensed lay workers, including Church Army sisters and church social workers, about 250, mainly engaged in diocesan and parochial work, were asked to make their views known, and over 150 responded. About nine-tenths of deaconesses were in favour, with or without qualification, and about two-thirds of licensed parochial workers, with the remaining third equally divided between those who were against and those who were neutral or uninterested. For many of the women this had become a live issue for the first time; Dr Una Kroll[39] had noted elsewhere the 'psychological difficulty' in admitting to a call which could not be recognised as such. Among the ten religious communities approached, two were against; two were convinced it would come; others saw no theological reasons against.

Ministry in the Church of England was affected by the legal situation of the incumbent. Because for centuries only men had been ordained, this was as much part of the law as if it had been the subject of legislation. Canon C1 assumes that only men can be ordained, and in order to change this General Synod would have to pass a measure. It was assumed that women priests ordained overseas were bound by the Overseas and Other Clergy (Ministry and Ordination) Measure 1967, section 1, which required written permission from the appropriate archbishop.

On 8 November 1972 the bishop of St Edmundsbury and Ipswich (Dr L. W. Brown), as chairman of ACCM, presented the report to Synod.[40] He said that it made no attempt to answer the question whether women should be ordained, and underlined two considerations arising from it. First, theological reasoning should underlie any change in the sense that 'we act in this way because we believe that God is giving us insights into the meaning of the new humanity in Christ which have not hitherto been fully understood. It is possible that such insights will make us believe that sex difference is as relevant or irrelevant to holy orders as racial or cultural differences' (686). Secondly, the question was part of the questioning going on in all churches about the nature of ministry.

When moving the acceptance of *WHO* in 1967 the bishop of Chester had expressed the opinion that the most important sentence of that report concerned the symbolism of the priest, to which he linked the questions of the symbolism of the sexes, as yet little explored or understood. In the 1972 debate this area, apart from occasional excursions into ecumenism, was the rallying ground of the opponents. Mr Clark (687–9) 'jettisoned' four arguments for and four against the ordination of women, adding that present practice could scarcely be altered by the Church of England alone, and so arrived at his

> most compelling . . . psychological argument about the widespread instinctive reaction and resistance which this proposal provokes. You may call it a taboo if you like . . . but this does not dispel the difficulty . . . Why does this subject bring up at once among so many an immediate antipathy? Until I get that illumination I must agree with Dorothy Sayers, Evelyn Underhill and many other notable women that for women to be admitted as priests is dramatically unsuitable since God chose to be born as a man.

Such 'immediate antipathy' was apparent in the contributions of Mrs V. Spencer Ellis and Miss L. M. Pobjoy. The former (709) acknowledged 'an instinctive feeling of unhappiness' at the idea of female ordination, and she was convinced that Jesus would not have acted differently in a different age. In her opinion he was perfect man, not perfect male: 'The priest before the altar is entirely sexless, and to think of a woman in that position is quite wrong.'

She added that the female's instinct was to deal with her family; 'that she should wish to become a priest is insulting to her human nature'. Miss Pobjoy (715–16) went further. She could not believe there was anyone present 'whose mind does not register a mental block at the suggestion that Almighty God might be a woman' adding,

> Man has the quality of detachment from his sex, and it is this detachment, this ability to stand before the altar as a representative of a sexless God, stripped of his sexuality or, if you like, of his specific masculinity, which speaks to the most basic instincts of so many worshippers, and which causes them to feel appalled – I do not think this is too strong a word – at the prospect of a woman celebrating at the Eucharist.

She continued somewhat dismissively, 'women from time to time are at the mercy of their hormones' (a link with the Orthodox position), and 'all women are basically in competition with one another'.

Two other speakers followed Mr Clark's argument about the difference between the sexes and its implications. Prebendary Cooper, acknowledging Miss Howard's reference to his letter in the *Church Times* (see above, p. 114), reiterated that a woman centres more obviously in the home, and a man in society at large, describing this as a sociological argument with a theological content. He also pointed out that there were no 'priestesses' in the Old Testament. The Reverend (from 1978 Canon) G. B. Austin (693–4) had grave hesitations about the ordination of women, wondering how far the conclusion that there was no theological argument against was based on the 'false premise that men and women are equal in kind in the sight of God'. He thought they were 'very different physically, intellectually, and psychologically', although they were 'certainly equal in worth'. There was 'something' in the role of a priest which made it a man's role: 'Instead of giving women a ministry which is equal in kind but inferior in status, which it would be, ought not we [*sic*] to be seeking for them a ministry equal in status and honour and worth but different in kind?' Linked with the same line of argument was Prebendary H. Riley's contribution concerning women and the episcopate. He referred to St Ignatius who spoke of the bishop being the son of the Father and who seemingly had at the back of his mind the image of Christ and the apostles being reflected in the bishop and his presbyterate.

Somewhat refreshingly, Canon C. R. Craston (710–11) pointed out that it would be a mistake to suppose that those who took a conservative view of scripture were necessarily opposed to the ordination of women. Within the theology of ordination there were many who would argue that if no grounds could be adduced against women leading worship and preaching, then there could be no bar to their celebrating communion or pronouncing the absolution. The crunch came with headship. He was not in agreement with the opinion attributed to conservatives in the document (para. 90); some thought that Paul's treatment and exegesis of the early chapters of Genesis presented a real difficulty, not least because if taken at face value he seems to be taking a line that God does not take. There was evident blessing by God of Deborah's leadership of Israel. He reminded the Synod that the woman ordained in Hong Kong had been for ten years the leader recognised by her parish. He thought therefore that the concept of headship should be seen in the context of the home and not of society generally. He ended with a plea that the theology of the sexes be developed.

Professor Lampe (689–93) prefaced his speech with the enigmatic statement that it was essential, in line with the opening paragraphs of the report, 'not to let the question of what is good for the Church and its mission in the present-day world become confused with what is good or may be good for women as a matter of women's rights'. He said that two theological questions were fundamental to the issue. First, whether sex differences must 'interpose a wedge between the ministry of the word on the one hand and the ministry of the sacraments on the other, which the whole tendency of theological and liturgical movements over the past decades' had been 'to try to bring together'. The second question concerned the relationship which this question of the ordination of women again focussed 'between vocation to ministry and baptism into the priestly body of Christ'. Priesthood was a sacred ministry. Both male and female were baptised into the body of Christ, yet the sacred ministry was open only to men. This raised questions about the meaning of vocation, and the meaning of complementarity, i.e. how to diversify the inner priesthood, rather than opposing clerical to lay. Both Deaconess H. Price and Mrs Ridley took up the question of vocation, the former making the point that there were women today, like Samuel, who hear God calling them, but the church, like Eli, discourages women from acting on that call. Mrs Ridley said that while no man had a right to be ordained, he had a right to have his vocation tested. She also pointed out the extreme imbalance between the sexes in the places where the affairs of the church were discussed.

A couple of speakers made more empirical points. The plea of the bishop of Chelmsford was 'away with expediences'! He said the overwhelming vote in the Chelmsford diocesan synod (unanimous in the house of bishops) the previous year in support of the ordination of women was linked with the fact that in the diocese were a very large number of women giving full-time service to the church. He also drew attention to a suburban parish in North London where the down-town end had been dominated by a Congregational church where the minister was a woman, namely the Reverend Elsie Chamberlain, who became in time the president of the Congregational Union. Mr T. L. Dye (703–5), referring to Dr Mascall's statements in *Women and the Priesthood of the Church* that the apostolic priesthood of Christ comes from its apostolic function and that apostles are those who extend and establish churches, said, 'If we consult the record of women missionaries throughout the world, we find that there are women in many places who have established new Churches, so that the women have been *de facto* the apostles of those Churches.' The motion was carried.

In May 1973 both Convocations debated the report. The motion in the Convocation of Canterbury[41] was that it saw 'no sufficient theological objection to the ordination of women'. Moving, the bishop of Derby stressed that they were concerned with theological issues (although the following day the bishop of Lichfield confessed to a feeling of unreality when one tried to keep practical and theological issues separate (54)). An openness to truth was required such that courtesy to other churches should not override their own denominational integrity. The Bible had to be interpreted by the church, its tradition and its living experience of worship and ministry, and by human reason and thinking, including scholarship. They in turn were judged by it. Shifts had taken place in other areas; in terms of priestly ministry they should be thinking in more dynamic terms. He questioned whether the current position whereby women were only barred from celebrating communion, pronouncing the blessing, and pronouncing absolution was right. Moreover, 'to say that on that basis of symbolism women must be excluded from the whole ministry of the Church was to press a particular symbol much too far'. Jesus symbolised fatherhood as essentially a caring, tender thing (22–6).

The Reverend D. A. J. Stevens moved an amendment to insert the word 'academic' before 'theological' and to add at the end of the motion 'or to the maintenance of the continuous tradition which prevents such ordination', postulating a 'bewildering gap between the things the theologians wrote and said and what the ordinary Christian believer believed to be the basis of the historic Christian faith'. Seconding, Prebendary Cooper (32–4) appealed to the Roman position (under the umbrella of ecumenism) and to the fact that a study commission on women, appointed by the pope, had been told in advance via an internal memorandum that the possibility of women becoming priests was to be ruled out. They needed, he believed, a new commission such as that which had produced *Gender and Ministry*, which could work out what their wives (although he had not got one), mothers and sisters and the ordinary women of the parishes – not bluestockings or masculine females, but ordinary feminine frilly women – should be as members of the church in their truly feminine vocation.

No new arguments were advanced during the debate, although some original clarifications were introduced. The Reverend J. Oldham (38–40), referring to different theories of ministry, compared Tillich: 'Protestantism demands a radical laicism', with von Allmen: 'The pastoral ministry is that of grace ... by which one of the faithful following on the Apostles is called to act in the name of Christ', and according to whom the subject must be debated in terms of the primary ministry, namely, the episcopate. Earlier, Professor Lampe had distinguished between representation and impersonation in this connection with some persuasiveness. The bishop of Exeter (36–8), returning to grave theological objections on the basis of scripture and tradition, said he did not derive his scriptural objections from proof texts but that scripture 'should be interpreted, and had been interpreted, by the tradition of the Church' – which seemed to suggest an up-to-date view of scripture, but not of tradition. He thought the culture was 'sex-obsessed', adding that the issue was touching on a very delicate nerve centre from which he shrank away with a shudder – he referred to C. S. Lewis, who suggested that the ordination of women might alter the prevailing concept of the deity and move the church in the direction of the old nature religions (thus following the line of Professor

Demant in *WHO* para. 99). Professor Nineham found this appeal to fear rather disquieting.

Mr Stevens withdrew his amendment. Next, Canon H. B. Marlow moved that added to the motion should be a requirement of proof on the part of the advocates, and that such an innovation should not be made unilaterally in any one part of 'the Universal Church'. It was agreed to vote on the two parts separately. The first was carried in the lower house (54:40) but lost in the upper house (11:8) and was therefore lost. The second was lost in the lower house (41:44) so the amendment was lost. Finally the bishop of Winchester moved that added to the motion should be recognition of 'a number of other important issues that have to be taken into consideration before the Church of England decides upon its future policy', and the amended motion was carried in both houses.

In the Convocation of York[42] the bishop of Liverpool (32–7) moved that *OWP* be commended to the study of the Northern province. He addressed himself particularly to the concept of ministry in ancient Israel, suggesting that the elements present in the Mosaic period were leadership linked with Moses; priesthood or cult linked with Aaron; judicial action linked with judges or elders. In the monarchical period leadership was linked with sacral kingship; pastor or teacher with prophetic ministry; cult with the Aaronic priesthood; and, in the post-exilic period, leadership with the high priest, cult with priesthood, pastoral care with elders. The church, he said, had inherited these concepts which had been part of Israel for 1400 or 1500 years, such that in the New Testament we find the leaders are the apostles, liturgy and cult are linked with elders and presbyters, service with deacons. His conclusions were that there was no consistent pattern of ministry; that the distinction between ordained and lay was elusive; that ministry was collective. This raised questions as to whether there was any reason for excluding women from a collective ministry; women could be debarred from those elements of ministry that were everywhere reflected in the Bible; what men were ordained for; what was meant by 'priestly, priest and priesthood'; whether the necessity of further study was implied in all this.

Seconding the motion, Canon G. O. Morgan moved from the Old Testament to the present day by distinguishing between a prescriptive and an intuitive theology. Both should be held in tension; scripture and tradition should be approached in the light of a new cultural and social pattern that might lead to a partnership of men and women in common service such as the world had never known. He did not want the church to be the institution which, above all things, held fast to attitudes which, above all others, had their origins in earlier social patterns, and added that sociologists were agreed that at first Christianity did improve the position of women in society – but that then the tides rolled back and existing cultural patterns took over. He referred to Don Cupitt's *Crisis of Moral Authority*, where it is argued that Christianity has tended to reinforce the subjection of women and where the church's failure to ordain them is cited as considerable evidence in support of the argument. Cupitt concludes that Christianity's adopted mythical world picture effectively taught the inferiority of women until the present century:

> Even Karl Barth ... still taught male primacy, but once stated, the feminists' case is irresistible and has now affected even Muslim countries. Christianity can fairly claim that it always carried latent within it the principle of the equal moral dignity of the sexes, but it will be unable to make the necessary changes in attitude without a very considerable effort to throw off the past, for in any culture the way the relation of the sexes is conceived reflects in a profound manner an entire world view. (40)

Speakers opposed seemed to differ in their ecclesiologies. Canon R. W. Phillips, referring to *MOW35*, said Jesus chose only men; women were 'inherently incapable' of receiving the grace of order; such action would raise a doubt in many that the Church of England was part of the catholic church of Christ; it would raise a very serious barrier with the Roman Catholic Church, the Orthodox Churches, and the Old Catholic Church; such an action should only be envisaged by an ecumenical council. Some of the opposition speakers, though, were moving, or had moved, to countenance female ordination providing male headship was preserved. Canon Craston (47–50), having divided the areas of opposition into those in the catholic tradition who dwelt on the concept of priesthood, and those in the evangelical tradition who centred on the concept of leadership and authority, and having aligned himself with the latter, said he saw no objection to a woman being part of a corporate presbyterate providing she were not the head. He postulated that *kephalé* can be translated 'source' rather than 'head' and referred to Genesis 1 and 2, where male and female together represent God. He also thought great weight should be given to Galatians 3: 28, where he thought the emphasis should be on its barrier-breaking implications. The idea of a woman minister as part of a team was also endorsed by the Reverend B. D. Jackson, provided she did not lead it. He saw female leadership such as Deborah's as part of a 'theology of extremity', where there was such a lack of men of courage; it was 'not normal theology'. With greater caution the Reverend W. A. Bretherton (66–7) accepted man's headship in the family, but asked whether the church was just a family; 'let the natural course of events take care of itself and not state in the woman's ordination that she must never be the leader of a team'.

Predictably, symbolism influenced the argument. The bishop of Chester (41–6), having acknowledged his shift in position since he had been asked to chair the 1966 commission, stressed the power of the symbolism of the priesthood, and compared the different leadership symbols of monarchies and republics to show how institutions are moulded in their characters by the symbolism of their chief officers. The Reverend P. H. Boulton (51–5) said he was glad to have such a weighty supporter as the bishop to his shrewd suspicion that the question would finally be settled on the basis of the inappropriateness of its symbolism. Taking up the bishop of Liverpool's question as to the meaning of 'priest'-derived words, he suggested that they concerned 'acts which are performed by the minister as he embodies and declares the acts of Christ to his people'. He reduced these acts to two: the eucharist and ordination, not having any strong feelings about absolution. Returning again to the bishop of Chester's stress on the importance of symbolism, he said that the church did not need a symbol, but Christ did, adding, 'Are we to pacify our guilt feelings about the way in which we have excluded women from the ministry of the church by upsetting this delicate balance of symbolism?' The answer was not to change the symbol, which was part of creation, but to give due dignity to the sex, bearing in mind such symbols as the madonna and child of Bethlehem, and the mother and St John of Calvary, which were not mutually exclusive but complementary. Moving in from an opposing perspective, the bishop of Southwell (56–9) said how closely a right theology of ordination was linked to the question of the ordination of women and hence to symbolism. Sexuality and the priesthood had to be thought about far more seriously; it was sometimes said with some truth that clergy had two hang-ups – sex and anger – and that it would certainly seem from the history of the church that sexuality had been dealt with by insulation; 'the question of the subservience of women is surely an instance of the way in which we have tried to ensure that no real, personal relationship between the sexes is possible in the ordained ministry'. He referred to 'a very real difference of interest and understanding and feeling and consequently of capacity to deal with life by women as opposed to men', adding how women would bring 'a whole new dimension to priesthood . . . in a way that does not deny sexuality but sees it as a good thing and capable of immense health and strength. Let us not fool ourselves into thinking that the male priest is sexless.' Ordained ministry in the future would be increasingly diverse, and he hoped they would not slide into offering an auxiliary form to women; it should be 'as fully ordination' as that offered to men. Eventually the two houses approved the motion.

2.4 Acceptance of principle: diocesan synods and General Synod

On 6 July 1973 the motion was proposed to General Synod[43] that before any answer was given to the ACC, the opinion of the dioceses should be obtained as to whether they accepted the principle, and as to whether they considered consequent action desirable at the present time. Surveying historical landmarks in the debate as from 1962, the archbishop of York (Dr F. D. Coggan), moving, said that the Church of England would be unable to reply to the ACC in time for its meeting in August 1973 as the question included matters of a doctrinal nature and that it therefore had to be regarded as article 7 business, and referred to the dioceses for discussion and report. In his opinion the fundamental question was whether the basic qualification for ordination was masculinity or redeemed humanity, and, underlying this, the 'doctrine of the Holy Spirit' particularly in relation to tradition and the ministry (534–7).

Mr Austin (539–41) said the General Synod should decide the point of principle before sending the question to the dioceses, thus giving them a lead. Then the dioceses could be asked whether they were in agreement with the principle established by Synod and whether they considered the implementation of the proposal was expedient. (In point of fact, the previous November the standing committee had stated that it would set a motion affirming the principle before Synod, and would only send the question to the dioceses if this were carried. Some regret at the change of plan was apparent in debate, and particularly in the tabling of an amendment.)

This proved to be a minority position. Mrs Haworth (542–3) said it was the dioceses' democratic right to have the question put, and Canon T. Barfett (543–4) suggested (*pace* Mr Austin) that their replies might indicate the direction in which the Spirit was leading. The Reverend S. W. Burrows (537–9) was interested in the psychological aspects of sending the question to the dioceses as it provoked such intense emotions. This last point was taken up anecdotally by Mrs A. Cameron (541) as illustration of how social conditioning can give rise to deep feelings which are then rationalised. She referred to a mission which had had a woman doctor for thirty years, and when the children were told they were having a Dr Harry Williams they said, 'But you cannot have men doctors; women are doctors and men are nurses.'

Miss Howard (545–7) believed that a start on the synodical process of consultation would be a proper answer to the ACC, and it would be a greater wisdom not to attempt to declare the principle. The ACC would not yet have a definitive answer from the Episcopal Church in the USA, from the Church in Wales, from the Church of the Province of South Africa, from the Church in Australia, and the debate had not started yet in Scotland and Ireland. However, once the principle were accepted, she believed the Church of England should do what was right, and not what was expedient. She asked that first, the experience of women involved in ministry should be considered because she found it odd to draw a line before the eucharist in the light of the New Testament silence on the subject of celebrants, and secondly that the Synod take seriously the call of those women who felt called to priesthood. She concluded, 'I plead that we shall not hear any more from men, and particularly from clergymen, about what it is like to be a woman, because that sort of talk is boxing women in, cutting them down to size, and stereotyping them.'

An amendment by Mr J. W. M. Bultimore (550) to include an assertion of principle in the motion having been defeated, the motion was carried.

Meanwhile, the second meeting of the ACC[44] took place in Dublin in July 1973. In its report it was noted that no church had ceased to be in communion with the Diocese of Hong Kong, whose action had been respected though not necessarily approved by other churches and provinces. A number of papers and reports had been received. Since ACC 1 the position was as in *OWP* (above, pp. 116–18), with the additions that now the Anglican Church of Canada had approved the principle, and preliminary action had been taken (final pending) in the Church of England in Australia. Having stressed its consultative status, the ACC made three statements. First, the decision on the part of one member to ordain women should not result in a break in communion (50: 2, abs. 3); secondly, that ecumenical relations should not be decisive (54: 1, abs. 0). In the section on 'ministry', the council requested a study 'of the relative status of the male and female principle and the symbolic authority they exercise upon our understanding of the nature of God and of leadership roles in Church and society' (37).

The General Synod met in July 1975 and voted without debate to take note of the report GS 252 on the diocesan voting.[45] The first motion ('no fundamental objections') had been carried in all three houses of 30 out of 43 diocesan synods and the second motion (removing legal barriers) had been carried in 15. The Synod then proceeded to debate the motion:

> That this Synod considers that there are no fundamental objections to the ordination of women to the priesthood.[46]

Moving, the bishop of Oxford (542–8) asked the Synod to consider other changes of comparable magnitude in the church's history: Paul's insistence that Peter was in the wrong for going back on his original decision to take meals with gentile converts; the change of norm from adult to infant baptism; the Reformation, effected by the conviction that God's free gift inspires the faith by which we are accounted righteous; the change of heart on slavery, and of attitude to mission and to sickness. He continued, 'The basic question which we have to decide is whether there have been any changes in our concept of God which would incline us to change our minds about the admission of women to the priesthood.' He indicated two such changes: first, in attitudes to eschatological beliefs, and secondly in questioning the description of God in article 1 as 'without body, parts or passions', by the suggestion that 'God was in a mysterious way involved in the suffering or passion of his children'. He referred to Dr Jürgen Moltmann's *The Crucified God*.

Then, dealing with arguments against the ordination of women, he described Dr Demant's position as lacking in substance because it was couched in old forms which had ceased to be 'theological tender'. He thought Mr J. R. Lucas' study of sexuality in Christian life in *Orders Disorderly* pointed in favour of the ordination of women in arguing for a representation of humanity. Next, he asked whether the ordination of women cohered with the rest of Christian doctrine as it had been received by the Church of England. It cohered with the present doctrine of creation; man and woman could no longer be thought of as lord and lady of a limited domain, such as the Garden of Eden or the Planet Earth, but instead as emerging, with other sentient beings, from the creative process and sharing in the creativity of God. To refuse to ordain one of them had a parochial ring. 'It lacks the humility of the scientist's openness to the undisclosed mysteries of the universe.' It cohered with the counter-claims of the Wisdom principle, and the motherhood imagery, in so far as both sides had to admit that the concept of gender can only be applied to God by way of analogy. Moreover, eschatologically, Christ, in his glory, is not a kind of divinised male, but one in whom all God's children of both sexes attain their perfection. 'I believe that a priesthood open to both sexes coheres better with the doctrine of the Incarnation.'

Turning to the doctrine of the Spirit, he pointed out that this had evolved in AD 235–381, but that most of the theological development had taken place during the last two decades of that half-century. The debate about women began just after the First World War, but most of the significant theology had emerged during the preceding twenty years. 'The two periods are directly comparable in size and character, and do not support the view that we have been hastier than the Fathers.' A theology of sexuality, as the gift of the Spirit, would have to be acknowledged and the quietly insistent call for ordination on the part of those women who believed themselves called, heeded. Above all, ecumenically, the Church of England had to bear witness to what was true. The tide could not be turned.

The bishop of Chichester (548–51), opposing, said, 'I cannot recall any other occasion when the Synod of these two provinces has been invited to reject a universal tradition of the Catholic Church to which we have hitherto subscribed.' He did not think slavery was a comparable example as slavery had resulted from sin. 'What we are concerned with is a fundamental change in the Christian ministry as received by the Church from her Lord and his Apostles and as handed down to our own day'. They were answerable to the church as a whole. The main issues were that our Lord chose only men as his apostles and the church following him chose only men as bishops and priests. This was a deliberate act of our Lord's, who initiated radical changes in relationships in other ways.[47]

There were two aspects of contemporary theology which created difficulties. First was the existence of

> a strong sceptical school, deriving from form criticism, and teaching that we can have little certainty about what our Lord said, did, or intended. This seems to me to lead either to a kind of Catholic modernism which says that Christianity rests upon its value in experience but has no historical base, or to a view that our only teacher and guide is the Church, unchecked by any Scripture and free to make what adaptation it thinks right to the circumstances of the day.

Studies of ministry in France were less sceptical, he said, adding, 'though there may be signs of a movement towards an ecumenical consensus that the ordination of women may be right, we are not nearly at that point yet'. Secondly, the issue of Christology and the related question of the incarnation, leading to the question of the true significance of the creation account, and the Pauline teaching about the headship of the male. He said that the supporters of the ordination of women refused to take them seriously. The whole area of anthropology and psychology needed study. Finally, he doubted whether it would be proper for a small part of Christendom such as the Church of England to make a unilateral declaration of such a kind.

On the whole, contributions to the debate developed points made in the opening speeches. On the one hand it was said that priesthood could not be fitted in between bouts of motherhood (560); a taxi driver's 'not natural, is it?' was quoted (564); bride and bridegroom symbolism put in an appearance (571). On the other hand Luther's remark that the Bible was not the word of God, but the word of God was in the Bible (567), and the example of the conservative Peter, who felt the onus on himself of keeping the doors closed to the uncircumcised (558), were quoted.

In response to Mr Austin (568–9), who referred to the discord in the Swedish Church, Miss Howard (569–70) replied that although there was division it would be a mistake to suppose the Swedish Church was rent from top to bottom. The situation was different anyway in so far as the Swedish Church had no proper system of synodical government, and they did not live in nearly so pluriform a society. She concluded, 'I have been unable to discover from the opponents what it is essentially in the sexuality of the male which is so intimately attached to the priesthood and which would absolutely debar a female from being ordained to the priesthood. Sexuality is a great mystery which we shall have continuously to discover.'

Interestingly, Mrs Mayland (561–3) referred to the WCC moves to remove sexist language from documents. She said that although the language of analogy was used for God, 'deep down many of us, clergy as well as laity, believe that God is masculine, that God is in a way a man'. She linked this with the concrete age of thinking, when God was conceptualised as a man or a woman, and as many people stopped thinking about religion at about that age, those concepts endured. She gave an example of a little girl brought up only by her mother, from whom had come all the love and care she had received, who thought of God as a woman, and who had difficulty in associating the word 'father' with religion.

The votes having been counted in the houses of bishops (28:10, abs. 0), clergy (110:96, abs. 2), and laity (117:74, abs. 3), the motion was carried.

2.5 Retention of legal barriers: the ecumenical dimension ...

Canon Paul A. Welsby (573–6) then moved on behalf of the standing committee[48] that in view of the significant division of opinion reflected in the diocesan voting 'it would not be right to remove the legal and other barriers to the ordination of women'. The motion had been proposed to avoid an intolerable strain on the dissenting minority, and for ecumenical considerations. Moreover, a draft measure would require overwhelming support; in the light of the lack of such support a disproportionate amount of Synod's time would be occupied; and it was desirable to have a period of calm reflection divorced from the controversy of debate.

Some speakers expressed regret that the standing committee had not been more positive; it was pointed out that they had failed 'to put these figures in the context of the very remarkable shift of opinion on this issue that has taken place over the last few years' (576); that debate should have been facilitated 'without prior guidance' (578); that what was right should be made effective as soon as possible (587); that if God were calling women, ecumenical worries could be left safely in his hands (577); that such a passion for unity had justified so many refusals and so few affirmations in recent years (584). Opponents thought more discussion was needed, and one referred to the feelings of 'several young priests who rang me up last week to say that if we in this Synod proceeded further to implement what might possibly have been carried this week they would feel that the ministry that they had entered would be radically affected by what the Church was doing' (591).

The bishop of Winchester (584–7) referred to action as often being 'the catalyst that enables the people of God to focus upon and grasp the ideas', a point which supplemented one made by Professor Lampe (578–80) when he had said that were the Episcopal Church in the USA to go ahead, this might have a significant effect on the Eastern Orthodox, much of whose intellectual strength lay in the United States at the current time. Also interested in the effect of the decision on other church bodies was the bishop of Chelmsford (582–4). He prefaced his remarks by referring to an Orthodox divine who had said that the Church of England should not spend its time calculating its moves on what others would do; and the extract from Fr Gerald O'Collins in the *Tablet*, 'If our ecumenical relations would be upset by recognising the full dignity of women in Church life (i.e. ordination) they are the wrong kind of relations.' However, within the Roman Catholic Church, he said, the papal utterances were unequivocal. Within the English ARC (of which the bishop was chairman) Bishop Butler had said that it would be difficult to estimate the Roman Catholic reaction were the Church of England to proceed, but he feared it 'might be an almost insuperable obstacle to ultimate union, although', Bishop Butler added, 'I cannot tell how our own ideas may change on the subject in years to come'. Cardinal John Willebrands had written to the archbishop of Canterbury on the subject. His letter drew attention to the study commission on women in society and in the church, and the work of the Pontifical Biblical Commission[49] and the International Theology Commission, the latter in particular having studied 'women's ministries on the basis of baptism, in the context of the universal priesthood'. He stressed that while such studies could not be read as indicating any prospect of change with regard to ordination, they may well raise points on which within the present context of Anglican/Roman Catholic dialogue, useful exchanges of ideas could take place. Indeed I might go further and say that our recent joint experience in dialogue has confirmed, in the perspective of history, the wisdom of taking common counsel on matters potentially divisive while they are still within our control.

The statement puzzled the bishop. The 'potentially divisive' sentence could be a warning to hold up proceedings. Yet it was no longer simply an English question. Hong Kong and Canada had acted; New Zealand and South Africa were likely to do so very soon. Change was already happening. He concluded by pointing out that the Churches' Unity Commission included the Free Churches as well as the Roman Catholics.

An amendment to add 'at present' to the motion having been accepted, the amended motion was carried in the houses of bishops (19:14, abs. 1), and clergy (127:74, abs. 0), but lost in the house of laity (80:96, abs. 0).

Canon G. D. J. Walsh (598) then moved that legal barriers to the ordination of women should be removed and legislation brought forward. The bishop of Norwich (598–600) had been opposed to women priests, but urged that this motion be passed so that the full diaconate could be opened to women, and then, should the church so desire, the priesthood.

Canon A. C. Hall (600–1) suggested some of the diocesan houses had followed the path of St Augustine, 'but not yet'. He listed possible reasons for these hesitations. First, out of deference to those against the principle: yet 'Why should we go in fear of the reactions of the reactionary, and have no respect for the positions of the positive?' Secondly, out of a wish to avoid division: yet unity would never be achieved if truth were believed to be one-sided. Thirdly, out of prejudice thinly disguised behind the prejudices of others: yet there was no refusal to ordain other groups who might be unacceptable in some parishes. Fourthly, because there was not yet a sufficient consensus: yet people needed to see it tried. Fifthly, because expediency had negative undertones: yet God surely spoke through the expediency of the situation in which one found oneself.

By way of illustration of the fifth point, Canon Hall gave an interesting account of the expediency of the Hong Kong events – interesting because of the difference in emphasis from the official line. In 1944 Florence Li Tim Oi had been deaconess in charge of a parish of 300 in Macao. A priest could not make the five-hour sea trip each month from Japanese-occupied Hong Kong. The bishop had consulted William Temple, who had privately advised him that Florence Li might be licensed to celebrate. That advice had seemed inadequate to one brought up in a Tractarian vicarage, and then acting presiding bishop in Free China of the autonomous Holy Catholic Church of China. He had decided to ordain her. They had arranged to meet on St Paul's day at Shin Hing, two or three days' journey from Macao, five days for the bishop on foot and boat, and had arrived within twenty minutes of each other. The bishop had reported fully to Archbishop Temple and had received after the death of the latter a hand-written letter saying, 'Whatever I may think of what you have done, it makes no difference to my affection for you.' The official letter discussed by the upper house of Canterbury had not been signed by William Temple, but had been sent by Archbishop Garbett. It was clear from the records that it did not fully reflect William Temple's own view,[50] as it even denied the existence of the earlier letter. A comparable sequence of events had led to the ordination of Jane Hwang. Surprisingly, no one to date had quoted Gamaliel: 'If this is of God, who will withstand it? If it is not, it will fail.' The canon believed that God was calling women to be priests, not just deacons, in the Church of England, and he wanted God to be eminently pleased. Finally the motion was lost in the houses of bishops (15: 15, abs. 0) and clergy (78: 108, abs. 4) but carried in the house of laity (101: 64, abs. 3).

Canon Craston (602–4) then moved that the house of bishops should be invited 'to bring before the Synod a proposal to admit women to the priesthood' when they judged 'the time for action to be right'. A move by Canon J. W. Roxburgh to amend this motion by inviting the bishops to produce a report was defeated, and Canon Craston's motion was carried.

The next in this series of motions was moved by the Reverend L. G. Moss (606–9) and into it were incorporated amendments by the bishop of Winchester (609–11). Not wishing to prejudice improving relations with the Roman Catholic and Orthodox Churches by prematurely removing legal and other barriers to the ordination of women, the presidents were requested to inform the appropriate authorities in those churches of Synod's belief that there were 'no fundamental objections', and to invite them to share in 'an urgent re-examination of the theological grounds' involved. In moving it he said it was in no way intended to be derogatory to the churches not mentioned. He thought the church of the Reformation and the churches of later origin were not in the same difficulty in their relationship with the Church of England as the two churches named. He felt that ecumenical dialogue needed to go ahead frankly, and quoted John Macquarrie, 'Unity ... must leave room for the continuing development of the rich heritage of different Christian traditions on which men and women of very different types have come to know the inexhaustible resources of the Christian faith.' He was supported by Canon R. G. Cornwell (609), who said, 'if we take this unilateral step of admitting women to holy orders we are creating a new animal, a Church of England minister who has been unknown in history and has no part in the general economy of the Catholic life of the Church'. The motion was put and carried.

Finally, the bishop of Guildford (611–12) moved that the house of bishops in consultation with ACCM should be requested to produce a report on the practical and pastoral implications of the issue, including the marriage relationship. He thought this would reassure ordinary people in the dioceses, where practical considerations could have caused the shift in vote. Mrs Haworth (612–13) opposed the motion, first on the level of practical overwork, particularly for the staff of Church House, and secondly, because of the impossibility of assessing situations before they existed. She agreed that the emphasis of priesthood might be changed with the introduction of women: 'We have heard so much about leadership and headship, perhaps it's time we heard a little bit more about serving and sharing.' She added that she thought it would be impossible to investigate the marriage relationship, 'but ... if we really do feel that it is something we ought to try to undertake, let us by all means be thorough and investigate the marriage relationship and its influence on the men who are already ordained. I think that might be very revealing and interesting.' The motion was lost (112: 128).

The ACC met in Trinidad on 23 March–2 June 1976. Points of interest in the report[51] concerned deaconesses and the ordination of women. The council asked that those made deaconesses should be 'declared to be within the Diaconate', and that appropriate canonical legislation should be enacted to provide for them. Movement had occurred since the Dublin report on the priesthood issue. The ordination of women had been accomplished in Hong Kong, where a third woman had been ordained and a fourth made deacon, and had been approved in principle in Canada, England, Scotland, Wales, the Indian Ocean, New Zealand, the USA, and Ireland. Preliminary action had been taken and final action was pending in South Africa and the West Indies, while no action or negative action had been taken in Sri Lanka and Singapore. From this list the council noted 'an increasing acceptance of the principle'. It was bound to listen to member churches and to describe the consensus it formed. The Anglican Communion had 'the opportunity to give witness to diversity without breaking the bonds of love'. In 1974 the Episcopal Synod of the Province of Central Africa had adopted the recommendation of ACC 2 that: 'Where any autonomous Province of the Anglican Communion decides to ordain women to the priesthood, this should not cause any break in Communion in our family.' In Southern Malawi, the Diocesan Synod resolved, by a 75 per cent majority, that any ordained woman priest on a temporary visit should be allowed to exercise a priestly ministry.

2.5.1 … and correspondence with Catholic and Orthodox Churches

At the General Synod in July 1976[52] the archbishop of Canterbury answered a question from Canon Welsby about his contacts with other church leaders on the subject of the ordination of women arising from the debate in July 1975. He had written to Pope Paul VI and also to Cardinal Willebrands, to the oecumenical patriarch Demetrios I, to the archbishop of Utrecht, Marinus Kok. He added that action in other parts of the communion had made the second part of the motion somewhat out of date, and that the current issue was the relationship between churches which did, and did not, ordain women. He said that the subject would be discussed in the Commission for Anglican–Orthodox Joint Doctrinal Discussions in Moscow at the end of July, in the Church of England–Old Catholic Conference in April 1977 at Chichester, and that it had been discussed informally at the Secretariat for Promoting Christian Unity in Rome the previous November, when Bishop John Howe and the bishop of Winchester were present. Additional unofficial consultations of Anglicans with Roman Catholics, Old Catholics and the Oecumenical Patriarchate had taken place the previous November and December.

Against the background of the 'serious dialogue' initiated in

Rome in 1966 between the Roman Catholic Church and the Anglican Communion, which had resulted in agreed statements, the archbishop wrote to inform the pope of 'slow but steady growth of a consensus of opinion within the Anglican Communion' that there were 'no fundamental objections in principle to the ordination of women to the priesthood'. They were aware that 'action on this matter could be an obstacle to further progress along the path of unity', and hoped that 'speaking the truth in love' they might 'grow up into Him in all things, which is the head, even Christ'. In reply, the pope spoke of 'our consolation at the growth of understanding' between the churches. The position of his church was that it was 'not admissible' to ordain women to the priesthood 'for very fundamental reasons'. These were detailed as the choosing of the apostles from among men, the constant practice of the church, and its teaching authority, which had constantly held that the exclusion of women from the priesthood was 'in accordance with God's plan for his Church'. He added that such a new course would introduce into their dialogue 'an element of grave difficulty', although such obstacles did not destroy 'mutual commitment to a search for reconciliation'.

The archbishop's second letter pointed out that the search for unity was taking place within a diversity 'of legitimate traditions' and that what might appear to one tradition to be a genuine expression of 'diversity in unity', might appear to another to go beyond such bounds. The pope replied that there was a strong likelihood that some Anglican churches would ordain women; he referred to his previously expressed hope that the Spirit would lead the two churches 'along the path of reconciliation'. 'This must be the measure of the sadness with which we encounter so grave a new obstacle and threat on that path', although it would be to miss the promptings of the Spirit 'to fail in the virtue of hope'. It is probable that when this last letter was written the Declaration on the Question of the Admission of Women to the Ministerial Priesthood (*Inter Insigniores*)[53] was nearing final draft by the Sacred Congregation for the Doctrine of the Faith. It was 'approved and confirmed' by the pope on 15 October of that year and published 27 January 1977. The Declaration was presumably aimed at parts of the Roman Catholic Church but had also an ecumenical intention.

The archbishop wrote substantially the same letter to the oecumenical patriarch as to the pope, and the Holy Synod instructed Archbishop Athenagoras of Thyateira and Great Britain (co-chairman of the Anglican–Orthodox Joint Doctrinal Discussions) to call on the archbishop and to make clear the Holy Synod's view. This view was detailed in the *Orthodox Herald* in May/June 1976.

On 14 July 1975 the archbishop wrote to the archbishop of Utrecht. He said the 'relationship of full communion which exists between our Churches' pointed to 'a unity in diversity in which would appear to be the way in which the longed for unity of Christ's flock could best be envisaged and hoped for'. Replying the following July the archbishop of Utrecht referred to the resolution of the International Bishops' Conference, which in July 1975 had stated that 'only men and not women can be the bearers of this priesthood of Christ, because Jesus Christ was a man and delegated His Work of Redemption to his apostles, who were also men'. He added that only the church as a whole could make this decision, and hoped that 'common counsel may lead to a common conclusion'.

It was in line with the sentiments expressed in the correspondence above that in February 1978 Cardinal Basil Hume addressed the General Synod:[54]

> There is an ancient practice in the Church of God whereby the faith and its formulation, tradition and ministries are matters to be decided in consultation with other local Churches. Now that our dialogue is progressing and we move in the direction of closer collaboration on the basis of mutual communion between the Churches, it would – to take an important example – be a matter for deep concern were the Anglican Communion to proceed further with the ordination of women without taking very seriously the position of the Roman Catholic Church, our brothers of the Orthodox Church and of the Old Catholic Church regarding so momentous a change.

The same year the reports of the Anglican–Roman Catholic International Consultation compiled at Versailles[55] and the Anglican–Orthodox Joint Doctrinal Commission[56] were published. The roots of Anglican–Roman Catholic discussions go back at least to the 1971 ACC resolution 28(c), which in turn referred to *LC* 1968, resolution 36, which had recommended metropolitans and primates of Anglican churches to consult with other churches in their area and report back to ACC. Locally, the Anglican–Roman Catholic Consultation in the USA had a whole meeting on the subject in October 1975 and had published its report and discussion papers the following year.[57]

Meanwhile the discussions referred to by the archbishop of Canterbury culminated in the Versailles report. This report examined how churches which did and did not ordain women could 'be reconciled in sacramental fellowship'. The Roman Catholic and Anglican positions are stated, and bearing in mind the Secretariat for Christian Unity's enigmatic statement that paragraph 6 should not be read apart from the respective statements, in paragraph 6 are noted 'two grounds for hope'. The first is that those Anglican churches 'which have proceeded to ordain women to the presbyterate have done so in the conviction that they have not departed from the traditional understanding of apostolic ministry (expressed for example in the Canterbury Statement of the Anglican–Roman Catholic International Commission)'. The second is that the Declaration 'does not affirm explicitly that this matter is *de jure divino*'. It was noted that these facts would 'seem not to exclude the possibility of future developments'.

The Anglican–Orthodox document describes this question as having brought the dialogue to a point of acute crisis. The respective positions are described in separate sections. For the Orthodox, the issue involves 'the basis of the Christian faith as expressed in the Church's ministries'. The warning is added:

> If the Anglicans continue to ordain women to the priesthood, this will have a decisively negative effect on the issue of the recognition of Anglican Orders. Those Orthodox Churches which have partially or provisionally recognised Anglican Orders did so on the ground that the Anglican Church has preserved the Apostolic succession, and the Apostolic succession is not merely continuity in the outward laying-on of hands, but signifies continuity in Apostolic faith and spiritual life. By ordaining women, Anglicans would sever themselves from this continuity, and so any existing acts of recognition by the Orthodox would have to be reconsidered.

The Anglican members of the commission were unanimous in their 'desire to accept and maintain the tradition of the Gospel', but were divided over the ways in which the tradition might develop and change in response to the world, and over the criteria for assessing such developments as 'legitimate and appropriate'. They noted that the present crisis in their conversations with the Orthodox had 'forced all of us to reconsider the way in which, in our Communion, decisions are made on matters of such fundamental importance'. Both sides wanted the dialogue to continue.

Lambeth Conference 1978[58] passed resolutions concerning the diaconate, the priesthood and the episcopate. It recommended that deaconesses should be made part of the ordained diaconate. Resolution 21 noted the position of member churches with regard to the ordination of women to the priesthood; it acknowledged the pain on both sides; it recognised the autonomy and legal rights of each of its member churches on the matter; it affirmed its commitment to unity with all member churches and encouraged them to remain in communion. The Conference requested the ACC 'to use its good offices to promote dialogue between those member Churches which ordain women and those which do not'. It recommended that ordained women should only minister with the agreement of the local community. Recognising the possible disappointment of the Roman Catholic, Orthodox and Old Catholic Churches, it made clear 'that the holding together of diversity within a unity of faith and worship is part of the Anglican heritage'. Finally, a recommendation was made that no decision be taken to consecrate women to the episcopate 'without consultation with the episcopate through the primates and overwhelming support in any member Church and in the diocese concerned, lest the bishop's office should become a cause of disunity instead of a focus of unity'.

Meanwhile the standing committee of General Synod invited Miss Howard to prepare a supplement to *OWP*, bringing up to date the sections on the Anglican Communion and on ecumenical evidence, so that it would be available to Synod in November 1978. Her report (*OWP(S)*) noted that in the Anglican Communion there were women priests in the Anglican Church of Canada, the Diocese of Hong Kong, the Church of the Province of New Zealand, and the Episcopal Church in the USA. The principle had been approved in the Church of England in Australia, the Church of the Province of Burma, the Church of the Province of the Indian Ocean, the Church of Ireland, the Holy Catholic Church in Japan, the Church of the Province of Kenya, and the Church in Wales. Action was pending in the Scottish Episcopal Church, the Church of the Province of South Africa, and the Church of the Province of the West Indies. A decision had been taken against in the Church of Ceylon, the Diocese of Singapore, the South Pacific Anglican Council, the Church of the Province of Tanzania, the Church of the Province of West Africa, and the Episcopal Church of Brazil. Nothing had been reported from the Holy Catholic Church in China, the Episcopal Church of

Cuba, the Episcopal Church in Jerusalem and the Middle East, the Church of the Province of Melanesia, the Province of Papua, the Anglican Council of South America, the Church of the Province of the Sudan, and the Church of Uganda, Rwanda, Burundi and Boga-Zaire.[59]

There had been some ecumenical movement. The Reformed Churches were gradually accepting, though not necessarily implementing, the idea. The Lutheran churches were gradually opening the ordained ministry to women, and one woman inspector had ordained a number of men. In the United Presbyterian Church of the USA ordained women were not being placed in ways to make full use of their gifts.[60] In Great Britain and Ireland the Methodist Church and the Presbyterian Churches in Wales and Ireland had begun to ordain women. The United Reformed Church had come into being as a union of Congregationalists and Presbyterians (both of whom had women ministers) and the Congregational Federation had been formed.

Miss Howard also updated the legal section with respect to women ordained abroad, legal language, and the law of the country. First, she noted that neither the archbishop of the province nor the bishop of the diocese has any power under the Overseas and Other Clergy (Ministry and Ordination) Measure 1967, or under any other enactment, to authorise a woman ordained abroad to officiate as priest – the bishops had expressed their view in May 1976. Secondly, the text of legal advice given to bishops in 1976 now read, 'that words importing the masculine gender include the feminine gender unless the contrary intention exists. In our opinion that contrary intention does exist and therefore the word clergyman for the purposes of this Measure or of any other part of the statute law or canon law of England does not include women so ordained' (43). Thirdly, the Sex Discrimination Act (1975) specifically excluded 'employment for purposes of an organised religion'.

2.5.2 . . . and legislation motion rejected

In November 1978 the General Synod debated a motion[61] asking the standing committee 'to prepare and bring forward legislation to remove the barriers to the ordination of women to the priesthood and their consecration to the episcopate'. The bishop of Birmingham (the Right Reverend H. W. Montefiore) (996–1004) said he was convinced that the 1975 vote was a recognition of truth as biblical evidence did not allow any final settlement of the question; tradition could grow and develop; the ministerial priesthood was representative of God in Christ, of *anthropos*, not *aner*, and women no longer felt they could be adequately represented by men;[62] the priestly ministry of women was already at work and recognised. He listed some objections raised against passing the motion, and replied to each one. First, the Swedish and American experience: but the situation would have been worse if women had not been ordained. Secondly, that a general council should be awaited: but the situation did not seem feasible and moreover Peter did not wait for the Council of Jerusalem before baptising Cornelius. Thirdly, that ordaining women would destroy the chances of reunion with Rome: but women priests existed in the Anglican Communion and ecumenism did not mean prevaricating over what was right – there was nothing in the ARCIC agreed statement on ministry that was opposed to the ordination of women. Fourthly, ordaining women would jeopardise the special relationship with the Orthodox: yet the Orthodox were asked only to accept the good faith of Anglicans, and they had just agreed to set up conversations with the Lutheran World Federation, some of whose churches had been ordaining women for twenty-five years. Fifthly, it would end the Bonn Agreement with the Old Catholics: true, they no longer took part in consecrations, but they were still in full communion (except the Polish National Church in the USA where there had been a unilateral break). Sixthly and seventhly, it would damage the ecumenical movement: but they had a record of closer official relations with the Free Churches than with the Roman Catholics. The executive officer of the Churches Unity Commission had said that mutual recognition should include all ministries, 'It would be unthinkable for the Free Churches to be asked to ditch their women ministers.' Moreover, it would be fantastic to recognise their women ministers and to refuse to ordain women in their own communion. Eighthly, more time was needed: but women's ministry had come to the forefront 115 years previously when Elizabeth Ferard was ordained deaconess, and the current debate had been sparked off by a report published sixteen years previously. Ninthly, it would break up the Anglican Communion: yet the Anglican Communion differed from the Roman Catholic and Orthodox Churches by holding together diversity within a unity of faith and worship. Tenthly, that if women were ordained, the Church of England would be torn apart: yet a decision that day would only initiate a long process and the very earliest final approval date was 1983–5. The bishop also pointed out the growing consensus on the subject, and that in a recent enquiry conducted by National Opinion Polls there had been two-thirds approval among church-going Anglicans.

The bishop of Truro (1004–11), opposing, referred to a book by Professor Stephen Sykes, *The Integrity of Anglicanism*, and said that the historic ministry was part of the framework maintained by the Church of England which had given it freedom of interpretation. The criteria whereby the Church of England discussed developments were tradition controlled by scripture, and this had to rule out 'developmental theology' for Anglicans, by which he meant 'the view that secular thought at any one point in history can justify theological changes which are not implicit in the revelation contained in Scripture and agreeable to the same'. He said that God created a world of which sexuality was an integral part, and did not believe that it was a historical accident that 'God was incarnate as a male, nor that the highest vocation of any created being was given to a female, Mary'. He added that although in Christ we have equal access to God, created distinctions between male and female were not abolished. When he examined the proponents' use of scripture he found that the 'whole symbolism' was culturally conditioned; that Paul and our Lord were regarded as being so conditioned by the culture of the time that they were incapable of transcending it; that there was no consistency among the proponents as to which parts of scripture to take into account and which to discard as culturally conditioned. He also referred to the divisive effects of ordaining women, and the need for obedience to Christ. 'A priest stands for that divine headship, not for human headship which can properly be exercised by queens, abbesses, prime ministers.' He linked this with the order of creation, where headship and authority were fundamentally and symbolically associated with maleness. He thought the verdict was 'not proven'.

During the five-hour debate points made in these speeches were developed. The archbishop of Canterbury (1015–18) referred to what he saw as the Paraclete's function of stimulating and arousing minds to 'the possibilities of new truth ... as the Church progresses down the centuries'. Tradition, he said, could petrify. The Reverend Professor D. R. Jones (1018–20) found contrary arguments singularly unconvincing, for example the choice of twelve men 'is not one we can defend in other aspects of the Church's life. It is a *non sequitur*. The slogan proposed by a would-be Athanasius *contra mundum*, that the very doctrine of the Incarnation is at stake, seems to me as great a *non sequitur* as you will find in modern theology.' A powerful reason for the ordination of women was the hitherto male dominance of the Judeo-Christian tradition. He referred to Jung's belief that the collective unconscious was at work in the appearances of Mary to children, that Marian doctrine was anchored deep in the needs of the soul. Although he did not share Jung's analysis, he did feel there was a gut reaction against this male domination and he thought that the ordination of women to the priesthood was necessary 'to the recovery of our true catholicity'. Mrs Mayland (1038–9) said that not only the wrong but also the right use of sexuality could be seen in the secular world. The attitudes of those believing themselves called to priesthood was raised, the bishop of Norwich (the Right Reverend M. A. P. Wood) (1041–2) referring to '211 men who say they feel they cannot stay in the ministry if this motion is passed', but the dean of St Paul's (the Very Reverend A. B. Webster) (1033–5) said that the question would not go away, and they had a duty 'to try to understand what the other person is saying and to listen to what she is asking us to do'.

Although Canon Hall (1049–50) decided not to move his amendment to omit consecration to the episcopate, three other amendments were moved. Canon J. M. Free's (1050) was that vocations claimed by women might be tested; Canon D. A. Rhymes (1051–4) and Professor Jones (1062) moved that no measure should be introduced until (in the case of the former) a consensus had been reached with the Roman Catholic and Eastern Orthodox Churches, and (in the case of the latter) the official dialogue requested by Synod in 1975 had taken place.

Miss Howard (1047–9) had earlier asked about the nature of the 'official dialogue' referred to in the amendments. Referring to the correspondence resulting from the passing of Mr Moss' amended motion in 1975, she said that there was an ambivalence in that the archbishop wrote both as president of the Lambeth Conference and as primate of all England. Thus it was basically an Anglican Communion dialogue, and she asked what was being requested in this case. The Anglican–Orthodox had already had a very full dialogue, and she very much doubted if they would at that stage be prepared for more – their views were clear. If the idea was to go forward only when there was a consensus, 'everything stops for tea'. With regard to the Roman Catholics, two things had occurred since that conversation: the Declaration and the Anglican ordinations. This had led to the Versailles conversations to see to what extent and in what ways churches with women priests could be reconciled in sacramental fellowship. The real question was whether they could go forward into sacramental unity with a diversity of practice. Another question at a different level arose from the Limuru resolution asking for local consultations. The only ones which had resulted in substantial published material were between PECUSA and the Roman Catholics in the USA. In Canada also there was a formal episcopal consultation, and here it was stated from the Roman Catholic side that there was no theological objection, and if the Canadian Church proceeded this would not halt the dialogue. In this church there was also episcopal concelebration at one of their General Synods. If it was dialogue with appropriate authorities in this country that was being asked for, there had been some conversations in ARCIC, which could proceed, she suggested, while consensus was forming.

Canon Rhymes replied that he did not think they should await until the Orthodox or the Roman Catholics ordained women, but until assurances were given that any such actions were not going 'to affect the ultimate unity of catholic Christendom'. The three amendments were lost. Synod then divided on the motion in the houses of bishops (32: 17), clergy (94: 149), and laity (120: 106), with 3 abstentions, and the motion was therefore lost.

At General Synod in February 1979 the chairman of the house of bishops[63] said that the issue of women in the diaconate, arising out of *LC* 1978, resolution 20, would be considered by ACCM and by full Synod in the near future. A wide-ranging study of ministry as a whole was to be prepared.

In a statement to Synod[64] he outlined his actions following the suggestion by the bishop of St Albans (Dr R. A. K. Runcie) concerning tripartite talks the previous November. He had been in touch with Cardinal Hume, had pointed out that his warning of 1 February 1978 had been heeded (above, p. 139), and had expressed a hope for his guidance as to how the debate should continue. The cardinal had promised to discuss the matter with the pope. The archbishop further pointed out that the bishop of St Albans was on sabbatical leave and was, as chairman of the Anglican–Orthodox conversations, visiting patriarchates in Istanbul, Jerusalem, Cyprus, Athens, Alexandria, Belgrade, Sofia, Bucharest and Moscow. He would take the opportunity of discussing the ordination of women to the priesthood. They would continue to keep in touch with the Old Catholics. Wisdom and courtesy required that they keep in touch with churches which ordained women such as the Methodists and the Lutherans. He added that it was for the Anglican Communion as such, and not for the Church of England as one part of it, to enter into dialogue with other churches. In pursuance of *LC* 1978, resolution 21(c), promotion of the dialogue concerning the ordination of women was on the agenda for the ACC which was to meet in May. As one dimension of these discussions, ARCIC agreed that statements on eucharist, ministry and authority revealed sufficient consensus to give hope that discussions on the place of women in Christian life and ministry could be profitably pursued.

The following three months saw developments in two of the areas referred to by the archbishop. First, in April 1979 the ARCIC document on ministry and ordination[65] referred in paragraph 5 to women:

> Since the publication of the Statement there have been rapid developments with regard to the ordination of women. In those churches of the Anglican Communion where canonical ordinations of women have taken place, the bishops concerned believe that their action implies no departure from the traditional doctrine of the ordained ministry (as expounded, for instance, in the Statement). While the Commission realizes that the ordination of women has created for the Roman Catholic Church a new and grave obstacle to the reconciliation of our communions (cf. Letter of Pope Paul VI to Archbishop Donald Coggan, 23 March 1976, AAS 68), it believes that the principles upon which its doctrinal agreement rests are not affected by such ordinations; for it was concerned with the origin and nature of the ordained ministry and not with the question who can or cannot be ordained. Objections, however substantial, to the ordination of women are of a different kind from objections raised in the past against the validity of Anglican Orders in general.

This[66] led to a question by Canon Rhymes in July as to whether the ordination of women to the priesthood constituted an obstacle *de jure divino* to a common recognition of ministry, or whether it was a matter of discipline. He returned to the question twelve months later during debate on a (successful) motion[67] to initiate official discussions with episcopally ordered churches on the ordination and ministry of women. He said he opposed the ordination of women because 'the whole ultimate unity of the Church was of greater importance'. Miss Howard's reply (624–5) is of interest. Having stated that she 'would rather not speak of a particular sacrifice being asked for a hypothetical situation', she said she had been present at Versailles and it was true that they had isolated as one of the signs of possible movement the fact that the Declaration contained no statement on this matter being *de jure divino*. However, in quite another context she had been present when a Roman Catholic bishop said that to read Vatican documents you look as much for what is not said as for what is said, and what is not said is not not said by inadvertence but very often quite deliberately. It should be taken that there is a deliberate desire not to make a statement, and it would not help either church to push the point.

The second area of development was the meeting of the ACC in May.[68] The ecumenical consequences of the ordination of women were considered in the report, and three problems were identified. The first concerned member churches which ordained women and non-Anglican churches which did not, and it was noted that dialogue with those opposed in principle had begun. The second involved member churches which had decided not to ordain women and those non-Anglican churches which did. It was said that the decision of the Church of England not to ordain women was likely to cause problems for ecumenical negotiations in England in the Churches' Council for Covenanting, especially on the question of the recognition or non-recognition of women ministers in the non-Anglican churches. The same problem was likely to arise elsewhere. The third concerned problems caused by Anglican sacramental disunity, for those non-Anglican churches with which Anglicans were seeking full communion. It was pointed out that within the Anglican Communion some Anglicans were unable in conscience to recognise the ministry of canonically ordained women priests. Likewise some provinces, and even dioceses within provinces, did not authorise women priests who were in good standing in their home province to exercise a sacramental ministry. These facts seriously called in question the reality of that acceptance of each other's members and ministry which 'being in communion' had up to then implied. They also constituted an anomalous situation which detracted from the proper universality of the ministerial priesthood. Though these were Anglican problems, they had ecumenical consequences, for at the heart of the current ecumenical debate lay the need for a mutually recognised ministry.

Three interrelated topics were to be the subject of considerable debate over the following decade: women ordained abroad; women deacons; and the ordination of women to 'higher' ministries. From here each strand is followed through separately. A comparative overview is available in Appendix C.

2.5.3 ... and women lawfully ordained abroad refused

After the defeat of the bishop of Birmingham's motion to remove legal barriers in November 1978, the standing committee had appointed a group to consider the position in this country of women lawfully ordained abroad. The group identified seven options,[69] ranging from a decision to take no action, and thus precluding such women from ministering as priests, to '(7) A temporary Measure with a non-renewable life of, say, five to seven years granting only the limited permission ... for the limited life of the Measure'.

Professor J. D. McClean moved reception of the report[70] on 6 July 1979. He said that although the issue was quite different analytically from that debated the previous November, emotionally there was not the same distinction. In Anglican terms the current diversity threatened the relationship of full communion between Anglican provinces. The ACC had asked for dialogue on theological issues, but it was for each member to decide whether to impose legal restrictions on recognition and interchangeability of ministries. The question had to be considered against the Lambeth Conference resolution 21. The ACC had invited primates at their meeting in November to develop guidelines for provinces regarding the sending or receiving of women priests, and, though useful, such could not be a substitute for clear legislation. Looking beyond the Anglican Communion, wider implications arose. He had in mind their partners in the Churches' Council for Covenanting. The report was received.

Canon Welsby (853–6) moved that the standing committee be asked to introduce legislation under option 7. He thought this option would achieve the greatest support, avoiding as it did the complications of benefices and other freehold offices. He argued, however, not from expediency, but because the principle had been agreed and legislation rejected only because of the consciences of a minority and because of ecumenical repercussions. They should recognise the orders of women ordained overseas and not object to their ministry in this country.

Mr Clark (856–60) preferred no action at all to option 7, over which no effective future control could be exercised. In this he was supported by Canon Austin (862–4), who saw option 7 effectively as a permanent step. Doubtless their fears were not allayed by the speech of Deaconess D. McClatchey (864–5), who said that the Movement for the Ordination of Women,[71] which was to campaign to change public opinion, had been launched two days previously.

The bishop of Leicester (the Right Reverend C. R. Rutt) (865–6) said that there were between twenty-five and thirty bodies in the Anglican Communion entitled to decide on the issue, and of these only three provinces and one diocese had so far actually ordained women. Within the three provinces there were dioceses which had decided not to ordain women or to receive the ministrations of those ordained elsewhere. In the light of factors such as these it was hardly fair to suggest that by not passing the motion relationships within the Anglican Communion would be spoiled.

Both the archbishop of Canterbury (851–3) and the bishop of London (860–2) drew attention to the problems facing bishops were the motion to fail, as conscientious views were held on both sides. The latter pointed out that many believed it to be 'conscientiously indefensible' for them to continue to refuse the fact of the ministry of these women who would be visiting the country. He added, 'If the Synod decides that the bishops have got to continue to say "No", then let us appreciate where the responsibility will lie if there is increasing defiance of the Canons and laws of the Church of England. That responsibility will lie not with the bishops but with the Synod.'

Supporting a point made by Deaconess McClatchey, Miss Howard (866–8) told the men to stop protecting the women in ministry, adding that though they could not be ordained themselves, she assured Synod they would like to have women from overseas there. Earlier, she said, Canon Stevens had been calling for peace where there was no peace, 'for let it be faced that this Church is deeply divided and the hurt is carried already on both sides. It is not possible to say "We will just have an academic debate about what options there are." Options demand a choice.' The crunch came with the Churches' Council for Covenanting. 'I do not know how I am going to face my Methodist, URC, Churches of Christ and Moravian colleagues in about a fortnight's time if we say "No" even to those of our Anglican Communion with whom we are in full communion.'

But the bishop of St Albans (the Right Reverend R. A. K. Runcie) (868–70) was negotiating at the other end of the ecumenical spectrum, and, as such, he was concerned about the clouding of the issue of authority. He referred to 'synodical fidgeting', adding, 'untidiness and disobedience, which, alas, the Orthodox definitely understand, may be less serious than an authority which does not know where it stands'. The ecumenical arguments which had had some influence in November were no less serious then.

Professor Lampe (870–3) disagreed. He thought that if to take no action would be divisive, to take action would be less so. He wanted what was least divisive within the Anglican Communion and least divisive in relation to the Churches' Council for Covenanting. Having mentioned his efforts to secure intercommunion with Roman Catholics, he added:

> Even if it were quite clear to us, which, of course, it is not, that by refusing to recognise our fellow Anglican priests who are women we should ensure that the Church of Rome tomorrow would recognise the orders of those of us who are Anglican men priests, again we should have to say 'No'. The price is not one that we ought to pay. It would be wrong. Reunion with Rome is a great and tremendous goal which we hope for, but it is not the paramount one to which everything else ought to be sacrificed.

Inaction would be disruptive within the Church of England. Those who believed Anglican women priests to be priests in the same sense that they themselves were would be compelled to act a lie by obeying the law. 'I disagree entirely, I may say, with the Bishop of St Albans, who seems to think that chaos and lawlessness is better than action under Option 7, better than legitimate action.' However, following a division in the houses of bishops (26: 10), clergy (87: 113) and laity (110: 65), the motion was lost.

On 8 July 1982 the issue came again before Synod[72] when Deaconess McClatchey moved that women ordained abroad should be received under the fifth of the seven options detailed in 1979. Option five was for a 'permanent Measure enabling women lawfully ordained abroad to be treated in the same way as men under the Overseas and other Clergy Measure only in certain specified circumstances, on certain specific recommendations or for certain limited periods of time'. She pointed out that the numbers of women priests had increased, as had their visits to this country. The eucharist had become a source of argument and controversy. It was no longer an issue of domestic concern; primates in the USA and Canada had made their feelings known. The preceding August the presiding bishop of the executive council of the Episcopal Church in the USA had been instructed by a majority vote to request the archbishop of Canterbury to bring this issue back to Synod, and the Reverend L. Clarke Raymond was reported in the *Canadian Churchman* of May to have refused to celebrate as a priest in England until all Canadian priests were so recognised. This was a measure of the discord within the Anglican Communion. Following the division of the houses of bishops (23: 4), clergy (106: 68) and laity (103: 60), the motion was carried.

The Draft Women Ordained Abroad Measure (GS 598) was presented to Synod for general approval in November 1983.[73] According to the measure a woman ordained abroad had to apply in writing to the archbishop of the province for written permission to minister there, and permission could only be granted for a period not exceeding six months in any period of twelve months. Any permission to officiate in the other province had to terminate at the same time. An application from a minister with the consent of his parochial church council could be granted at the discretion of the bishop for a period not exceeding fourteen days in any one parish.

A contentious point was whether the measure was article 8 business,[74] which would involve reference to diocesan synods, and a two-thirds majority in each house of General Synod at final approval stage. It was agreed that the measure came under article 8 in so far as it proposed 'a permanent change in the Service of Holy Communion', and although the temporary nature of the measure should have excluded it, it was argued successfully that to admit a temporary change in practice meant 'the admission within our tradition irreversibly of a principle which the Synod has yet to write into Canon and Statute Law, namely, that a woman can carry out priestly functions in the Church of England'. Yet in the debate the Reverend B. M. M. O'Connor (995–6) had argued that it was clear to many that the matter had absolutely nothing to do with article 8, and he asked whether it was true that the decision flew in the face of legal advice, what the reasons were for the decision 'other than a desire to defeat this Measure by any means apparently, fair or foul?', and who has so voted – although he acknowledged that nothing in standing orders required that he should receive a reply to his question. He added that the decision played into the hands of those cynical about synodical government and these would justify their stance by indicating this 'kind of skulduggery and manipulation'. Certainly the frustration expressed here evokes that of Dr Maltby in the face of the procedural delaying tactics in the Wesleyan Methodist Church during the second period identified above (see pp. 36–42), and some of the comments by Taft during the first (pp. 12–13).

Professor McClean's starting point in introducing the debate was that 600–700 women were validly ordained priests of 'the true and apostolic Church of Christ', since validity of ordinations was a matter of canon law. The Reverend P. J. Geldard (985–8) was not convinced: 'To put the question rather bluntly, are there actually women priests in the Anglican Communion at all?' Ordination to ministry in particular churches, he argued, did not imply ordination to the whole of the Anglican Communion, and the legal rights of an autonomous province 'in no way authorised the theological or ecumenical rightness of that decision'. Only four autonomous churches had taken the decision to ordain women, and they had been criticised three times by the Orthodox and five times by the Roman Catholics.

The archbishop of York (997–9) said that behind the question as to whether there were women priests in the Anglican Communion lay the major issue of authority, and it was quite clear that member churches had such authority: 'it seems to me that the whole of our Anglican heritage does depend to a very considerable extent on the belief that unilateral action in matters touching authority and touching ministry is possible. What else is the Reformation about?' and Professor McClean (1006–7) added later that paragraph 3(a) of Lambeth 1978, resolution 21, 'must mean Holy Orders in the Church Catholic'. Deaconess Anne Jennings (1001) asked: 'perhaps somebody afterwards will be kind enough to explain to me how this [claim not to be ordained] could possibly happen. Perhaps it is because some people regard women as inferior, or perhaps they think that ordination would not take on a woman. I do not know, and I would be glad to hear' – an intervention that must evoke Pauline Webb's raising of the issue at the 1959 Methodist Conference.

While Canon R. T. Greenacre urged that it would not be responsible for Synod to agree to a measure which committed the Church of England for the first time to the validity of the priestly orders of women from abroad, and to heed the shadow of ARCIC currently hanging over them, Canon Austin, who described himself as 'a Catholic, as a hard-line opponent of the ordination of women', begged his 'fellow Catholics and opponents' to abstain as the measure was so limited as a gesture in response to Professor McClean's plea for generosity. His plea may have been heeded by some as there were 19 abstentions when the motion received majorities in the houses of bishops (24: 9), clergy (112: 73), and laity (130: 71).

In introducing the revised measure in July 1984,[75] the bishop of Wolverhampton (the Right Reverend B. Rogerson) said four areas of concern had been considered. First, the revision committee had accepted an argument that the measure should be temporary, for a period of seven years, to give time to resolve the question of the admission of women to the priesthood. Secondly, advice had been taken with regard to the implications of the Sex Discrimination Act 1975, and the outcome had been that whilst the six-month term amounted to discrimination, it was not unlawful discrimination, because the intention was to reduce discrimination. Thirdly, the implications of the EEC directives would not be breached as long as the ministry of female priests was kept under review, and finally the ecumenical implications were not in any one direction.

Canon A. J. S. Freeman (643–5), who described himself as a supporter of the ordination of women to the priesthood, opposed the measure because he thought the principle should be decided before hospitality was extended, to which the bishop of Birmingham replied that he thought the principle had been decided already when Synod passed the motion that there were no fundamental objections to the ordination of women (in 1975). A similar point was made by the archdeacon of Dudley (the Venerable C. R. Campling) (640–3), who said this was not a claim to synodical infallibility, but simply a statement that currently 'in synodical life we believe theologically in the ordination of women'. It is interesting to see how in this series of debates this point was largely ignored, and the ground ceded to the opponents on the decision of Synod in relation to the principle. He returned to the article 8 factor: 'I still do not understand why this particular Measure which seems to be to be about human gender should be thought to affect the service of Holy Communion'.

The archbishop of Canterbury (648–51) noted that students 'of archiepiscopal form in the *Report of Proceedings* will correctly discern some development' – in 1979 he had been critical of a measure which he thought had at heart the conversion of the recalcitrant, and the motion debated against a background of a decision just taken (to reject legislation) amounted to 'synodical fidgeting'; three years later he saw the time as ripe for movement, and two years further on he was convinced was the time for action. Travelling in the Anglican Communion as archbishop of Canterbury he found it difficult apparently to reject canonically ordained women in full communion; he was in a position which embodied rejection and division rather than providing a focus for identity and affection. Moreover, he did not think 'the carefully hedged provisions in this draft' would affect relationships greatly with the Catholic Churches. Subsequently the motion was passed and the matter referred to the dioceses.

The diocesan synods were asked to consider the motion: 'that this Synod approves the proposals embodied in the Draft Women Ordained Abroad measure and in draft Amending Canon No 13', and this motion was carried in thirty-five diocesan synods and lost in eight, thus easily achieving the required 50 per cent majority. In February 1986 this report was received by Synod, and the measure passed to the house of bishops.[76] In July there was a long debate[77] prior to the vote on final approval. As the measure had been declared to come under article 8, two-thirds majorities were required in all three houses, which was achieved in the house of bishops (28:12), but lost in the houses of clergy (128:95) and laity (147:88); there were 6 abstentions. Thus the motion and measure were rejected finally.

2.6 The deaconess order and the diaconate

On 12 November 1981[78] the bishop of Portsmouth moved that *The Deaconess Order and the Diaconate: Report by the House of Bishops*[79] be received by Synod. This bishops' report had arisen out of 1968 and 1978 Lambeth Conference resolutions, and had taken as its starting point an updated paper prepared by ACCM. The central recommendation was to have a single order of deacons, open to both men and women. The bishop acknowledged that there was dissatisfaction because the diaconate was almost exclusively restricted to apprentice priests, but said he was concentrating rather on the dissatisfaction surrounding the uncertainty of the relationship of the historic diaconate to the existing order of deaconesses. After some discussion on scripture and tradition, the nature of 'order', and what the bishop of Norwich described as 'underlying anxieties about a policy of gradualness in relation to women priests' (1086), the motion was carried.

The bishop of Portsmouth moved[80] next that the standing committee be asked to prepare legislation to bring this recommendation into effect, and to make provision for the admission to the order of those deaconesses who so desired. Four amendments were moved. Dr O. Wright Holmes wanted to postpone the decision until the bishops had responded to a motion passed by Synod in 1981 to explore the subject of a renewed diaconate, and to assess the implications for the Churches' Council for Covenanting. Deaconess Jennings had earlier made the point that the ordination of women to the diaconate could be positively helpful to the process of covenanting because the United Reformed Church could relate a distinctive diaconate to their eldership, and the Methodists were considering establishing a single order of deacons. This amendment was lost. Then the Reverend Dr G. V. Bennett wanted the bishops to consider the matter further and to bring forward proposals – to which the bishop of Portsmouth replied that were this amendment to be passed, he would be prevented from asking the standing committee to prepare legislation, and it was lost (154:267). Mr Dye moved that 'recognising that the Diaconate can be a lifelong Ministry', legislation should be prepared to admit men and women, but the amendment was worded in such a way that it left open the possibility of continuing the deaconess order (the bishop of Portsmouth's reservation). The bishop of Durham (Dr J. S. Habgood) (1114) said it was a theological solecism to say that the diaconate could be a lifelong ministry: 'This is not a sophistical point but an extremely important theological point, that the diaconate is and remains a theological and sacramental reality, and it is into this ... that the Order of Deaconesses is being invited to come by the main motion.' The amendment was lost, as was the Reverend B. D. F. T. Brindley's recommending no action unless the voting figures seemed to imply that the legislation would be carried through all stages with requisite majorities. The motion was carried, and it was also agreed that the standing committee should consider the appropriate representation of deacons within the synodical structure.

In November 1982 Mr J. F. M. Smallwood presented *The Ordination of Women to the Diaconate: Report by the Standing Committee* (GS 549) to Synod.[81] He pointed out that the issue was how women were to be made deacons: in November 1981 the statement 'within the historic threefold ministry the Order of Deacons is an order open to women' had been carried by the Synod by a substantial majority. In the Lambeth Conference report of 1968 it was said unequivocally, 'The diaconate must by its nature remain a Holy Order', and thus a woman ordained deacon would be in holy orders in both the legal and the canonical sense. These proposals were consistent with the motion to widen the diaconate. Although in future ordinations would be *ab initio*, conditional ordination was proposed for deaconesses as an interim measure as recruitment to the order was to cease. It will be remembered that in the Methodist Church recruitment to the Wesley Deaconess Order was terminated after discussions following the admission of women to the ministry.

Although Mrs A. L. A. E. Treen thought that to permit the ordination of women to the diaconate would finally destroy it, Dr Bennett (924–6) found it difficult to separate the admission of persons to the diaconate from a serious consideration of the kind of diaconate wished for. In his opinion the motion was in conflict with a motion of Mr Dye's passed earlier for the reform of the diaconate which had implied its declericalisation. He was not prepared to vote for women to become clerks in holy orders – what might be a principle of inclusion for current deaconesses was a principle of exclusion for many other men and women who had no wish to become professional clergymen or clergywomen. These, he argued, were the people who ought to be considered for a renewed diaconate. He acknowledged that some saw the motion as a first step towards the ordination of women to the priesthood, but rather than considering that this could influence his own argument, pressed, rather, his 'passionate desire' for a more radical renewal.

Mr Clark (929–31) focussed on the issue of deaconesses. He said that the significance of Lambeth Conference 1920 was that it deliberately did not adopt the recommendation made to it by 'a weighty committee of bishops' that the ordination of a deaconess conferred on her holy orders, neither had the recommendations of

Lambeth 1968 been adopted by the Church of England. 'All resolutions of the Lambeth Conference, all statements of this Convocation, have carefully refrained from attributing Holy Orders to the Order of Deaconesses', and he urged 'absolute and unequivocal ordination'. Finally he argued that the suggestion to interpret 'he' to include 'she' to avoid changing the ordinal in the prayer book was a means of 'conveniently and effectively' bypassing the safeguards of articles 7 and 8 of the constitution of the Synod.

Sister Marion Eva's (926–9) point was that the debate was about the third order of the historic ministry – which would certainly be reformed by the entry into it of women. Currently those most concerned were the deaconesses, and all the uncertainties surrounding this order had to end. She quoted the words of the archbishop of Canterbury, 'For over a century now deaconesses have made an invaluable contribution to the life of the Church of England. They have given their services in the midst of uncertainties about the place of the deaconess in the historic ministry of the Church, more particularly about their relations with the Order of Deacons.' The uncertainties between Lambeth Conferences of 1920, 1930, 1968 and 1978 were to be resolved, but now uncertainty surrounded the resolution. In Wales ordination *ab initio* had been preferred, and in Canada a simple declaration had sufficed: 'let us get it straight, once and for all' was her plea. Deaconess M. Parker drew attention to a resolution passed at the recent conference of deaconesses held in Birmingham to the effect that while they would stress their preference for a form of conditional ordination so that the previous ordination would appear confirmed rather than questioned, they would nevertheless accept 'whatever form of admission to the Order of Deacons the Church may deem appropriate' (79:15, abs. 2).

Mr Brindley (938–9) argued that in the past, conditional ordination had been selected either to avoid conferring the same sacrament twice or to remove doubts in the mind of the church, and not to 'flatter the personal belief of the recipient of the order'. Although it was perhaps the private opinion of some women that they had received ordination, and the private opinion of some bishops that they had ordained them, the only appropriate move forward was by absolute ordination. The bishop of Gloucester (the Right Reverend J. Yates) (941–2) wondered if the working party had been hijacked – 'I think Dr Bennett wants us to hitch the wagon to a star, but I do not quite know where he is bound for'. He urged a return to reality, which was legislation to admit women to the order of deacons as they knew it. The point of conditional ordination was to remove doubt in the church.

Miss Howard (939–40) replied that there was a limit to how much more women could go on 'being messed about with by the Church'. She argued that if the bishops had voted by 35:2 for conditional ordination they were not such fools as suggested by Mr Brindley, and she wondered whether he really believed in the episcopal church to which he belonged (to which he replied with a suggestion of humour that he did, and that though the bishops were not fools, some of them were knaves). It was the bishops, she understood, who were responsible for ordination. 'I do not think that we can have riveted on us in this Church the particular theological interpretation that Father Brindley and Mr Clark have produced.' That the ensuing applause signified the support of Synod was remarked on later by Mr Smallwood, and this observation was confirmed by the passing of the motion.

An amendment to postpone the introduction of a draft measure while the house of bishops considered an earlier motion concerning a lifelong diaconate was defeated, but not before a suggestion by the archdeacon of Leicester (948–9) to make use of 'supplemental ordination', which had been revived by Lambeth 1920 to deal with Free Church ministers, which was to add considerable fuel to the following debate. Finally, the motion received majorities in the houses of bishops (35:1), clergy (120:63), and laity (127:53).

The Draft Ordination of Women as Deacons Measure (GS 580) came before Synod the following July for general approval.[82] The main focus of debate was the proposed supplemental ordination, and Deaconess McClatchey (640–3) found it very puzzling that her 'Catholic friends should see supplemental ordination as a more acceptable way forward in this instance than conditional'. She preferred the latter, on the basis that the apostolic commission was received, or not received, and asked what, precisely, was to be added. 'We should not, I fancy, believe in a few years' time that the Church could add a little extra and turn a deacon into a priest.' After an adjournment the debate was saved by Professor McClean (783–5), who proposed an amendment inviting the revision committee to enable liturgical forms based on models in the report to be received, and so to put labels aside. The candidates would 'for the first time, be admitted unambiguously and with the full authority of the Church to the office of deacon, and that is and must be described as ordination – it is nothing else'.

There was a last-ditch stand by Mr Geldard (791–3), who urged that past arguments should be remembered, if not repeated. Moreover scholarship had not stood still, and he referred to A. G. Martimort's *Les Diaconesses: Essai historique*, where it was argued that there were 'two branches of deacon'. Martimort was a contributor to the *L'Osservatore Romano* series following the Declaration, and reference to this book was to be made to support the Anglo–Catholic position in future debate. In this instance appeal to such authority was unsuccessful, the motion being carried by majorities in the houses of bishops (28:0), clergy (118:33) and laity (111:33).

Draft Deacons (Ordination of Women) Measure (GS 580Y) came before Synod in a radically revised form in February 1984.[83] The committee had decided in favour of Mr Clark's argument that whilst parliamentary approval was necessary for women to be ordained as deacons in the Church of England by the use of a measure, matters concerning worship, doctrine and order were properly dealt with by canon. Notably, the committee had accepted a proposal by Professor McClean and had inserted into the measure clause 1(4): 'Nothing in this Measure shall make it lawful for a woman to be ordained to the office of priest.' This insertion should be seen against the proposed reintroduction of a motion to remove legal barriers to the ordination of women to the priesthood, which was to be debated the following November, and the forthcoming final approval stage of the Draft Women Ordained Abroad Measure, to be determined (unsuccessfully, as we have seen) in the July.

The final revision took place in February 1985[84] so that the measure could go before the house of bishops in May following the completion of the reference to the dioceses. The diocesan voting results duly came before Synod in July.[85] The official motion was carried in 42 diocesan synods and lost in 2 (Exeter, and Gibraltar in Europe), in each case in the house of clergy. Canon H. Williams thought that the figures were inadequate and reflected inadequate preparation 'for this fundamental change in the life of the Church of England' – an argument which, it will be recalled, was used in the Methodist Church in the second period with some success. It was replied that to report back was a voluntary option, and the motion to receive the report was carried.

The final approval of the measure was then debated.[86] With some justice Miss Howard remarked that they had 'exhaustively and at times exhaustedly considered this matter'. Historical arguments were apparent during the debate. Although Mr Dye said they would be righting an ancient wrong dating from around the time of Nicaea when the clergy became imperial officials, and thus by custom excluded women, Mr Geldard said they were altering a principle. The Church of England, he argued, possessed a sacrament in three forms, and to alter eligibility to one would be an implicit argument to alter the others later, and he mentioned Athanasius, who became a bishop straight from the diaconate. He was supported by the Reverend B. R. Tubbs both in his reference to Athanasius and in the argument that to pass the legislation would change the sacramental order. Mr J. M. Coombs, on the other hand, thought the legislation was acceptable as deacons remained outside the priestly barrier.

The archbishop of York (Dr J. S. Habgood) (450–1) considered Mr Geldard's claim to be 'old-fashioned' as explicable in that he seemed to separate the ordained ministry from 'the whole body of the Church', and that lurking behind his position was the fear of the place of the Church of England in the whole of Christendom. Miss Howard said that to act, and then to reflect theologically on something they had actually done, was 'often the way theology is done' (a position clearly in line with the theology of Schillebeeckx).

Seemingly Synod did not heed the warnings of Miss Treen, who compared the supporters to the bogus mother in Solomon's judgement in terms of what she perceived as the potential damage 'to our dear Church', and of the Reverend J. G. Bishop, who saw ahead a path leading 'to the free-floating gnosticism of Rosemary Ruether or Mary Daly'. The motion received majorities in the houses of bishops (36:0), clergy (147:49) and laity (137:34), with 4 abstentions.

The Legislative Committee prepared a report on the measure which was then considered by the Ecclesiastical Committee of parliament. The latter thought that in the service of ordination the prayer asking to be found worthy to be called to higher ministries should (rather than might) be omitted. This revision was agreed by Synod (367:104), and the draft canon was referred to the house of bishops and thence for the petition to the crown and for royal licence.[87] In February 1987 Synod agreed 'That the new Canons entitled "Canon C 4A" and "Amending Canon No 12" be promulged and executed' (335). Thus the way was open for existing deaconesses to become deacons, and the order of deaconesses was closed to new recruits. In the following weeks the first ordinations of women in the Church of England to the order of deacons took place.

2.7 Renewed moves towards priesthood

When on 15 November 1984 a motion was moved[88] 'That this Synod asks the Standing Committee to bring forward legislation to permit the Ordination of Women to the Priesthood in the Provinces of Canterbury and York', Synod had before it the third in the trilogy of reports produced by Miss Howard, *The Ordination of Women to the Priesthood: Further Report*. Access to the previous two, *OWP* and *OWP(S)*, was presupposed.

> Miss Howard noted that the question is approached within traditions which influence one's assessment of the arguments offered. At issue is whether a fundamental change is involved, and, if so, how such a decision would be made. While on the one hand arguments in line with the Declaration would imply that to ordain women as priests would be contrary to the normative practice of the church, on the other hand Professor John Macquarrie addressing Lambeth 1978 placed the ordination of women on the periphery of a hierarchy of truths. Those who would argue that a fundamental change *is* involved, often appeal to 'the Catholic doctrine of Priesthood' in the context of 'Catholic Christendom', and for them the priesthood is *essentially* male, while the proposers question how far details of clerical order are theological. This leads to questions about the nature of biblical authority, the normative character of tradition, and the nature of men and women. For those who hold that a fundamental change is involved, the ecumenical-authority argument is seen as a fundamental theological one, and along with this argument two objections of a more pragmatic nature are anxiety about damaging unity proposals with the Roman Catholic Church and anxiety about creating divisions within the Church of England. However, when one moves from the arguments involved to 'doing theology', understanding and appropriation are seen as a fusion of horizons (this approach to hermeneutics is considered briefly in Part Two), and Dr Mary Tanner is quoted: 'It is in an interplay of

Scripture and Tradition, Reason and Experience that we renegotiate inherited doctrines and beliefs ... and ... are led to new insights' (20).

Next the changes in the experiences of women are considered in society, in the church, and in ministry. While the Sex Discrimination Act and the Equal Opportunities Commission improved the position of women in employment, the recession had a negative effect, and this, coupled with the increase in female single parent families, led to the critiques developed in the women's movement, notably in the effects on women of role models in our society. Christian feminists within and without the church have considered this institution from the same critical perspective. Women in ministerial roles meanwhile have positively affected the attitudes of other people, and have had an effect on the self identity of the women themselves. Since *OWP(S)* the numbers of women offering for ministry had increased, there having been a very marked increase in deaconess recruits, and in women filling posts of responsibility. On the whole these women exercised a traditional kind of ministry, although some questioned the pyramidical model, preferring more cooperative ones. In the Tiller report, *A Strategy for the Church's Ministry* (CIO, 1983), it was said that 'the Church is surely impoverished by its failure to make full use of the potential ministry of women', and in *Women in Training* (ACCM Occasional Paper 16, 1984) it was noted that women in mixed theological colleges received 'exactly the same training as the men to be ordained to the priesthood in spite of the fact that the Church has no intention of ordaining them as priests'.

Since *OWP(S)* there had been movement in the Anglican Communion. By the summer of 1984 Canada had approximately 127 women clergy (97 priests and 30 deacons). In 1980 the General Synod of the Anglican Church of Canada had recommended affirmative action to counteract the discrimination that some women priests reported, which stemmed to some extent from the conscience clause. Misapplication of the clause was deplored by the house of bishops in 1983, and General Synod of the same year passed resolution 60, 'Be it resolved that: in this Church now all functions, offices and ministries, in the jurisdiction of General Synod, be open equally to men and women.' In Hong Kong in 1983 there were

4 serving women priests – the Reverend Li Tim Oi was listed among the Toronto clergy in the Anglican Church of Canada. In Kenya the house of bishops accepted the principle in 1976, and although the Provincial Synod in 1982 decided that no ordinations should take place until discussions had been completed, Dr Henry Okullu, bishop of Maseno South, acting with the support of his diocese, ordained Mrs Okuthe priest on 2 January 1983. In New Zealand in 1984 there were approximately 55 women clergy of whom about 25 per cent were deacons. There was no conscience clause, but there was some resistance to appointing women priests in sole pastoral charge, and lack of acceptance appeared to coincide with the general conservatism of the area. In Uganda, following some irregular ordinations, the house of bishops and the Provincial Assembly voted that there was no objection in principle and left the matter to individual bishops. In the USA in April 1984 there were 744 women clergy (474 priests and 270 deacons). These were unevenly distributed, and their employment situation was not easy. The ordination of women had been approved but no subsequent action had been taken in Brazil, the Indian Ocean, Japan, and Wales. In Australia draft legislation currently before the dioceses appeared likely to be defeated (in the event, it was). Provinces which had postponed or rejected positive action were Central Africa, Diocese of Singapore, Sri Lanka, the South Pacific Anglican Council, Tanzania, West Africa, and West Indies. Meanwhile women deacons had been approved in principle, and action was pending in South Africa, while in the Scottish Episcopal Church this motion had failed to achieve the required two-thirds majority in the first chamber of the General Synod and the matter had lapsed. No action had been recorded in Burundi, Rwanda and Zaire, Jerusalem and the Middle East, Nigeria, Anglican Council of South America, and The Sudan.

As far as the general ecumenical situation was concerned, 'a cautious retreat', perceived by Dr Tanner, between the WCC Faith and Order Commission texts at Accra (1974) and at Lima (1982) in connection with the eucharist was noted, and according to the report seemed to relate 'to the increasing involvement of the Orthodox and their nervousness at any reference to women's ordination in ecumenical texts'. Among other communions, the Old Catholics did not perceive the Women Ordained Abroad Measure as a threat to full communion, but in a 1975 meeting at Assisi it had been said that were women clergy to be introduced to their church in combined functions, either intercommunion would have to cease or, if it were simply a matter of procedure, the ordination of women would be expedited in their own church. With regard to specific churches, in the Church of Scotland in December 1983 there were approximately 1451 ministers of whom 50 were women. They represented 3 per cent of the total ministry, but 13 per cent of the candidates in training. In the Baptist Union of Great Britain and Ireland there were 58 women ministers. The Methodist Church did not keep male/female figures, but there were 6 female superintendents. Of the 24 ministers in the Moravian Church, 3 were women and there was one woman in training, while the United Reformed Church had 165 women ministers. Turning to Europe, the Church of Finland rejected the proposal to admit women to the ministry in 1984; in the Church of Sweden in January 1984 there were approximately 500 women presbyters out of a total of approximately 3,000 clergy. In this church a conscience clause had operated in 1958, and this was abolished over twenty years later. In India there were 2 women presbyters in the Church of North India, and 4 in the Church of South India. Currently it was impossible to ordain women in the Church of Pakistan, which existed in a Muslim state.

The interrelatedness of various issues such as sacrifice, priesthood, eucharist was noted, as was the fact that traditional positions on ministry were being challenged. One such challenge appeared in Richard Hanson's *Christian Priesthood Examined* (Lutterworth, 1979), where he argues that no ministry 'can justly claim that it was instituted by Christ or his apostles' and that certainly no Christian priesthood could be found in the New Testament. A similar position was found in Schillebeeckx (1981), 'Apart from apostleship or the "apostolate", the Christian communities did not receive any kind of church order from the hands of Jesus when he still shared our earthly history'. Questions at issue were whether bishops could be said to be derived directly from the twelve, the meaning of priest and priesthood when used of Christian ministers and their relation to Old Testament conceptions of ministry, and whether there was such a thing as a common mind on such matters concerning ministry in the Church of England. In this connection, relevant factors were the divergence of scholarly opinion concerning the accuracy, historicity, and purpose of the New Testament documents, and the difficulty of moving from description to prescription in church order. There was also the question of the right of an Anglican province, or a Christian communion, to decide on the ordination of women unilaterally.

Finally the issues of headship and the nature of God were considered. There is a wide spectrum of opinion among evangelicals, with whom the former is generally associated. Dr Gordon Wenham in an article in *Churchman* (92: 4, 1978) links the issue of ordaining women with 'the crisis of morality in our society'. To give a woman teaching authority over men in church would upset the created order, which he sees as supported by anthropology and biology. On the other hand, Paul K. Jewett in *MAN as Male and Female* (Eerdmans, 1975) offers a consideration of the relevant Pauline passages in relation to Genesis 2 as well as Genesis 1, concluding 'theologically, or perhaps we should say hermeneutically, the problem with the concept of female subordination is that it *breaks the analogy of faith*' with its implied equality. A number of writers would understand *kephale* as 'source' rather than 'head', while others would argue for the principle of subordination but would allow that in some situations women could teach men as long as the principle is not infringed. Occasionally those in the catholic tradition appeal to this argument, notably the bishop of London in the *Epworth Review* (January 1984): 'When I look at the biblical relevation, in particular at the early chapters of Genesis, I find there what can only be described as the principle of subordination. It is so deeply rooted in scripture that, I believe it is normative for us.'

When debate is centred on the nature of God, it is the trinity and the incarnation that are the points at issue. Miss Howard notes that 'deep-rooted feelings' are aroused. 'These feelings may well go far deeper than the rational element in us, but if they touch a *non*-rational element it is not to be assumed that this is to be equated with the *irrational*.' On the other hand the bishop of London has argued: 'we are dealing with the deepest primaeval truths about what we are and about our relation to

> God'. It is, of course, in this context that the ikon argument arises, and Miss Howard has included an interesting quotation from an unpublished paper by the bishop of Salisbury (the Right Reverend John Austin Baker), who takes issue with it:
>
> > it may be worthwhile pointing out that the supreme example in Christianity of a symbolically representative material object through which Christ is made personally present, namely the bread and wine of the Eucharist, media which have the ultimate authority of Christ himself, is actually almost defiantly *unlike* the spiritual reality which it mediates. The bread and wine have absolutely no outward features in common with Christ . . . (In the RC Church the use of white wine was specifically enjoined for the Sacrament in order to avoid superstitious notions that might arise from the likeness of red wine to blood.) [Quotation edited by the bishop] (87)
>
> Arguments about the maleness of God bring us into the area of language and its feminist critique: Dr Rowan Williams sees the crucified Jesus as God's judgement on 'the world's patterns of dominance'.

Although at the beginning of the debate the chairman ruled that the basic argument was relevant, there was some justice in the conclusion of the bishop of Birmingham towards the end that the theological debate was becoming sterile (1125). Among points made, the bishop of Southwark argued that to ordain women was the only way to safeguard the doctrine of God in its fulness, and this had the support of the dean of Durham, who argued that representation demanded that both pure act and pure receptivity should be imaged. Among the more cautious, Canon G. Grainger showed some concern about the emasculation of the priesthood by some 'extremists', while, opposing the debate, Mr Clark (1085–90) said it could not be presented as development 'totally to banish the Fatherhood of God – as revealed – to the margins of metaphor, nor to think it wholly explained away by adept appeal to Dame Julian of Norwich and the femininity of Wisdom, still less to let it be profaned by a female crucifix in an Anglican cathedral'.

The archbishop of Canterbury (1092–6) said he was still driving down the middle of the road. He thought the theological argument tipped in favour, but wanted the introduction of women deacons and women ordained abroad first as part of a process of 'gradualism'. Deaconess McClatchey replied that it was on the point of where the process of gradualism ended that they differed, and Miss Howard (1118–20) pointed out that there was some inconsistency in that it had been consistently argued that women should be made deacons as distinct from the priesthood, and the process should not be regarded 'as a sort of relentless bandwagon'. 'But how long they are taking!', she added. Deaconess McClatchey pointed to the implications of the passage of time in the dilemma expressed by a student of 'staying in the Church at all, if you are a woman and a Christian'; she added, 'If you want a Church which retains the atmosphere of an exclusive men's club on ladies' night, you will have little sympathy either with Christian feminists or with this motion', and Miss C. Barker-Bennett said that the exemption of the church from equal opportunities legislation resulted in it dragging its feet in an area when it should be in the lead – an argument similar to that of Dr Maltby in the Methodist Church of the 1920s (above, p. 27). Although on the other hand Mrs V. E. Ffinch (1102–4) believed 'that a woman's true vocation is to be wife, mother and helpmeet to her man', she did not think of herself as prejudiced: 'I do not like terms such as "gut reaction". I like to feel that if I had deeply felt convictions about something they would be coming from a little nearer the heart.' More rationalised convictions were criticised by Deaconess McClatchey, who said that some of the argument about the deep-lying dangers to the Christian faith of ordaining women put her in mind of the hysterical witchcraft trials of the seventeenth century.

That the time was right to put pluralism into practice, as part of the current reformation in the church, was argued by the bishop of Southwark. Mr M. D. Oakley drew attention to what he called the 'scaremongering tactics' of a *Times* article the previous Monday that had forecast 'mayhem', 'with the founding of an independent church and large sections taking the express way to Rome'. Seemingly Synod was not influenced unduly because the motion was passed in the houses of bishops (41: 6), clergy (131: 98), and laity (135: 79).

That the standing committee asked to bring forward legislation was 'about equally divided' on the issue was suggested by the tenor of their report, *The Ordination of Women to the Priesthood: The Scope of the Legislation* (GS 738), where a great deal of ground had been ceded to the opponents. Article 8 would apply to the measure; a special provision excluding the consecration of women to the episcopate would be included just as the diaconate measure had excluded the ordination of women to the priesthood; and 'safeguards' would be 'entrenched' – that is, could only be removed by a two-thirds majority vote in each house of General Synod. The safeguards were designed to protect those who would not accept the ordination of women. Thus a bishop could refuse to ordain, license, etc. 'solely on the ground of the gender of the person concerned ... whatever the preferences of parishes, or indeed of the diocesan synod', but the suggestion by an opponent was turned down that henceforth no person opposed to the ordination of women should be consecrated to the episcopate (9). The incumbent was already 'protected' under canon C8 paragraph 4. Special rights should be extended to the laity through legislation. Safeguards should also surround the appointment of incumbents and priests-in-charge. Special arrangements were considered for those 'who would be left in difficulties related to the exercise of episcopal ministry and jurisdiction by a bishop who had ordained, or who accepted the principle of ordaining, a woman to the priesthood' (an issue of particular interest to the bishop of London, Dr Graham Leonard, who attended the meeting when it was under discussion). These people 'would not wish to repudiate the Anglican tradition as they have received and lived it – so they would not wish to join any other communion', and consequently five possibilities were examined in the report: the delegation of episcopal ministry; the exemption from the jurisdiction of the diocesan bishop; the creation of 'non-geographical' dioceses; the creation of a separate body in some continuing relationship with the Church of England; and complete separation. Finally various financial proposals were outlined.

The shock waves caused by the report were apparent during this debate[89] – the Reverend R. F. Sainsbury put his finger on the fear in Synod, although Mr O'Connor (653–5) commented that it would have been greeted more appropriately by 'a great gale of laughter', and to him the contents in the light of the composition of the committee came as no surprise. Indeed the comments of the proponents were more overtly critical of the tactics of the opponents than hitherto. Mr O'Connor referred to the tactic of some opponents in the debate on women ordained abroad who had asked for concessions to enable them to vote in favour, and who had then voted against, and the negative tenor of the proposals was noted by another speaker. Mrs Penny Granger asked how the group members in favour could have 'allowed themselves to be hijacked by the opponents'. Mr O'Connor said the report was based on bad theology and bad prophesy: 'just a scare story to frighten the children', although he warned that not to receive it would play into the opponents' hands. He offered a suggestion – to be taken as seriously as those in the report – that those threatening to leave should be required to offer a post-dated deed of resignation so that the seriousness of the threat could be assessed. Mrs Granger made the point that the group

> has bent over backwards in providing sensitivity towards those who cannot accept the ordination of women, with almost no corresponding sensitivity towards those who can and do. For example, women in what would inevitably be a 'no go' diocese who have to move to be ordained or, worse, parishes in such a diocese which are deprived, against their own inclinations, of the ministry of a woman priest. (651)

However, the Reverend D. N. Gibbs (664–5) thought that everything 'looks as if it will be taken away from men who have committed their lives to the Lord, and who have been accepted by the Church for priesthood', and the bishop of London expressed his hope that 'the realism of the report' would be 'recognised and accepted'.

It did not imply necessarily an endorsement of these sentiments that the report was received by Synod because an amendment was then moved on behalf of the house of bishops by the archbishop of York to the effect that further consideration on the report should be postponed 'to enable the House of Bishops to report to the Synod before steps are taken to prepare legislation, the Bishops' Report to be presented not later than February 1987'. Mrs Mayland expressed the hope that this all-male group should consult some women theologians, and Deaconess McClatchey said that if Synod really wished to write safeguards against women priests into legislation 'it should pause mentally and replace woman with another category – perhaps "black" or "Jew" – and then consider whether it really wishes, open-eyed, in 1987 to draft such discriminatory legislation for the guidance of our patrons and PCCs' (679). Mrs C. A. Watson reflected on the nub of the debate, catholic order and the nature of authority, and asked for clarification of the former in the light of the events of the sixteenth century.

The Reverend D. C. Hawtin contributed a lighter note in

summing up the mood of Synod as '2, 4, 6, 8. Who do we appreciate? Our own beloved episcopate', and indeed, the bishops' amendment was carried.

In February 1987 *The Ordination of Women to the Priesthood: A Report by the House of Bishops* (GS 764) was duly presented to Synod.[90] It was in three sections. First, the theological presuppositions were considered. Basically at issue was whether the ordination of women to the priesthood was a 'legitimate development in' or a 'fundamental change to' the historic ministry, and it was from here that a complexity of issues arose. Opponents appealed to article 34: 'Every particular or national Church hath authority to ordain, change, and abolish, ceremonies or rites of the Church ordained only by man's authority ... ' Next the church as communion or fellowship in relation to the ministry, and then in relation to the structures of decision-making was considered; and finally the process of decision-making when there is division in the universal church. The matter of the second section was the principles underlying the legislation, and it was stated that whichever way the decision went, 'actively to seek to frustrate the Church's order and decisions would be to act against the ministry of the Church which is the bond of communion of the Church'. Interestingly it was added that legitimate synodical means could be used by the disappointed to change the decision. Any safeguard legislation would have to be understood as interim as it upheld the non-recognition of ministries and legislated for the continuation of impaired communion and disunity. For these reasons its scope was of particular concern in relation to the episcopate. In this report the position of women who wished to be priests and who lived in the dioceses of opposing bishops was 'recognise[d]'. There followed nine specific reflections on the scope of the legislation. The third section was concerned with the framework for legislation and safeguards. A one-clause measure was not considered an option; two separate measures, one dealing with the principle and with safeguards and the second with financial provision, in conjunction with a code of practice, were proposed – furthermore it was not envisaged that safeguards should be entrenched. These safeguards were in relation to bishops, clergy and parishes; what is not clear is the position of a parish that wanted a woman priest when the bishop did not. Finally some financial provisions were outlined.

The archbishop of Canterbury moved the reception of the report.

It had the unanimous agreement of the house of bishops. He regretted the 'premature panic' of which it had been the occasion and reminded Synod it had been produced following the McClean report on the scope of the legislation (GS 738), which some had perceived to be more about the dismembership of the Church of England than the ordination of women. He mentioned that those who left might 'claim that they represent the traditional faith and believe themselves to be entitled to some of the resources of the Church of England' but added that while 'the bishops note that some may so claim and so believe, they do not themselves endorse this'. Continuing debate on theological issues was required; consideration of the reserves of the Roman Catholic Church in the light of his recent correspondence with Cardinal Willebrands as well the theology 'of our ecumenical partners' and ARCIC debate had to be taken on board. Moreover, the earliest date that any legislation could be implemented would be July 1992, but it could take years longer. To console Anglo–Catholics he pointed out that at the Council of Trent debate about bishops had become so heated that opponents branded each other 'damned heretics' and blood had been shed in the streets.

There was some debate about ecumenical authority. The provost of Southwark (the Very Reverend David Edwards) wanted to know why the consent of a General Council or Vatican or Eastern Orthodox was required 'when, since the Reformation, which did not involve a General Council, our holy orders, female or male, have never been recognised by those bodies?' He added that the sixteenth-century Elizabethan Settlement was established 'in explicit defiance of the papacy and without reference to the East' and that to be any sort of an Anglican one had to believe that the Reformation was 'in some sense right' (312). The Right Honourable J. S. Gummer said their church's orders had been inherited from the universal church, and Canon P. J. S. Armstrong replied that Anglican orders were recognised 'by the Ecumenical Patriarchate in 1922, by the Patriarchate of Jerusalem in 1923, by the Church of Cyprus in the same year, by the Patriarchate of Alexandria in 1930 and by the Patriarchate of Rumania in 1936' (319). Still on the issue of authority, Deaconess Una Kroll said that she did not notice the Roman Catholic Church waiting for the Anglicans before making 'unilateral decisions of profound consequence, such as the declaration of the infallibility of the Pope or the Assumption of the Virgin Mary' (321).

Mrs Petra Clarke referred to the effect on the report of its all-male compiling body. She quoted paragraph 8: 'Other issues in the current debate include . . . the discovery of gifts exercised by women in secular life. Does the discovery of these gifts have a bearing on the ordination of women to the priesthood?' She wanted to know who was doing the discovering: 'As women, surely we always knew that these gifts were there: we did not have any discovering of gifts to do. I suppose the House of Bishops is making discoveries about women in secular life. Is there no morsel of regret that these gifts have for so long actively been repressed?' She wanted at the very least the text of the report amended to 'the wider and welcome rôle of women in secular life' (309).

Following the formal acceptance of the report, the archbishop of Canterbury moved that the standing committee should be asked to bring forward legislation based on its guidelines, and that meanwhile the house of bishops should begin to prepare the code of practice. There followed a long debate during which a number of amendments were lost and little of note emerged. The Reverend Dr John Sentamu said that had the early church waited for the Council of Jerusalem before admitting gentiles, only the bishop of Birmingham would be present, and Dr Margaret Hewitt described as 'yo-yo theology' the idea of ordaining women and then not ordaining them. Eventually the archbishop's motion received majorities in the houses of bishops (32:8), clergy (135:70), and laity (150:67), with 2 abstentions.

The Ordination of Women to the Priesthood: A Second Report by the House of Bishops of the General Synod of the Church of England (GS 829) was the promised theological reflection accompanying the legislation.[91] It was admitted in this report that some of the bishops who voted in favour of legislation in February 1987 might have 'regarded the drawing up of specific legislation as a way of bringing to the attention of the Church of England the real threat to the unity of the Church of England that such legislation might involve' (5). The bishops identified five issues underlying the debate: priesthood and representation in Christ; priesthood, headship and the exercise of authority; priesthood, the unity of the church, and the authority of the ordained ministry; how the sources of authority (scripture, tradition, reason) were used in this debate; and decision-making when there is division in the universal church. That debate had already occurred and reports (notably by Dame Christian Howard) been presented was acknowledged by the bishops – their concern, rather, was 'to set out the degree of theological agreement' that existed among themselves.

One does not therefore expect to find anything of original theological note in this report. What is significant is the priority and weight given to the (originally) Roman Catholic ikon argument. Certainly the refrain 'some of us think ... others are of the opinion' recurs, yet the resulting effect of this juxtaposition is that the minority positions receive a great deal of official episcopal emphasis, with little or no relative evaluation. During the ensuing debate the Reverend (formerly Deaconess) Anne Jennings remarked that the report 'never actually states how much weight is behind any one view'.

When the archbishop of Canterbury (Dr R. A. K. Runcie) asked Synod to 'receive' (rather than 'take note of') the report in July 1988,[92] he said that while some said the theoretical decision had been made in 1975, others argued that at that stage the theological issues for and against were very inadequately set out. During this debate they were most adequately aired. Among points raised, Prebendary Michael Saward said that tradition is 'formulated by the people who are in charge'. He counselled members to look at the patristic views on 'woman, the temptress', notably Augustine's description of 'Woman, a temple built over a sewer'. These writings he thought expressed 'a deep-seated fear of the power of women'.

Sections of the debate centred on Roman authority, its extent and limitations. The bishop of Birmingham (the Right Reverend Mark Santer) said that in the context of ecumenical dialogue 'we and other Christians are coming to realise that, within the Christian community as a whole, the Bishop of Rome has a special place as focus and guardian of unity', and that 'we must listen very carefully [to] ... the Bishop of Rome'. He quoted from the archbishop of Canterbury's letter replying to the pope's 'expression of that responsibility in pastoral care for the unity of all God's people which is part of the office of the Bishop of Rome'. But following him Canon Craston wanted to know 'how we define the one Catholic Church', which was not the same as the 'Church of Rome'. The bishop of Durham (the Right Reverend David Jenkins) asked whether 'the reasonable tone of this debate so far is altogether reasonable', and he found distasteful the forthcoming decision as to whether £30,000 was appropriate compensation 'for the cost of the possible effects of certain things on certain consciences'. He thought the present argument and behaviour were 'putting over a picture of God which can only promote atheism', for example in the 'selective and evasive fantasy' that God can be 'absolutely perceived and definitively discerned for decisions and actions'. He queried the decision-making procedures of traditional churches: 'Terrible decisions have been taken in past history by Roman Popes and Roman Councils, not least, for example, about the Jews.' He added, 'We seem to be suddenly kidding ourselves that life would be easier in this troubled world and in our present worries if we could go back to Mother rather than on to God's future.' After further debate the report was received.

The following day Professor McClean moved that general approval be given to the Draft Priests (Ordination of Women) Measure. He stressed the need to test the mind of the church, and pointed out that the resolution limited women to the priesthood: the question of their consecration to the episcopate was excluded. It is interesting to see how over a decade the priesthood and the episcopate were gradually divorced in relation to this issue, a trend reinforced by the appearance of the Grindrod report on women and the episcopate, which was available to Lambeth Conference in 1988. After considerable debate the motion received majorities in the houses of bishops (28:21), clergy (137:102), and laity (134:93), with 1 abstention. A number of related motions concerning the legislation also received majorities.

Accordingly, the draft measure and draft canons were referred by Synod to the diocesan synods, who were requested to reply by 30 November 1991. They were contained in the first of two consultative documents, *The Ordination of Women to the Priesthood: Reference of Draft Legislation to the Diocesan Synods 1990: Memorandum by the Standing Committee and Background Papers* (GS Misc 336) and *The Ordination of Women to the Priesthood: A Digest of the Second Report by the House of Bishops (GS 829)* (GS Misc 337), which were made available to aid discussions. A majority vote in favour by the dioceses would enable Synod to proceed to final approval stage in 1992. Meanwhile, the appointment of Dr George Leonard Carey, who is in favour of the ordination of women, as archbishop of Canterbury from 1991, could be read as a propitious omen for women seeking ordination to the priesthood in the Church of England.

SECTION THREE

THE ROMAN CATHOLIC CHURCH[1]

The Roman Catholic Church would claim New Testament antecedents. Dissenters would distinguish between it and the 'Church Catholic' of early Christendom. Henry Chadwick (1967) notes that the 'rapid emergence of the Roman see as a preeminent centre of both leadership and juridical authority' was a 'striking feature of the life of the Western churches from the second half of the fourth century onwards' (237). The authority claimed by the papacy on matters of faith and morals reached its zenith with the declaration of papal infallibility at Vatican 1 (1869–70) – which has been interestingly reconstructed by Hasler (1981).

This move should be seen in the context of the church's fear of the new liberal society which had arisen out of enlightenment thought and developing industrialisation and which threatened traditional order. Indeed, Vatican 1 was preceded by Pius IX's publication of the *Syllabus of Errors* (1864). Leo XIII believed in the building of a new social order, and with this in view he restored Thomism as the church's official theology in his encyclical *Aeternae Patris* (1879). This is a subject addressed by Gregory Baum in his contribution to *Sociology and Theology: Alliance and Conflict*.[2] Baum notes three functions of Thomism. It accepted the dignity of human reason, while beyond the limits of reason revelation was defined by the magisterium. It provided the model of an organic society derived from times past which could provide a critique of liberalism by putting the 'common good' above class, and of socialism in asserting the independence of classes and the need of common (Christian) norms and values – from here, I would suggest, arises the Durkheimian view of the function of religion in society. Thirdly, Baum notes the political function of Thomism wherein the historical human reality is divided into the spheres of the natural and the supernatural order mediated by the church; the church is needed to guide the sin-affected world in its limited independence by clarifying the meaning of the common good. This apartheid of order was apparent explicitly in the post-Vatican 2 contribution of Cardinal Joseph Ratzinger to *L'Osservatore Romano*, which he wrote to support the Declaration (below, pp. 191–3).

In the 1950s Roman Catholic theologians borrowed increasingly from modern philosophies. Karl Rahner and colleagues developed the 'transcendental method' and integrated into Roman Catholic theology such concepts as 'the turn of the subject' and 'the historicity of consciousness', while the Jesuit Teilhard de Chardin used evolutionary concepts as a basis for 'Christogenesis'[3] – although prior to Vatican 2 church authorities refused him permission to publish. This Vatican Council, which opened in 1962, allowed greater freedom to Roman Catholic theology, which became increasingly pluralistic. Those influential in bringing about church renewal through the Council belonged to those industrialised nations where Catholics represented either a majority or a significant minority with great cultural influence, such as France, Germany, Belgium and Holland. Collegiality and the recognition of the plurality of local churches in *Gaudium et Spes* balanced to some extent the definition of papal infallibility of Vatican 1 and the publication of the *Syllabus of Errors*.

Baum introduces four social considerations which could aid a study of this pluralism. The first is that the social location of the Christian community affects the theology it produces. He suggests for example that English theologians were not influential in drafting documents for Vatican 2 because in England theology still followed the old Scholastic orthodoxy and was not applied to a critique of culture. The significant community of educated people who had often made their own decision to join this church, produced a culture of their own which stood out against the dominant culture. Secondly, theology is a function of the dominant culture to which it belongs. As an example he contrasts the tendency towards empiricism in the Anglo-American world with that to explore consciousness among German thinkers. In Roman Catholic theology these differences emerge in the differing emphases of the writings of Bernard Lonergan and Karl Rahner, and in the contrast between Anglo-American process theology inspired by Alfred North Whitehead as opposed to German process thought which is always based on some dialectics of unfolding consciousness. Thirdly, theology depends on the dominant academic institutions in which it is taught, notably their means of funding. Baum expresses some concern that the move of theology to university estranges the former from the life of the church. He makes the point that it was pastoral concern which influenced the renewal of Vatican 2 in so far as the demand for renewal made by the bishops was enthusiastically supported by large numbers of Roman Catholics in their home dioceses. The argument that pastoral expediency carries more weight than academic argument would be interesting to consider in terms of the issue of birth control, where in the event neither carried much weight against previous Vatican pronouncements.[4]

The fourth consideration relates theology to economic class. This position arose from the Latin American bishops' conference held at Medellin in 1968,[5] where the perspective and conclusions contrasted with the westernised, middle-class, optimistic perspective of the Council of the 1960s. From the Latin American perspective the New World being created was not a world of hope. The industrialised centre became rich at the expense of the periphery – where countries such as Latin America were located. The bishops saw a need for an economic analysis to throw light on material conditions, and did not wish the Christian religion to be used to console people for hard conditions which required, rather, social change. As a result of the influence of these bishops, the third synod of bishops held in Rome in 1971 produced the teaching document 'Justice in the World'. In it the idea of social sin was adopted, and the notion that divine salvation included the liberation of people from all the oppressive conditions of life; a Christian praxis for social change was advocated.

> What emerged here, even at the highest ecclesiastical level, was a new orientation in theology, one which holds that the gospel can only be understood ... *after* a person has identified himself or herself with the oppressed, the marginalized, the crucified in this world. This new trend recognizes that religion and theology always fulfil some sort of political role and insists that unless Christians engage themselves in the emancipation of humankind, their religion and their theology, however learned, will actually be an ideology legitimising the existing unjust power relations.[6]

This new political theology – or liberation theology – emanating from Latin America has spread well beyond that continent's borders. It shares similar (critical) roots with feminist theology, in which patriarchy and the androcentrism of recorded history, particularly biblical history, subsumed under the social sin of sexism, are perceived as the forces of oppression to which salvific liberating forces need to be applied. This is the starting point adopted by Elisabeth Schüssler Fiorenza in her analysis of New Testament origins, where she seeks to uncover the liberating impulses emanating from the life and praxis of Jesus and his community of disciples. I will return to a consideration of her work in Part 2. The paradigm shift required by feminist theology is, arguably, no different in kind from that required by the Latin American bishops.

I THE THIRD PERIOD: THE ISSUE EMERGES IN THE ROMAN CATHOLIC CHURCH

1.1 The question raised and the report of the Pontifical Biblical Commission

Roman Catholic canon law is unequivocal on the subject of the ordination of women to the priesthood. The 1917 canon 968: 1 and the 1983 canon 1024[7] state: 'Only a baptised man can validly receive ordination' even though the antecedents for the original canon have been challenged.[8] Interestingly, both codes of canon law followed in the wake of a feminist wave which led eventually to discussion and decision in the Vatican. In 1968 the World Congress of the Lay Apostolate requested a study of the role of women in the sacramental order and the church.[9] The national synods of Holland in 1969, of Austria in 1974, the synods of three Swiss dioceses in 1975 and the Canadian delegates to the third synod of bishops in Rome in 1971 all asked for this question to be studied. In 1975 the Vatican study commission on women in society and the church was set up but was debarred from discussing ordination. The Pontifical Biblical Commission and the International Theological Commission both embarked on studies in the same field, although the studies of the latter concerned the possibilities of women's ministries on the basis of baptism in the context of universal priesthood.[10] These two commissions passed their reports to the Sacred Congregation for the Doctrine of the Faith, which was responsible for the 1976 Declaration on the Question of the Admission of Women to the Ministerial Priesthood (*Inter Insigniores*).

The Pontifical Biblical Commission was asked to study the role of women in the Bible with particular reference to the priesthood issue.[11] The commission pointed out that such an enquiry was limited for a number of reasons. The role of women was not central to biblical texts (but see the work of Schüssler Fiorenza below). The contemporary concept of priesthood was foreign to the New Testament, where the whole people was priestly and *hiereus* was never used for the Christian ministry and *a fortiori* in relation to the eucharist. Little was said about eucharistic ministry. *Episkopos* and *presbuteroi* were never linked with eucharistic function.

The symbolic arguments I have linked in particular with this church begin to appear in this report, although not to such a marked extent as in the Roman Catholic documentation that follows. First the commission considered 'Woman's place in the family', basing their observations on the Bible and/or biblically-associated symbolism. Equality in the image of God, with woman as man's 'helper'[12] (Gen. 2: 18), was taken as God's fundamental plan, subsequently upset by sin. There was 'no sexuality in the God of Israel', but very early on the symbolism of father and of spouse were used: 'the prophets gave value to the dignity of women by representing the people of God with the help of feminine symbols of the wife ... and of the mother'. (227). Jesus' teaching and behaviour were striking. He moved from rabbinic casuistry with regard to divorce (Mk 10: 1–12), and referred to the inauguration of the reign of God. This observation provided the commission with an understanding of celibacy where sexuality is eschatologically transcended, and, arguably, there is an implied link here between 'the full restoration of feminine dignity', and celibacy 'for the sake of the kingdom of God' (Matt 19: 12). Marian symbolism[13] was perceived as bridging the Old and New Testaments: 'The value[s] proper to femininity that the Old Testament presented are recapitulated in her, so that she accomplishes her unique role in the plan of God.' Her maternal role anticipates the new covenant through her son. Through the Spirit she gives birth to Jesus, and through the same Spirit a new people is born at Pentecost. 'Her historic role is therefore linked to a resumption of the feminine symbolism used to evoke the new people: from then on the church is "our mother"' (Gal 4: 26) and the eschatological 'spouse of the Lamb' (Apoc [Revelation] 21). Finally, in this section, Paul's[14] nuptial imagery evoking the mystery of Christ and his church (Eph 5: 22–3) is understood in terms of mutual submission (Eph 5: 21). Marriage is seen to have 'received its full meaning, thanks to its symbolic relationship with the mystery of Christ and the church (Eph 5: 32),

[and] can regain also its indissoluble solidity' (1 Cor 7: 10–12; cf. Luke 16: 18). The saving value of maternity (1 Tim 2: 15), the honour of consecrated widowhood (1 Tim 5: 3), and virginity as eschatological witness (1 Cor 7: 25–6) are noted.

Christian society, according to the commission, lives on the government of the twelve and on sacramental life in which Christ as high priest communicates his Spirit. The problem is whether women can be called to participate in this liturgical ministry and in the direction of local communities. In general ecclesial terms, in the Old Testament women could have sacrifices offered, could participate in worship, were prophetesses and intercessors; in the New Testament they followed and served Jesus (Lk 8: 2–3), were exemplary disciples (Lk 10: 38–42), witnesses, and announcers of the resurrection. They helped spread the gospel, lending their houses for meetings and were collaborators of Paul, and 'in Christ' (Rom 16: 3–4). They number nine or ten of the twenty-seven people mentioned in Romans 16, and a female *diakonos*[15] is mentioned. Junia or Junio (Rom 16: 7) is placed in the rank of apostles.

The specific question concerning priesthood is then considered. Historically, Jesus chose twelve men symbolising the twelve patriarchs to be leaders of a renewed people. After his death Christ confided evangelisation to his apostles.[16] Acts show that the first community of Jerusalem knew only apostolic leadership. Very early the Greek community received its own structure presided over by the seven (Acts 6: 5). At the end of their first missionary journey Paul and Barnabas installed presbyters at Ephesus (Acts 20: 17) to whom were given the name of bishop (Acts 20: 28). The question posed by the commission was what normative value should be accorded to this 'masculine character of the hierarchical order'. Turning to the sacramental economy, and its relationship to the hierarchy, it is pointed out that in the New Testament the primary leadership role was preaching and teaching; no text attributed leaders with a 'special power' either in eucharistic terms or to 'reconcile sinners'. The commission add, however, that the relationship between the sacramental economy and the hierarchy (a statement not developed) means that the administration of the sacraments 'should not be exercised independently of this hierarchy'. Although there is no proof that women performed these ministries in the New Testament, it is possible that certain situations call on the church to assign to women the role of teaching, and to minister sacramentally in terms of eucharist and reconciliation.

In plenary session the seventeen members of the commission agreed unanimously that the New Testament by itself did not seem able to settle the issue. Five members thought that there were sufficient indications in the scriptures to exclude the possibility; twelve wondered if 'the church hierarchy, entrusted with the sacramental economy, would be able to entrust the ministries of eucharist and reconciliation to women in the light of circumstances, without going against Christ's original intention'.

1.2 The negative response: the Declaration

Meanwhile Pope Paul VI was engaged in the correspondence with the archbishop of Canterbury on the ordination of women to the priesthood (see above, pp. 137–8). The Declaration can be seen as a development of his remark to the archbishop, 'it is not admissible to ordain women to the priesthood, for very fundamental reasons'. This letter was dated November 1975: the Declaration was approved and confirmed by the pope on 15 October 1976. The Declaration was also for internal consumption and was directed particularly towards the English-speaking world. The English translation together with the 'Commentary' was released and published on 27 January 1977 before the Latin text was circulated in the *Acta Apostolicae Sedes* (which did not include the 'Commentary').

The Sacred Congregation for the Doctrine of the Faith, who prepared the document quote from *Pacem in Terris* (1963), which links women with public life, and the Conciliar document *Gaudium et Spes*, which condemns discrimination, to argue that the resulting equality should be based on the harmonious unification of distinctions. Although women have played a historical and play a contemporary role in the church, the congregation judged 'it necessary to recall that the Church, in fidelity to the example of the Lord, does not consider herself authorized to admit women to priestly ordination'. This refusal will 'help in deepening understanding of the respective roles of men and of women'.

The congregation pointed out that the 'Catholic Church has never felt[17] that priestly or episcopal ordination can be validly conferred on women'. The few heretical sects which did so were condemned by the fathers, whose 'prejudices had hardly any influence on their pastoral activity'. The canonical documents of the Antiochene and Egyptian traditions called 'only men to the priestly Order and ministry in its true sense'. The same conviction is found in medieval theology, although the supporting arguments are sometimes such that 'modern thought would have difficulty in admitting or would even rightly reject'. The tradition had been so firm that it had not been felt necessary for the magisterium to formulate a principle or defend a law. This tradition had been firmly safeguarded by the churches of the East.

Jesus did not call any woman to be part of the twelve, even though his attitude was quite different from that of his milieu (cf. Jn 4: 27, Matt 9: 20–2; Lk 7: 37ff; Jn 8: 11; Mk 10: 2–11; Matt 19: 3–9; Lk 8: 2–3; Matt 28: 7–10; Lk 24: 9–10; Jn 20: 11–18). It is admitted that 'a purely historical exegesis of the texts cannot suffice. But it must be recognized that we have here a number of convergent indications that make all the more remarkable the fact that Jesus did not entrust the apostolic charge to women', not even to his mother (cf. Pope Innocent III: 'Although the Blessed Virgin Mary surpassed in dignity and in excellence all the Apostles, nevertheless it was not to her but to them that the Lord entrusted the keys of the Kingdom of Heaven').

'The apostolic community remained faithful to the attitude of Jesus towards women.' Although Mary occupied a privileged place in the upper room (Acts 1: 14), it was Matthias who was called to 'enter the College of the Twelve'. On the day of Pentecost both men and women were filled with the Spirit (Acts 2: 1), 'yet the proclamation of the fulfilment of the prophecies in Jesus was made only by "Peter and the Eleven" (Acts 2: 14)'. Although certain women worked with Paul, 'at no time was there a question of conferring ordination on these women'. The congregation then draw a distinction between the designation 'my fellow workers' (Rom 16: 3; Phil 4: 2–3), when referring to men and women helpers, and 'God's fellow workers' (1 Cor 3: 9; cf. 1 Thess 3: 2), depicting Apollos, Timothy and Paul himself as set apart for apostolic ministry.

The congregation argue that the 'attitude of Jesus and the Apostles' is normative. They broke with prejudices in a number of ways so expediency in excluding women from the twelve could not have been determinative. Paul's prohibition based on custom must be distinguished from prescription 'bound up with the divine plan of creation' (cf. 1 Cor 11: 7; Gen 2: 18–24) in relation to 'the official function of teaching in the Christian assembly'. The congregation here cite Galations 3: 28 as a disclaimer against any charge of Pauline prejudice. Furthermore, they quote Pius XII (supported by Trent): 'The Church has no power over the substance of the sacraments, that is to say, over what Christ the Lord . . . determined should be maintained in the sacramental sign.' Such are natural, not conventional, signs, because they respond to the deep symbolism of actions and things, and also link the recipient to 'the supreme Event of the history of salvation'. Thus the eucharist is both meal together and memorial; the priestly ministry is not simply 'pastoral service' but ensures the continuity of the functions and powers 'entrusted by Christ to the Apostles'.

The congregation note the 'profound fittingness that theological reflection' has discovered 'between the proper nature of the sacrament of Order, with its specific reference to the mystery of Christ, and the fact that only men have been called to receive priestly ordination'. The bishop or the priest 'in the exercise of his ministry, does not act in his own name, *in persona propria*'. He represents Christ (2 Cor 5: 20; Gal 4: 14), and does so particularly in the eucharistic celebration where he 'who alone has the power to perform it, then acts not only through the effective power conferred on him by Christ, but *in persona Christi*, taking the role of Christ, to the point of being his very image, when he pronounces the words of consecration'. As sacramental economy is based on signs, Christ's role in the eucharist would not be expressed sacramentally, there would be no 'natural resemblance' if the role of Christ were not taken by a man;[18] 'in such a case [i.e. of a woman] it would be difficult to see in the minister the image of Christ. For Christ himself was and remains a man.' Christ is the first born of all humanity, but the fact that 'the Incarnation of the Word took place according to the male sex' they insist 'cannot be disassociated from the economy of salvation'.

1.3 Extension of the negative arguments: *L'Osservatore Romano* articles

A series of articles appeared in *L'Osservatore Romano* to extend the arguments of the Declaration.

'Women Priests' by Louis Bouyer[19] appeared on 20 January 1977 as a *mise-en-scène* for the document. The author's concern is to dismiss as flimsy and ill-informed those arguments which had been put forward in favour of the ordination of women to the priesthood. To the argument that antiquity could not accept women priests he replies, 'One thinks one is dreaming when one hears people who consider themselves enlightened and unprejudiced, calmly come out with such a gross blunder.' He asserts rather that Jesus' originality lay in the fact that he did not take as a model the female priesthoods of the surrounding cultures.

He replies next to the argument that exclusion implies inferiority. The Judeo-Christian religion was the firmest and clearest tradition advocating sexual equality, on the basis of 'complementarity', to safeguard the originality and identity of women from annihilation. He says it would be naive and false to see purification rites of a woman after childbirth and of a man between intercourse and worship as implying impurity of or contamination by the female. He argues that just as contact with the Torah 'soils the hands', and after the eucharistic celebration the vessels are 'purified', so the sexuality of the partners is sacred but must be purified against 'possible sin in every contact with them on the part of fallen man'. Rabbinic thankfulness at having been 'made men and not women' is intended to inculcate in the reluctant man the awareness of the honour in bearing the whole yoke of the Torah. Thus woman is excluded from the responsibility of public worship because her own responsibility lies in the family, where she must prepare (but not preside over) the paschal meal. She has a more constant intimacy with the sacred than man, which is why 'Wisdom, which ... will come to mean the closest association that can be conceived of humanity with divine thought and life, will always be represented by Israel as female.'

To those who assert lack of theological justification for excluding women from priesthood, he claims a self-evident principle which the proponents just do not see (rather like the emperor's clothes, one suspects). He argues that pursuit of equality based on the elimination of sexual differences is ruinous for the real liberation of women. By 'taking care not to crush her femininity' in conferring on her an unsuitable ministry, the way will be clear to uncover the 'unique beauty of her femininity', her 'mystery' will be revealed. This mystery is seen as the 'final mystery of creation ... redeemed, saved, divinized by the incarnation of God, in the flesh that He took from woman'.

The first in the series following publication of the Declaration

'The Advancement of Women According to the Church' by Raimondo Spiazzi, appeared on 10 February. He confesses to 'certain reserves' on the part of the church towards the 'excesses' of the feminist movement which threatens the 'meaning of things' such as femininity, the family and society. Yet he acknowledges that the movement had led to 'a new ecclesial awareness' on the role of women. The author approves juridico-political evolution of rights, but finds 'painful' the 'extreme aberrations' found among feminists, and stresses how the magisterium has pointed out several times the paths to take for women's 'real' advancement – the reader may recall a similar attitude in the nineteenth-century Convocations *vis-à-vis* the independent sisterhoods. According to Paul VI this advancement should be 'according to their own particular nature' (*Gaudium et Spes*, section 60), although he encouraged 'all initiatives that wish to implement the justice often lacking in women's status'.

Spiazzi believes that a 'dispassionate and calm' reading of the Declaration can bring enlightenment. The value of a 'sign' whereby the priest acts *in persona Christi* leads on to the further symbolism of covenant between God and mankind (*sic*), where woman symbolises the church, and he draws attention to the appreciation shown in the document of women's role in that context. Although priesthood is linked with '"professional graces" which are certainly of superior level', it is to other roles that women are called. He quotes Cardinal Journet: 'In the Church there is the greatness of hierarchy and the greatness of charity: the Blessed Virgin was placed at the summit of the latter greatness', and he finds himself drawn irresistibly to the following conclusion:

> if the ministerial priesthood reflects the image of Christ, the head and bridegroom, the Christian woman is called to reflect in herself and reveal the identity of the bride-Church, the supreme figure and type of which is a woman whose name is Mary ... The principle of the 'eternal feminine' in Christianity did not clothe itself in myths, but became history in the Mary–Christ pair.

'Significance for Us Today of Christ's Attitude and of the Practice of the Apostles' by Albert Descamps was the second in the series, appearing on 17 February. At issue for Descamps is the meaning Christ gave to not choosing women. He contrasts the traditional view of *actus humani* with contemporary anthropology, which favours the concept of conditioning, and argues that both 'environment *and* genius' must be safeguarded. He further distinguishes between 'spirit' and 'mentality': 'The spirit is the new, original contribution of a really original, creative individual; poured out right into the mentality, it questions it and obliges it to change.' This he applies to the 'deep innovations' made by Jesus towards women. Thence he reaches his 'clear and inevitable' conclusion that Jesus' actions were not based on 'a concession, conscious or not, to a certain prevailing anti-feminism, or out of a kind of absent-minded conformism with the customs of the time'. He believes that 'the specificity of the concept of Apostle' was exceptionally original, and if Jesus never exercised ministry alone and was so original in this, 'how is it possible to suppose he chose men only out of mere conformism?' This was a sufficiently precise plan in which women have been called 'to help'. This divine plan, revealed in a certain historical period, 'is marked by it for ever'.

Hans Urs von Balthasar's 'The Uninterrupted Tradition of the Church' was the third in this series of articles, and appeared on 24 February. He believed the Declaration pointed into 'the depths of the mystery' in a 'thorough consideration of "appropriateness" (*Convenientia*)', which he defined as 'coming together, inner harmony, such as an organism achieves in the balance of its various organs'. The sacraments 'have their own hermeneutics', accessible to believers who 'let themselves be led by the mystery of Christ ... into the depths of their inner harmony and plausibility'.

The unchangeability of tradition hinges on whether the issue belongs to the essence of the structure of the church. For Balthasar crucial here is 'the essential harmony between the order of Creation and the order of Redemption ... The redemptive mystery "Christ–Church" is the superabundant fulfilment of the mystery of the Creation between man and woman', in which analogy the 'natural sexual difference is charged, *as* difference, with a supernatural emphasis, of which it is not itself aware, so that outside of Christian Revelation it is possible to arrive at various deformations'. In the post-Reformation churches constructed on the priesthood of the faithful, 'deviations' exist in their weakened relationship with apostolic office. In the Catholic and Orthodox Churches apostolic succession is decisive: full powers, christological and representative, have always been invested in the episcopal office, although there is an ambiguity in this representation in that the 'superiority or dignity' present cannot be claimed by the representative. This ambiguity is mirrored in the natural order of the sexes in the *doxa* of God in man (1 Cor 11: 7).

Balthasar refers to Bouyer's book, *Mystère et Ministère de la Femme* (1976, Aubier), in which he aims to elucidate with even greater clarity than the 'femininity' of the church,

> the sexual–personal role of woman. While man, as a sexual being, only represents what he is not and transmits what he does not actually possess, and so is, as described, at the same time more and less than himself, woman rests on herself, she is fully what she is, that is, the whole reality of a created being that faces God as a partner, receives his seed and spirit, preserves them, brings them to maturity and educates them.

This recall of 'a great tradition' coincides with a '"masculinization" of a whole civilization, marked by a male technical rationality' which has become confused with and pursued as equality. One facet of the true difference in equality of nature is the masculinity of Christ in his eucharist,

> in which he, on a plane above the sexes, gives himself to the Church entirely as the dedicated seed of God – and the participation, difficult to formulate, of the apostolic office in this male fertility which is above sex. Only if this aspect were fully brought to light, would man's latent inferiority to woman be overcome in some way.

Balthasar concludes that God can and wishes to be received into the world in woman, 'particularly in the virgin-mother Mary'. Men in this Marian church must participate in its comprehensive femininity: apostolic office remains secondary. Thus the tradition goes down to unfathomable depths which can only be expressed 'in stammering words'.

'The Ministerial Priesthood and the Advancement of Women' by Joseph L. Bernardin, the fourth in the series, appeared on 3 March. Bernardin, president of the United States Episcopal Conference, wrote from the centre of the controversy.[20] The bishops had only to 'explain' the Declaration to the people, and women to see it 'in a positive fashion'. He thought now the situation had been clarified, it remained simply to apply this understanding to the advancement of the role of women. Patience would be required while women reached their 'right and proper place within the Church, society and family'. Meanwhile, 'creating awareness' in Paul VI's words was primary, and those 'called to the ministerial priesthood' had a special reason to promote the advancement of women because of the attitude of Jesus.

Although women 'should ponder' opportunities for advancement offered in the New Testament, this did not provide a blueprint. Converging insights pointed to the necessity of unselfish love: 'Sacramental ministry is not the only rank of greatness, nor is it necessarily the highest ... "The greatest in the Kingdom of Heaven are not the ministers but the saints."' Suggested openings for women were as catechists and as ministers of music. Meanwhile spiritual progress was required of the clergy:

> The ministerial priest acts not '*in masculinitate Christi*' but '*in persona Christi*'. If he is to be an effective sign, especially if he is to lead and inspire others, *particularly women* [italics added], in the apostolate, then he must display the virtues and the godlike qualities of the man Christ. It is not maleness which must be accented and brought forward as the significance of the priesthood, but rather Christlike qualities: humility, gentleness, self-effacing service must be easily recognizable.

Within the sacramental structure it was baptism which enabled women to share in the apostolate in a position of equality which does not exclude distinctions. This equality had not been achieved because of 'longstandinghatreds and oppressions', and should be pursued.

On the strength of nuptial imagery, Bernardin moved in conclusion first to 'women's role in the home', where 'the role of the mother is essential' in order to give meaning to the analogy of faith within the doctrine of the church. Next, single women, especially those with professional training, were to be 'fully recognized and used' to merit the promise, 'I will espouse you in fidelity, and you shall know the Lord' (Hos 2: 22). Finally, the 'consecrated religious woman (or man) remains the privileged sign of espousal with the Lord and should be of all the most totally available for the work of the Gospel'.

Between the fourth and fifth articles, on 10 March appeared 'The Value of a Theological Formula, "*in Persona Christi*"' by A. G. Martimort. The author traces the history of this formula used in the conciliar documents *Lumen Gentium* and *Presbyterorum Ordinis*. Aquinas gave the phrase classical expression when writing on 2 Corinthians 2: 10; 5: 19–20. It came to mean that bishops and priests are 'ambassadors of Christ, that they speak in his name'. But they not only speak effectively, they also carry out Christ's role.

Therefore the phrase is equivalent to 'take the place of Christ'. The idea of copying Christ's place was used typologically by Ignatius of Antioch, and later by John Chrysostom in connection with 2 Corinthians. A mid-ninth century Byzantine liturgy, *Protheoria*, says priests '*play the part of Christ the high priest* (*ôs tou megalou archiereûs tou Christou ferousi prosôpon*)', which may be 'a discreet allusion ... to the mask of the theatre, by means of which the actor disappears, giving way to the character whose part he takes'.

The priest's role in the eucharistic celebration is the strongest test of his link with Christ, Martimort continues. At the consecration he proceeds in a historico-narrative manner, uses the words of Christ in the first person, and completes it with Christ's actions. While acknowledging 'discussions' with the orientals with regard to *epiclesis*, the Western tradition held that the priest 'utters Christ's words with the same efficacy as Christ. His personality is therefore effaced before the personality of Christ, whom he represents and whose voice he is: representation and voice which bring about what they signify.' Hence Christian thought has taken '*in persona Christi*' to mean that the priest is firstly an image of Christ and secondly the presence of Christ – from which is derived the 'natural resemblance' argument whereby Aquinas held that women were unable to receive holy orders.

The fifth article in the series, 'The Mystery of the Covenant and its Connections with the Nature of the Ministerial Priesthood' by Gustave Martelet, appeared on 17 March. First he contrasts what he perceives as the structural weakness of the Old Testament institution of priesthood with what it was a shadow of in the New. Here the covenant offered access to the Father in Christ not primarily biologically, but 'in a specifically spiritual way': 'While he bears within him all man's [*sic*] authenticity ... he also contains in himself (this is the paradox) all the newness of God, all the hidden power of the Spirit, who conceived him, moreover, in the Virgin's womb.' Martelet then asks how this new covenant still implies a priesthood, and suggests that the priesthood became in Christ 'no longer a *particular institution* but *the very form of the life of the whole Church*'. It is not primarily a function but a '*charism of existence*'. He adds that this is so clearly manifested in the scriptures that 'our Protestant brothers [*sic*] are unable to go beyond this evident fact, which, however, implies something which is not affirmed in this place but which nothing excludes or denies'.

The bride–bridegroom imagery (which Martelet introduces by way of the reference to prostitution in Ezekiel 23), modelled on 'the conjugal life of man and woman', is 'precisely the foundation of a quite specific ministry, which can be called priestly in the real sense of the word'. In this, the self gift of the bridegroom 'must not mask the identity of the Donor'; it must not 'give rise to a gradual cancellation of Christ'. He continues,.

> Now, since Christ, having become invisible for her, can no longer appear personally to affirm his irreplaceable presence and action, there will be in the Church a visible and efficacious reminder of her absolute and vital dependency on her irreplaceable Bridegroom. The ministerial priesthood is this sign.

It is an efficacious sign of the identity and action of the 'Absent one', pointing to 'the moment of complete communication between the Bridegroom and the Bride, which is, as is known, the Eucharist, the climax of the espousals of the whole Church with her Lord'.

Ministerial priesthood is best explained not by the Old Testament model, but by the 'incomparable originality' of Jesus Christ. Martelet refers to the Eastern debates about 'a unity of the two natures in Jesus Christ that would be confusion, and of a distinction that would become opposition or conflict', and applies this to the union of Christ with his church. Only the Spirit can guarantee this union, but the ministerial priesthood is necessary to remind the bride 'efficaciously of the incomparable personality of the Bridegroom'. He concludes:

> since it is a question of a ministry which depends entirely on the identity of the bridegroom, it can be understood that the priestly service of the New Covenant should be carried out by men. Are they not by nature bridegrooms and not brides? Man is, therefore, better suited than woman to symbolize in the new conjugality that defines the communion of the New Covenant, the Bridegroom from whom the Bride knows she receives both Love and Life.

The 'seventh' article appeared on 12 May. Whether this was a printing error, or whether a prepared article was not accepted for publication, or whether there was another reason for the gap we are not told. 'The Male Priesthood: A Violation of Women's Rights?' by Joseph Ratzinger concluded the series. He distinguishes two principal forms in which the concept of a fundamental right emerges: the

'Anglo-Saxon type with its Christian foundation', expressed in the American Constitution; and the 'declaration of the rights of man of the French revolution', 'a merely human institution' based as it was on reason. Here he points to an opposition between authority and rationality. He cedes that priesthood is not a consequence of creation, yet argues that the bringing up of human rights in the matter 'betrays a dulling of the sense of the "supernatural", of the new, non-deducible and specific aspect of Christianity'.

He considers first the argument that the principle refers not to creation but to discrimination. This, he says, is the position 'defended in Protestant circles', where the church is seen 'as a functioning apparatus and her relationship to right is conceived in the perspective of the concept of right of Enlightenment'. He counters that the priesthood is a sacrament which has 'with regard to the Church, a position similar to natural law with regard to the civil legislator'. In the last analysis this is 'a dispute between the functionalist conception of law and the sacramental conception of the Church'.

He looks next at the argument that the church has a considerable area of discretionary action, and that 'nothing proves that being male belongs to the inalienable substance of the priesthood'. Ceding that no one can bring forward compelling metaphysical proofs, he says that the Declaration 'tries to understand the admittedly contingent fact from the inner structure of the faith'. He uses von Allmen's[21] argument which binds the species of the eucharist to Christ's initiative, and links this to the son of God's salvific initiative in becoming a Jew: 'its "accidental" historical form is the concrete expression of God's action for men [*sic*]'. The sacrament, essentially symbolic in form in contrast to the rationalistic outlook above,

> knows pre-existing symbolic structures of creation, which contain an immutable testimony. The symbolic place of man and of woman also falls within this interpretation of reality; they both have equal rights and equal dignity, but each has a different testimony. It is just this that functionalism cannot admit, for its complete activism implies also complete equality, in which everything receives its definition only from the activity of man himself.

Ratzinger agrees with Bouyer that such equality through uniformity 'contains the sole dominion of the male form and produces equality through the negation of woman'. Furthermore he finds it significant that the two 'qualifications' of femininity – virginity and motherhood – 'should be slandered and ridiculized in an unprecedented way today' and, in the final analysis, forbidden. He discerns a Manichean feature in 'a masculinization of unprecedented proportions' where the human being is ashamed 'of his [*sic*] masculinity or femininity, because here is something which eludes complete planning and modelling and binds him [*sic*] to his [*sic*] created origin'. Woman is the first to pay for this Manichean slant because the 'incarnation of the spirit is manifested in her in a more radical and essential way than in man'. It is easier to limit fatherhood than motherhood to a biological parenthesis; it is 'easier for him to escape from the preconstituted structure of created life to the fictitious emancipation of operating rationality than it is for women'. Behind the 'mask of emancipation' lurks the 'complete assimilation' of the 'right of being a woman'. His conclusion is that the defence of symbolic representation, on which the Declaration is based, is the defence of women: 'The finest ideas remain incredible, and are even falsified, if the facts of the Church's life do not correspond to them.'

1.4 Negation reinforced: *Mulieris Dignitatem*

The matter rested there until 15 August 1988, when John Paul II published an encylical 'on the dignity and vocation of women on the occasion of the Marian year'. Written in the Vaticanese one has come to associate with these official documents, it eulogises Mary, 'The Virgin-Mother' (26), as the great (yet paradoxical) role-model for women. One might be forgiven moreover for suspecting that this argument, or 'meditation' (8), is subsidiary to the encyclical's primary function, namely a reiteration of the central argument of the Declaration:

Since Christ, in instituting the Eucharist, linked it in such an explicit way to the priestly service of the Apostles, it is legitimate to conclude that he thereby wished to express the relationship between man and woman, between what is 'feminine' and what is 'masculine'. It is a relationship willed by God both in the mystery of creation and in the mystery of Redemption. It is *the Eucharist* above all that expresses *the redemptive act of Christ the Bridegroom towards the Church the Bride*. This is *clear and unambiguous* [italics added] when the sacramental ministry of the Eucharist, in which the priest performs acts '*in persona Christi*', is performed by a man. This explanation confirms the teaching of the Declaration *Inter Insigniores*, published at the behest of Paul VI in response to the question concerning the admission of women to the ministerial priesthood. (98)

It is interesting to note that just as the Declaration (1976) appeared between Church of England debates to remove legal barriers to the ordination of women and followed Paul VI's correspondence on the subject with the archbishop of Canterbury Dr Coggan, so *Mulieris Dignitatem* (1988) has appeared before final approval stage in another series of debates in the Church of England on the same issue. Moreover, it follows another exchange of letters between the archbishop of Canterbury Dr Runcie and the Vatican – and in this case the correspondence was initiated by John Paul II.[22]

1.5 A brief word on the democratic process and the Roman Catholic Church in England

On 3–6 May 1980, in the wake of Vatican 2, 2,000 delegates to the National Pastoral Congress (NPC) met at Liverpool. The status of the NPC was advisory to the Bishops' Conference of England and Wales. The diocese of Westminster's preparatory *Report to the National Pastoral Congress: Liverpool, May 1980* (1979), which made it clear that 'the views expressed do NOT necessarily reflect the official teaching of the Church, nor are they a statement of diocesan policy' (i), nevertheless contained a reference to ordaining women as the expressed opinion of an organisation, Roman Catholic Feminists:[23] 'The exclusion of women from the ministerial priesthood cannot be sustained theologically' (70). At the congress any resolutions passed reflected opinion rather than affected practice; there was no voting on issues raised beyond topic level.[24] The report[25] of sector B, 'The People of God', addressed the issue of women and ministry.[26] 'The request for women's admission to the permanent diaconate was again firmly made. The question of the eventual ordination of women was raised in this context, with a plea that the matter be explored seriously at this time.' No mention of the issue was made in the report of sector G, 'Justice and Peace', although at topic level within this sector the resolution had been passed:[27]

16. In view of the fact that Jesus came to liberate women as well as men, the Congress is asked to endorse,

(a) The teaching of Vatican II [opposing] discrimination [against] women (*Gaudium et Spes*: 29);

(b) Acceptance [by] the Church that women can be Doctors of the Church;

(c) Taking account of the close connection between teaching and preaching and the importance of the role of preaching in the ministerial priesthood, all levels and structures of the Church reflect the participation of women in the preaching/ministerial function of the Church.

37 for; 7 against.

Interestingly, the same topic group rejected:

18.

(a) The involvement of women in the selection and formation of seminary students

11 for; 24 against.

(b) The admittance of women to the ministerial priesthood

18 for; 35 against.

(c) The elimination of sexist language in the liturgy

9 for; 40 against.

Following the congress, on 21 March 1981, there was a meeting of the Westminster delegates to the NPC to discuss the topic reports from the 'Justice and Peace' sector and to see how the recommendations could be translated into action in the diocese. The following was among the agreed recommendations to the bishops.[28]

1. That the Westminster bishops recommend that the Bishops' Conference of England and Wales, having examined the statement prepared by ICEL's[29] Advisory Committee 'The Problem of Exclusive Language with Regard to Women' which has been circulated to all bishops of member conferences, adopt the draft text of the Green Book 'Eucharistic Prayers'. (This contains eucharistic prayers revised to eliminate discriminatory language. We would add that this text has already been approved by the American and Canadian Bishops' Conferences.) (Topic G4 – recommendation 16c.)
   [**Passed unanimously**]
2. In view of the fact that the 1976 Roman document on the 'Admission of Women to the Priesthood' has only the status of a declaration; that there is no unanimity of theological opinion on the subject; that there are no theological objections that cannot be successfully refuted; that there is a variety of opinion and practice in the Christian Church as a whole (EP [*Easter People*] 96), we consider that there are, rather, 'serious and impressive' reasons (EP 96) for raising the matter at the present time,

and we recommend that the bishops consult with interested persons. We would not wish the Church to fail in its Jesus-given mandate to witness to the equality of women and men, particularly in view of the positive efforts now being made in society at large.
(Topic G4 – recommendation 16c.)
[**Passed unanimously**]

A section of the meeting wished to raise the question of women being admitted to the diaconate; any opposition to this was on the basis that such a project would diffuse the priesthood issue, and the voting was 17 in favour; 2 against; 7 abstentions. When the proposals were considered by the Council for Diocesan Affairs, the priesthood issue disappeared, the appropriate minute reading simply:[30]

1. Discrimination against Women: the CDA will take note of the request to eliminate discriminatory language in the Liturgy when this issue is discussed by the Episcopal Conference of England and Wales.
12. The CDA believes profoundly in the leading role that women can play in the Church, but it notes that some issues are beyond the competence of Diocesan Bishops to change (e.g. women Deacons, female altar servers) . . . (5)

Another body which addressed itself to the issue was the Laity Commission, in its document *Why Can't a Woman be More Like a Man?* (1983), where the example of opposition 'gradually changed to acceptance' was cited. In 1983 the Laity Commission was dissolved by the church authorities. By publishing a final report[31] that December the commission 'resisted the temptation to fade quietly into oblivion'. In this report they suggested that the bishops were ignoring the National Pastoral Congress *per se* and were basing their strategies on their own reflections on it, as contained in *The Easter People*, and that the proposed new ecclesiastical structures did not provide a forum for ordinary people to voice their opinions. In short, 'the *Review*[32] . . . lays itself open to the charge of attempting to build an impressive bureaucracy on sand' (5). The commission made three recommendations: that another National Pastoral Congress should be held in 1985; that the committees of the bishops' conference should be composed of not less than 25 per cent women and not less than 25 per cent men; and that a framework should be developed for a 'permanent, national lay forum which could take its place alongside the National Conference of Priests' (7). These recommendations were not implemented.

The National Pastoral Congress, which appears to have sunk without trace, was not regarded favourably in Vatican circles. The official follow-up meeting at London Colney revolved around the topic of prayer, and discussion of strategy was not permitted to arise – analogously one recalls Michael Winter's book, *Whatever Happened to Vatican II?* References to the NPC were conspicuously absent from John Paul II's speeches during his subsequent visit to this country. Of course Vatican/Roman Catholic authority is not based on democratic processes for the theologised reasons already noted. The *sensus fidelium* is increasingly perceived by official theology to function like the 'informed conscience' – that is, under the guidance of the Vatican.

PART TWO

INTERPRETATION

SECTION ONE

UNDERCURRENTS

In the documentation it is possible to discern three periods when women were variously successful in their attempts to take part in the official ministry of their churches. These three periods fall into two classifications. The first concerns the entry and then gradual disappearance of women from the ministry of emergent connexions/churches as institutionalisation progressed; the second and third were marked by two separate ongoing movements in which women attempted to enter the ministry of established institutions. The three periods can be seen to coincide with challenges to institutional (state) hegemony, while the repulsion of the women happened when defensive strategies were at work in society at large. In proportion to their degree of institutionalisation the churches followed in the wake of the wider institutional trends. With these trends the relationship between individual and institution, and hence the perceived role of women and conceptualisations of female sexuality, are interconnected.

Before examining these trends a further word on the concept of 'institutionalisation' may be helpful. By it I mean the process whereby new imagination, initiatives and ideas are formalised into belief systems and structures by their androcentrically orientated adherents, though often amidst protest by others. Henceforth these belief systems and structures cannot develop freely, but only within the constraints of these structures which are always in some degree hierarchical, and in which even the most charismatic leadership is limited in some degree by that established structure.

If and when the new group expands, it tends to mirror dominant structures in the society, which are related to state structures. Sometimes by its very success the group will take on political functions and replicate state structures, which are strongly hierarchical or even authoritarian. Developments of this sort occurred in the early Christian communities, and apart from occasional reversals, have persisted ever since. (The kinds of structure existing in the nineteenth and twentieth centuries in the three communions examined in this book are described in Appendix D.)

Together with the development of structures of power and decision-making goes development of beliefs and moralities which justify the structures – or criticise them in times of upheaval. As these structures formalise, symbols evolve, and become 'frozen' and form 'tradition', which is subsequently appealed to to fend off change. Such symbols are used to justify androcentric hierarchies which have been dominant in societies, including Christian ones. Hence the tendency to see authority in terms of maleness. Conver[illegible]ely, when tradition and symbols are used to criticise authority, to [illegible]mand freedom from established structures and a more egalitarian [illegible] informal community, symbols are reinterpreted and evaluated, [illegible] female, as symbol of the oppressed, of revitalisation and sp[illegible] comes to the fore (cf. Joanna Southcott (1804)) – reac[illegible]tically with the use of female symbolism employed by the dom[illegible] institution (cf. Mary – it is interesting how she is now presented as the liberated woman). I have considered this line of argument further in 'Interpretations' (Part Two, Section Three), where I have attempted to show how unconscious processes have come to link maleness with masculinity and thence with subjectivity, and femaleness with femininity and hence with what-differentiates-the-subject. I apply this argument at both the group and the individual level. The state is the dominant group structure within which unconscious processes are operative, and in 'Interpretations' I will consider how unconscious processes can be perceived to affect the institutionalisation process.

I THE FIRST PERIOD: LIBERATING INFLUENCES INSTITUTIONALISED

1.1 Radical writings

The greatest threat to institutional hegemony of the first period arose from the revolutions in France and America, which activated strands of criticism and unrest reaching back into English history. In the early 1790s the American Tom Paine published his *Rights of Man*, in which he challenged the 'arbitrary power' of all governments (excepting those of America and France) which divided the populace into the propertied and the unpropertied. His iconoclastic feat was simultaneously to destroy 'century-old taboos'[1] and to send eddies for social reform reaching even into the twentieth century – and Mary Wollstonecraft's *A Vindication of the Rights of Women*, published the same year the Republic was declared, could be similarly described. But if the 1792 proclamation of the Republic was an inspiration to those struggling for reform, her dedicatory letter to Talleyrand, which prefaced the book, focussed on the 'flaw':[2] the Constitution, based on reason and written from first principles, failed to extend the rights of *citoyens* to *citoyennes*.

Enlightenment thought underlay these works and related movements, and if it prepared the way for the French Revolution which overthrew the *ancien régime* and established the Third Estate in power, it was in fact a stage in the thought of the bourgeoisie which in England was already established. Goldmann[3] has shown the centrality of individualism to these thought patterns. Individual consciousness appeared as the absolute origin of consciousness and action, and individual understanding was recognised as the supreme arbiter.

Individualism also generated bonds between Enlightenment thought and the bourgeoisie through related concepts. Society was the product of a contract between a large number of autonomous individuals. The social contract resulted in the general will, which implied the equality of all citizens. The market was universal in that the contracting partner's personal qualities were irrelevant, while the religious or moral concerns of this partner were viewed with tolerance. The prerequisite of liberty had led to the *jus fori* to counteract the lack of freedom of serfs to buy and sell in the emergent market economy of the twelfth and thirteenth centuries, to the freedom of towns (accorded in 1989 in London to the Prime Minister Margaret Thatcher), and the status of citizen. Property carried the right to dispose of one's goods as one wished.

Enlightenment empiricism and rationalism succeeded traditional Christianity, which based norms on the divine will or on reason accorded to us by God. They preceded dialectical thought wherein the human being was perceived as an active part of the whole, such that all value judgements formed a part of reality, which in turn had itself an active value-conferring character. Thus empiricism and rationalism had no hold on the problem of morality. Just as supra-individual reality was separated off, so now rational knowledge and evaluation parted company. It was regarded as an axiom that individualism was morally neutral[4] in relation to values of content such as love, hate, indifference to others, etc. This very neutrality however meant that even the formal virtues linked to individualism, mentioned in the previous paragraph, could be abandoned and replaced by an opposite (this, I would suggest, was the problem facing Mary Wollstonecraft). Enlightenment thinkers were united at least in their search for a reference point in their common hostility to traditional Christianity, whether they embraced atheism, deism, or theism. Although religion might appear as the concessionary 'opium' for the masses, for the rationalists at least the 'watchmaker' image was an internal theoretical necessity, while the empiricists declared the problem insoluble.

Politically, philosophers differed as to whether, for example, equality should extend to the economic sphere or should be purely judicial[5] (in the case of married women it would be a long time before either would apply). There were more fundamental contradictions arising from the perception of human kind as unchanging and the human will as derived from natural and social factors, which gave rise to the question as to how an ideal state could have been lost. That tyrants and priests had exploited the fear of the ignorant and that education would provide the answer was the most general explanation – and one favoured, above all in its solution, by Wollstonecraft.

Mary Wollstonecraft's initial statement of position disclosed the extent of her Enlightenment heritage:

> the perfection of our nature and capability of happiness must be estimated by the degree of reason, virtue, and knowledge, that distinguish the individual, and direct the laws which bind society: and that from the exercise of reason, knowledge and virtue naturally flow, is equally undeniable, if mankind [*sic*] be viewed collectively.[6]

Yet universal reason, she argued, was unavailable to women because an adequate education was denied to them. Confronting the discrepancy she perceived with regard to Enlightenment 'equality', she wished to extend Rousseau's blueprint for men, the achievement of independence through rationally acquired habits of virtue, to women. Such, she argued, was woman's right as a citizen, and the path to 'true civilisation'. This right and this path were blocked by the 'disorderly education' given to women, and by the ideas spread by popular authors such as Dr Gregory and Rousseau, who substantially advocated total dependence on and orientation towards men: 'All the ideas of women, which have not the immediate tendency to points of duty, should be directed to the study of men, and to the attainment of those agreeable accomplishments which have taste for their object',[7] wrote Rousseau. The effect on women, claimed Woolstonecraft, was that women were:

Confined . . . in cages like the feathered race, [where] they have nothing to do but to plume themselves, and stalk with mock majesty from perch to perch. It is true they are provided with food and raiment, for which they neither toil nor spin; but health, liberty, and virtue are given in exchange.[8]

Such an upbringing would not lead to individuality based on universal reason, and certainly could not equip women for true companionship with men or for responsible parenthood as educators of children, but resulted in a capricious and self-centred sensuality.

Moreover, the Enlightenment abandonment of supra-individual authority was waived in the case of women, whose superior authority was decreed to be man, who was elevated to a god-like position of authority. Women's opinions were to be based, not on reason, but on trust in man, who intervened like a priest between her and God:

Every daughter ought to be of the same religion as her mother, and every wife to be of the same religion as her husband: for, though such religion should be false, that docility which induces the mother and daughter to submit to the order of nature, takes away, in the sight of God, the criminality of their error[9]

wrote Rousseau, and whereas in traditional Christianity God saw the heart, women were now told to mind not what only heaven saw, but to dread only the eye of man. This 'prevailing opinion that woman was created for man' was traced by Wollstonecraft to 'Moses' poetical story', which she interpreted as without factual foundation, but as mythologising man's use of physical strength 'to subjugate his companion . . . for his convenience or pleasure'.[10] Moving from a biblical to a theological perspective, she argued that the primacy accorded to omnipotence in God was at the expense of the harmony of attributes characterising the Divine Being. For Wollstonecraft the soul or the rational individual transcended sex, and was destined to submit, not to power or strength, but to Wisdom.

Women, meanwhile, were defined by their sexuality. All was sacrificed to render women an object of male desire for a short time – 'only created to flutter our hour out and die?',[11] queried Wollstonecraft, advocating instead a passionless relationship between husband and wife to allow reason full play. Yet the double standard decreed that sexual desire should appear only in men – Dr Gregory had counselled his female reader to conceal her gaiety lest 'she darkly ... be told that men will draw conclusions which she little thinks of',[12] thus setting in train a form of repression which could and would lead to illness. Rousseau had justified the great disparity between the education of Emile and that of Sophie on the basis that women should be weak and passive because they had less bodily strength – and a century later the post-Darwinian Freud was to distinguish between the 'passivity' of ovum and 'activity' of sperm in his analysis of female sexuality. Between the two writers, the ideal of wifely purity was emerging in a home increasingly separated from the state (which in turn countered with a prostitution explosion) – which would create the 'hysterial woman' analysed by Sigmund Freud and categorised by Michel Foucault.

1.2 Religious enthusiasm

If social turmoil was a catalyst for radical writings, it also accompanied the explosion of religious enthusiasm, predominantly Methodist, which was a phenomenon of the years 1790–1830. The fragmentation of churches and sects related to the individualistic, anti-authoritarian philosophy, while on the other hand the characteristic enthusiasm was the antithesis of rationalism. When, to distinguish Methodism from the Old Dissent, Wesley described Methodism as a religion of the 'heart', he appeared to mean an emotional, experiential assent to biblical revelation – in contrast to Wollstonecraft, who by 'heart' meant understanding guided by reason. Yet such an epistemological divergence, as Goldmann has shown, is in harmony with the tenets of individualism.

1.2.1 Psychological pressures

Differing interpretations of the relationship between the Methodist explosion and the development of the market economy have been offered. In E. P. Thompson's opinion, neither Weber[13] nor Tawney[14] addressed the fact that Methodism was simultaneously the religion of the industrial bourgeoisie and of a wide section of the proletariat (or of those representing the institution/state and of those who might challenge it). His argument was that it weakened the poor by inner submission. On offer to those who remained in grace through service to the church, through the cultivation of the soul in religious exercises and especially in the reproduction of the emotional convulsions of conversion, and through methodological discipline in labour, was membership of an egalitarian brotherhood and sisterhood. Crucial, in his opinion, was the emotional upheaval of the conversion experience, 'the psychic ordeal in which the character-structure of the rebellious pre-industrial labourer or artisan was violently recast into that of the submissive industrial worker'.[15] Socially dangerous emotions and economically unproductive energies were harnessed, and sublimated in love feasts and other devotional practices often involving sexual imagery.

Deborah Valenze,[16] on the other hand, has focussed particularly on sectarian Methodism and has argued that with the submergence of cottage industries under the wave of industrialisation in the first half of the nineteenth century, the self assertion of the poor took on a religious form. The itinerant preacher was the bearer of tradition in the face of change, symbolising perseverance in the face of a shifting economy – there was a strong link between these sects and politically radical movements, which was one of the sources of tension with orthodox Methodism. Another was the presence of women preachers, yet they would have arisen naturally from a cottage industrial context where women had an importance and role which was lost when women became a source of cheap labour in towns, and, moreover, the meetings were held in houses, which were the conventional domain of women. Plainness of dress and 'modest' demeanour were expected of the women – to contrast with the fashion of the towns. Plainness was expected particularly of the female preachers, whose existence was a novelty.

In fact, the egalitarian offer referred to by Thompson was extended decreasingly to the sisterhood as institutionalisation progressed within Methodism, and was never absolute, particularly with regard to the ministry. Taft frequently drew attention to the comparative alacrity with which such a 'call' was acknowledged in men. Women, on the other hand, had not only to discern the 'call' within themselves, but also had to contend with social expectations and symbolisations of women, together with their own internalisation of scriptural injunctions to women.

Overtly, there was opposition from men (and from preachers in particular), occasional threats of expulsion from the society, or from the family home.[17] But there were more subtle obstacles which applied even in the sects admitting women preachers. In 1825 Taft argued that women were allowed to address mixed groups in public theatres, markets, fields and shops,[18] yet in 1815 Sarah Kirkland, the first Primitive Methodist female travelling preacher, declined to preach in the market place because 'her modesty and timidity forbade her'.[19] The internalisation of 'modesty' fundamentally gave a sexual significance to moving outside the private sphere of the female in the sense of revealing to foreign eyes what should have remained hidden. When Wollstonecraft considered 'modesty' she rejected the conventional interpretation as propriety of behaviour, on the basis that by mis-education women were slaves of sensibility, making it hard to resist impulsive acts and by the same token leading to over-familiarity among women. For her, modesty was a rational and balanced self-esteem which would lead to a reclamation of the person – Jesus Christ was her exemplary model. In Sarah Kirkland's case there was tension between her internalised 'modesty' and the very self-assertion postulated by Valenze as a defence against loss of economic identity. Her self identity was at issue. And if 'modesty', ignorance and inexperience created problems for women preachers, a similar clash of internalised symbols occurred in potential converts. Margaret Adams' tussles with her curls in the face of her internalisation of wishes attributed to God resulted in a graphic description of her 'conversion':

> At that time I wore false plaiting under my bonnet, and I felt as if that and my curls were fire about my face; so I threw it under the table, and should have cut off my hair had I had any scissors, so great was the evil that I now saw in those things which I before took so much delight in.[20]

This was a far cry from the rational approach of Wollstonecraft; while on the other hand one might say, 'from such tangles, O Freud, deliver us'.

Not all women who felt drawn to preach were psychologically suited to running the gauntlet of the opposition, yet if they sidestepped they found themselves in the metaphorical fire. Elizabeth Hurrel wrote: '*I am going to die . . . I am entering the eternal world, but all is dark before me: neither sun, moon, nor stars appear. O that I had my time to live again, I would not bury my talent as I have done.*'[21] Those women who did preach could be seen to appropriate a conventionally male symbolic structure:

About this time, I had a particular dream. I dreamed that there was war proclaimed, and that young women were called to fight, and I for one; but I refused to go, pleading the not being skilled in war. I was told that I was drawn, and must go; I said I could not fight; in answer to which, it was said, – I should be taught. I thought that after some more conversation and reasonings, I yeilded [*sic*]. I then had put into my hand a shining instrument, and, with many more young women, went into the field of battle; where, before I began to fight, I began to pray. Whilst on my knees, the enemy gave me a stroke on my cheek, but the hurt I received was but little; and I was brought off conqueror, shouting praises to God who hath been my strong helper. This dream made some impression on my mind; yet, I thought, I may have such a dream as this, and not be called to the work of the ministry.[22]

1.2.2 Political implications

Having considered the 'moral machinery' of contemporary Methodism Thompson interpreted its social timing as the 'chiliasm of despair'. While acknowledging the obscurity of the precise nature of the recognised relationship between political and religious excitement, he has suggested that religious revivalism took over just at the point where political or temporal aspirations met with defeat.[23] He employed Mannheim's utopian model to account for the individual's submission to the practices referred to above: 'Chiliasm has always accompanied revolutionary outbursts and given them their spirit. When this spirit ebbs and deserts these movements, there remains behind in the world a naked mass-frenzy and a despiritualized fury.'[24] Beginning at the time of the French Revolution and of the associated publications of Paine and Wollstonecraft, he used selected dates notable for the linkage of political activity and Methodist revivalism to plot a 'spiritual graph' in support of his reading of the situation: the early 1790s; the later 1790s and 1800s; 1811–12; 1816–17; and 1831–4.

This marks an interesting link with my own interpretation. If momentarily, one disregards the earlier dates on the basis that towards the turn of that century Wesleyan Methodism was no longer in its incipient stage, but was fast becoming institutionalised and hence state-orientated, and so women preachers who had earlier received limited support were virtually prevented from functioning by the 1803 resolution, then the two final dates are of particular interest. The penultimate date marks the secession of the Bible Christians and the Primitive Methodists over tensions between the stipendiary ministry and lay preachers, over political radicalism and over female preachers. Moreover, this and the final date, the only ones involving these connexions, mark the two peak periods of their female preachers, after which the women gradually disappeared (even if, briefly, only rendered invisible by initials among the Primitive Methodists) from their *Minutes*. There is, then, apparently a link between charismatic, pre-institutionalised, beginnings, politically radical critiques, and female ministry – and hence with the perception of and self-perception of women. Returning to the earlier dates, the late 1790s and 1800s witnessed the preaching of Joanna Southcott and her followers. Thompson's proposed reading of an oscillation between intense political activity and chiliastic fervour has been rejected by Barbara Taylor[25] as too narrow a definition of radical consciousness. Taylor prefers, rather, the interpretation of religious 'heresy' used as a weapon of ideological subversion – epitomised by the example of Joanna Southcott. For Thompson, although Southcott's appeal was to the poor, who saw one of themselves as an agent of revolution, and, moreover, lacking the organisational stability, money, and benign attitude of the authorities linked with orthodox Methodism, her effect was startling, but transitory. Taylor interprets her message, rather, as the incipient stages of working-class expression of feminist doctrines.

Her argument is that feminist doctrines had been articulated in the language of spiritual mission – for example, during the civil wars[26] – and the radicalism of such women writers was not confined to specified goals and reforms as instead they saw women as victims of sexual and intellectual archetypes. She went on to consider the links in the 1830s between the Southcott prophets and the Owenites[27] – the latter being communities of mutual cooperation in terms of social production, common property and a loving disposition towards one's neighbour.[28] The women, drawn mostly either from the artisan layer of the working class or the impoverished gentry of the lower middle class, adopted an explicitly feminist perspective, and by the early 1830s had become active in trade unions. The conflict between the Owenites and the Established Church centred mainly on attitudes to marriage and divorce – or female sexuality – Taylor notes the slippage between 'spirit' and 'reason' in terms of the perceived new moral world.[29] It is here that she sees heresy and scriptural interpretation as an important weapon of the working class; the appropriation and subversion of the language of scripture as a key moment in the development of emancipatory ideals.

The challenge of Paine, Wollstonecraft and Robert Owen among others to the divine authority of the Bible led, by the 1830s, to an offensive by the Established Church, which could not have been heartened by the 1835 publication of D. F. Strauss' *Life of Jesus* (which was translated by George Eliot).[30] The campaign was brought together by the bishop of Exeter's speech in the House of Lords in 1840, when he dwelt particularly on the issues touching women.[31] By this time there was a sharply defined separation of the sexes – the working wife was decreasingly socially acceptable – and in the division of the public from the private sphere, women were placed firmly in the latter. There is a parallel between the increasing opposition to the right to speak of women trade unionists and the gradual disappearance of women preachers among the Primitive Methodists and the Bible Christians at about this time as the connexions became more institutionalised, and an increasing Methodist presence appeared in trade unions.

A battle over symbols was taking place. The troubled world which had produced the various conceptualisations of radical thought, either in the works of Paine and Wollstonecraft or in the preaching of the Methodists, was giving way in Britain to a firmly established institution at the head of an empire where the issues of concern to the radicals would be taken up within the institution and modified – the emancipation of women was a middle-class movement with limited and specific aims. In the earlier 'feudal' economy the church had decreed the 'revealed' place and role of the sexes and of the nature of women, and it was the aristocratic interpretation of this which so incensed Wollstonecraft. With the development of the Enlightenment thought of the bourgeoisie, the individualism of the market economy did not have a place for sexuality, which was to become a 'problem' and a means of control. It is here that Thompson's thesis of psychological manipulation, complementing the Weberian position, is of interest, and Mary Wollstonecraft's rational attempt to bring sexuality under the banner of equality, which, as we have seen, was only a formal virtue, was both economically premature and frantically resisted. With the waning of 'divine law', religion was linked only externally to the economy and was separated from the state and placed firmly in the home, while women were placed firmly in the home on the basis of the old ideology; the Augustinian dualisms[32] would reappear sharply. The symbolic fight over scriptural language noted by Taylor in the decades preceding the development of biblical studies is important. Yet the ideas about the revealed place of women which created the most acrimonious confrontations were in fact what recent hermeneutical advances in biblical studies would encourage us to question.

2 WOMEN, MINISTRY AND INSTITUTION

2.1 The second period: undercurrents converging in the 1920s moves towards ministry

The 1920s post-war (and post-Russian Revolution) attempts by women to gain access to the ministry coincided with the granting of the ultimate demand of the nineteenth-century women's emancipation movement – suffrage (though initially selective) to women. Dr Maltby referred specifically to these advances,[33] and in 1925 there followed the resolution that women were not disqualified from the ministry merely on the basis of sex. In fact, disagreement over 'many difficulties' was to ensure the delay of legislation for forty-nine years: overtly at issue were the itinerant ministry and the relationship between the respective vocations of ministry and marriage, the latter resting on the assumption that the married woman's place was in the home. Underlying this was the argument as to what constituted the sexual equality acknowledged by both sides in terms of difference, non-interchangeability and complementarity. The opponents advocated a 'spiritual' equality, and for them only in the deaconess order could women truly be equal and 'dare to be themselves'; entry to the ministry was seen as an imitation of men and therefore a subordination to them. The proposers argued that personality rather than sexuality was paramount; that the deaconess order did not meet the aspirations of educated women who were denied responsibility in the church. Within the Church of England requests by women to enter the ministry were more muted, yet such as surfaced were part of a trajectory beginning with the emergence of the sisterhood and deaconess movement. It is therefore necessary to return to the beginning of the nineteenth century in order to follow through the developments leading to these moves of the 1920s. Around this trajectory revolved similar argument and assumptions – and, I shall argue, unconscious resistances.[34]

2.1.1 Liberating impulses and the sisterhoods

The emergent sisterhoods harnessed a number of interwoven and contradictory forces, which guaranteed them a stormy passage until their recognition and hence institutionalisation by the Lambeth Conference of 1897. Although they interacted with the Oxford Movement and their beginnings coincided with the women's emancipation movement,[35] interesting undercurrents were operative. Among them was the concept of community living, which was in the air because of the heated debates between the Established Church and the Owenites (and the tiny Communist Church), and which, together with feminism,[36] had acquired a radical label. Meanwhile, although extreme separation of home and state was symptomatic of the general conservatism of the time, the 1830s were also marked by the famous Norton case, which was to be a stimulus for the reforms referred to eighty years later by Dr Maltby.

First, the emergence of the Oxford Movement. The downfall of the restored monarchy in France in July 1830 sent ripples of concern among conservatives, while within the Established Church the chilly winds of change were blowing following the repeal of the Test Act in 1828 and Catholic emancipation in 1829. These were strengthened by the agitation for the reform of institutions which characterised preparations for the passage of the Reform Act of 1832: the bourgeoisie were extending their grip on the institution in general, with the implications for traditional religion noted above. In the event Robert Peel's commission (1835–6) ensured the survival of the Established Church, although the principle on which it was established remained unclear. An infusion of spiritual life was needed at this point, according to Alec R. Vidler,[37] and was realised principally in the Oxford Movement, yet he does not explore why it occurred precisely then. I suggest that it was a defensive move on the part of the institutional church, which was no longer intrinsically and thus symbolically linked with the state, which was under attack from representatives of Enlightenment thought, and which was engaged in a losing battle about and within biblical language without the tools of modern hermeneutics. The Established Church chose to return to its historical roots in its quest for meaningful symbols, yet the origins chosen were themselves the product of institutionalisation and appropriation of symbols, which I shall discuss in the final section.

One of the effects of the Reformation had been the dissolution of the monasteries, which had harmonised with the developing economy and ideology. As the Religious Life became a misnomer, the Holy Family began its ascendancy.[38] Virginity was no longer the ideal life for women, but wifehood: motherhood would be an emphasis of the early twentieth century in particular.[39] As women were placed in the home, the relation of home to state and hence to public life took on an additional importance for women, and as their monastic source of education had been removed they had become dependent on the sporadic information so decried by Wollstonecraft. She had argued that women's rational running of the home and education of children as future citizens would bring together home and state and would facilitate women's passage as rational citizens into the latter. Earlier, Mary Astell[40] in *A Serious Proposal to the Ladies* (1696; 1697) had argued for an educational establishment based on religious community living, but the ghosts it raised ('Popish Orders', 'nunnery')[41] proved inexorcisable. Yet it was a modest suggestion aimed merely at unmarried women, who she wished to withdraw from the superficial social life of the time in order to embrace 'duties' currently believed to lie beyond women's grasp. The Platonic and Cartesian tendencies in her thought can be compared with the Enlightenment rationalism of Mary Wollstonecraft: she believed in the equality of souls, Wollstonecraft in the equality of rights; she accepted male and female 'nature', Wollstonecraft believed rational human nature transcended sexuality. It is significant that at the time the industrial expansion and the ascension of the bourgeoisie were at their height towards the mid-nineteenth century, religious community living reappeared in the Church of England, and that its overriding specialisation for women was not education but rescue work.

Such a departure would not have been totally without precedent in the post-Reformation world. A century earlier Wesley contrasted his own circle (favourably) with the Anglican Little Gidding community.[42] When Robert Southey pleaded for protestant sisterhoods in 1829 he appealed to the Methodists and to the Quakers – it was Elizabeth Fry who initiated the process when she founded an institute to train nurses in 1840 following her visit to Kaiserswerth. He urged women to alleviate their position in society by harnessing and directing their 'enthusiasm' to such an end, using a 'mad woman (sc. Joanna Southcott)'[43] as an – albeit misdirected – example. Six years before following in Elizabeth Fry's footsteps to Kaiserswerth, Florence Nightingale wrote of her plans for 'something like a Protestant Sisterhood, without vows, for women of educated feelings'.[44]

The legal and economic position of women of whatever 'feelings' was not enviable. By marriage a woman became a 'feme covert',[45] such that the property, earnings, freedom, responsibility before the law, and children, all belonged to her husband – and prior to 1857 there could be practically no escape in divorce. General endorsement for this rested on the belief that men were intellectually, physically and morally the superior sex. Yet paradoxically, the 'moral' part of this legal person was sited in the home, over and against the amoral world of work, and the 'angel of the hearth' became the depiction of purity. The 'pure' woman stood over and against the 'fallen' one; the licit, reproductive sex of the conjugal home contrasted with illicit, erotic sex of outside, and for women there was a one-way ticket between the two. In 1869 W. E. H. Lecky wrote:

> there has arisen in society a figure which is certainly the most mournful, and in some respects the most awful, upon which the eye of the moralist can dwell. That unhappy being whose very name is a shame to speak; who counterfeits with a cold heart the transports of affection, and submits herself as the passive instrument of lust; who is scorned and insulted as the vilest of her sex, and doomed, for the most part, to disease and abject wretchedness and an early death, appears in every age as the perpetual symbol of the degradation and sinfulness of man. Herself the supreme type of vice, she is ultimately the most efficient guardian of virtue. But for her, the unchallenged purity of countless happy homes would be polluted, and not a few who, in the pride of their untempted chastity, think of her with an indignant shudder, would have known the agony of remorse and despair. On that one degraded and ignoble form are concentrated the passions that might have filled the world with shame. She remains, while creeds and civilisations rise and fall, the eternal priestess of humanity, blasted for the sins of the people.[46]

This was a flagrant exposition of the double standard – which existed not entirely without question, but the questioning was muted partly because there was no satisfactory discourse which women could use to rebut it – that would begin to emerge at the end of the century. It lurked behind Victorian 'morality', and attempts to challenge it stretched from Wollstonecraft's criticism of male 'passion' to Christabel Pankhurst's 'Votes for women and chastity for men' slogan. Foucault has termed sex 'The Secret' which permeates everything as a means of control.

Among the voices raised in protest was that of Florence Nightingale in *Cassandra* (1852).[47] Passion, intellect and moral activity had never been satisfied in women who were only allowed to devote their time and energies to trivia, she claimed. This resulted in an accumulation of nervous energy which could lead to illness,[48] or to a life lived in phantasy:

> Nothing can well be imagined more painful than the present position of woman, unless, on the one hand, she renounces all outward activity and keeps herself within the magic sphere, the bubble of her dreams; or, on the other, surrendering all aspiration, she gives herself to her real life, soul and body.[49]

Interestingly, she looked toward a female Christ – a link with the vision and language of Joanna Southcott. Working-class women were covered by the same ideology, but economic factors rendered them less 'moral' than their middle-class sisters. Necessity drove them to work (for little pay) when this was socially acceptable; the marriage licence was expensive so many formed partnerships without it; and above all, in Judy Walkowitz's words, 'There is perhaps no more telling commentary on the exploitative character of Victorian society than the fact that some working women regarded prostitution as the best of a series of unattractive alternatives.'[50]

Many women followed Florence Nightingale's second alternative, giving themselves up to 'real life' as it was defined for them, and as it had earlier been captured wryly in literature by Jane Austen. A century later Dr Maltby was to suggest that it was on these novels that the opponents based their ideas of women. 'It is a truth universally acknowledged, that a single man in possession of a good fortune, must be in want of a wife',[51] she balanced elsewhere by 'A single woman with a very narrow income must be a ridiculous, disagreeable old maid – the proper sport of boys and girls; but a single woman of good fortune is always respectable, and may be as sensible and pleasant as anybody else.'[52] In fact, 'surplus women' – who were no one's wife, nor daughter, and who were not in possession of a fortune – were a growing problem in the mid-century. The association of the sisterhoods as a place of refuge for such women, with education and with philanthropic work, was a middle-class, utilitarian strand in the formation of sisterhoods.

Most generally recognised was the influence of the Oxford Movement on the emergence of these Church of England sisterhoods. The quest for a holy life modelled on the example of Christ was seen to point backwards to monasticism of the patristic period, of seventeenth-century France, and of medieval times which had such strong links with the contemporary Romantic movement. Emphasis was on the sacramental structure: on the priest, communion, frequent confession, liturgical and mental prayer. Bridal imagery abounded: 'He has given you the power of coming to His help in a way in which few women can come; not by doing anything unwomanly, but by your very position as Brides of Christ',[53] preached J. M. Neale, although in a sense power was simply transferred from a father or theoretical husband to the priest – and the documentation shows how concerned were the 'fathers in Christ' that they should have dutiful and obedient 'daughters' in the sisterhoods. T. T. Carter doubted the ability of the community at Clewer to manage without male guidance and this was reflected in the all-male governing body.[54] That women struggled for autonomy in the sisterhoods is everywhere apparent, a striking example being between the archbishop of Canterbury and the Church Extension Association, which removed the names of patrons (including his own) from their literature and announced their future intention of having only patronesses.[55] The sisterhoods did indeed offer an alternative way of life to women, and one can read their struggle to take vows as a symbolic rejection of the trivia of life.

I have suggested that many tensions converged in the Church of England sisterhoods, which stood between the service-giving Protestant institutions and the eucharistically orientated Roman Catholic convents, the latter's authorities not recognising the Anglo-Catholic orders which facilitated the emulation of the convents by the sisterhoods. This pragmatic–spiritual conflict ws reproduced in the varying orientations of the clergy. While J. H. Newman praised

Methodism for satisfying the 'heart', Bishop Samuel Wilberforce warned against the 'sentimentalism' that led to Rome (here he did not have Newman in mind). When Wilberforce ceased to be diocesan of the community at Clewer, there was a linguistic shift in the community annals from 'sister probationer' and 'consecration', to 'novice' and 'profession'.[56] Florence Nightingale commented acidly on the sisterhoods which made their object the spiritual good of their members and who prepared her patients for death when her secular nurses were struggling to prolong life. There was also a conceptual tension between the middle-class background of the sisters, and their 'rescue' work. Underlying these was the contradiction between the amoral bourgeois ideology and the pragmatically fashionably linked philanthropy on the one hand, and, on the other, the spirituality related to a feudal background where the power and centrality of the institutional church and hence of the priest was paramount. In the final analysis, at issue were power, identity and sexuality.

2.1.2 A word on the ambiguity of the deaconess

Not surprisingly, contributors to the nineteenth-century Convocation debates expressed preference for the deaconess who made a direct promise of obedience to the bishop and who was not 'professionally' related to other women. But subsequent to the formal restoration of sisterhoods and the order of deaconesses in the early twentieth century, the focus of dissenting debate shifted to the Trojan horse that had been brought into the institution: as bearer of an 'order' she was an intrinsic challenge to the traditional concept of 'holy orders' as a woman-free state. Lambeth Conference in 1920 declared her to be a member of an 'Order of the ministry' which had 'the stamp of Apostolic approval', but in 1930 the second phrase was dropped and she was declared to be a member of 'an Order *sui generis*'; thus her status was effectively diminished while her functions were slightly extended, a repetition of an earlier pattern noted in *MOW19*,[57] where her decline in status coincided with increasing institutionalisation.

2.1.3 The ideology of family and motherhood

The request for ministerial status by women in the 1920s was a request for equality within the institution, just as the various legislative reforms which occurred during that time stemmed from the pursuit of equality within capitalist society and were not primarily linked with radical critiques of sexual relations. That the request for ministry was more obviously a Methodist phenomenon suggests that within this church there was less insulation from societal currents. Yet there was a consensus on the limit of equality: a deaconess' or a (theoretical) woman minister's marriage would imply her resignation. Trajectories converging on the family and motherhood which dominated the first half of the twentieth century can be traced back to a complex of interrelated factors such as the controversies surrounding the Contagious Diseases Acts and the rise of the social purity movements, the popularisation of birth control and its linking with eugenics, and the gradual acceptance of the work of theorists such as Havelock Ellis and Freud.

The double standard had long ago been highlighted and challenged by the campaign to repeal the Contagious Diseases Acts (1864–9)[58] aimed at military towns and allowing for the registration and regular examination of any woman suspected of being 'a common prostitute'. While many vested interests rallied to the defence of the acts, the Ladies' National Association led by Josephine Butler[59] (and due to her efforts supported by working men) produced a 'ladies' manifesto' where it was pointed out that the acts were an example of class and sex discrimination. Poor women were denied their constitutional rights and subjected to a humiliating internal examination while a double standard was being sanctioned – women were penalised in order to make it safe for men to engage in the same act. Butler was firm in her assertion of the economic basis of prostitution, and in her refusal to discriminate between the 'fallen' and the 'pure':

> One group of women is set aside, so to speak, to minister to the irregularities of the excusable man. That section is doomed to death, hurled to despair, while another section of womanhood is kept strictly and almost forcibly guarded in domestic purity.[60]

Butler rejected Lecky's notion (above, p. 215) as a travesty of Christian teaching. She believed that the special influence of women, characteristically maternal though not to be confined to the home, could be a great asset to society. After the acts were repealed in 1886 and there was a mutation of the mainstream repeal movement into various social purity groups,[61] she left. An opposing ideological perspective developed in which the emphasis on the control of 'male lust' and the defence of its victims, women, shifted to greater control and stigmatisation, rather than to the defence of the individual rights of women engaged in prostitution and other manifestations of 'illicit' sex.

An important effect of the campaign was to originate both a discourse on and a platform for the discussion of sexuality. The conceptual shift from women as temptresses to women as passionless victims of passionate men took hold. On the one hand this conceptual shift underlay the suffragette movement epitomised in Christabel Pankhurst's *The Great Scourge and how to end it* (1913), where votes for women were presented as the panacea for all such ills, and it reappeared in the feminist movement of the 1970s in the anti-pornography campaigns. On the other hand, it was turned into an oppressive force against women in the social purity campaigns of the turn of the century and in the campaign for moral rearmament in more recent decades. Walkowitz makes the point that the women tried to set standards of sexual conduct, but lost control of the movement because they did not control the institutions of state that ultimately enforced those norms.[62] Stepping further back, I suggest that this appropriation and re-presentation by institutions of 'breaks-through' in feminist theory is a recurring pattern, and one which leads to the heart of 'identity' and the power to define 'reality'.

There was a second, though smaller, strand of feminism in the early decades of the century whose journal, *The Freewoman*, was the forum of debate between those advocating celibacy and those in favour of developing the understanding of female sexuality along the lines of Havelock Ellis' work. While the position of celibacy as autonomy was hounded from the scene,[63] motherhood and female enjoyment were appropriated and re-presented in the new family ideology. Whereas a typical marriage manual of the 1870s stressed a young woman's need for support, guidance, protection and help, which her partner should meet, while children were not mentioned, a 1917 book proposed three main reasons for her marriage: mutual comfort and support; the maintenance of social purity; and the reproduction of the race.[64] Here motherhood and eugenics converged, supported by the writings of theorists such as Havelock Ellis, who held that women were misguided to concentrate on suffrage rather than motherhood, while voluntary organisations to support the process of child-bearing multiplied. (That some action was necessary was shown by the publication of the *Maternity Letters* in 1917[65] and illustrated in the BBC 2 programme, *Out of the Dolls' House*, in 1988.) The twin concerns of feminists – voluntary motherhood and sexual pleasure – were shadowed by the belief that the impetus of the sex act for men was pleasure while for women it was motherhood. Marie Stopes' mystical representation of married bliss did much to advance the respectability of birth control within the family (by distancing it from free love) in the 1920s, and by the 1930s it had official endorsement and was approved by Lambeth Conference in 1930 – although significantly the Vatican lost no time in replying with the encyclical *Casti Connubii* in December of that year. As this trajectory of discourse and control developed, it was underlined by a significant change of name, noted by Jeffrey Weeks, when in 1939 the National Birth Control Association became the Family Planning Association: 'Nothing better reflects the change from the feminist aspirations of many of the early birth-controllers to the social-planning emphases that were to become dominant from the 1940s'.[66] It was in the context of the dominant ideology of family and motherhood during these decades that procedural delays kept Methodist women from entering the ministry, while in the Church of England any such emergent ideas were firmly dismissed in the 1919 and 1935 reports.

If the problems of Victorian working women were at the origin of one strand in the twentieth century perception of the family and motherhood, another emanated from the hysteria which could affect their middle-class sisters. Freud's studies of hysteria on the continent led him to his perception of the unconscious origins of dreams and neuroses, and to his discovery that the unconscious operated according to certain laws. As he developed a theory based on clinical case-histories he concluded that sexual repression was at the basis of neurotic behaviour. This in turn led him to formulate his theories of sexuality, which he modified slightly over the years, and which culminated in the 1920s debates on female sexuality. Freud always insisted, in contrast to his opponents, that his theory (which will be considered in Section Three) was psychical:

> I object to all of you (Horney, Jones, Rado, etc.,) to the extent that you do not distinguish more clearly and cleanly between what is psychic and what is biological, that you try to establish a neat parallelism between the two and that you, motivated by such intent, unthinkingly construe psychic facts which are unprovable and that you, in the process of doing

so, must declare as reactive or regressive much that without doubt is primary.[67]

The popularisation of his work in the first half of the century, however, was biologically orientated, and to some extent this is apparent in the appendix of psychology by Professor Grensted attached to *MOW35*.[68] It was instead Melanie Klein's emphasis on the mother–child relationship[69] which gained ground in this country.

Two areas of interest to feminists were named over these decades: voluntary motherhood and sexual pleasure; and both, having been named, were appropriated and transformed. The autonomy at the basis of both disappeared. Motherhood became idealised within the family, which became subject to increasing institutional control. Pleasure became linked to sexuality within marriage and then, in the sixties, the advent of the pill coincided with a sexualisation of 'woman' – notably in advertising. The moral-rearmament campaigns focussed on the holiness of the family and the 'Christian' values surrounding it – in fact the Christian symbols they appealed to were already appropriations by church institutions of conservative historical trends which became the 'tradition' of the institution. This movement is related to the fact that bourgeois rationalism has no intrinsic place for sexuality or the emotions ('heart' in Wesley's or Newman's terminology). Yet both are appropriated in varying ways as a means of control or method of catharsis, although the use to which they are put can conflict with their use under different economic conditions. The moral neutrality of capitalism caused advocates of the intrinsic values of the family to turn to an ideology which could support their argument. Arguably, however, traditional, institutionalised Christianity and the bourgeois ideology are equally subversive of feminist insights. At issue, more fundamentally than economics, is identity.

2.2 The third period: the 1960s movement and ecumenism

The weakening of institutional hegemony in the 1960s coincided with the third period when moves were made by women to enter the ministry. Their position in society was such that in the Methodist Church agreement on principle was quickly forthcoming, although there was a delay pending a decision on Anglican–Methodist union.

In the Church of England the social status of women was differently interpreted by the two sides in the debate. The proposers of women's ordination argued that the improvement in the position of women was a significant factor, while the opponents ranged from considering it a minor argument to regretting the entry of women into 'traditionally masculine' spheres at all. This contrast was underlined by the differing perspectives of the two reports separated by only four years – the central advisory council's *Gender and Ministry* (1962), and the archbishops' commission's *Women and Holy Orders* (1966). The former, approximating to the Methodist position, pointed to the great changes in traditionally masculine and feminine ways of life, and requested a re-examination of the nature of ministry together with the reasons for withholding the priesthood from women. The latter considered the changed status of women a minor argument, and did not directly address the questions posed, as was pointed out in the debate (above, p. 97). The proposers argued that any moves towards women priests in early times would have been too radically disruptive for the early church, (cf. above, p. 90) or, perhaps more perceptively, that at first the role of Christian women had improved but that then the tides rolled back and existing cultural patterns took over (cf. above, p. 125). They were in agreement that if the ancient and medieval assumptions about the social roles and inferior status of women were no longer accepted, the appeal to tradition was virtually reduced to the observation that there was no precedent, and the New Testament did not encourage the belief that nothing could be done for the first time. The theological backing was a new *kairos*: it was argued that the ministry should be adapted to the current ethos of egalitarian responsibility and opportunity. Marriage and authority were discussed theologically, but not socially, but it was pointed out that celibacy could not be imposed on one sex alone (cf. above, p. 94). The social line of argumentation unfortunately seems to have been largely ignored, and the debate closed on the opponents' ground of symbolism, which arguably is basically a reading of tradition.

The official Roman Catholic response to such requests was categorically negative. Vatican 2 statements such as:

> every type of discrimination, whether social or cultural, whether based on sex, race, color, social condition, language, or religion, is to be overcome and eradicated as contrary to God's intent. For in truth it must still be regretted that fundamental personal rights are not yet being universally

> honored. Such is the case of a woman who is denied the right and freedom to choose a husband, *to embrace a state of life* [italics added], or to acquire an education or cultural benefits equal to those recognized for men (*Gaudium et Spes* 29)[70]

were simply assumed to exclude ordination. The increasing part women were playing in public life was noted, and the elimination of discrimination was said to be desirable, but in terms of the 'harmonious unification of distinctions' between the sexes. The magisterium, it was asserted, had set itself to discover the 'originality' of 'woman's nature' and to uncover suitable roles in the church, family and society. Yet also asserted was the position of the church as a society apart. Ratzinger's[71] linking of the issue with the 'concept of right' of the Enlightenment had its internal logic – but he left unexplored the basis of his own 'traditional' position.

The influence of the Roman Catholic Church on the issue was not negligible. The twentieth-century ecumenical tendency towards convergence resulted in a domino effect whereby churches with a 'higher' or more symbolic theology tended to influence the attitudes towards the ministry and women of churches aspiring to union with them. That the Church of England gave ecumenical priority to Orthodox and Roman Catholic Churches was illustrated on the one hand by the failure of Anglican–Methodist union in 1969 (prior to which the Methodists in turn were looking towards the Church of England) and by the use of ecumenical argumentation in the debates from the mid-seventies; moreover, the effect of Cardinal Hume's intervention in 1978 was predictable.

The motive for the ecumenical movement in general appears to have been economic and political under the cloak of a theological pursuit of 'oneness'.[72] Its antecedents can be traced to the sixteenth century but the contemporary movement dates from the 1910 International Missionary Conference, this movement paralleling – perhaps not surprisingly – the origins and twentieth-century expansion of industrialisation with its inherent tendency towards mergers. Also not surprisingly, the Roman Catholic Church remained aloof. I suggest that a deeper motivation for the movement was the uncertain relationship between church and state, which led the churches to aspire towards hegemony and to seek to defend symbols structuring an identity under threat, and associated with happier times. Although the Roman Catholic Church remained apart from the movement at least until the 1960s, the ultramontanism, anti-modernism and general triumphalism of the pre-Vatican 2 church (hints of which, the documentation suggests, are still alive) can be interpreted as another form of the same defensive strategy. Here the self-sufficiency was an additional defence against the churches which shared a philosophical base with the bourgeois economy which had shared their time of birth. During this period the churches were drawn towards symbols which held the promise of an identity apart from the industrial state. 'Holy Orders' was the point of convergence.

SECTION TWO

STRATEGIES

This section considers strategies of the various assemblies and speakers aimed at the frustration of the movement towards the presence of women in ministry.

I THE METHODIST ITINERANT PREACHERS

Strategies to oppose the presence of women in ministry have always been more apparent in Methodism because the 'window effect'[1] of theological argumentation in the Church of England and the theologised magisterial statements of Roman Catholicism were lacking. In spite of Wesley's concept of an 'extraordinary' call, female preachers were constantly under pressure. Some became ill while others adopted devices such as preaching from the pulpit steps or to women only, billing 'meetings' and, later, appearing on the plan as an asterisk. Then Bunting gradually threw the weight of the institution behind the prohibition. He redefined an 'extraordinary call' as 'every fanatic's plea' and used his authority to censor references to women's preaching from the *Methodist Magazine* on the basis that such would provide encouragement to others – a move Taft's publication sought to rectify. When a letter from a woman on the subject did appear, a masculine title was accredited to the writer. Finally the 1835 Conference expressed its strong disapproval of women's preaching, which disappeared. It was during the same decade that significant moves were afoot among the Primitive Methodists. They, together with the Bible Christians, had allowed female preachers, although in both connexions these women were paid lower wages than their male counterparts. Expressed hardship such as hers who could not 'dress smart enough for the people' was greatly augmented when in 1826 the Primitive Methodists decided that women could no longer join the Primitive Methodist Itinerant Preachers' Fund, thus allowing women no insurance against sickness. This was undoubtedly an overriding reason for the dwindling number of recruits – although the Primitive Methodist practice dating from this time of using initials in their listings makes detailed analysis impossible. Additionally in 1832 came the Primitive Methodist ruling that their women preachers could not travel with a male companion, thus making their position increasingly difficult and dangerous. By the turn of the century institutionalisation had reached such a stage that it was possible simply to require the remaining Bible Christian female preacher to resign in the interests of union in 1907.

2 THE MOVES OF THE 1920S

In the twentieth century, as already noted, there were two peak periods of moves by women to enter the ministry: these began in the 1920s and the 1960s. As in the previous century, the moves corresponded to currents in society generally, and in the first twentieth-century period were more apparent in Methodist than in Church of England documentation, while in the pre-Vatican 2 Roman Catholic material they did not appear at all. In Methodism this pressure was at its peak in the early 1920s, but was (just) kept alive for twenty-six years. The loss of momentum was due to the delays preceding Methodist union in the early 1930s, and to the war years. Opponents' strategies were predominantly procedural and took the form of a variety of resolutions and delaying amendments based on 'many difficulties'. These were detailed as the itinerant ministry, its relationship to marriage, and supplemented by the thesis that an equal but separate ministry for women could be provided by an expansion of the scope of the Wesley Deaconess Order. The arguments of the proposers – that women were sent as missionaries to labour single-handed in lonely tropical stations miles from their nearest neighbours; that proposed schemes dealt with the marriage issue as far as was possible and that it was contrary to the spirit of Methodism to be stopped by practical difficulties; that the deaconess order could not meet the aspirations of all educated women – proved unavailing. In 1948 Conference finally declined to declare its willingness to receive for ordination to the ministry of the word and sacraments women who believed themselves called of God to that work.

Meanwhile moves by Church of England women towards priesthood which culminated in the 1930s memorandum *Women and Priesthood* were preceded in the later decades of the previous century by struggles surrounding the establishment of sisterhoods and the revival of the order of deaconess. These have been followed through already as part of the ongoing movement leading to the period under consideration (see pp. 213–18 above). In the 1861 Convocation debate the two issues were blended, the bishops amending a motion to establish rules for women's communities, to accord them only general 'sanction and guidance' on the basis that 'the time was not yet ripe' – which was to be a recurring argument. But alarmed by the 'independence' of 'these ladies', the bishops later agreed rules, and with this impingement of the institution the impetus of the sisterhoods lost ground in a manner comparable to the effect of institutionalisation on Methodist female itinerant preachers. Yet the alternative pleased neither all women nor all bishops. The underlying ambiguities which had bedevilled the diaconate of women from the earliest times re-emerged. Some women joined the deaconess institutions as a way of furthering their ministry, while others perceived the scope as limited and unsatisfactory and were driven towards the sisterhoods instead. Meanwhile the bishops viewed the submission of the deaconess to her bishop with approval, in contrast to the independence of sisterhoods, seeing in the deaconess' office a satisfactory and official ministry for women. They were apparently genuinely puzzled at the relatively small number of applicants, while on the other hand they expressed reservations about its scope and status in relation to priesthood.

Thus in the Church of England the priesthood issue explicitly or implicitly underlay discussions on the ministry of women. In the very first 1861 debate it had been argued that the deaconess would not receive 'ordination', and subsequent debates, resolutions and regulations had this issue as a point of reference. When the 1919 motion to allow women to speak in consecrated buildings was debated, it was argued that tradition could not be ignored here, but could be appealed to on the issue of priesthood. *The Ministry of Women*, presented the same day, and focussing particularly on the history and status of the deaconess and underlining the historical ambiguity of her position, also asserted the continuous tradition of a male priesthood. The 1935 report, triggered by the 1930 memorandum, reasserted on the one hand the continuous tradition of a male priesthood, and on the other hand that a new great order of ministry specifically for women was on the table. Meanwhile the note by the dean of St Paul's took the position that tradition was not irreversible and that policy (he saw the time as 'not ripe') and principle should be distinguished.

With the acceptance of this report the priesthood issue faded in the Church of England. It was however kept alive in the wider Anglican Communion when the 1945 ordination by the bishop of Hong Kong was judged to be *ultra vires* and contrary to all laws and precedents. Yet here too the debate was brought to a close by the reply to the 1948 question about an experimental period. Such a move was declared to be against Anglican tradition and order, although it was added that the reply did not rest on a discussion of the underlying principle because (still) 'the time was not ripe', and it was stated somewhat doggedly that the deaconess order could satisfy the deepest aspirations of women. Thus 1948 temporarily brought to an end the issue in both Methodism and in the Church of England through the Anglican Communion. Interestingly, two years later Pope Pius XII, in defining the dogma of the Assumption, implicitly asserted the creative power of tradition.

Thus strategies in the Church of England to circumscribe the ministry of women can be seen as operating at a level somewhere between the procedural strategies of Methodism and the later strategies of authoritarian pronouncements of Roman Catholicism. The issue having been raised, the archbishop's committee and archbishops' commission prepared reports which were subsequently debated – before 1919 by the clerical Convocations and after that date by the newly constituted Church Assembly – but the reports nevertheless set the tone and boundaries of debate. Argument at this stage rested on tradition and law (especially article 34), although there was admitted to be little consideration of the principles on which tradition and law were based, and it was stated the time was 'not ripe'. The aspirations of women could be met, it was claimed, in the deaconess order.

3 THE MOVES OF THE 1960S

The 1960s marked the beginning of the second twentieth-century period of moves by women to enter the ministry. All three churches were affected and, arguably, the traditional strategies of the institutions in dealing with the issue determined the respective outcomes.

In Methodism Pauline Webb's 1959 and 1966 strategic interventions proved decisive. The first reopened discussion and resulted in the 1961 report, which was offered for consideration by the whole church. This time the delaying factor was conversations about union with the Church of England, yet five years later a reluctance to overburden the conversational agenda (which included discussion on fermented wine) with 'this particular issue' was noted. This led to Pauline Webb's amendment, which affirmed the principle of the ordination of women, admitted that unilateral action would be unwise, and desired discussion with Church of England representatives about the implications of the principle in relation to the ministry of both churches and to women ordained elsewhere. The resulting *Women and the Ordained Ministry* (1968) concluded that Methodist ordination of women would be problematic at stage two of the plan for union. However, when the plan for proposed union failed to obtain a sufficient majority in the Church of England, the Methodists implemented the principle. It is interesting to speculate whether the 1966 stand arose from the fact that Methodism was more closely bound to social forces and less insulated by traditional argumentation; whether it marked a revival of the freedom of judgement which had been an important factor in Methodist origins; or whether knowledge that the Church of England was looking towards Rome for recognition of Anglican orders gave rise to doubts as to whether the proposed plan would indeed achieve a majority in the Church of England vote.

Within Church of England documentation, *Gender and Ministry*'s 1962 reopening of the argument was comparable to Pauline Webb's intervention at the 1959 Methodist Conference. In it was considered the changing role of women in society in relation to the church's ministry, and a request for an examination of the reasons for withholding the priesthood from women. The resulting *Women and Holy Orders* was notable for its emphasis on symbolism – of the sexes and of the priest – while, as was pointed out, it contained 'questionable definitions of women', but none of holy orders, and it provoked the request to distinguish between theological reasons and prejudice. It was, of course, produced against the background of the Swedish ordinations, which had resulted in a great deal of (predominantly clerical) bitterness, and of Archbishop Pike's proclaimed intention in the USA to ordain a deaconess deacon – to which the Vatican secretariat had responded with the warning that such a move would be an 'insurmountable obstacle' to unity. Thus at the very beginning of this second twentieth-century period the two areas which were to be the rallying ground of the opponents had been marked out: ecumenism and symbolism.

In the 1970s the Church of England stood uneasily between (but facing churches with a 'high' theology) Christian communions which had women ministers and those which did not. The dividing line extended even into the Anglican Communion after the 1971 ACC resolution 28 and its subsequent implementation in Hong Kong. The ACC was also the catalyst for the Howard Report, in which for the first time the areas of biblical scholarship and tradition were critically considered, and which resulted in the 1975 resolution that there were 'no fundamental objections' to the ordination of women. On the one side was the argument of new insights; on the other the assertion that the whole area of anthropology and psychology needed study: strangely, both sides seemed to agree that a distinction should be made between women's rights and what was right for the church. Christian Howard summed up the division in her question as to what it was in the sexuality of the male which was so intimately attached to the priesthood and which would absolutely debar the female from being ordained.

The stalemate following the subsequent resolution on legislation was to bring together the two areas of argument – symbolism and ecumenism – via the conversations of the archbishop of Canterbury with the Roman Catholics, the Orthodox and the Old Catholics, which were reflected in the reports of 1978. The Old Catholics asserted on the basis of 'Holy Scripture and Tradition' that only men and not women could be bearers of the priesthood of Christ because he and the apostles were men, and that a change could only be made by the church as a whole. The Orthodox saw the issue as one of 'acute crisis', as a threat to the basis of the Christian faith as expressed in the church's ministries. They warned that the ordination of women to the priesthood would have a decisively negative effect on the recognition of Anglican orders, as hitherto any such recognition had been on the ground that the Anglican Church had preserved the apostolic succession not merely as a laying on of hands but as continuity in apostolic faith and spiritual life. For the Roman Catholics, interestingly, the 'insurmountable obstacle' prior to Anglican decisions on principle became in 1976 'a grave new obstacle', while the issue was addressed in the Declaration (1976), published with the English-speaking world in mind. That the Roman Catholic Church sought to influence the Church of England is undoubtedly the case, and Cardinal Hume's intervention in February 1978 prior to the vote on legislation later that year was not coincidental. Two 'grounds for hope' were noted in the English Anglican–Roman Catholic consultation (1978): that Anglican churches ordaining women did so in the conviction that they had not departed from the traditional understanding of the church's ministry, and that the Declaration did not affirm explicitly that the matter was *de jure divino*. ARCIC (1979) noted that the principle on which doctrinal agreement rested was not affected as it was concerned with the nature and origin of the ordained ministry and not with the question of who could or who could not be ordained. This made objections to the ordination of women of a different kind from past objections to the validity of Anglican orders. Meanwhile Lambeth Conference in 1978 recommended that no decision should be made on the consecration of women to the episcopate. Thus Anglican orders were safeguarded; ordained women were not an insuperable ecumenical obstacle, and by halting any consecration of women to the episcopate it would theoretically be possible in future to make the move – foreshadowed in the Anglican–Methodist stage two – of ordaining no more women and even of reviewing the position of those already ordained. Indeed, such a possibility was hinted at in the 1987 bishops' reports.[2] However, the subsequent consecration of the Reverend Barbara C. Harris to the episcopate of PECUSA made this strategy difficult to pursue.

Interestingly, in the 1980s procedural strategies enjoyed a higher profile in the Church of England, while ecumenical and symbolic argument still dominated debate. Possibly with a closer democratic voting result looming, further displacements of theologised argument temporarily seemed a less promising strategy. A successful petition to bring under article 8 the measure allowing women ordained abroad to officiate in this country resulted in the loss of motion and measure at final approval stage. The proposers' argument that the measure had a limited life and so should not come under article 8 was overruled on the basis that a permanent principle would have been established even though in 1975 the principle had already been accepted by Synod. This point was largely ignored and debate closed again on the opponents' ground.

When the admission of women to the diaconate was debated, a

move to renew (and possibly demote) the diaconate before admitting women failed, as did the moves to introduce 'supplemental ordination' for deaconesses (presumably its effectiveness could be later put into question). It was successfully argued that a clause should be put into the measure divorcing it from moves towards priesthood, and when it came before the Ecclesiastical Committee of parliament it was ruled that the ordination prayer asking to be found worthy to be called to higher ministries 'should' (rather than 'might') be omitted. In the renewed moves to open the priesthood to women, their admission to the episcopate was explicitly excluded. The 1980s moves to consider priesthood separately from episcopate on the basis of preserving the latter as a focus of unity effectively met objectors' doubts about the validity of a female bishop's subsequent ordinations. Further strategies were the implied threat to split the Church of England together with the acquisition of 'safeguards' in the legislation for dissenters, and the move further into ecumenical and symbolic terrain, which means effectively into the orbit of official Roman Catholic theology and ecumenical influence. The 1988 bishops' report safeguarded the bishops' external unity; effectively it revolved around the opponents' arguments, and gave disproportionate space and weight to their positions.

Yet strategically where Methodism has led, the Church of England is likely to follow. Ultimately, it lacks the Roman Catholic facility of simply stating a position to be adhered to even though that position or the circumstances which gave rise to that position might change. It has a democratically elected governing body, which includes the house of clergy, which must operate by persuasion in the context of late twentieth-century expectations concerning the place and role of women. Such a shift, of course, is in harmony with the pattern already noted whereby when the movement of women is too strong to be simply repressed, it is assimilated by the dominant structures and the demands defused and represented. Furthermore, the possibility does not resolve the questions either about the recurrence of this pattern, or about the related and temporally prior questions concerning the displacement of argument and the persistence of the strategies of opposition. Now I return to the source of both argument and ecclesial institution, namely, the New Testament texts, to consider the struggle between the forces of liberation and the forces of oppression from which have sprung these arguments and strategies.

SECTION THREE

INTERPRETATIONS

I have suggested a relationship between weakened institutional hegemony and the acceptance of women ministers by the churches in relation to their own degree of institutionalisation (Part Two, Section One, 'Undercurrents'). I also suggested that strategies to oppose the presence of women in ministry were obscured in Roman Catholicism by theologised magisterial statements, and to some extent in the Church of England by the 'window' effect of theological argumentation (see Part Two, Section Two, 'Strategies'). It is to this contemporary shift into symbolic argumentation that the argument now turns – first by tracing the shift from biblical to traditional, to symbolic argument in the texts, and secondly by interpreting the shift. This interpretation moves from Baum's sociological considerations of theology, notably liberation theology, which links salvation with social transformation, towards Schüssler Fiorenza's feminist reconstruction of Christian origins based on the critical hermeneutics, which was absent from the documentation. Finally I suggest a theoretical relationship between sexuality, self identity, and institution to explain the unconscious forces underlying the repulsion of the impetus of women through the displacement of argument I have identified. (By institution here I have in mind people united by a traditioned symbolic structure, which may vary between institutions – and individuals belong to more than one but which increasingly mirrors that of the state as the institution grows and becomes established.) A similar process is discernible in Schüssler Fiorenza's reconstruction of Christian origins, so neither the impetus nor its repulsion is novel.

I THE BIBLICAL-TRADITIONAL-SYMBOLIC MOVEMENT THROUGH THE CHURCHES

Interpretations of the pivotal text (Bible, especially New Testament) on which the texts (documentation) focus became increasingly traditional–symbolic in the move from Methodist to Church of England to Roman Catholic material. The Church of England documents, which in the early stages revealed a concern to preserve Reformation principles, later showed a marked swing towards the Roman Catholic position, coinciding with the increased ecumencial emphasis of the 1970s. Interestingly, neither the Methodists nor the Roman Catholics concentrated much on the biblical texts.

In early Methodism, opposition was based on texts. Wesley disagreed with the Quaker position which dismissed the 'rule' of 1 Corinthians 14: 34 and 1 Timothy 2: 12, and argued instead in favour of the rule which allowed of 'extraordinary' exceptions based on an extraordinary dispensation of providence[1] – a view endorsed by Taft, who nevertheless thought that no woman was called to pastoral office.[2] The influence of the Quakers on the Bible Christians and the Primitive Methodists was greater. The former supported their admission of women preachers with reference to Joel 2: 28–9 as applied in Acts 2: 17–18, sweeping aside as nonsensical objections based on 1 Timothy 2: 12 and 1 Corinthians 14: 34–5[3] – although female travelling preachers never had their male counterparts stationed under their authority.

In the twentieth century the Wesleyan position developed into an explicit distinction between principle and practice. This distinction was sketchily demonstrated in the 1926 report which followed the 1925 Wesleyan Conference's agreement on the principle, and in which, the example of slavery and the state having been cited, Galatians 3: 28 was opposed to 1 Corinthians 14: 34 and 1 Timothy 2: 12. In the 1961 report more texts were cited in favour of the distinction. Genesis 1: 26–8 was contrasted with Genesis 3; Jesus' attitude to women (their function in accompanying him and as resurrection witnesses), with their non-inclusion among the twelve or as far as was known the seventy; the restored status of women in the early church, with 1 Corinthians 14: 33b–35 (interpreted as an antidote to disorder) and 1 Timothy 2: 12 (interpreted as post-Pauline ambivalence towards the freedom claimed by women); and the contentious translations of 1 Timothy 5: 2 were juxtaposed. In conclusion, the principle was linked with Galatians 3: 28 and with the gifts of charismata to all, while the subjection of Genesis 3, explicitly stated in 1 Corinthians 11: 3, Ephesians 5: 22–4 and 1 Timothy 2: 13,14 was seen as underlying the non-normative practice of excluding women from among the presbyter bishops and from the administration of the Lord's Supper. Argument based on the concept of a priest who represented Christ as opposed to the priesthood of all believers was explicitly rejected in the report as alien to the New Testament. In Conference debates, Mr Cartwright's 1925 plea to go back to 'Apostolic practice'[4] and Mr Niles' 1948 statements that in the Bible the succession to which the ministry belonged was a male ministry, and that God [*sic*] did not choose women, and that at stake was entry not into the Methodist ministry but into the church of Christ,[5] were among the few recorded biblically linked objections. The latter in particular was a rare example of 'high' argumentation. Although in the brief 1926 report the New Testament was taken as backing up the distinction between principle and practice, in general, biblical argumentation, in the guise of scripture unencumbered by tradition, featured rarely in Methodist documentation, as objections to female ministry were seen at least overtly as practically rather than scripturally based.

Not surprisingly, traditional and symbolic argument was not used – a point underlined during the 1939 debate when it was stated that the Methodists held no theory of apostolic succession but that traditionally men from the humblest backgrounds had been able to offer for the ministry.[6] Historical considerations appeared in the 1961 report. Here it was pointed out that after New Testament times there had been no question of ordaining women presbyters until after the Reformation. As the emphasis on priesthood had increased, so the likelihood of women's ordination had decreased, linked as it was to the idea of representation of Christ. It was also noted that with the possible exception of the letter to Trajan in AD 112, the first reference to the diaconate of women as an institution was in the fourth century(which could have pointed to a lapse in the order). After this it had continued until the eleventh century, when the functions of the deaconess had been gradually taken over by the monasteries (the frequent references to what was forbidden to deaconesses from the fourth to the eleventh century suggested that they were in fact doing these things). It was pointed out that the Reformation was a protest at the power of the monasteries and at the influence of women behind the clerical scenes, and the resulting emphasis on family life had left indeterminate any role for the single woman until the revival of deaconesses in the Reformed Churches of the nineteenth century. Symbolically, the Methodist position was quite clear. Explicitly rejected as alien to the New Testament was the notion of a minister who administered the Lord's Supper as a priest who represented Christ: preferred was the doctrine of the priesthood of all believers.

Polarised against this was the Roman Catholic interpretation. The main biblical document was the Pontifical Biblical Commission's report, which considered woman's place in the family: in Genesis 2: 18 as 'helper'; in the Old Testament symbolism of the fatherhood and husbandhood of God as against the feminine people of Israel; in the teaching and behaviour of Jesus (Mk 10: 1–12; Matt 19: 12) and the symbolism of Mary in terms of motherhood–church (Gal 4: 26; Rev 21); in the mutual submission of Ephesians 5: 21. Then woman's place was considered ecclesiastically: in the Old Testament as 'prophetesses'; in the New as resurrection witnesses; in Acts; and notably in Romans 16. In the context of the ordination debate, attention was drawn to the twelve as a symbol of the twelve patriarchs, and to the exclusively apostolic leadership of the community of Jerusalem, which soon spread. The question of the normative value of the masculine character of the hierarchical structure of the early church was raised. The Declaration simply took up the issue in terms of the practice of Jesus, which was interpreted as of particular significance in the light of his radically 'different' attitude to women. Generally, the biblical material in the Roman Catholic documentation was heavily entwined with traditional and symbolic interpretations.

This church claimed as its constant tradition (and that of the East) that the priestly ministry had never been conferred on women. It was argued that the few heretical sects which did not conform had been condemned by the fathers, and that although the latter showed prejudice against women such prejudices had had little influence on their pastoral activity. The same conviction had animated medieval theology, although supporting arguments were admitted to be questionable.

The predominantly symbolic character of Roman Catholic biblical interpretation has been noted and exemplified. Additional examples were Jesus' eschatological transcendence of sexuality and his inauguration of the reign of God and celibacy, and the maternal imagery of Mary projected onto the people in their nuptial relationship with the Lamb. It was above all in the sacramental structure that symbolism took form. The argument ran that the church had been entrusted with the sacramental economy, but that its power over the sacraments was limited by what Christ had decided was to be maintained in the sacramental sign. In the sacrament of order the minister did not act *in persona propria*, but *in persona Christi*, to the point of being his very image when pronouncing the words of consecration. There would be no natural resemblance if the role of Christ were not taken by a man as the incarnation took place in the male sex.[7] This was intrinsically linked to the economy of salvation: the priest represented the church because, first, he represented Christ. Following from here was a strong link between sacramentality and sexuality. It was argued that the church was original in its structure and nature and apart from other societies, so equal rights were not an issue (throughout Roman Catholic documentation recurs the claim to be a defence of the 'true rights' of women): full power, Christological and representative, resided in the episcopal office. The feminine symbolism of the church was depicted as shedding light on the sexual–personal role of woman, who was what she was whereas man represented what he was not. This type of argument extended into assertions such as that Christ 'in which he, on a plane above the sexes, gives himself to the Church entirely as the dedicated seed of God – and the participation, difficult to formulate, of the apostolic office in this male fertility which is above sex',[8] and the evocative mention of the 'moment of complete communion between the Bridegroom and the Bride, which is, as is known, the Eucharist, the climax of the espousals of the whole Church with her Lord'.[9]

Between the Methodist and Roman Catholic polarisations stood, though oscillating slightly, the Church of England, with the conflict of interpretations extending into the church itself. Biblical interpretation here was more traditional than in Methodism. As early as 1862 Mr Mackenzie argued that the 'ordination' of a deaconess was contrary to 1 Timothy 2: 12.[10] The 1919 report selected New Testament examples similar to those of Methodism (1961) concerning Jesus' attitude and choices, but interpreted them as supplying 'proof' that certain functions were assigned to men (alongside equality of spiritual privilege). This position was said to have been confirmed in Acts, and a distinction was made between prophecy and public teaching (1 Cor 14: 34–40; 1 Tim 2: 12). The contrast between oneness in Christ and mundane differences was attributed to either social custom, Jewish attitude, or fundamental differences inherent in the variety of sex. In the 1966 report it was admitted that no clear answer was given in the New Testament; the checks to female freedom of 1 Corinthians 11: 3–16; 1 Corinthians 14: 34, 35; 1 Timothy 2: 12 and Ephesians 5: 22–33 could have meant that the new emphasis on individuality was proving too disruptive. It was asserted on the one hand that the ordination of women was against the example of Christ: on the other Isaiah 49: 15; 66: 13 and Galatians 4: 19 were offered against the arguments based on divine fatherhood, the maleness of Christ, and Ephesians 5. The 1972 Howard Report detailed contrasting views on the nature of biblical authority: the authority of scripture as accepted by faith on the one hand, and on the other the use of biblical and historical scholarship to assess how far the Bible was authoritative for thought and action. The position of and hence attitudes towards Jewish, Greek and Roman women were contrasted to the actions and attitude of Jesus. Among examples given were his reactions to Martha and Mary (Lk 10: 38–42) and to the woman in the crowd (Lk 11: 27,28) etc.; the fact that women were first at the empty tomb and first news-bearers of the resurrection; and their depiction in Acts and the epistles (cf. Gal 3: 28; Rom 16: 1–3 (*diakonos* of common gender); Acts 18: 26; 21: 9; 2: 18 (quoting Joel 2: 28); 1 Cor 11: 5). But 1 Corinthians 11: 3–16; 14: 34–6; 1 Timothy 2: 12 were identified as subject to conflicting interpretations. A conservative view held as a permanent principle the subordination of women based on the patriarchal structure of Israel's life, its male priesthood, the fatherhood of God, the incarnation of Jesus as male, his appointment of male apostles, the depiction of women as the weaker sex (1 Pet 3: 7), and the household codes of Ephesians, Colossians, Titus and Peter. Galatians was seen as irrelevant to the issue in hand, and it was further pointed out that the only biblical quasi-official function of women was as deaconess (*sic*). The alternative interpretation of these passages stressed the innovative choice of women as witnesses at the resurrection, the fact that Jesus chose no gentiles, and the lack of any New Testament plan for the abolition of slavery. Acts, it was argued, said little about ministry although the designation of Phoebe as *prostatis* was noted, and in the epistles the social codes were a question of practical adjustment rather than ethical practice. The anachronistic attribution to the New Testament situation of words such as 'eucharist', 'apostolic ministry', 'church order' was underlined. In the debates a recurring theme was that scripture should be interpreted according to 'the tradition of the church'. There were occasional references to the Roman Catholic position and at one point concern was expressed about 'a sceptical school' linked with 'Catholic modernism', and about the suggestion that Jesus could have acted differently in a different age.[11]

The Church of England's use of historico-traditional material changed in emphasis with the increase in ecumenical activity *vis-à-vis* Roman Catholicism. The 1919 summary of the history of deaconesses was in general agreement with that in the Methodist report of 1961, although the Church of England preferred the suggestion that there was no hint of a lapse in the order between the first and the fourth centuries. The 1919 report additionally drew attention to the debate over the words *χειροτονία* and *χειροθεσία* in the *Apostolic Constitutions*, and concluded that the older Greek Euchologia justified the assumption that the diaconate conferred was as real a diaconate as that conferred on men. Meanwhile two tendencies were indicated, the first to give the deaconess and other women definite positions, and the other to ignore or curtail her position. Whereas the 1919 report did not consider traditional attitudes to women and priesthood, that of 1935 drew attention to the contemporary challenge, but stressed that it was a modern phenomenon with the possible exception of the first four or five centuries, and it was to these centuries that sections of the 1966 and 1972 reports turned. The former pointed to the depiction of women by the majority of the church fathers as frail, emotional and subordinate to man on account of the fall and perhaps even by the original creation, although a minority stressed the sanctity and spirituality of selected females. The report noted that from the fifth century onwards there was a succession of prohibitions against women assisting in the sanctuary during the eucharist on the ground that their presence constituted a threat to the chastity of the clergy. The fathers based their case on the Pauline epistles and Genesis 1–3. The 1972 report pointed out that little was written about women and priesthood by the fathers; the work of Tertullian, Irenaeus, Chrysostom and Epiphanius was more generally about heretical sects. The reinforcing of the New Testament texts mentioned with the Aristotelian doctrine that a woman was a defective male provided the possibility of a more developed doctrine. The report cited Aquinas as arguing that women could not receive the sacrament of order because they were 'under subjection'. Some added that women could not teach in public because men might be tempted to lust. For the Scholastics the question was part of a theological system linked with natural and divine law, although there had been a hardening of position in the late Middle Ages. The 1972 report distinguished between the concepts of tradition in the different churches. For the Orthodox, tradition was the church in its continuous life; for the Roman Catholic Church it was divine truth not expressed in scripture alone but orally transmitted (at Trent both were said to have equal authority, *pace* the Reformers). The Protestant churches pointed to scripture alone. Ecumenical study over the previous fifteen years had reached a consensus that tradition was the actualised preaching of the word. The Anglicans saw it as the context of a living fellowship which was the church universal, against the background of which was the Anglican tradition. Thus, it was argued, traditional perspectives could be challenged on the basis of a renewed concept of tradition.

A growing Roman Catholic influence was apparent in the Church of England material in the gradual move over the years from arguments concerning the maleness of Jesus, to a linking of priesthood with a theologising of sexuality. These perspectives merged in the 1988 bishops' report, in which considerable space was given to the (originally Roman Catholic) ikon argument. Opponents argued that the ministerial priesthood was of a different order from the priesthood of believers. They stressed a 'transcendent' symbolism of the male priesthood and the psychic implications of tangling with deeper symbolism. They also appealed to the Orthodox view that the bishop represented Christ the bridegroom.[12] Reference was made to the lively discussions among Roman Catholics as to the kinds of ways in which the changed position of women in contemporary culture could be theologically interpreted.[13] Moving to the respective symbolism of the sexes, arguments were developed from the order of creation, from natural law, from the different involvement of the sexes in the incarnation. Language in terms of the fatherhood of God was cited. The argument of the proposers, that Jesus in his humanity transcended sex and that women ministers were the logical outcome of women's full humanity, was swept aside in the wider tendency to create a theology around the symbolism of priesthood and the symbolism of sexuality. This tendency was encapsulated in the 1973 ACC request 'for a study of the relative status of the male and female principle and the symbolic authority they exercise upon our understanding of the nature of God and of leadership roles in Church and society'.[14]

The question requiring an answer is: How to interpret this interpretational process? The search for an answer leads towards new perspectives.

2 HERMENEUTICS AND THE CHURCHES' INTERPRETATIONAL PROCESS

A sociology of hermeneutics has yet to appear, but some tentative conclusions can be reached by viewing the varying positions in contemporary hermeneutics in the light of perspectives gleaned from Baum's contribution to *Sociology and Theology: Alliance or Conflict?*[15] As already indicated, Baum introduced four social considerations which could aid a study of the theological pluralism which has characterised Roman Catholic theology since Vatican 2, and which, arguably, is having in some areas a knock-on effect on Church of England theology. These are that the social location of the Christian community affects the theology it produces; that theology is a function of the dominant culture to which it belongs; that theology depends on the academic institutions in which it is taught; and that theology is related to economic class – and here I added 'to gender' in the light of the common critical origin of liberation and feminist theologies. There are two main debates within hermeneutics:[16] one between the Italian Emilio Betti and the German Hans-Georg Gadamer and the other between Gadamer and his co-national Jürgen Habermas. Their respective positions can be viewed in the light of the social considerations outlined by Baum, and can be related broadly to the three churches I am considering, particularly in the light of the varying views of tradition in both hermeneutics and churches. This subsection is not intended as an in-depth analysis of the relative positions in contemporary hermeneutics; it indicates simply some pointers that can help to clarify the three churches' differing interpretations of the biblical material and thus to throw some light on the question of women and ministry. I have pegged out the ground with the names of various writers to enable the reader to explore further the ideas which converge here.

Betti, a lawyer, seeks to establish criteria of authoritative decision. He rejects Gadamer's use of tradition, and is even more opposed to his 'fusion of horizons' – the change effected in the interpreter as part of 'real' understanding. At issue are truth values and authorities. Betti is in the line of theorists rooted in the

Reformation decision to reject developing institutional tradition in interpreting the Bible. On the other hand, Gadamer, following Martin Heidegger, argued that understanding is a historical act and so is always connected with the present. He reinstated developing tradition to span the temporal gap between past and present, and indicated the role of prejudice(s) in constituting the horizon-bounded field of the subject. Understanding was achieved through a fusion of horizons. As any historical situation contained its own horizon, he required a mediation in the fusion of horizons and developed a theory of the universality of language. For Gadamer, being *is* understanding in language. In Betti's debate with Gadamer he has been joined by Eric Donald Hirsch, who sees hermeneutics as the logic of validation, i.e. the author's intentions abstracting from historical development must be the norm and these can be disclosed through objective evidence. Betti and Hirsch would claim that Gadamer has threatened the quest for objectively valid interpretation in the human sciences. Gadamer's basic reply is that he is describing understanding, not evolving a methodology, and that the human sciences cannot aspire to the same kind of objective certainty as can the natural sciences.

It is not surprising that hermeneutical theory, rooted in German Romanticist thought, has been taken up recently within the Anglo-American positivist tradition, notably by Hirsch, while Gadamer's hermeneutic philosophy has allies in the theological positions of Rudolf Bultmann, Ernst Fuchs and Gerhard Ebeling. These two divergent tendencies can be related to the two theological orientations identified by Baum under his second point, namely, American scientific knowledge and German self-knowledge. The emphasis on relatively objective interpretation along the lines of Betti/Hirsch throws considerable light on the Methodist documents in their historical approach to the New Testament (an approach shared by the Church of England 1919 report), the avoidance of 'traditional' interpretation, and the unwillingness to apply historical practice to the present day.

Perhaps at this point a caveat should be heard. It could be argued with justice that the Reformers' encounter with the Bible was (at least anachronistically) existential. This case would be supported by referring to such theological works as Luther's on *Romans* and Bultmann's on *John*. From this perspective, what was being rejected by the Reformers was tradition-as-underwritten-by-the-institution, not the 'fusion of horizons' between the individual and the 'Word of God'. These considerations would line them up behind Gadamer rather than Betti and Hirsch. It is arguably less clear that the Methodists should be associated per se with such perspectives either historically or theologically. It is certainly true that in the early Methodist connexions the conversion experience was hyper-existential, and possibly some contemporary Methodists are moved by the writings of Karl Barth or Bultmann. But as one moves away from the individual level we find that in the documents that we are considering, which determine and describe institutional policy, existential interpretation is not in evidence. The Bible Christians attempted briefly to compare biblical texts, and decided quickly it was best 'to be pressing on'. In more recent debates New Testament principle and precedent were considered, but objections to women ministers were (at least overtly) practical, whether in social or ecumenical terms. In short, when institutional policy is to be determined, it is English pragmatism and associated philosophies rather than German self-knowledge and allied perspectives that carry the day in Methodism.

It is interesting to note that it was after Vatican 2, when the Roman Catholic move to assimilate (for example) German theological ideas was becoming apparent, that union negotiations between the Church of England and the Methodists failed, although these were long-standing. It was at this time that the Church of England began to aspire towards closer links with Rome, which may help to explain the shift into symbolic argument when the ordination of women was under consideration in the Church of England in the 1970s. This fits well into the linguistic ethos of hermeneutic philosophy. Hermeneutic philosophy has affinities with the second view of biblical authority in the Church of England 1972 report, where 'the real urgency in using the Bible' was seen as enabling 'God to speak through it to us today' (the implied contrast with *MOW19* is intended). It was also apparent in *Women and Priesthood* (1978), a reply of American Roman Catholic scholars to the Declaration, particularly in the analysis of 'the living, historically-situated character of tradition'.[17] This perspective, adopted by those who argue for the ordination of women to the priesthood on the basis of the development of tradition, does not of itself provide the means either to evaluate 'different' readings of the Bible, or critically to examine traditional church structures.

This absence of a fundamentally critical tool in the hermeneutical theory and hermeneutical philosophy discussed to date can be further illustrated. The historical and empirically orientated developments of hermeneutical theory influenced the varying historical stages of biblical exegesis, notably the nineteenth-century quest for the historical Jesus. Then the development of form criticism in the mid-1950s, and the sociological explorations of more recent decades, occurred with the realisation that the interaction between text and community, and between text and interpreter, had to be considered. These considerations may throw some light on the factor noted by Baum under his third point – namely, the tendency in America to separate 'theology from the life of the Church'. In the light of Betti's separation of interpretation, understanding and application, application becomes an optional extra to interpretation, while, conversely, the collapsing of the three into a unitary happening, as in hermeneutic philosophy, points to the fusion of historical and dogmatic interpretation and their application in the face of biblical texts. It is interesting to remember that it was the inability of liberal theologians to challenge Hitler that caused Barth to formulate his dialectical theology, which was to some extent indebted to Heidegger. This is not to argue that a 'right' application is intrinsic to hermeneutic philosophy – indeed Heidegger's own pro-Nazi political position could be cited here to the contrary in so far as it was opposed to Barth's – but application is part of the act of understanding in language in hermeneutic philosophy.

3 AN ALTERNATIVE CRITICAL PERSPECTIVE

Critical hermeneutics aims to locate the means of discriminating between different interpretations within the 'ideal speech community'. As Josef Bleicher (1980) points out, it arose because previously hermeneutics could not sufficiently explain experiences such as lies, censorship, the manipulation or oppression of thought, and also the force over people's minds exercised by ideological structures in the formation of false consciousness. While Gadamer allowed for the review and correction of prejudices in the fusion of horizons, Habermas, as a representative of critical hermeneutics, would go further. To tradition Habermas would apply reason, and where Gadamer assumed accessibility of meaning, Habermas would argue that Gadamer's dialogue was not necessarily an open one because ontological understanding, which excluded factors such as labour and domination, put limits on the horizon. The socio-political interests and forces which were absorbed into social institutions and language resulted in pseudo-communication, which required further in-depth analysis. It is here that he turns to psychoanalysis in as far as it shows a method to uncover how and where socially unacceptable behaviour has, first, been repressed until becoming unconscious, and then, secondly, rechannelled into acceptable forms of expression. The meaning could be retrieved by general interpretation and the events that lay behind the disturbed communication could be pinpointed.

3.1 Critical theologies

I have noted that critical hermeneutics developed in order to interpret the various manifestations of false consciousness. Critical theologies arose in response to specific areas of oppression: the poor, and women. Liberation theology emerged from the irrelevancy of the Vatican 2 view of the modern world to the Latin Americans, as Baum noted under his fourth point. This view was expressed in the Conciliar document *Gaudium et Spes*, which was rooted in the (limited) perspective of European culture. Liberation theology is based on a religious experience that looks for the fulfilment of God's will on earth. The guiding concepts are of divine salvation including the liberation of women and men from all oppressive conditions of life, or praxis for social change being an integral part of Christian life, and of social sin. Liberation theologies have been taken up by other groups suffering from institutionalised oppression, such as the black Americans and the original inhabitants of North America.

It is from this same critical base that feminist theology arose. It views liberation theology as inadequate in its analysis of the forces of oppression to which women specifically are subject: women are potentially doubly oppressed as poor and as women. From here of course arise the debates among such theologians about the weighting given here to 'third world' women – debates which, though important, take us beyond our present project. Suffice it to say that feminist theology is critically directed against the oppression of women *qua* women of whatever 'world'. Feminist theologians argue that because the authors of the Bible were submerged in their own culture, as were its traditional interpreters, the Bible and its historico-traditional interpretation have been oppressive forces towards women. Consequently a critical feminist perspective is brought to bear on biblical texts together with traditional gendered images and derived roles. Feminist theologians have appeared in a number of countries – for example, Catharina Halkes in Holland; Elisabeth Moltmann-Wendel in Germany; and Elisabeth Schüssler Fiorenza, Rosemary Radford Ruether, Phyllis Trible, among others, in the USA.

The work of no feminist theologian was considered in the biblical, traditional or symbolic argument outlined at the beginning of this section. As biblical interpretation takes on new life when viewed from a feminist perspective, I thought it helpful to remedy the omission, not least in order to see what light is thrown on issues such as institutional leadership and cultic presidency. There follows an overview of the work of one feminist theologian, Professor Elisabeth Schüssler Fiorenza, on the basis that an in-depth presentation of one theologian is more helpful than a more eclectic overview. Moreover, Schüssler Fiorenza is eminently suitable for our purposes as she has Roman Catholic roots and the displacement of argument we have traced has brought us into Roman Catholic theologising. Furthermore, her interest in ministry originally brought her to women's issues. Above all she is primarily a biblical scholar and we are currently concerned with the interpretations of biblical texts.

Her book, *In Memory of Her*, created a great deal of interest when it appeared in 1983. No fewer than twenty-eight reviews appeared both in scholarly journals and in less academic publications.[18] As the reviewers include eminent people in the field, and therefore the main strengths and weaknesses of the book come under scrutiny, I thought it useful to site an overview of her reconstruction of Christian origins within the network of the reviewers' comments. This is intended to stand against the interpretations reproduced in the documents considered in Part One. It is also helpful to view it in the light of the strategies of opposition traced above, as history appears to have repeated itself not least in the theologising of dominant social trends to impede the liberating impulses of women.

3.1.1 *In Memory of Her*

The author of *In Memory of Her* (1983) is a New Testament specialist from the University of Münster, West Germany. She has held the post of professor in the theological faculty of the University of Notre

Dame, Indiana (*Docli* 398) and more recently of Professor of New Testament Studies at the Episcopal Divinity School, Indiana. She moved to Harvard Divinity School as Stendhal Professor of Divinity in the autumn of 1988. She was the first woman in her diocese to study theology and to do so needed the bishop's permission (speech to Women's Ordination Conference, 1978). Her early studies of the Apocalypse led her to ecclesiastical questions, and from the beginning she has been interested in the declericalisation of the church. Her doctoral thesis (published in 1972 – see Bibliography of references) arose from her interest in new models of the church, but the writing of it made her conscious of feminist issues and by 1972, when she participated in the 'Women doing theology' workshop in Grailville, she had claimed women's issues as her own (*CrossC* 459). *In Memory of Her* was developed as the result of lectures and seminars (*Fur* 203). Among previously published papers which relate to the subject are: 'Feminist theology as a Critical Theology of Liberation' (*Theological Studies* 1975); 'You are not to be called Father' (*Cross Currents* 1979); 'Word, Spirit and Power: Women in Early Christian Communities' (in Ruether & McLaughlin *Women of Spirit* 1979); 'Sexism and Conversion' (*Network* 1981); 'Gather Together in My Name: Toward a Christian Feminist Spirituality' (*Women Moving Church Conference Proceedings* 1981); and 'Discipleship and Patriarchy: Early Christian Ethos and Christian Ethics in a Feminist Theological Perspective' (in Rasmussen, ed., *The Annual of the Society of Christian Ethics, Selected Papers* 1982) (*CrossC* 459).

In Memory of Her: theoretical framework and critique

That the title, *In Memory of Her*, probably evokes for the reader the words of Jesus at the Last Supper (Lk 22: 19) (cf. *RevPhLou* 275), rather than his response to the woman who anointed his head and whose prophetic action he promised would be told 'in memory of her' (Mk 14: 3–9), lends support to Schüssler Fiorenza's argument that women have been erased from their place in history by an androcentric perspective or 'mindset' (*Amer* 353) which is the product of patriarchal 'false consciousness'. Her perspective is consciously emancipatory, that is, within this theology, feminist, and her intention, to empower[19] women to reclaim the centre of the *ekklesia* within which they have been marginalised through its progressive patriarchalisation.

While the insights of Heidegger, Gadamer, and Paul Ricoeur

have led biblical scholars to take seriously the historical 'strangeness' of the text, the prejudices of the interpreter and the interrelated effects of language, tradition and community, these insights have been limited in that they do not extend the critique to the cultural and socio-political context of interpreted and interpreter (*RelStRev* 2). The model of liberation theology has highlighted the presumptions of interpreters and texts within the context of class struggle, and feminist theology has brought into focus patriarchal structures and androcentric perspectives. But whereas liberation theology would root revelation within the biblical canon – for example the hermeneutical circle suggested by Juan Luis Segundo begins with the analysis of social reality and moves to reinterpretation of the text (*EAJT* 149) – Schüssler Fiorenza combines insights from the Frankfurt School with liberation theology, and her controlling insight is that revelation is located not in the canon, but in the ministry of Jesus and life of the community called forth by him.

Historically this is not the first feminist reading of the Bible. In 'Undercurrents' (Part Two, Section One above) I indicated some nineteenth-century political uses of biblical interpretation in England. In the USA Elizabeth Cady Stanton's *The Woman's Bible* was a reply to the anti-emancipation arguments of the 1890s, when proof texts were used to argue against women's suffrage. For her, as for Schüssler Fiorenza, the Bible *is* androcentric and political in its collaboration in the oppression of women, but the model used by each woman was determined by the contemporary stage of biblical exegesis. Cady Stanton (1895 and 1898) subjected the passages about women to an ethical critique which is at the root of the tendency to segregate passages about women in more recent studies – as was apparent in the documentation where a section on 'Women and Jesus' or 'Women in the New Testament' unfailingly appeared. Schüssler Fiorenza (1983) uses 'imagination' to reconstruct the submerged praxis of women behind and beyond the canonical texts.

Since Cady Stanton, feminist theologians have moved through a number of stages (in fact Mary Jo Weaver has identified six 'logical steps' (*CrossC* 455)), ranging from becoming aware of the absence of women in the field, moving through retrieving texts and traditions, and thence towards the construction of a new, feminist, symbolic structure and system of knowledge. Broadly speaking, feminist theologians fall into two categories. There are those, such as Mary Daly, who perceive the biblical tradition as irretrievably patriarchal. Daly views as anachronistic the revision of texts, and calls for new reality construction and vision.[20] In so doing, Schüssler Fiorenza argues, she ignores the history of the struggle of women for freedom in biblical religion and thus its liberating potential – whether or not biblical religion is acknowledged, its culturally imbibed power to oppress remains. The second category of feminist theologians seeks to re-form biblical religion by a drastic reinterpretation of the canon, and includes writers such as Trible, Ruether, and Schüssler Fiorenza. Schüssler Fiorenza perceives as 'neo-orthodox' the interpretive models of Ruether and Trible in distinguishing between revelatory essence and historical accident – rather as in the documentation the Methodists distinguished between principle and precedent. She argues[21] that such a model puts the burden of historical action on God, not women; that this model (unintentionally on the part of the users) idealises the biblical and prophetic traditions by not facing up to the oppressive and androcentric elements in those traditions; and that it posits an 'Archimedean point' which presumes a liberating nucleus in the patriarchal overlay (*RelStRev* 3). Spurred on by Johann Baptist Metz's 'Christian *memoria* [which] insists that the history of human suffering is not merely part of the pre-history of freedom but remains an inner aspect of *the* history of freedom',[22] Schüssler Fiorenza's intention is to uncover the history of women at New Testament origins. Her reconstruction, or writing (*JouRe* 83), both moves the locus of revelation beyond the texts to the movements behind them such that the New Testament is perceived as a prototype rather than an archetype, and also extends the scope of texts to include those which are not within the officially recognised canon of the New Testament (*Ecumt* 86).

Schüssler Fiorenza's views have had a varied reception. Her reading of New Testament origins has been described as a 'Hermeneutics of Reception' in its new and challenging interpretation (*ThStu* 729) which highlights the importance of the imagination the reader brings to the text (*Amer* 354), in this case by providing a female reader as a counterweight to traditional biblical reading (*SecCent* 177). Origen's view that the exegete had the liberty to reinterpret stories to make a case was mentioned (*JouRe* 84). Less sympathetic was Jean-Yves Lacoste, who found 'la thèse centrale ... s'avère hors d'atteinte de toute preuve' (*RelPhLou* 276). The French reviews listed showed less appreciation of Schüssler Fiorenza's heuristic perspective than did the Anglo-American, and it would be interesting to see if an extension of Baum's geographical divisions in his sociology of theology would throw any light on this. The one review listed from East Asia found the new paradigm of interpretation helpful in countering proof texts, which were used there in order to categorise women. This dogmatic approach on the part of the East Asian churches was seen as a defensive strategy in regions where the Christian churches represented only a tiny minority of the population. That these churches were firmly opposed to the ordination of women was apparent in the documentation.[23] Kwok Pui Lan, the reviewer, wondered if Schüssler Fiorenza's interpretive model was inclusive and adequate enough to integrate the struggle for liberation from the multiple oppressions of Asian women (*EAJT* 151).

A number of methodological questions were raised. Among these were whether yet another reconstruction of the 'historical Jesus' can bear the weight of the reconstruction and the reconstructor's purpose (*ThStu* 730); whether in selecting an extra-biblical principle of critique, Schüssler Fiorenza establishes a new canon within the canon and this fixes the principle in a new form of Roman Catholic neo-orthodoxy (*Amer* 353, cf. *Ecumt* 89); and how much historical accuracy can be claimed by theologically motivated history (*RelStRev* 6). These questions have been touched on by Cornel West. A dilemma which 'haunts' Schüssler Fiorenza's interpretive method and discussion is why, if revelation is located in the feminist struggling for freedom, and if the biblical texts are fundamentally androcentric, the adjective 'biblical' is used in 'biblical revelation'. West thinks that although she pushes us to the brink of the Christian tradition, she does not push us over the edge. Her implicit ontology and epistemology provide clues to the resolution of the dilemma. West distinguishes three basic philosophical strategies within hermeneutics relating to truth and justification. The first follows Hegel in perceiving truth in the depths of the historical process. The second is Kierkegaardian, incorporating the transiency of historical claims with the ultimate mystery of God in Jesus Christ. Third is Gadamer's historical perspective where the criterion for truth rests in the anticipation of perfection on the way to continually deferred unity. West argues that the third strand is present in Schüssler Fiorenza's work, yet she stops short of the (in this model, necessary) deprivileging of Jesus Christ, and at this point rests on Kierkegaardian ground. For Schüssler Fiorenza Jesus Christ is not subjected to a critique; he is 'a woman-identified man' with a particular vision of 'kingdom'. Such a presentation of Jesus Christ suggests the Christian confessionalism and a-historical moralism which Schüssler Fiorenza criticises in the neo-orthodox model and points to the fact that 'the Kierkegaardian-Barthian touchstone of modern Christian identity remains intact in Schüssler Fiorenza's work' (*RelStRev* 4). Thus the adjective 'biblical' is retrieved for Schüssler Fiorenza, concludes West, although he remains unconvinced that it follows from her new hermeneutical model.[24]

In Memory of Her: method and model of reconstruction and critique

Methodologically, Schüssler Fiorenza's first move was to examine the various stages of New Testament formation: translation, selection of traditions, canonisation, as well as their interpretation, which takes her beyond the New Testament canon. Issues of inclusive lanaguage, of the assumption that the texts refer to men when women are not mentioned, and of mistranslation are notable. Moreover, the methodological insights of form criticism, source criticism and redaction criticism[25] lend support to the argument that the church was not male dominated from the beginning, but that the lack of information on women and their initiatives was due to the androcentric 'prejudice' and redaction of the early Christian authors – indeed, one recalls a comparable situation in the Methodist documentation, where information about women preachers was censored out of the official magazines, and, but for Taft's work, would have been lost. New Testament discrepancies are seen to lend support to this view, notably those surrounding the attribution of the role of primary resurrection witness to either Peter or Mary Magdalene. Peter is preferred by Luke, but the struggle to cast Mary Magdalene in that role continued in the *Gospel of Thomas*, the apocryphal *Gospel According to Mary*, and the Gnostic *Pistis Sophia*, while the *Apostolic Church Order* indicates that the prejudice against Mary Magdalene attributed to Peter reflected an actual ecclesial situation[26] – an analysis with which Ross S. Kraemer agrees (*JouBibLit* 722). Schüssler Fiorenza argues that which texts were accorded apostolic status was determined by the result of the struggle of the patristic church with Marcion, various Gnostic groups, and Montanism, all of which were linked ministerially with women, and that it is in this context that women's leadership became identified with heresy. From here arises her description of the canon as the record of the historical winners, and her preferences for a more heterodox – or 'ecumenical' – approach to sources (cf. *DocLi* 398–400).

Schüssler Fiorenza's privileging of the socio-historical dimension in biblical exegesis is not novel as a method, but it is novel in its extent and perspective. Social models have been applied in recent years, notably by Robin Scroggs, S. R. Isenberg, John Gager and Gerd Theissen.[27] The first three have used the 'sect' model in order to throw light on the early Christian movement. While Scroggs has shown simply that this movement fulfilled the characteristics of a religious sect, Isenberg and Gager have added a millenarian dimension to the analysis. Isenberg links the millenarian character with the quest for religious power and Gager with the search for social power. Unlike Gager, Theissen distinguishes between the early Jesus movement and Hellenistic Christianity; he uses a functionalist model, relying on conflict analysis to reconstruct the Jesus movement, and an integrative model in his consideration of Hellenistic expansion.

These models have been critically considered by Schüssler Fiorenza (68–84). Despite their differences, there seems to be general agreement between the various studies about the a-familial and anti-familial character of early Christian groups. Schüssler Fiorenza would appear to have a good case in her criticism of Theissen's assumption that the Jesus movement was composed of groups of wandering charismatic men, as 'wives' are listed among those left behind only in Luke 14: 26 and 18: 29 (*DocLi* 401) (a revision of Mk 10: 2–9), and not in the earlier 'Q' ('Q' = *Quelle*, i.e. source) traditions (145). There is also agreement between the studies that Christianity as a sectarian protest movement existed for a long time. Gager sees the distinctive gift of Christianity as a sense of community, thus presenting as an a-historical ideal what was, arguably, the communal reality described in Galatians 3: 28. For Theissen it is 'love patriarchalism', whereby status inequalities are 'lovingly' accepted, which provides the binding power of Christianity, and in this he uses as his theoretical model the hierarchically ordered patriarchal family (*oikos* or *familia*). That the 'gift' of Christianity was the internalisation of the status inequalities of patriarchal society is questionable, as is the argument that such was necessary for the survival of Christianity. Sociological or political expedience became all too easily theological orthodoxy, and the cost was the gradual marginalisation of women within the *ekklesia*.

If the 'prejudices' of androcentric exegesis evaluate the 'success' of Christianity in sociological terms, and accept as 'necessary' the conditions for women which inevitably accompanied institutionalisation, it is necessary to find new exploratory models to make the emancipatory struggle of women visible in history. Among those on which Schüssler Fiorenza draws are sociologist Elise Bouldings' model of 'overlife' structures, which are male-dominated, and political and into which the 'underlife' structures sometimes 'erupt', which can be used to counter the church/sect model; classicist Marilyn Arthur's model, which charts social change in women's roles and status with respect to politics, economics, and social relationships between the sexes; and Sheila Johansson's work, which shows that misogynist polemics can be traced to the attempt by middle-class men to emphasise the 'natural' difference between the sexes in order not to be replaced by women[28] – in parenthesis, it is interesting to note that the move into symbolic argument in the documentation seems to have had a 'holding' effect. Such heuristic models suggest that when the social–institutional interaction between women and men was examined, religion functioned as a 'half-way house' between the public (male) state, and the private (female) household (90). Hellenistic religious cults and associations which were sited in the house had an emancipatory function as an individual choice was made to join them. It is part of Schüssler Fiorenza's thesis that it is this emancipatory function which drew women to early Christianity, and that these associations, rather than the patriarchal family proposed by Theissen, were the bases of the early Christian gatherings. Thus rather than considering Jewish, Greek, Roman and Asian women as 'background' (cf. *OWP* 16–18), the point is to consider how the conversion of these women intruded into the cultural patriarchal ethos and how far it supported emancipatory tendencies in Roman Hellenism. Both tendencies appeared in the early Christian movement, and the struggle lasted for a long time before women's leadership was submerged – yet it was never eliminated and has remained as an undercurrent into the twentieth century.

In Memory of Her: egalitarian origins(?)

When the Christian corpus is viewed from the perspective described above, a different interpretation arises from that described in the documentation.

Schüssler Fiorenza's 'very tentative and preliminary' (152)

reconstruction of the Jesus movement in Palestine perceived it as one of several prophetic revewal movements with which it shared the central concept of *basileia*, while differing from them in its non-cultic interpretation of associated symbols: the central symbol of guests at a royal banquet or wedding feast rather than a cultic meal as among the Pharisees; the understanding of holiness as the 'wholeness' intended by God in creation rather than sited in cult and Torah (although these were respected); and, ultimately, the refusal to conceptualise Jesus' suffering and death in cultic terms. The shift from cult to all-inclusive community as the locus of God's action meant that not only were large numbers of women likely to have been involved as they would have formed a large section of the destitute poor and social marginals, but also that the intervention of Galilean women would have been decisive in preserving and extending the movement after Jesus' death. Jesus is remembered as the female Sophia in the earliest texts, and then as Sophia herself, who is put to death because of the challenge to imperialism. Finally the pre-gospel traditions are interpreted as addressing patriarchal structures, examples including: the pre-Markan controversy stories on patriarchal marriage; the a-familial ethos of the movement and the rejection of biological motherhood; and the exclusion of the power and status accorded to fathers – with 'father' it is suggested the group associated the gracious goodness usually associated with a mother.

While the presentation of the inclusive and egalitarian character of the Jesus movement has been described as 'the most persuasive I have ever read' (*DocLi* 402), and 'the most important section [of the book]' (*JouRe* 85), doubt has been raised also about 'what might be called the "Camelot" view of Christian beginnings' (*SecCent 180*), and a number of reviewers raised questions about 'equality' (e.g. *RelStRev* 6; cf. *Horiz* 144–6), Marie Isaacs wondering if it is not 'a vision of the church to be hoped for in God's future rather than a historical reality of the past' (*Theol(BNS)* 484). There is little evidence either to validate or to invalidate conclusively Schüssler Fiorenza's reconstruction. Jesus' sayings *may* go back to 'Q', and *may* suggest that the structure of the group was not based on the paterfamilias model. Since the source 'Q' on which the New Testament writers are assumed to have drawn is also hypothetical, there must remain the uncertainty attached to any reconstruction of the Jesus-context. There is also the question as to how far any historical sociological analysis is possible. Yet these considerations must allow for the possibility of Schüssler Fiorenza's reconstruction. I would suggest that although 'equality' is essentially an eighteenth-century concept, a similar underlying challenge to institutions could have motivated the praxis of the community. Among other queries raised were Schüssler Fiorenza's interpretation of the Sophia motif (e.g. *LexTheolQuart* 59–60; *CathBibQuart* 568; *JouBibLit* 724–5); the contrast between God's healing 'wholeness' and the holiness in cult and Torah; and the point has been made also that a sacrificial metaphor, the Passover theme, underlies most Last Supper accounts.

In so far as the emphases in interpretation outlined above are accepted, their implications for the documentation are at least threefold. First, questions are raised about the validity of a ministry modelled on the cultic concept of priesthood; cultic eucharistic celebration as the primary task of ministry underlies the symbolic argument in particular in the documentation. Secondly, the arguments about the fatherhood of God and the maleness of Jesus must be modified by the Sophia imagery. Thirdly, the praxis of the early women would not appear in this interpretation to have been simply as 'helpers' – or as 'complementary'.[29]

In Memory of Her: patriarchal house code movement: prescription rather than description

The setting of the early Christian movement was the Jewish diaspora, and Schüssler Fiorenza identifies the Hellenistic cults and associations as the model of the early Christian groups. These were located in the house, and were in all probability structured on a patron/client relationship (hence *prostatis* in Rom 16). Women were predecessors and collaborators of Paul, and Schüssler Fiorenza suggests that some were more powerful than he.[30] These early Christians were inspired by Sophia-spirituality, and it is to this missionary-diaspora setting that the pre-Pauline Galatians 3: 28 belongs as part of this theology of the Spirit that engendered new – egalitarian – behaviour.[31] But Paul, Schüssler Fiorenza suggests, set in motion two patriarchalising tendencies. To the baptismal formula Galatians 3: 28, 'There is neither Jew nor Greek There is neither slave nor free There is neither male and female For you are all one' (208–18), he introduced minor qualifications in 1 Corinthians 12: 13 and 1 Corinthians 7: 17–24 (218–20), which were developed in the deutero-Pauline codes and the pastorals. The very existence of the alternative community in the midst of the Greco-Roman city was threatening to the institutions of the patriarchal family and state, and the codes interpreting these modifications were an attempt at accommodation with the dominant class – the counter arguments of women and slaves have not survived. Secondly, Paul opened the door to patriarchal imagery in describing his apostleship as fatherhood (cf. 1 Cor 4: 14–17) and in using betrothal imagery for the church (2 Cor 11: 2–3).

The interpreters of Paul, the writers of Colossians, Ephesians and the pastorals, dispensed with the commitment to an egalitarian community, and began a gradual absorption of the values of the patriarchal household and thus of empire. This strategy was intended to help in missionary work, and to reduce the possibility of persecution. Colossians, dated in the third part of the first century, contains the first and most precise household code within which three pairs are addressed, including husbands/wives and masters/slaves, and the subordinate 'half' is exhorted to obedience. The writers'/writer's principal interest is in the behaviour of slaves, and Schüssler Fiorenza considers E. A. Judge is right to discern 'the voice of the propertied class'.[32] Thus Galatians 3: 28 is 'spiritualised' and moralised, and the Greco-Roman household ethic is made part of the Christian social ethic. 1 Peter does not mention three pairs, but slaves, wives/husbands, and stresses the duties of the subordinate members of the household. No masters are addressed, so the majority of addressees would seem to be wives, or slaves in pagan households. They appear as a deeply alienated group within their society, 'exiles in dispersion' who were persecuted for belonging to an illegal religion. The code reads as an apologia for the Christian faith,[33] and sacrifices the new freedom of women and slaves so to do. But this strategy was doomed to failure precisely because the religion of the paterfamilias was being abandoned by these Christians. Among second-century writers Christians were attacked for destroying the household by attracting women, slaves, and young people.[34] Whereas the author of Colossians was interested in the good behaviour of slaves, Ephesians focusses on the relationship of husband and wife in marriage, which is compared with the relationship between Christ and the church. The traditional house code form is merged with the church-body theology and Paul's bride–bridegroom metaphor first found in 2 Corinthians 11:

2. This reinforced the patriarchal pattern of submission in so far as the relationship was clearly not an equal one; moreover submission was justified christologically.

In the second century ministry underwent significant changes. Whereas some theologians have detected a shift from charismatic leadership to institutional consolidation,[35] Schüssler Fiorenza described a shift whereby the charismatic authority of prophets and apostles and the community's power to make decisions were eventually all subsumed by local leaders. Thence three developments occurred. First, local church ministry was patriarchalised. According to Timothy and Titus, desirable behaviour in the household of God was modelled on the age and gender lines of the patriarchal household. In 1 Clement the Corinthian heads of households were praised for maintaining patriarchal order in the community, while certain female members were called to repentance for not accepting patriarchal values. Ignatius of Antioch took this development a step further by arguing that the bishop represented God the Father and Master and thus legitimised the patriarchal order theologically and christologically. Secondly, the pastoral office of bishop was merged with prophetic and apostolic leadership, which contrasted with the presence everywhere of prophecy in the early Christian movement. It is from this perspective that the substantial body of anti-Montanist literature that focusses in particular on the leadership of women can be viewed. Moreover, the struggle between radically different church structures influenced the selection of canonical writings. The rise of the monarchical episcopacy and the patriarchalisation of the early Christian movement resulted in the segregation and marginalisation of women, who were placed increasingly under the control of the bishop (285–315).

There is agreement with the broad sweep of this analysis among reviewers, William S. Babcock asks whether the church's decline into patriarchy was quite so thorough, quite so bleak, as Schüssler Fiorenza intimates, and attempts to extend her analysis into the 'patristic' period in order to uncover there the action of women (*SecCent*). On more specific points, Kraemer wonders whether it was not first-century synagogues rather than voluntary religious associations which were the model for the house-churches and whether such associations were in fact egalitarian simply because they admitted women, slaves and freedpersons (*JouBibLit* 724). Jerome Murphy-O'Connor asks about the consequences for a professedly egalitarian community if prominent women were attracted to Christianity because of the possibility of patronage and scope to exercise influence, and suggests that they themselves were in part responsible for the shift from egalitarianism to patriarchalism (*DocLi* 403–4). Lan wonders about the critical issues between the church and impoverished women, if fighting for leadership was an issue for these rich women when the pastorals prescribed limitations on their freedom (*EAJT* 152), although Schüssler Fiorenza has replied that her intention was not to imply that all early Christian women performing leadership roles were wealthy (*Horiz* 157). The answer to Lan's question has implications for many contemporary Asian, Latin American and African women.

Meanwhile, the women whose concerns are addressed in the documentation would appear to find themselves at the end of this patriarchalising trajectory, namely, under the control of the bishop rather than in the position of aspirants to the episcopate. The Church of England bishops in the nineteenth century brought the sisterhoods under episcopal control, and the Roman Catholic hierarchy of the twentieth century retains legislative powers over women's canonical communities. The limiting point in ministerial status in the Church of England is currently the office of deacon, although this may change, while in the Roman Catholic Church the exclusion of women from the ministry is officially justified christologically.

In Memory of Her: alternative movement and conclusion

There was another, divergent, movement emanating from Galatians 3:28 and converging in contemporary feminist praxis, which Schüssler Fiorenza terms the *ekklesia* of women.[36] While the majority of Christian communities succumbed to the patriarchalising influences, Montanist and Gnostic communities lent support to alternative, Spirit-guided ministries. Meanwhile the gospels of Mark and John (which was nearly excluded from the canon because of Gnostic tendencies) provided an alternative vision of community which emphasised love and service as the core of Jesus' ministry and as the mark of discipleship.

Discipleship in Mark is understood as a literal following of Jesus and of his example. Persecution and sufferings of the community are sited within the tensions of the patriarchal household (cf. Mk13: 12), which complements the Markan emphasis on those in authority being the servants of those of lower status. This community still experiences the fear of Mary Magdalene and the women as it struggles to avoid the pattern of dominance and submission that characterised the socio-cultural environment. Jesus' sign action in washing the disciples' feet, interrupted by the misunderstanding and protest of Peter, marks the alternative structure of the Johannine community. The Johannine Jesus advocated leadership and power through alternating love and service among the disciples among whom the special leadership of the twelve is never stressed. He celebrated the Last Supper with all his disciples, appeared to them after the resurrection, and accorded to all the power to forgive sins, to bind and loose (20: 19–23, cf. Matt 16: 18–19). Peter is implicitly contrasted with the beloved disciple, and although he is reinstated in the redactional Chapter 21, the bulk of the gospel points in the opposite direction. Discipleship and leadership in the Johannine community is inclusive of women and men, and women hold a prominent place in the narrative. This pre-eminence and its apostolic tradition caused consternation among other Christians (Jn 4: 27). The last woman mentioned is Mary Magdalene, who represents the disciples' situation after the departure of Jesus. Her great sorrow is turned to joy when she seeks (*zetein*) Jesus, and recognises him when he calls her by name.

Thus on the one hand the post-Pauline literature recommends adaptation to the dominant structures in order to ease the tensions within the communities, while on the other the primary gospel writers insist that such persecution and suffering cannot be avoided. The communities of the former claim the authority of Peter and Paul while the alternative communities point to Jesus' stress on the love and service demanded of all. For apologetic reasons the post-Pauline and post-Petrine literature limits women's ministerial roles, while the writers of Mark and John accord women apostolic and ministerial leadership. Historically the social and theological stress on patriarchy was victorious over the social and theological stress on love and service. But, concludes Schüssler Fiorenza, this cannot be justified theologically as it cannot claim the authority of Jesus for its Christian praxis (334).

I would suggest that Schüssler Fiorenza's argument points to deeper questions concerning the all-pervasive nature of patriarchal structures, which reasserted their dominance within the liberated Markan and Johannine communities, and which appropriated theologically symbols from within the patriarchal social fabric to legitimise the structural shift. The struggle within the structures, though related to economic factors, also stems from deeper, unconscious roots, namely, the way masculinity and femininity and their relationship to institution have been structured. Jesus' prophetic vision challenged not only patriarchal structures but also unconsciously appropriated and displaced symbols. That self identity must be restructured was, as I will argue, what was unconsciously at stake in the vision and praxis of Jesus and his community of disciples. It is to such considerations that we now turn.

4 THEORETICAL EXPLORATION OF ASPIRATION, RESISTANCE AND RESULT: THE RELATIONSHIP BETWEEN SEXUALITY, SELF IDENTITY AND INSTITUTION: AN INTERPRETATION

4.1 Symbols and praxis

4.1.1 Aspiration and resistance: unconscious processes and the documentation

In the introduction I pointed out that as women have sought to harmonise with the life and praxis of Jesus and his community of disciples, they have interpreted this impetus as aspiration towards ministry/priesthood within institutionalised churches. I have followed through this movement in three churches over a period of two hundred years. I have noted the recurring resistance, and have pointed to the operation of unconscious processes which are of fundamental significance.

I have shown that critical hermeneutics allows us to consider such factors as censorship, manipulation (cf. 'Strategies', Part Two, Section Two), as well as the force over people's minds exercised by 'false consciousness'. Habermas has drawn on psychoanalytic theory to disentangle these forces and orientate us towards the ideal speech community. This might be an appropriate point to cast a 'suspicious' eye over the documentation to see if any clues to the operation of unconscious resistance emerge.

Debate in the Methodist Church was characterised by an overtly rational approach. Underlying this, the existence of strong unconscious forces was indicated on one occasion by Dr Maltby, who remarked that 'the worst obstruction was that which was in the deep, subliminal parts of the mind. (Laughter.)'[37] While for Freud, dreams were the royal road to knowledge of the unconscious activity of the mind, in the absence of dream material he would settle for jokes to provide the signposts, and Mr Walters' facetious comment: 'Why, if a woman was not to be debarred from the ministry by the fact that God had made her a woman, why is she to retire if she gets married? Why did not he (Mr. Walters) retire from the ministry when he married? (Laughter and cries of 'Why?')'[38] is an interesting example. Habermas, building on Freudian theory[39] (Freud had stressed the social nature of jokes as opposed to dreams[40]), wrote:

> In our response to a joke, which leads us to retrace, virtually and experimentally, the dangerous passage across the archaic boundary between pre-linguistic and linguistic communication, we become re-assured of the control we have achieved over the dangers of a superseded state of consciousness.

The laughter, that is, betokens relief that 'identity and resemblance' are not confused after all.[41] That Mr Walters' joke was also questioned would point to a fundamental questioning of his basic assumptions, which could be taken for granted no longer. Such, of course, is but one example, but psychoanalytic method would claim that all such paths lead towards unconscious processes. Be that as it may, eventually in the Methodist Church a rational application of societal expectations of the relationship between the sexes in capitalist society prevailed, and the ministry was opened to women. Yet this decision was not based on a critical interpretation of the biblical texts, nor of societal forces. It was, I suggest, fundamentally a repetition of the assimilation–re-presentation pattern I have already noted, where the insights of women are subjected to this process by the institution when they can be resisted no longer.

In the Church of England the displacement from biblical to traditional to symbolic argument over the years suggests a constant underlying resistance. The debates drew on tradition and symbol, and analogously, 'secondary elaboration' was more successful in that the masquerade of the unconscious processes was safeguarded. 'Prejudices' about women and ministry in relation to biblical interpretation were re-viewed and even cor(r)-ected,[42] but the object of interpretation, the Bible, was not critically interpreted. For example, varying hypotheses about the existence of the contentious Pauline, post-Pauline and Pastoral texts were posited, but there was no consideration as to whether the writers themselves were prejudiced in the sense of acting oppressively – the tendency was to excuse the writer and to blame the women for over-enthusiasm. The perception of a liberating impulse on the part of women, subsequently repressed, was not a consideration. Similarly, when horizons were 'fused' in the consideration of traditional attitudes, these attitudes were related to the social context from which they emerged. An example cited was the patristic writers, but there was no consideration of their writings as a deliberate source of oppression against the liberating impulses of women linked with 'heretical' sects. When 'traditioned' meaning in symbolism such as the fatherhood of God was questioned, the symbolism was acknowledged briefly to be analogous, but any suggestion of change or any critical examination of the concept was resisted. In the Church of England documentation the most recent mystification was the settling of the horizon of debate around the symbolic, i.e. traditioned, meaning of sexuality and priesthood, with an emphasis on further exploration through anthropology rather than through critical sociology coupled with psychoanalytic insights.

The fundamental issue is that of unconscious resistance. Psychoanalytic theory is the only tool available to uncover unconscious processes, and among theorists, Freud's work is primary. His theory evolved from the initial insights of Anna O, who became the first social worker in Germany and devoted a major part of her life's work to women's causes and emancipation.[43] Freud built on the insights she had found during her analysis to develop a theory which has been described as patriarchal and circumscribed by Western culture. This last point was illustrated by the Jones–Malinowski debate in the 1920s, a debate re-examined more recently by Rosalind Coward (1980) from a Lacanian structuralist perspective. Freud stood in the scientific positivist tradition, and claimed to describe only what clinical practice revealed, and as he lived in the West and in a patriarchal society, not surprisingly unconscious processes were revealed through Western cultural concepts. I suggest that unconscious processes are a universal phenomenon, while their particular manifestations together with their interpretations are culturally relative.

4.1.2 Result: the limiting point in traditioned symbolism

Significantly both the symbolism of the priest acting *in persona Christi* and the Marian symbolism of the encyclical *Mulieris Dignitatem* (1988) offer a double-bind to women. The sacerdotal imagery appears to endorse the direction of the impetus of women because of the close linking of the priest with Christ, while on the other hand they are told officially that they cannot be an image of Christ at this limiting point of sacramental symbolism. For the Orthodox 'he became *man*' is significant with regard to ministry, and for this church means precisely what it says. The bishop represents Christ and is wedded to his diocese, a part of the 'church' which is conceptualised in feminine terms, namely, as passive and receptive. For the Roman Catholic Church the limiting point of this traditioned symbolic process is that a priest acts in the cultic eucharist '*in persona Christi*' and that only a man can represent Christ. Meanwhile 'woman' (and hence women) is required to symbolise the church, which could appear as organic and impersonal, but which is in turn imbued with ecclesiastically constructed Marian symbolism. Of course the political implications of such symbolism are not novel. I have already noted the timing of the institution of the Feast of the Holy Family in 1893, 1921 and of the Motherhood of the Virgin Mary in 1931 in relation to underlying currents of social thought and feminist aspiration. Quite apart from the politics on the one hand, and on the other the unattainability of the virgin-mother imagery as any sort of role model, the Marian symbol of mother has a deeper dimension. In *Mulieris Dignitatem* Mary's function as mother incorporating '*theotokos*' imagery is stressed. Her function is to offer Christ, and his ultimate subjectivity has to be differentiated from her 'otherness'. She is a function of him – the 'unselfish love' demanded of women in fulfilling their church-appointed role (cf. Bernardin (1977)) is deeply significant.

Not only mother–child imagery, but also sexual imagery appears (although it is claimed to transcend sex). In *MOW35* it was argued that the priest was sexless, and Professor Grensted pointed out the inaccuracy of such a position from a psychological perspective. Sexual symbolism is particularly apparent in *L'Osservatore Romano* articles, notably when Balthasar speaks of the masculinity of Christ in his eucharist, 'in which he, on a plane above the sexes, gives himself to the Church entirely as the dedicated seed of God –

and the participation, *difficult to formulate* [italics added], of the apostolic office in this male fertility which is above sex'. Again, 'woman' (and thence women) are required to differentiate the divine. Man becomes God, and woman provides the difference. Both these themes of mother–child and of sexual imagery are of significance in psychoanalytic theory.

So too is language. Language and symbolism are intrinsically entwined. Unfortunately an overview of linguistics and its applications to the subject is beyond the scope of this book. The fundamental importance of linguistic considerations to symbolism is everywhere assumed, however. This is an area which has informed some feminist praxis, and in the 1970s and 1980s there has been some very limited response. ICEL in the Roman Catholic Church, and recently the Church of England liturgical commission's report, *Making Women Visible* (1988), have initiated some moves to include women linguistically in liturgies. These moves (for a long time ridiculed and resisted) can be seen as part of the assimilation–representation process I have identified. Moreover, those changes that have been suggested or implemented have by contrast highlighted the masculinity implied in the phrase 'he became man', which is at the heart of the matter, by leaving it untouched. It could not easily be amended and the ikon argumentation retained. Significantly in March 1988 John Paul II turned down proposals from the Bishops' Conference of England and Wales to remove discriminatory language from Eucharistic Prayer 4 in the Roman missal. This eucharistic prayer revolves around the maleness of Jesus, and papal refusal can be construed politically *vis-à-vis* current debate on the ordination of women to the priesthood within the Church of England, where the ikon argument is being propagated by Rome – notably in Cardinal Willebrands' letter (1986) to the archbishop of Canterbury (GS Misc. 245).

4.2 A feminist method

Faced with this resistance and result, some women have diverted their aspirations away from institutionalised Christianity; others, such as Mary Daly, who has developed a new sociology of knowledge model, have decided that Christianity itself is beyond salvation. Others again have not been deflected from their aspirations towards ministry/priesthood, and others have reconceptualised their aspirations. I am in agreement with Schüssler Fiorenza's argument that what is liberating for women in past history must be saved rather than uniformly discarded. I would argue that a critical feminist hermeneutics cannot afford to jettison patriarchal history as recorded in texts, etc., or androcentric derived theories, but would view both with 'suspicion'. It would seek to uncover androcentric presuppositions/prejudices/traditions and related symbols, and would operate on the assumption that what purports to be descriptive is very often prescriptive. In tension with this critique would operate a 'sifting' process which on the one hand roots text or theory in its socio-historical context, and on the other uncovers the emancipatory tendencies on the part of women, which were embedded and often camouflaged in the work – for example, at Christian origins as noted by Schüssler Fiorenza; the attempts by women to enter the ministry in the modern times of weakened institutional hegemony; and, as I shall show, the flickers of protest discernible in Freud's case histories. If canonisation represented the record of the historical winners (Schüssler Fiorenza), tradition, I would argue, is the symbolic structure of the socio-historical winners. A feminist integrative–interpretive framework would aim to reclaim history/'reality' and hence its symbolic structure as the heritage of both sexes. What emerges, then, is a battle over symbols, dialectically related to the social context, where the unfreedom of women has roots which are deeper than those revealed by a Marxist materialist analysis and reach into the unconscious. If with Paul Ricoeur one accepts that I am not such as I think I am,[44] I would go further and assert, *pace* Ricoeur, that symbols, and that of 'father' in particular, are not such as they have been traditionally perceived.[45]

4.3 A new perspective

I suggest the following relationship between sexuality, self identity and institution. Related to economic structures, institutions determine cultural concepts,[46] and their androcentric identity requires a differentiator which is femininity. Women, to whom 'femininity' has been attributed, have remained a constant 'other' to this socio-historical androcentric trajectory. Such a tendency has not remained unchallenged by women, but because of the power of institutions their protests have been only fleetingly effective when institutional hegemony was weakened. When such moves were too powerful simply to be repressed (cf. 'Strategies', Part Two, Section Two), insights have been appropriated and re-presented (cf. the 'motherhood' emphasis following the suffragettes). Schüssler Fiorenza[47] has shown how women were gradually marginalised in the early Christian movement. As the emerging movement took on institutionalised structures modelled on the state, and the praxis of women was submerged, so the state appropriated the Christian movement and their identities were fused. When reality was perceived in terms of dualisms such as male/female,[48] the male priesthood reigned supreme. With the emergence of Enlightenment individualism and of capitalism, at the same time as supra-individual reality was separated off, so the self identity of the church came under threat, a development not immediately perceived, although unconscious anxiety had been apparent well before in the emergent stages of economic change, manifesting itself in phenomena such as witch burning, which significantly was linked with heresy. The Roman Catholic Church retains the medieval symbols surrounding its self identity, which are not mirrored in a social reality, and identifies itself, significantly, as a society apart; the Church of England, which split off for political reasons, found its eventual self identity in the English state, but this security proved ambiguous and it is currently looking towards Rome for its symbols; the Methodist Church, which eventually seceded for pastoral reasons, moved closer towards the Reformation position and acquired the associated problems with supra-individual reality *vis-à-vis* institutional identity. So whereas symbols surrounding leadership in Methodism and in strands of Church of England thought merge more easily with social institutional conceptions, in Roman Catholicism and Anglo–Catholicism the appeal is to traditional symbols, which coexist uneasily with present-day ideologies. Feminist theology, based on feminist theory, reveals the hope of something better for women; required is praxis through analysis – a rediscovery and re-presentation of symbols surrounding self identity.

4.4 The patriarchalisation of the unconscious

In order to get to the 'unconscious' of the matter, a tool is necessary which is not yet available. Critical hermeneutics points towards political liberation and can throw light on liberation theology more easily than on feminist theology. Habermas draws on psychoanalytic theory, as does Ricoeur, but both writers accept without question its androcentric presuppositions. In order to follow through the method I have suggested and view the material from the proposed new perspective, it has been necessary to develop a critique of psychoanalytic theory.

There follows an attempt to trace at once the patriarchalisation of Freudian theory, and also to show that this theoretical construction was not built without protest on the part of his analysands. I offer here an interpretation of the tension between these two tendencies in order to throw light on the relationship between sexuality, self identity and institution.

Freud's aspiration towards value-free description and theorisation was, arguably, ultimately a desirable ideal. Yet the assumption that such was possible meant that the description of the internalisation of patriarchal attitudes and their application in clinical practice became prescriptive. I have suggested that Freudian theory did not evolve without protest on the part of his analysands. I would argue that discernible in Freud's work are two trajectories. The first began with Anna O's discovery of her 'talking cure', moved through the childhood seduction theory, and *The Interpretation of Dreams* in 1900, and ended with Dora's premature departure from analysis on the last day of the same year. The second trajectory began with Freud's self-analysis following his father's death in 1896, moved through the Oedipal theory, intrinsically entwined with the shift from suppressed reminiscences to repressed desires as the roots of neuroses,[49] and hence to his exploration of childhood sexuality, and thence through a succession of male case histories to his writings on metapsychology, on feminine sexuality, and on civilisation and religion. The move from the first to the second trajectory entailed a shift from a more gynecentric to an androcentric perspective. The former brings to mind the liberating potential uncovered by Schüssler Fiorenza in the earliest Jesus community, which was retained for some time in the Markan and Johannine communities, and the latter development of Freudian theory and psychoanalytic practice can be compared to the patriarchal house-code movement, which developed into contemporary theologies and forms of worship. In the latter strand in each case the androcentric symbols of patriarchy are uncritically imbibed.

I shall argue that Freud's theory works psychoanalytically precisely because this false consciousness of women has been internalised by both sexes and given cultural credibility, and more over that it is in relation to this false consciousness and illusory identification that the male self identity is constituted. This father identification, being the androcentric perspective, will be interpreted in terms of the subjective power to define reality, and hence to define self and the difference-from-self which takes symbolism in sexuality. It is from the internalisation of this (for her) objective symbolism that false consciousness in women is constituted. Particular emphasis will be placed on the concept of identification on the basis that a father identification is unconsciously refused to the little girl. If the reader does not wish on this reading to join the psychoanalytic excursion, the thread is taken up again on page 286.

4.4.1 The first Freudian trajectory: from Anna to Dora

In Freud's writings the initial impetus is from clinical experience to theory. Here the enigma of resistance was determinative for Freud as it is for this critique. It was his failure to overcome resistance by hypnosis and suggestion that led him gradually to the free-association method and to his theory that the unconscious is structured according to certain laws. It was to the decipherment of these laws that Freud's efforts were henceforth directed.

Freud's earliest case histories were of women; the study of Little Hans did not occur until 1909. *Studies on Hysteria* (1895), published in collaboration with Joseph Breuer, contained the case history of Anna O[50] under Breuer's name together with the four case histories of Freud. Hitherto the fashionable subject of hysteria, which Freud had studied under J.-M. Charcot, had been seen as a function of brain research and entailed a positivistic approach. Freud's treatment of Emma von N shows him as being under the influence of H. Bernheim's method of suggestion, and his clinical manner and methods contrast with those of Breuer, who is with little difficulty persuaded by Anna O to listen to her thoughts. It was Anna O who coined the phrase 'talking cure' to describe the cathartic effect she discovered of talking through, under auto-hypnosis, the phantasies of her 'private theatre' that had come to her during her 'absences'. Other aspects of her method have been noted by Donald Meltzer:[51] she talked out the corresponding events of the corresponding day the previous year; she set as the time limit to her treatment an anniversary following her father's death (Freud later linked such timing of a cure with the mourning process); she traced back her current symptoms to their original appearance;[52] she linked symptoms and dreams; she investigated the problem of 'the unconscious'[53] and its relation to the powerlessness of her will to control her 'naughty' behaviour during her second state of consciousness. To this publication can be traced the seeds of Freud's interest in amnesia, unconscious resistance, the force of the sexual instincts, and the phenomenon of transference, and it is here that the first reference to repression in its psychoanalytic sense appears. The theoretical papers show that Freud had extended his 1891 criticism of the then fashionable theory of cerebral locations, by developing rather the theory of psychical locations and by attributing to each a character and operational mode.[54] He always acknowledged to Breuer the idea that the psychical apparatus is composed of different systems, but that each has its functional significance. He never acknowledged Anna O as inspiration and source of the theory he was to develop.

If the original inspiration belonged to Anna O, the early development of method and theory was through Freud's self-analysis. This followed his father's death in 1896. Until 1897 he had held to a childhood seduction theory (thus safeguarding the innocence of Victorian childhood), but he reached the conclusion that such was more likely to exist in the phantasy of patient and clinician than in the real life of the patient. This reversal took the form of an Oedipal theory intrinsically entwined with the shift from suppressed memories to repressed desires as the roots of neuroses. We should note in passing the significance of the shift to this critique. Here the reality shifted from the female patient to an internalisation of androcentric desire, and this shift, arguably, betokens great resistance to female autonomy. Whereas in a footnote in the *Studies* Freud had indicated that he was analysing his own dreams in the interests of interpretation, by this time he was exploring his own dreams with the purpose of self-analysis. This led to a strengthening of his hypothesis of a separation between psychical systems, and to the crystallisation of his historic discovery of an unconscious system functioning under its own laws. The theatre of dreams was not an extension of waking ideas, but was irreducible to any quality of consciousness.

The Interpretation of Dreams appeared in 1900. Although its evolution from Freud's self-analysis and its one Oedipal reference link it with the second trajectory, I have positioned it here because the important description of mental functioning in Chapter 7 is not linked with a theory of sexuality. Thirty-one years later Freud wrote: 'Insight such as this falls to one's lot but once in a lifetime.'[55] Dreams are the royal road to a knowledge of the unconscious activity of the mind, which operates under its own laws of the primary process, hidden from conscious thought by repression, but these strategies of desire can be deciphered by free association and by dream interpretation. Thus dreams are the fulfilment of repressed wishes which telescope desire and satisfaction by achieving fulfilment in phantasy. The meaning of the dream lies in the latent content, and each element becomes manifest by its own path, while the dreamwork ensures its disguise through the processes of condensation and displacement. This process is of particular interest because through it instinct is symbolically represented. At this point I would indicate two links with the second trajectory. First, in later editions as his theory of sexuality developed, symbolism received increasing emphasis, and secondly, Freud's identifying of certain basic symbols (he refers to primal language) has a-historical implications. Analogously one recalls Paul setting in motion the patriarchalising tendency already noted in 1 Corinthians 4: 14–17 and 2 Corinthians 11: 2–3. In the theoretical Chapter 7, the first topographical description of the psychical apparatus distinguishes three systems: the unconscious, the preconscious and the conscious, each with its own function, processes, affects, and systems of representation. Between the three systems censorship acts to inhibit and control any movement between them. Distinct laws of association give rise to mnemic systems, and the three systems must be crossed in order. The psychical apparatus is constituted between a perceptual and a motor extremity, and at this stage Freud saw its relationship to the nervous system as basically metaphorical. Associated to this topographic point of view is a dynamic view according to which there is conflict between the systems. There are two possible though not mutually exclusive aetiologies for this topology: on the one hand the genetic, whereby the agencies of consciousness gradually evolve and are separated from the unconscious system, 'everything that is conscious has first been unconscious';[56] and on the other hand the unconscious is constituted in terms of repression, and hence the notion of primal repression. Thus at this stage Freud had not opted definitely for the intervention of culture – whether or not subject to critique.

Dovetailing into the publications of this period appeared his 'Fragment of an Analysis of a Case of Hysteria',[57] which brings this first trajectory to an abrupt end. Although Freud delayed publication until 1905, the analysis took place in 1900, when he was completing *The Psychopathology of Everyday Life* (1901), and he described it to Wilhelm Fliess as 'a continuation of the dream book'. An exploration of the importance of two dreams and the peculiarities of unconscious thinking are Freud's dominating interests. Although he was by then convinced that hysterial symptoms had a sexual, organic basis, in the published case history he admitted there were 'only glimpses' of that organic side but that a way was paved for an exhaustive study of it another time.[58] Such an exhaustive study in the format of a case history of a woman never materialised, a fact perhaps not unconnected with Dora's premature departure, after which he did not publish another case history of a woman for fifteen years. His theory was sufficiently developed to mask Dora's protest at its imposition on data which would have required a more liberating interpretation, and which led to her departure. I suggest that Freud's interpretation rested ultimately on his working concept of what was 'masculine' and what was 'feminine',[59] and because of his failure to perceive femininity as the internalised male phantasy, his interpretation in Dora's case was descriptively accurate, but ultimately 'false'. I have reconstructed a deeper layer of interpretation among the already fragmented 'finds'.

Freud's Dora case re-viewed

This is a reconstruction of another layer of interpretation of the Dora case.[60] In this reconstruction the case is interpreted as Dora's defence of self identity, which took the form of an identification with her father because of his power over 'reality', i.e., the appropriation of subjectivity which he represented. This move had to be repressed, was forbidden, because of the normative androcentrism whereby female sexuality is phantasised and hence symbolised, and with which she had to identify instead. I discuss below the origins of this symbolism, the nature of the 'self' that is being defended, and the implications of the use made of this symbolisation of 'woman'.

Dora's father used his authority to bring her to Freud on account of her hysterical symptoms, dyspnoea, *tussis nervosa*, aphonia, and *taedium vitae*, and particularly over an argument following the discovery of a suicide note, and Dora's collapse followed by amnesia. The argument was over an affair with Frau K. that Dora wanted her father to terminate, and which he denied was taking place. The situation had been brought to a head by a lakeside proposal made by Herr K. to Dora, which she had angrily rejected and reported to her mother two weeks later, but which Herr K. described as phantasy. This was corroborated by Frau K., who had attributed it to Dora's overriding interest in sexual matters, which explanation had been accepted by Dora's father.

The importance accorded by Freud to the analysis of the two dreams make them an appropriate starting point. Dora brought as an addendum to the recurring first dream the smell of smoke, which, in line with his theory of the importance of forgotten elements, Freud diagnosed as masking particularly repressed material. He immediately made the link with his own saying, 'There can be no smoke without fire' (109), but Dora objected that the memory of smoke had accompanied the earlier appearances of the dream, and that not only were both her father and Herr K. smokers, but that she herself had smoked during her stay with the K.s by the lake and that Herr K. had rolled a cigarette for her before he began his 'unlucky' proposal. I do not reject Freud's view, i.e. that the smoke evoked the scene of the earlier kiss by Herr K., in which the smell of smoke would have been perceptible and to which Dora had responded by feelings of disgust, and that these feelings were in conflict with the more recent repressed temptation to yield to the man, feelings that had been transferred to Freud in the desire for a kiss during the analysis. But it is interesting that, beyond noting it, Freud ignores Dora's own association. I posit that it masked an identification of Dora herself with Herr K., and behind him with her father, manifested in this case through her smoking, which had been accepted by the rolling of the cigarette, but immediately deeply threatened by Herr K.'s words. Freud's counter-transference, in which he identified with Herr K., and behind him with Dora's father, led him to resist the identification (as Herr K. had done) by failing to see the implication of her own association, and by offering his own association and interpretation as 'the' meaning of this part of the dreamwork.

Support for this deeper level reconstruction may be derived from the dream as recounted by Dora. A key word was the ambiguous 'jewel-case', with which Dora first associated the fact that in spite of her earlier fondness for jewellery she had not worn it since her illness began. She then remembered a parental quarrel over a bracelet her father had brought her mother, despite the fact that her mother had badly wanted some pearl ear-drops, because her father '[did] not like that kind of thing' (104), upon which her mother had threatened refusal of the gift, and finally she remembered a jewel box given to her by Herr K. Freud eventually arrived at the interpretation that she was conjuring up her old love for Herr K., and that she was more afraid of herself and of the temptation that she might yield to Herr K. because of a deep love for him. Furthermore, the current appearance of the dream was attributed by Freud, because of transference, to Dora's warning to herself that the situation had once more arisen, and that she had better give up the treatment (106) – a diagnosis which proved accurate in the final part.

But again, Freud did not include Dora's first association: that she, though fond of jewellery, had not worn it since the beginning of her illness, and her linking of this with her father's 'gift' (104). Freud did not ask her why she stopped wearing jewellery, but her association of it with her parents' quarrel is a clue. It could also have symbolised for her the powerlessness of the symbolism of female sexuality, which could only 'receive' what was determined by someone else,[61] and which Dora had rejected by her illness. There is, of course, an economic dimension to the powerlessness of women, but here my concern is with repression. Freud moved from this dream to consideration of the interrelated enuresis–masturbation concepts, leading to Dora's reproach against her father for making herself and her mother ill, and the underlying self-reproach for her own actions. But he also pointed to the identification with her father, 'I have a catarrh, just as he has' (120), symbolised in her cough, and although she perceived her mother's attention to cleanliness as a reaction to the illness her husband had inflicted on her, Dora did not identify with her mother primarily, but identified rather with her father's critical stance, and resisted efforts to draw her into housekeeping, while attending lectures for women and devoting herself to serious studies (53).

Also arising from the enuresis–masturbation train of associations, Freud drew attention to Dora's admission that in childhood she had always followed her brother's contagious illnesses, catching them in a severer form, and this had lasted until the time of her first illness, at which point she had fallen behind him in her studies. This Freud described as a 'screen memory':

> It was as though she had been a boy up till that moment, and had then become girlish for the first time. She had in truth been a wild creature; but after the 'asthma' she had become quiet and well-behaved. That illness formed the boundary between two phases of her sexual life, of which the first was masculine in character, and the second feminine (119, note 1).

It was also the point at which Dora stopped wearing jewellery, and the point at which she took as a model the aunt who was intelligent, who had had an unhappy marriage, and who suffered from psychoneurosis (49). I suggest that this was the point at which Dora gave up her overt struggle to identify with her father, manifested in her modelling of herself on her brother, and that the then repressed struggle manifested itself in disguised form through identification with her father's cough. This easily reaches back to the scene to which Freud attached such significance, of Dora, still an infant, sitting on the floor in a corner sucking her left thumb and at the same time tugging with her right hand at the lobe of her brother's ear as he sits quietly beside her (85). Dora's behaviour here is unquestionably active. Freud had an ultimately deterministic working concept of 'masculine' and 'feminine' and was not in a position to perceive femininity as the internalised male phantasy of 'woman'. A further example of his determinism occurs in his discussion on the motives of illness, in which he cites an example of flight into illness on the part of a woman subjected to her husband – allowing not for the possibility of change, but only of knowledge, control, and hence of a little more happiness. Significant are his words, 'It is in combating the motives of illness that the weak point in every kind of therapeutic treatment of hysteria lies' (78).

Through analysis of the second dream it emerged that Herr K. had said, 'You know I get nothing out of my wife' (138), the same words Dora's father used about her mother, and that Herr K. himself had uttered to the governess who had subsequently given two weeks' notice, and whom Dora imitated in her notice to Freud. These associations, converging on Dora by the lake, and opposed to the identification in the cigarette, brought Dora sharply up against the unconscious demand to cede the power attached to male sexuality by identification with the father, and to become an object of desire by acceptance of the dominant symbolism. Her contemplation of the Madonna can be seen as of one she perceived as having attained power and retained subjectivity. Moreover, it was in the second dream that the phantasy of revenge in the form of her father's death had full play.[62] Freud makes little of the fact that it followed and symbolised the death of the aunt of whom she had been so fond, an event which must have affected her greatly, and could well refer to the annihilation of self which Herr K.'s words seemed to demand of her.

At no point did Dora object to the affairs of her father or of Herr K. until it was clear that she herself was being treated as a pawn in a game, as the story of her own governess illustrated. I would further argue that her much discussed 'homosexual love for Frau K.' (162, note 1) was, in fact, the effect of her identification with her father. This was the one identification she could not relinquish, and would also explain the erotic element in the relationship. It would also throw light on her desire to terminate the relationship through her father as her final revenge. These same most deeply repressed feelings would explain another fact that puzzled Freud: the fact that she made so little of her persecution by Herr K. When he took the key it was an act of power over her, whether he used it or not, comparable to her father's choice of a bracelet for her mother. If she dwelt on the persecution she would have to relinquish a deeper identification with her father – and with Herr K. Her disgust at the first kiss was at a deeper level the fear of annihilation at being made into an object of desire.

A brief word about Freud's counter-transference,[63] i.e. his identification with Herr K. and behind him with Dora's father. He sees Dora's mother through her father's eyes and although he has never met her he describes her as 'an uncultivated woman and above all . . . a foolish one' suffering from 'housewife's psychosis', and attributing to her some 'intolerable behaviour' on Dora's part (49). Herr K. he described as 'young and of prepossessing appearance' (60, note 2), which he linked with his own deterministic attitude concerning sexual stimuli in describing the fourteen-year-old Dora's rejection of an unsolicited kiss thrust on her unawares and in the dark as 'already entirely and completely hysterical' (59); and in his explanation of her disgust, he overlooked the fear of annihilation. He described Herr K.'s second attempt by the lake as 'unlucky', despite its effect on the eighteen-year-old young woman. He continually interprets Dora's love for Herr K. as the final truth, although he allows for its eclipse in the 1923 footnote by the theory of her homosexual love for Frau K. (162). But neither, I suggest, is the final truth.

Freud's unconscious motivation in the choice of the name 'Dora' can be read as corroborating my position. He named her after his sister Rosa's nursemaid, whose name, also Rosa, had been changed to Dora for the duration of her employment. Recounting the incident elsewhere,[64] Freud wrote, ' "Poor people," I remarked in pity, "they cannot even keep their own names!" ' Dora is indeed the analysis of a woman who took refuge in hysteria in order to protect her subjectivity, symbolised in her identification with her father as the cultural source of subjectivity and power, and to protect herself from the annihilation of self implied in becoming an object of desire. But in choosing the name, Freud unconsciously asserted his own power, removing her identity from her in a significant manner. Thus he took Herr K.'s revenge on her for her rejection of his proposal. Furthermore, in his discussion of the case he considered the hypothetical result of Herr K. being told of Dora's love, but decided to do nothing in the light of the possibility of a greater act of revenge on Dora's part. Be that as it may, protection for Herr K. was more heavily weighted than opportunity for Dora. Neither did he give her priority when he considered the question of pleading with her to continue analysis. But in spite of his motivation, doubtless his hunch was effectively correct; just as she opted for hysteria as the only path open to her to escape becoming an object of desire, so she walked out of Freud's treatment as the only means of side-stepping the annihilation of her identification with her father – and the smell of smoke provided a timely warning from her unconscious of the threat to this identification. Freud's determinism left her with no other option.

4.4.2 The second Freudian trajectory: the patriarchalisation of the unconscious

In 1897 Freud's self-analysis led him to replace his childhood seduction theory by an Oedipal theory from which stemmed a trajectory in which male case histories (which replaced female ones) interacted with his theoretical progress. Meanwhile the male Oedipus complex was uncritically taken as the norm, and led eventually to the formulation of the castration complex. A more or less parallel development was attributed to the female until the second theory of the personality led to a varying theoretical formulation. It was along this trajectory that his writings on morality, religion and society occurred. Bearing in mind my argument that his brilliant description was in fact the prescription of androcentric subjectivity through the imposition of a symbolisation of sexuality, I will indicate three markers. These were the ontogenetic, comprising the case of Little Hans (1909) in relation to the *Three Essays on the Theory of Sexuality* (1905); the phylogenetic material of *Totem and Taboo* (1912–13), where Hans appears again briefly; the drawing together of both in *Group Psychology and the Analysis of the Ego* (1921) in the light of the developed formulation of identification, which in turn influenced the second theory of the personality and his theories on femininity. As this programme includes most of Freud's work, in a subsection on this length it must forcedly be selective and schematic. I have placed greater emphasis on the earlier work, particularly on the case of Little Hans, which for Freud was very influential.

Ontogenetic dimensions: Little Hans opts for 'masculinity'

The *Three Essays*[65] highlighted the importance of pre-history, subsequently covered by amnesia, in which groups of themes later appearing in formulations of the Oedipus complex are found, and included a prototype of identification in the oral, cannibalistic phase. It also shows civilisation as built up by a process of 'sublimation' at the expense of the sexual instincts, which are diverted from their aims – institutionalisation demands instinctual renunciation. Freud was writing primarily of male sexuality, and not surprisingly in his eyes the case of Little Hans[66] provided the vindication, besides providing him with material for subsequent addenda. It confirmed the existence of infantile sexuality, and seemed to him to illustrate the principle of phallic monism, a pivotal concept in his later formulation of 'femininity'. It was the nucleus of a constellation of publications around that time: 'The Sexual Enlightenment of Children' (1907), where Little Hans appeared as Little Herbert; 'On the Sexual Theories of Children' (1908); and following the appearance of the case history itself in 1909 it influenced discussion on totemism and animal phobias in *Totem and Taboo*. Its importance in confirming his ontogenetic and phylogenetic theories points to a vital missing link: a case history of a Little Hanna.

The 1915 insertion of the sexual theories of children into the *Three Essays* was based on Little Hans. Here the sublimations of the latency period and the appropriation of civilisation were rooted in the instinct for knowledge and research, which on the one hand corresponded to a sublimated manner for obtaining mastery (for Freud a 'masculine' characteristic), and on the other made use of scopophilia, while its object was originally sexual. Such theorisation was activated not by theoretical interest but by external events, which were used as clues to the child's (*sic*) evolving theories (7: 192) – an example of occasional slippage in language. Freud thought that the denial of knowledge by adults brought in its train 'psychical conflict', which could turn into psychical dissociation, from which the nuclear conflict of a neurosis could spring. The sad example of Lili provided corroboration for the view (7: 178), while the phobia of Hans disappeared as items of information were accorded to him.

The case of Little Hans came after the failed Dora case. It confirmed the material of the *Three Essays* but it confirmed Freud's theory from an androcentric perspective. Freud was successful with Hans for the very reason he was unsuccessful with Dora: the little boy confirmed the initial insights he had discovered and his subsequent attempts to formulate a theory which were rooted in his own self-analysis.

The knowledge of one genital organ led Hans to the deduction that women were crippled – hence the crumpled giraffe – and this slotted in with Freud's footnote: 'as is so often the case with the sexual researches of children, behind the mistake a piece of genuine knowledge lies concealed. Little girls *do* possess a small widdler, which we call a clitoris, though it does not grow any larger but remains permanently stunted.'[67] Hence too Hans' fear lest he be made 'into a woman', which he saw as an undesirable possibility. Within these ideas lay the seeds which Freud later developed into this theory of feminine sexuality.

Allied to this was the theory of intercourse as a sadistic act performed on the woman (an observation doubtless fuelled by women's protests arising from fear of pregnancy). The importance accorded by Freud to the primal scene in the formation of neurosis is a recurring theme in his work. The first plumber phantasy would seem to confirm this, and I suspect that Hans' ambiguous words, 'because I would like to have children, but I don't want it', might well be connected with this syndrome, although Freud did not take it up. Moreover the giraffe 'sat on' or 'took possession of' the crumpled one, a perspective Freud accepted unquestioningly. There are examples elsewhere where he 'factually' discusses the issue in terms of taking possession. Unquestioning too was Freud's acceptance of the male sexual instinct as aggressive, and in the *Three Essays* he linked this to a historical need to take possession of an unwilling object – a thesis which reappears in *Totem and Taboo*. Hans' desire to violently break into somewhere forbidden seems to confirm this construction (Freud's interpretation of the incest barrier meets the 'forbidden' but not the 'violent' ingredient), but whereas Freud accepts this violent and aggressive wish as 'normal', he never offers a parallel example or hypothesis of the pre-pubertal desires of the little girl.

Meltzer[68] argues that Hans' masculinity complex was emphasised at the expense of his 'femininity', but he does not critically examine either concept. He remarks that Freud had noticed but showed little interest in Hans' 'femininity'. Janine Chasseguet-Smirgel[69] links phallic monism with the defensive amnesic effect of the splitting of the ego, thus eradicating the narcissistic wound common to all humanity which springs from the infant's total dependence on the mother figure: the conflict here is between the generations. Her hypothesis of the projection of power onto the father (here penis envy is common to both sexes) in order to differentiate self from, and overcome helplessness in relation to, the omnipotent maternal *imago* is of interest to the thesis I am proposing of the struggle between identification and differentiation, and, if correct, would provide the basis of a double-bind for the little girl to whom a father identification is forbidden.

In my opinion the evidence of Hans' identification with his mother represented in 'his children' was not primarily a compensation for his mother's withdrawal during her pregnancy (as Meltzer rightly points out). It was primarily a desire for femaleness interpreted here as the ability to bear children and exercise control over their production. It was not merely as Freud interprets it: identification in terms of object choice. However, Hans had to balance this with his internalised concept of 'femininity'. This he rejected in the first plumber phantasy, namely his 'realisation' that birth and intercourse were painful for women based on the sadistic view of intercourse and his sighting of blood coupled with his mother's groaning at Hanna's birth. This was symbolised in turn by the subjection of his mother to his father, who 'possessed' her. Indeed the case has many examples of the living out of 'masculine' and 'feminine'. The component instinct of sadism was activated in him as an extension of 'masculine' aggression symbolised in the beating phantasy and the teasing of his father (NB mental *vis-à-vis* the masculine; physical *vis-à-vis* the feminine). In the second plumber phantasy he overcame his womb-envy and appropriated 'masculinity', which was his cultural birthright on the basis of his biological gender. This was represented in the final phantasy where he cared for 'his' children in true patriarchal style, when the concept of 'having' them had been displaced. By way of a rider, I would add that the testing of his father, after the case, with questions to which he already knew the answer, evokes Dora's attitude to Freud. Both could be interpreted in line with Freud's theory as symbolising the powerlessness of the ignorance then imposed on children and young women and their uncertainty *vis-à-vis* 'reality'.

Phylogenetic dimensions: *Totem and Taboo*

The focus of Freud's attention moved beyond early childhood towards ethnology as analogous to the first stages of human development in his search for a 'first cause' in the constitution of the unconscious. *Totem and Taboo* (1912–13)[70] was the resulting attempt to bridge the gap between social psychology and psychoanalysis; to provide the phylogenetic confirmation for his theories rather as Little Hans had provided ontogenetic substantiation. Thus in order to formulate a hypothesis which would explain the two basic laws of totemism – not to kill the totem and not to have sexual relations within the totemic kinship – Freud drew on Charles Darwin's theory of the horde, where the jealousy of the oldest and strongest male prevented sexual promiscuity; on J. J. Atkinson's perception that the practical consequence of this was exogamy for the younger males; and on W. Robertson Smith's totem meal: 'One day the brothers who had been driven out came together, killed and devoured their father and so made an end to the patriarchal horde.' By eating the violent primal father, the object of their fear and envy, they achieved identification with him and each brother acquired a portion of his strength. The festive totem meal would thus seem to be a 'commemoration of this memorable and criminal deed, which was the beginning of so many things – of social organization, of moral restrictions and of religion'.[71] Ambivalence between satisfied hatred and remorseful guilt arose: 'deferred obedience' gave rise to the two laws of totemism, and the subsequent development of religion was affected by this ambivalence and guilt. The concept of God which had emerged 'from some unknown source', became attached to the totem meal under the guise of the father figure; meanwhile the family was the restoration of the primal horde. In time the totem meal became a simple offering, while the deity became so exalted that priests were necessary; the subjected sons further unburdened their guilt to the point where God demanded the sacrifice, symbolically, of himself.

Freud's own perception of the 'proven-ness' of the 'Deed' oscillated between a 'Just-so story' and the conviction that he had uncovered the 'first cause' relayed by the collective unconscious and transmitted to the individual through the inheritance of psychical dispositions. There follows an alternative 'Just-so story' on a deeper level of interpretation than Freud's, and it is intended no more seriously than is his. Freud's *Totem and Taboo* is based on the male Oedipus complex; in my 'reconstruction' below, women are the primary actors. Here the castration complex arises from an event, while identification with the group's symbol of power is forbidden to women:

> The women, resenting the oppression of the dominant male, came together to immobilise him sexually, and the mother ruled over the sisters and brothers. But the brothers, fearing castration themselves, united and overcame the women: they killed and ate the mother and divided the

women among themselves as spoils of victory. The women were not allowed to share the brothers' meal to prevent identification with the powerful mother, but nevertheless the totem was descended through the female line because it represented the mother. The horror of the brothers at their deed was such that the memory was displaced onto one of patricide. Thus the castration complex would arise from an 'event', would be activated at the prospect of union with a woman, initially the mother, and so symbolised in the incest prohibition. This would be the root of masculine ambivalence towards women – desire and fear – a fear displaced such that penis envy would have been attributed to women, and women would have assimilated this false consciousness partly to survive, and partly because the signifier of masculinity had become linked with power – but the path to power, namely identification with the father, was forbidden to them. The women, after their thwarted bid for freedom and now divided from each other, adapted strategically to survive and their unrest only emerged in flickers of protest, or when male hegemony was weakened, yet because of their own diaspora through exogamy they could not organise. Moreover, as androcentric culture evolved, women had only such systems of representation to express themselves – and survived by internalising that phantasy of women that was completely non-threatening to those who internalised it (passivity). Above all, the rigid insistence on a male God served by a male priesthood would screen a tremendous resistance to female imagery lying behind it, where the revived totem meal has links with the oral stage, thus reactivating the ambivalence of assimilation and differentiation on which sexuality had become 'hooked'.

René Girard[72] would retain the deed, but not the psychoanalytic interpretation and hence not the Oedipus complex, which in his opinion obscured the issue – that of sacrificial crisis and surrogate victim. For him the problem of violence and the sacred included sexuality, which was subject to solemn sacrificial prohibitions. His theory of the primacy of violence is an alternative interpretation of the androcentric paradigm whereby the original, sexual violence is by men over women, who are, still, the 'spoils' – and when he describes the breakdown of difference conducive to the sacrificial crisis, it is the breakdown of the status quo and of sexual difference that he cites.[73]

Towards 'Femininity'

Having traced the Oedipus complex first to its ontogenetic and to its phylogenetic roots, where the origins of society, religion and morality converged, in *Group Psychology and the Analysis of the Ego*

(1921)[74] Freud turned his attention to the dynamics of the group within this society. Family-linked relationships constituted the essence of the group mind concealed behind a screen of suggestion: his examples were the army and the Roman Catholic Church. He turned to identification to throw some light on contagion (the tie between members) and suggestion (the tie with the leader) and the difference between them. Identification, the earliest emotional tie with another person, operated when the small boy took his father as a model; he also developed 'a true object-cathexis towards his mother according to the attachment [anaclytic] type',[75] and by defining the latter as sexual, the Oedipus complex was the result of their convergence. Freud drew attention to the ambivalence of identification, rooted in the oral stage, and comparable to the cannibal's devouring affection for his enemies. He thought identification in the form of a perception of a common quality shared with another person who was not the object of the sexual instinct was the nature of the tie between members of a group (he would notice the cohesive and integrative effect of homosexual tendencies in groups as against disruptive heterosexual tendencies), while the emotional quality seemed to lie in the nature of the tie with the leader, concluding: '*A primary group of this kind is a number of individuals who have put one and the same object in the place of their ego ideal and have consequently identified themselves with one another in their ego.*'[76] The group was a revival of the primal horde, and the leader, the primal father whose freedom from libidinal ties recalled the Superman of Nietzsche's future. Individual psychology evolved from group psychology; nowadays, Freud added, people were members of various groups and shared in numerous group ideals – they also rose above the group towards a little independence and originality, ideas he would return to in his writings on culture.

Primarily to explain the occurrence of the varying identifications which constitute the personality and the permanent structures they leave behind, in 1923 Freud superimposed the id, ego and super-ego, all of which have anthropomorphic characteristics, on his first topology of the unconscious, preconscious and conscious. He bracketed the super-ego with the id and part of the ego as unconscious, and thus the unconscious is not only characteristic of the repressed, but also of the operations by which societal imperatives, initiating from the parental agency, are internalised. Freud derived this second study in part from his studies of melancholia, where he had perceived how a lost object could be internalised and the object-cathexis replaced by an identification. This operation, together with the desexualisation which accompanies it, is the key to all sublimation. He posits its equivalent in the Oedipus complex, which the little boy resolves by identification with the father, which takes the place of his wish to supplant him; the erotic object is mourned, the parents are abandoned as erotic objects, and are internalised and sublimated. The shift in emphasis in the use of identification between *Group Psychology* (1921) and *The Ego and the Id* (1923)[77] has been noted by Girard:[78] the boy's identification with the father in the former work suits his own theory of the mimetic nature of desire and rivalry as the source of violence. In the latter, he argues, Freud does not specifically repudiate the mimetic elements, but in mentioning the mother first he removes the causal connection and opts for object-choice such that identification is interpreted as the internalisation of prohibition resulting in the repression of desire. Again, he argues, Freud obscures the issue, this time by the insertion of the flash of incest–patricide desire subsequently repressed, as the experience of a violent refusal of mimetic desire would be sufficiently traumatic to account for the link between desire and violence.

A year later, for the first time, Freud laid theoretical emphasis on the differing sexual development of little girls. In 'Some Psychical Consequences of the Anatomical Distinction between the Sexes' (1925)[79] the central concept in the development of the little girl was 'penis-envy', and its corollary, the 'masculinity complex': 'Thus a girl may refuse to accept the fact of being castrated . . . and may . . . behave as though she were a man.'[80] From her narcissistic humiliation arose a sense of inferiority: 'She begins to share the contempt felt by men for a sex which is the lesser in so important a respect, and, at least in holding that opinion, insists on being like a man.' From here her desire moves in a penis–baby trajectory and she adopts the father as a love-object although there is a risk of a later identification with him when it has to be abandoned, which would mean fixation in the 'masculinity complex'. Not surprisingly this paper led to the great theoretical debates of the 1920s and 1930s, the eddies of which are with us still.[81] This led to the acknowledgement by Freud for the first time of an intense pre-Oedipal attachment of the little girl to the mother, which he interpreted as an ambiguity, a fear of being killed and devoured by the mother. Two years later in

'Femininity' (1933)[82] he returned to the recurring problem of defining 'masculinity' and 'femininity', urging caution, but still repeating his tendency to link character traits with a specific sex: 'The suppression of women's aggressiveness which is *prescribed for them constitutionally* and imposed on them socially [italics added]'[83] assumes a wedge between women and aggression – which, of course, links in with Girard's position. He addressed himself to the question of how a woman came into being from a child with a bi-sexual disposition, 'a little man', quite as aggressive as her male counterpart, particularly as there did not seem to be any inherent attraction between the sexes. He thought the girl blamed her mother for the anatomical distinction, to which was linked envy and jealousy, which in turn implied a weaker super-ego, capacity for sublimation, and entry into culture.

I have suggested that Freud's theory of female sexuality was an addendum to his general theory, which was derived primarily from male case histories, and that it grew out of his second theory of the personality, after he had opted for the intervention of culture. His perception of culture was ultimately uncritically androcentric, and he applied its concepts as to what character traits constitute 'masculine' and 'feminine', hence attributing as 'masculine' any appropriation of initiative on the part of the female, to whom any identification with the father was forbidden. Freud's brilliant achievement is his description of the unconscious androcentric phantasy of 'woman', which is internalised by both sexes and whence is derived the dominant paradigm which underpins ideological formulations including the theological.

5 CONCLUSIONS AND DIRECTIONS FOR FURTHER EXPLORATION

At issue is a struggle for self identity, a struggle dating from a very early stage between symbolic identification to extend the boundaries of the self and symbolic differentiation to maintain boundaries which guarantee difference. This conflict of desire between difference and identification is at the root of ambivalence and aggression; at a very early stage it becomes fused with sexuality, which epitomises unity–difference, but it nevertheless precedes it; aggression here is not necessarily a 'masculine' character trait as Freud ultimately thought.

Another factor coming into play is that of unequal force, and in the face of greater violence the weaker would turn aggression inwards – hence the roots of the 'masochism' Freud linked with femininity. This would enable the more powerful to extend their identifications, and to define and impose difference; to appropriate subjectivity and to demand objectivity as this difference. This marking out of boundaries would require psychic negotiation, resulting in an androcentric paradigm and derived symbolic structure which appropriated language and culture and which imposed femininity on femaleness and appropriated masculinity for the male – exogamy coupled with patrilocality and patriliny would be an appropriate symbol, while to the little girl a father identification as the epitome of subjectivity would be forbidden. I have attempted to show how such is not achieved without resistance. The same argument would apply in the case of groups/institutions – Freud's argument about the threat of heterosexual relations to groups could be read as a threat to the boundaries of subjectivity.

I argued that a critical feminist hermeneutics would be anchored in the social context, and here I would draw on the work of Foucault, who has sited Freud within the development of discourses on sexuality, discourses which aim at power and control. This development coincides with the Enlightenment and has been linked with capitalism, but it is on individualism that I have placed the primary emphasis. Because of individualism the symbolism of sexuality was no longer fundamentally linked to institutions, and was potentially 'floating freely'. This was an implicit threat to the theological and liturgical structures which had been developed when Christianity was patriarchalised in line with the dominant institutions and the state was Christianised. While the Methodist Church and the Church of England could derive their self identity from the state, although the Enlightenment rejection of supra-individual reality brought in train its own problems, the Roman Catholic Church defended its self identity with the traditioned symbolic structure of other times, namely, in terms of institutionalised sexual difference. It is from this perspective that current moves in the Church of England in particular, inspired by the Roman Catholic position, to 'explore' sexuality in relation to the ministry would be viewed with suspicion.

Discourses can be used not only to control, but also to liberate. Elsewhere[84] I have linked this critique of Freudian theory with a critique of ideas expressed by Ricoeur to suggest that Jesus unerringly put his finger on the central cultural concept when he prayed, 'Abba, Father'. I argue that the paterfamilias was the all-powerful symbol of the dominant and oppressive culture, and the familiarity of Jesus' prayer in the use of the informal word 'Abba' reversed and subverted its meaning. *This would imply, not that the father symbol is the most revealing metaphor for God, but that central to the praxis of Jesus was the reversal of the dominant symbol of oppressive subjectivity.* I therefore suggest that the concept of God, so closely linked with the identification–differentiation pattern, needs to be unhooked from its links with sexuality. This in turn would affect symbols of institution and leadership. Attempts to reintegrate the father symbol in hermeneutics, notably by Ricoeur in 'Fatherhood: From Phantasm to Symbol',[85] would be viewed with suspicion. Based on the male Oedipus complex, Ricoeur's work describes the development of the dominant paradigm. A 're-view' of language is of more fundamental importance than ministry as an object of feminist concern, and it is not accidental that sections of the documentation revealed greater resistance to such a proposal expressed in greater ridicule/avoidance of it.

Freud's argument that the concept of God became linked early with the symbol of father is persuasive. As the authority of God and the guilt of 'his' subjects resulted in an ever-widening rift between the two, so the necessity of a masculine sacrificing priesthood was required to bridge the awesome gap. As the subjectivity of God is seen in terms of masculinity, which is shared by the 'brothers', the sexual 'otherness' of women (symbolised non-subjectively as 'woman') is emphasised – leading eventually to female purity taboos.[86] It is in this context of sexuality hooked to subjectivity[87] that the admission of women to the priesthood would be seen as a threat to 'the nature of the Church', as was argued in the documentation. It is also from this context, I would argue, that the overtly sexual symbolism that is attached to the church and its symbolic liturgical structure, particularly in Martelet's article but in the Roman Catholic material generally and to some extent in the Anglo–Catholic, originates. From this same critical perspective, arguments in favour of the ordination of women on a 'complementary' basis would be viewed with suspicion, and I would extend this argument to those contemporary women's liturgies which emphasise female sexuality – for example those constructed around the symbolism of birth. Moreover, the actual admission of women for example into the Methodist ministry, and more recently into the Church of England diaconate and probably soon to 'higher' ministries, can be viewed as part of the assimilation–re-presentation process I have underlined, which absorbs and diffuses protest. The great plasticity of the unconscious is capable of multiple displacements along multiple dimensions of symbols, and thus of varied forms of resistance and adjustment.

Schüssler Fiorenza's reconstruction of the earliest strata within the gospels appeared to show a rejection of patriarchy and a reversal of its 'father' symbol, which emanated from Jesus. This reversal was a move, not into the gentleness generally associated with a mother *per se*, but towards a detachment of power and 'masculinity' from the representation of subjectivity. Held out was the hope of a resolution of the differentiation–identification struggle, but one requiring a displacement of repressed and unconsciously activated symbols. Offered to women and men was a dialectical relationship to the group, expressed in a feast between equals – it is here that I would site Galatians 3: 28. Bearing in mind the challenge this represented to the subjectivity of the institution, the strength of the unconscious forces activated into resistance would come as no surprise.

EPILOGUE

'Neither in Rome nor in Lambeth will you worship . . . but in spirit and in truth' is a conclusion. Indeed, many women are no longer asking for the 'power' of eucharistic presidency, but within alternative groups are discovering within themselves the power they already have to so preside.

At the beginning of this book I suggested that the aspirations of women to identify with the life and praxis of Jesus and his community of disciples had been diverted towards institutionalised roles such as priesthood, which misrepresent that original impetus, primarily at women's expense. At the unconscious of the matter are institutionalised power relations which from earliest times hooked subjectivity to masculinity, epitomised in a 'father' identification, and projected ultimate subjectivity onto the 'fatherhood' of God; simultaneously femininity became what-differentiates-the-subject. Any attempt to rectify these identifications and projections meets with tremendous resistance as self identity is threatened. Analogously one recalls the entry of tanks into Tiananmen Square, when institutional hegemony – the power and ideology – were challenged; similarly psychical 'hardware' is brought to bear on the liberating impulses of women. Alternatively, when these impulses can no longer be repressed, they are partially assimilated and the status quo re-presented. Schüssler Fiorenza began to uncover the liberating impulses of women at New Testament origins, and showed how institutionalised power relations reassumed their supremacy soon after Jesus' death. A masculine priesthood appeared to be justified later by ikon argumentation. The resumption of these power relations was not completely successful however; they are weakened and reforged as they are analysed and re-cognised. That knowledge is power is true both of China and of the unconscious processes.

A great deal of thought is necessary about inspiration and praxis within emerging groups and their relationship to reconstructed institution. Such thought could ensure that church his-story is retold and redirected, so that the words of the Johannine Jesus to the woman of Samaria recorded in John 4 do not appear a desirable alternative – or remain a desirable ideal.

APPENDIX A

THE US CONNECTION

I METHODIST CONNECTIONS

The interaction between the early Methodist connexions and the Society of Friends has been noted, and in collections of lives of female preachers the English and American experiences are interwoven. Before briefly considering two strands of American Methodism, an equally brief look at the Friends would be appropriate. Here two issues are of interest: the ministry of women and women's meetings. From the beginning George Fox supported the right of women to speak during worship, and his first interruption in a 'steeplehouse' was made in defence of a woman silenced by a pastor.[1] The right to speak was taken up eloquently by Margaret Fell.[2] Within the society women had from the start an equal opportunity to so minister. In Victorian times, interestingly, they outnumbered men,[3] but as the role of pastor became more institutionalised over the next hundred years, the men came to outnumber the women. As preaching was essentially a lay role, power in the society was concentrated in its Yearly Meeting.[4] In 1671 Fox set up the women's monthly and quarterly meetings to come together at the same time as the men's. Opposition from Protestants led to some diffidence on the part of the women, who received encouragement from the Yearly Meetings of 1675, 1691, 1707, and 1744.[5] At the Yearly Meeting of 1697 leave was given to women ministers to hold a meeting by themselves the following day, and the same year it was agreed that in future they could sit with their brethren at the Yearly Meeting of ministers. Yet in 1701 an incipient meeting of women ministers was suppressed, and women were cautioned against too much speaking.[6] In England a women's yearly meeting was not established until 1784. This notwithstanding, the (men's) Yearly Meeting remained the authoritative body. In America women's yearly meetings had been in general use, though with limited powers, and it was with American support and encouragement that the 1784 move came about.[7] In the early Victorian period the unequal arrangement was generally acceptable, but by the 1870s the subjection of women was no longer taken for granted. From 1907 joint sittings were gradually adopted in England: in America such joint sittings had been the practice from 1875 to 1885.

A brief excursus into American Methodism uncovered some interesting points. In the Methodist Episcopal Church (North) Maggie Newton Van Cott was the first woman licensed to preach in 1869. The issue was taken up by Conference in the same year, but sanction was not given to the licensing of women as preachers.[8] In 1880 the office of deaconess was instituted in the church, but the same Conference rejected an appeal to vote on the recommendation to grant orders to Sister Anna Oliver.[9] In 1903 it was again stated that women should not be licensed to preach.[10] Then in 1924 it was agreed to recognise women as local preachers, but ministerial rights and privileges were not granted to them.[11]

In the humbler Methodist Protestant Church, Anna M. Shaw was elected to eldership in 1880, but the move was declared 'unauthorised' by the Judiciary Committee, although the New York Conference continued to recognise her work.[12] In 1892 General Conference recognised Eugenia F. St John as an elder. Effectively the matter was left in the hands of Annual Conferences, and if a woman changed her Conference she had no guarantee of recognition by another. Women ministers in the Methodist Protestant Church, unlike their Methodist Episcopal sisters, were given appointment, pension, and Annual Conference membership rights equal to male clergy.[13]

In 1939 at the uniting Conference of the three main branches of Methodism, full Conference membership for women ministers was narrowly defeated. Subsequently the presence of the Methodist Protestant women proved somewhat embarrassing, but their membership continued to be recognised although other women were not admitted.[14] There was no change in official policy until in 1956 General Conference granted women limited clergy rights. It was not until 1968 that they received full clergy rights.[15]

2 PECUSA AND THE CHURCH OF ENGLAND

The issue emerged in the Protestant Episcopal Church in the USA during the same (second) period as in the Church of England. In

1885 the bishops of Alabama and New York 'ordered' deaconesses with the laying on of hands. The status and function of such deaconesses were the subject of debate until the 1940s. That 'women of devout character and proved fitness' should be unmarried (amendment by the house of deputies, 1889) was a resolution that carried the day,[16] and continued to be a condition, though occasionally challenged, throughout this period. In 1919 (the year of *MOW19*) a joint commission was appointed to consider how to adapt the office of deaconess to current church tasks,[17] and in the spirit of Lambeth Conference 1920 it produced a progressive report in 1922, but the proposed canon was referred back by the General Convention. The reasons given for the referral were: that a canon was not a place for statements with respect to ecclesial history and policy; that the proposed canon implied that the deaconess should bear sole responsibility for various functions rather than continue in the role of assistant – indeed there was the possibility that she might preach 'greatly to the displeasure and distress of many devout worshippers'.[18] The self-described 'restrained and conservative' conclusions of the consequent 1925 report made clear that the deaconess should not attempt to emulate a man but should make proper use of 'those feminine qualities and gifts' peculiar to a woman.[19] In 1934, in the wake of Lambeth Conference 1930, majority and minority reports were produced, the minority dissenting from the substitution of 'making addresses' for 'preach', and the inclusion of the phrase 'unmarried or widowed'.[20] Some debate in the 1940s led to the reiteration of the 1930 Lambeth Conference resolution that the deaconess order was the only order of the ministry open to women.[21]

The third period in this church was marked by the entry of women into the diaconate and the presbyterate. Each institutional step was preceded by unendorsed action by certain bishops, in 1965 and then in 1974. In 1964 some movement was indicated by the dropping of the words 'unmarried or widowed' and the use of the word 'ordered',[22] but deeds outmatched words when in 1965 Bishop James A. Pike of California declared deaconesses to be within the diaconate and recognised Deaconess Phyllis Edwards as a deacon by virtue of her prior ordination as a deaconess. In a San Francisco ceremony he conferred on her the New Testament and stole, the historic marks of the diaconate.[23] In 1970 the General Convention declared deaconesses to be within the diaconate.[24] The same year, following a 1966 report on the ministry of women[25] (the same year as *WHO*), a resolution in favour of the ordination of women was defeated in the house of deputies.[26] Consequently the house of bishops referred the issue to a special meeting in 1971, where they appointed a new committee to undertake an 'in-depth study' (which appeared in the same year as *OWP*) prior to the General Convention of 1973.[27] At this 1973 Convention the house of bishops reaffirmed the principle of the ordination of women, but the motion was defeated again in the house of deputies as a result of the rule which counted 'divided' votes with the 'noes'. The house of bishops also affirmed the principles of collegiality and mutual loyalty in the light of certain 'rumours' – rumours which proved to be well founded and indicative of the developments which resulted in the Philadelphia ordinations.

In that city, in July 1974, eleven women were ordained to the ministry, without the approval of the General Convention. Although subsequently in 1976 a motion in favour of the ordination of women was carried in both houses, the General Convention was left with two problems before it. The first comprised those who had been ordained before the motion to ordain women was legally carried, and what to do about them. After debate, in which argument was polarised broadly between promptings of the Spirit on one hand, and ordination in and for the community on the other, two options were proposed: either a 'completing' ceremony, or else 'conditional' ordination.[28] The second problem lay in what to do about those who dissented from the majority vote: although dissenting statements were read in both houses the problem was not contained there. In September 1977 the Congress of Concerned Churchmen was held in St Louis, bringing together about 1,800 people, and from this meeting emerged the Anglican Church of North America, which later adopted the title of the Anglican Catholic Church. At that first meeting the congress affirmed its determination 'to continue to confine ordination to the priesthood and the episcopate to males'. In 1980 this church incorporated about two hundred parishes and five bishops; there was also a women's religious order and a male Franciscan order which had a third order for men and women; no deaconess (*sic*) existed although the opening was available.[29] Undeterred, in 1988 PECUSA took another forward step and elected the Reverend Barbara C. Harris as the first female bishop in the Anglican Communion. She was consecrated in Boston on 11 February 1989. Present at the ceremony was the Reverend Florence Li Tim Oi, who was the first woman to be ordained priest in the Anglican Communion in 1944.

The ripples caused by American decisions and actions spread across the Atlantic. The refusal by the General Synod of the Church of England to remove legal barriers to the priesthood in 1975 and 1978 ensured continuance of the debate and the possibility that if women legally ordained in the USA came to England there might be breaches of canonical discipline. In October 1977 an invitation to officiate at services in their churches was extended by the Reverend Ian Harker and the Reverend Alfred Willetts to the Reverend Alison Palmer, and the ensuing service resulted in public reprimand from the archbishops of the Church of England.[30] Then, perhaps more seriously, the Reverend Elizabeth Canham returned from New Jersey, where she had been legally ordained in December 1981, to her home in this country. She was the first Englishwoman to become an Anglican priest. Her practice of celebrating the eucharist in private houses was viewed with some displeasure, and her action in conducting a communion service in St Paul's Deanery was described by Dr Graham Leonard, the bishop of London, as 'unauthorised'.[31] Six months later General Synod agreed to prepare legislation to allow women lawfully ordained abroad to celebrate the eucharist in this country. The story did not end happily as this legislation was put under article 8 and did not achieve the required two-thirds majority in all three houses at final approval stage in 1986. The issue became the subject of media attention once again when in 1988 the Reverend Suzanne Fageol of Chicago was reported to be conducting communion services at St Benet's Chapel, the University of London. She claimed that technically speaking such services were not officiated in accordance with the liturgy of the Church of England because the text had been amended to address God as 'she'. The situation again attracted the attention of Dr Leonard and the group of women and men was evicted from the chapel.

Thus events relating to the Church of England and to the Protestant Episcopal Church in the USA were confined broadly to two similar periods. Significant reports appeared at about the same times. In the course of the second period they were produced in 1919 and 1922, and then in 1935 and 1934 respectively and were aimed at informing the deaconess debate; those of 1966 and 1972 in both churches were within the third period and engaged firmly with the issue of ordination.

In the USA dissident action preceded Convention decisions with respect to both the diaconate and the presbyterate, while in the Church of England any such action was not concerned directly with ordaining people but was associated with the presidency of legally ordained priests from abroad, although this too influenced the decisions of Synod. Moreover, in the USA the ordination of women led to the founding of a dissident church, and although in England such a move has been the implied threat of Dr Leonard, the break with the Established Church of this country could have different (e.g. economic) implications from a break from the Protestant Episcopal Church in the USA.

APPENDIX B

BIBLE CHRISTIAN 'FEMALE ITINERANTS' AS LISTED IN CONFERENCE *MINUTES*

The names are listed in order of appearance in the *Minutes*. Italicised dates indicate years 'on trial'; a break for whatever reason (which could simply be an oversight) is signalled. In the third column I have also drawn on Beckerlegge's *United Methodist Ministers and their Circuits*; comments and dates taken from there are given in brackets with a page reference.

Elizabeth Dart	1819–32	(1832 Mevagissey supernumerary; B62.)
Betsy Reed	1819–20	
Elizabeth Gay	1819	'desisted' *Minutes* 1820/3.
Ann Mason	1819–23	(Joined Society of Friends; B156.)
Patience Bickle	1819–29	(1827 Davenport supernumerary; B23.)
Margaret Adams	1819–21	Obituary *Minutes* 1822/3.
Susan Furze	1819–23	
Mary Ann Soper	1819–22	(1822 Kingsbrompton supernumerary; B220.)
Ann Cory	1819–29	(1828 Kilkhampton supernumerary; B55.)
Catherine Reed/Thorne	1819–25	Married James Thorne – from 1824 appears under this name.
Elizabeth Trick	1819–20	'desisted' *Minutes* 1821/3.
Grace Mason	1819	'desisted' *Minutes* 1820/3.
Sarah Cory	1819–20	'desisted' *Minutes* 1821/3.
Susan(nah) Baulch	1819–30	(1829 Truro supernumerary; B17.)
Mary [Ann?] Mason	1820, 1822–4	'desisted' *Minutes* 1821/3. Is the 1822 entry same person? (Is this

		the Mary [Ann] Mason who married John Beadon? B156.)
Elizabeth Courtice	1820–31	
Ann Vickery	1820–31	(1831 married Paul Robins; stationed in Jersey after birth of second child; died Bowmanville, Canada before 1854; B245.)
Ann Arthur Guest	1820–41	(Married James Brooks; 1841 Northlew Mission supernumerary; B96.)
Mary Toms	1820–3	(1824 married; B236.)
Grace Barrett	1820	'desisted' *Minutes* 1821/3.
Mary Ann Werrey	1820–4	'desisted' Pyke (1941) 28.
Mary Runnal(l)s	1821	'desisted' *Minutes* 1822/4.
Ann Slooman	1821–2	'desisted' *Minutes* 1823/5.
Ann Edmunds	1821	
Hannah Pearce	1821, 1825–30	
Eleanor Turner	1822	'desisted' *Minutes* 1823/5.
Mary Billing	1822–7	
Ann Brown	1822–32	
Mary Cottle	1823–31	(1830 Kilkhampton and Chasewater supernumerary; B56.)
Grace Palmer	1823–7	
Mary O'Bryan	1823–5	Daughter of Catherine and William O'Bryan. (Born Gunwen, Cornwall, 3 April 1807; local preacher 1823; married Samuel Thorne 28 November 1825; died Plymouth 12 November 1883; biography by S. L. Thorne; B173.)
Frances Davy/ey	1823–6	
Jane Bray	1823, 1825–33	(1833 married W. Hill; B30.)
Elizabeth Carne	1823–33	
Eliza Jew	1824–7	
Elizabeth Ann Sinclair/ear	1824–9	
Elizabeth/Betsy Nicholls	1824–8	(1827 Michaelstow supernumerary; B170.)
Mary Gale	1824	(Married John Roberts; B85.)
Hannah Pearce	1821, 1825–30	
Catherine Harris	1825–73	(Born 1804; supernumerary 1852; disappears from *Minutes* 1874; 'as

		she then was the only woman supernumerary, suspect she remained so, though not listed in the Minutes'; died Medland 9 January 1896; B101.)
Ann Tremelling	1825, 1827	If the 1826 omission was simply an error, there would have been 28 female itinerants in the peak year of 1827.
Jane Bird	1825–7	(1827 Ringsash supernumerary; B23.)
Winifred Champion Rowland	1825–9	(1829 Forest of Dean supernumerary; B204.)
Mary Urch	1825–6	(1826 Weare supernumerary; B244.)
Mary Hewett	1825–7	(Born Chitterwell, Somerset, 20 December 1803; married William Mason 22 August 1827; died Launceston 5 June 1853; B107.)
Jane Bray	1823, 1825–33	(Married W. Hill; B30.)
Ann Potter	1825–34	Obituary *Minutes* 1835/5. (Born Southtawton, Chagford; converted 1820 via Andrew Cory; 1831 Exeter supernumerary; died Exeter 25 February 1835; B186.)
Lavinia Dunn	1826–8	
Elizabeth Hilborn	1826	
Joan Lock	1826–7	(1827 Kingsbrompton supernumerary; B147.)
Charlotte Bunce	1827–31	(1831 Isle of Wight supernumerary; B36.)
Mary Coffin	1827	
Fanny Tremain	*1828–30*, 1831–2	(1831 St Ervan supernumerary; B239.)
Mary Husband	*1828–30*, 1831–46	(1846 St Austell supernumerary; B123.)
Elizabeth Rowcliffe	*1828–9*	
Mary Biddick	*1829–30*	
Ipsa Parnall	*1832–4*, 1835–7	
Mary Ann Taylor	*1832–4*, 1835–53	(Married Paul Robins 1854; 'still alive in 1890', B231.)
Ann White	*1834–6*, 1837–50	

Am(e)y Terry	*1834–6*, 1837–46	(Married William Drew; B232.)
Mary Elson	*1835–6*, 1837–45	Received from Arminian Bible Christian Connexion, *Minutes* 1835/4.
Harriot Mary Hurle	*1835–7*, 1838–41	
Susanna de St Croix	*1835–7*	
Margaret Pinwill	*1836–9*, 1840–1	Remained an extra year on trial on account of the 'delicate' state of her health, *Minutes* 1839/5.
Eliza Wheeler	*1837–9*, 1840–1	
Jane Gardner/iner/ener	*1838–40*	Obituary *Minutes* 1841/7. (Born Worldham, Hampshire, 28 November 1815; converted 1834 via F.J. Pudney; died Flushing 19 March 1841; B85.)
Susanna(h) Walter	*1842–4*	
Martha Hutchings	*1846–7*	
Susanna(h) Hobbs	*1851–3*	Health was a problem for her. (1853 Faversham supernumerary; B113.)
Mary Jullif	*1855*	
Sarah Hutchings	*1859–61*, 1862–4	
Elizabeth Dymond	*1861–3*, 1864–9	
Elizabeth Ann Jollow	*1861–3*, 1864	
Eliza Giles	*1890–2*, 1893–7	'resigned' *Minutes* 1898/10.
Lillie Edwards	*1894–6*, 1897–1906/7	'ceases to be recognised' because of 1907 union, *Minutes* 1907/10.
Lily L. Oram	*1894*	'resigned' *Minutes* 1895/10.
Annie E. Carkeek	*1894*	Retires to become an evangelist, *Minutes* 1895/10.

APPENDIX C

COMPARATIVE OVERVIEW OF KEY EVENTS

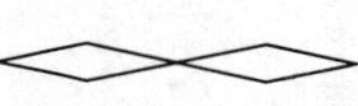

Year	Lambeth Conference	Church of England	Methodist Church	Roman Catholic Church
1862		Elizabeth Ferard ordained deaconess by Bishop Tait		
1890			Wesley Deaconess Order founded	
1897	Recognition of the revival of the office of deaconess and of the revival of sisterhoods			
1919		*The Ministry of Women* (report of the archbishop's committee)		

Year	Lambeth Conference	Church of England	Methodist Church	Roman Catholic Church
1920	Resolution that the diaconate of women should be formally and canonically restored. Inclusion of phrases: 'Apostolic approval'; 'Order of the Ministry'			
1922			Pastoral session of Conference appointed committee to consider the admission of women to the ordained ministry and to the work of a deaconess	
1923		Convocation of Canterbury formally restored office of deaconess	Pastoral session received report. Joint committee appointed to look into the question of women candidates for the ministry	
1924		Both upper houses agreed the service for making deaconesses	Both sessions received the report. Standing committee appointed	

Year	Lambeth Conference	Church of England	Methodist Church	Roman Catholic Church
1925		Convocation of York formally restored office of deaconess	Committee report received and the resolution that 'in principle . . . not disqualified . . . merely on the ground of sex' adopted. Enlarged committee to explore biblical grounds	
1926			Report accepted by representative session but rejected by pastoral session so not confirmed by legal conference	
1927			On amendment, question remitted to a committee to explore larger opportunities for consecrated women, and the further development of the existing diaconate	
1928			Report received and generally approved, but sent back for clarification on practicalities	

Year	Lambeth Conference	Church of England	Methodist Church	Roman Catholic Church
1929			Report received. Uniting Methodist Conferences to be invited to form a joint committee the following year and to report to all three Conferences	
1930	Order of deaconess declared to be: 'for women the one and only Order of the ministry'. 'Apostolic' reference dropped; emergence of *sui generis* phrase			
1931			Report received and adopted subject to confirmation by the Conference of 1933	
1933			Report received and adopted and so sent to synods. Also referred to committees of Wesley	

Year	Lambeth Conference	Church of England	Methodist Church	Roman Catholic Church
1933 *cont.*			Missionary Society and Wesley Deaconess Order for consideration	
1934			Report received. Representative session viewed response from synods as 'not sufficient support' while ministerial session wanted adjustments to give women 'full scope' for the exercise of their ministry	
1935		*The Ministry of Women* (report of the archbishops' commission) referred to the deaconess as in 'a Holy Order'		
1937			Committee appointed to consider adjustments to give women 'full scope'	

Year	Lambeth Conference	Church of England	Methodist Church	Roman Catholic Church
1938			Report generally approved. Returned for further consideration and details	
1939		Convocation of Canterbury agreed to regulations on the status and functions of deaconesses	Report received but not approved. Committee appointed to look into ministerial implications of present scheme	
1941		Convocation of York brought deaconess regulations into line with those of Canterbury		
1945		Letter to the bishop of Hong Kong describing his act of ordaining a deaconess to the priesthood as '*ultra vires*'	Report received and remitted to district synods	
1946			Report on synod results received and referred to an enlarged committee with direction to consider the enlargement of the sphere	

Year	Lambeth Conference	Church of England	Methodist Church	Roman Catholic Church
1946 *cont.*			of service of the Wesley Deaconess Order, and the women missionaries overseas to receive presbyters' orders	
1948	Negative reply to the request by the bishop of Hong Kong for a trial period during which a deaconess might be ordained to the priesthood		Conference received the report but declined to agree to ordain women	
1959			Pauline Webb's intervention. Committee appointed on the status of deaconesses and the admission of women to the ministry	
1961			Report of committee adopted and committee directed to confer with Overseas Missions	

Year	Lambeth Conference	Church of England	Methodist Church	Roman Catholic Church
1961 *cont.*			Committee. Report sent to synods	
1962		*Gender and Ministry* (report of CACTM)		
1964		Canon D1, para. 4: 'The Order of Deaconess is not one of the Holy Orders of the Church of England'		
1966		*Women and Holy Orders* (report of the archbishops' commission)	Pauline Webb's amendment passed, i.e. agreement on principle but implementation delayed during discussions with the Church of England	
1968	Theological arguments found to be inconclusive. Request to churches to study and report to the ACC and to seek advice of the ACC before taking a decision	*Women and the Ordained Ministry* (report of the Anglican–Methodist commission on women and holy orders) *Women in Ministry* (report arising out of *WHO*, which stressed the primacy of the question)		

Year	Lambeth Conference	Church of England	Methodist Church	Roman Catholic Church
1969		Anglican–Methodist scheme failed to achieve required majority.		
1970			Proposals to admit women to the ministry accepted subject to confirmation in 1971. Decision referred to ministerial sessions of district synods	
1971	ACC's first meeting at Limuru. Resolution 28: 'action will be acceptable', and two women ordained in Hong Kong.	GS referred Limuru res. 28 to ACCM and CWMC with request they advised by September 1972	Ministerial session resolved to accept women into the ministry on the conditions of the 1970 Faith and Order Committee	Issue of women and priesthood raised in the Synod of Bishops
1972		*The Ordination of Women to the Priesthood* (report compiled by Christian Howard and presented by ACCM)	Report and resolutions on practical problems accepted	
1973	ACC Dublin underlined significance of remaining in communion	Revised canon D1 omitted 'the Order of Deaconesses is not one of the Holy		

Year	Lambeth Conference	Church of England	Methodist Church	Roman Catholic Church
1973 *cont.*		Orders of the Church of England' and gave to deaconesses the same functions as to deacons	Final decision taken. Candidates accepted to train for the ministry	
1974			Seventeen ordinations	
1975		Report on diocesan results received. 'No fundamental objections' motion passed in all three houses. Removal of legal barriers motion rejected		
1976	ACC Trinidad proposed deaconesses should be declared within the diaconate	Publication of archbishop of Canterbury's correspondence with other churches on the ordination of women (1975–6)		Report of Pontifical Biblical Commission. Declaration (approved by Pope Paul VI on 15 October)
1978	LC resolutions 20–2: women ordained to diaconate recommended; no fundamental objections to priesthood declared; unity in diversity urged; no			

Year	Lambeth Conference	Church of England	Methodist Church	Roman Catholic Church
1978 *cont.*	female consecrations to episcopate advised. ARC report published	Cardinal Hume's warning to GS; motion to remove legal barriers rejected. *OWP(S)* (compiled by Christian Howard)	Recruitment to Wesley Deaconess Order to cease	
1979	ARCIC document on ministry and ordination published. ACC 4 Canada recommended dialogue	Motion to grant women lawfully ordained abroad the same status as other clergy rejected		
1980				National Pastoral Congress in England. *The Easter People* (bishops' comments on the NPC). *Eucharistic Prayers* (report by ICEL on discriminatory language) approved by US bishops
1981	ACC 5 notes tension caused by England's refusal to allow women priests to minister	Motion to open the order of deacons to both men and women carried		*Eucharistic Prayers* approved by Canadian bishops

Year	Lambeth Conference	Church of England	Methodist Church	Roman Catholic Church
1982		Issue of women ordained abroad revived. Agreement to prepare legislation. Report on women as deacons (GS 549) received. Draft measure to be prepared		
1983		Draft Women Ordained Abroad Measure (GS 598) generally approved. Draft Ordination of Women as Deacons Measure (GS 580) generally approved		*Why Can't a Woman be more Like a Man?* (report of the Laity Commission). Laity Commission dissolved by church authorities
1984	ACC 6 recommends that women ordained in other provinces should be permitted to minister on particular occasions during temporary visits	Draft Women Ordained Abroad Measure (GS 598) finally rejected. Draft Deacons (Ordination of Women) Measure (GS 580Y) revised. *OWP (Further Report)* by Christian Howard. Motion		

Year	Lambeth Conference	Church of England	Methodist Church	Roman Catholic Church
1984		to bring forward legislation for the ordination of women to the priesthood carried. Archbishop of Canterbury receives letter from Pope John Paul II describing ordination of women as 'serious obstacle'		
1985		Archbishop of Canterbury's letter to Cardinal Willebrands describes experience of women priests as 'generally beneficial'		
1986		Legislation by standing committee causes shock, but received. House of bishops to prepare a report on scope of legislation. Cardinal Willebrand's letter reiterating RC position		

Year	Lambeth Conference	Church of England	Methodist Church	Roman Catholic Church
1987	ACC 7 focuses on episcopate in terms of acceptability	All stages completed for ordination of women as deacons. First ordinations. Report by house of bishops (GS 764) received. Agreement to prepare legislation on ordination to women to the priesthood		
1988	Grindrod report *Women and the Episcopate* sent to all bishops prior to Lambeth Conference, 1988	Second report by house of bishops (GS 829) taken note of. Draft Priests (Ordination of Women) Measure (GS 830) generally approved		Papal encyclical *Mulieris Dignitatem*. Vatican turns down Bishops' Conference of England and Wales' proposals to remove discriminatory language from Eucharistic Prayer 4

APPENDIX D

STRUCTURES OF THE THREE INSTITUTIONALISED CHURCHES[1]

I THE ROMAN CATHOLIC CHURCH

The Roman Curia is the papal court together with its functionaries, especially those through whom the government of the church is administered, and it acts with the delegated authority of the pope. It emerged from the fourth-century Apostolic Chancery, was established by Sixtus V in 1588, reorganised by Pius X in 1908, and a post-Vatican 2 reform was effected by the decree *Regimini Ecclesiae Universale* in 1967.

Currently it consists of the office of the pope, including the Secretariat of State and the Council for the Public Affairs of the Church, nine congregations headed by the Sacred Congregation for the Doctrine of the Faith, which are the executive departments responsible for ordinary central administration, three tribunals, together with various offices and permanent commissions. Each congregation consists primarily of cardinals under a cardinal-prefect assisted by a secretary and supporting officials. Each has attached to it seven diocesan bishops chosen by the pope from various parts of the world, along with a panel of consultants also papally selected – in April 1968 six nuns were named as consultants to the Sacred Congregation for Religious and Secular Institutes[2] – for renewable five-year terms of office. Official information is given through the *Acta Apostolicae Sedis*.

With the *motu proprio*, *Apostolica Sollicitudo*, the Synod of Bishops came into being in September 1965. The synod was described in the document as a permanently constituted body of bishops responsible for advising the pope on matters of importance to the whole church. This sprang from the concern for collegiality expressed during

Vatican 2 (*Lumen Gentium* 22), a concern which went a little way towards balancing the definition of infallibility of Vatican 1. The synod is directly and immediately subject to the pope, who has authority to order its agenda, to convene it, and to give its members deliberative as well as advisory authority. In addition to a limited number of *ex officio* members and heads of religious institutes, the majority of the members are elected representatives of national or regional episcopal conferences. The pope reserves the right to appoint the general secretary, special secretaries and no more than 15 per cent of the total membership. This synod meets generally every three years.[3]

Episcopal conferences, functioning under general norms and particular statutes approved by the pope or his representatives, are official bodies in which the bishops of a given country or territory act together. Each conference has its own advisory bodies – for example, the Laity Commission (prior to its dissolution in 1983) functioned in relation to the Bishops' Conference of England and Wales. Also advisory to this last conference was the event unique to and in this country of the 1980 National Pastoral Congress, at which diocesan representation was based on the ratio of one delegate to every 1,000 church attenders. According to Michael Hornsby-Smith, 'Among our 1276 respondents 49% claimed they had been elected, 41% had been invited or co-opted and 7% had volunteered. 75% of the respondents represented their diocese, 8% Catholic organisations, 9% special groups, and there were 16 members of the bishops' national commissions.'[4]

A comment about power in this church springs to mind. Although the power centre is theoretically the pope, it is interesting to note that when John XXIII asked the curial cardinals to resign so that the curia could be completely restructured, they refused. As power is linked to economics, one must also consider factors such as the Banco Ambrosiano affair. It would be most interesting at some future date to compare the symbolism and the effective power of the bishop of Rome with those of the president of the United States.

2 THE CHURCH OF ENGLAND

The two ancient provincial assemblies of the clergy of the Church of England are the Convocations of Canterbury and York. They have had a stormy history culminating in their prorogation by Royal Writ in 1717, and they began to discuss business again only in 1852 and 1861 respectively. At first the bishops and lower clergy sat together but since the fifteenth century the Convocations have sat as two houses. The respective archbishops preside over the upper house and in full synod while at the beginning of each Convocation the lower house elects a 'Prolocutor' or 'Reverendary' to preside. Although the houses are exclusively clerical assemblies, since 1895 a house of laymen (subsequently house of laity) has been associated with the respective Convocations. In 1904 a Representative Council consisting of the members of both Convocations together with the two houses of laymen was initiated, but this had no legal position or authority. It was superseded by the Church Assembly, the powers of which were defined in The Church of England Assembly (Powers) Act of 1919. The Synodical Government Measure, 1969, transferred most of the functions of Convocation to the General Synod, although provision was made for each Convocation to meet separately to transact formal business.

The Church Assembly consisted of a house of bishops, composed of all the members of the two upper houses of Convocation; a house of clergy consisting of all members of the two lower houses of Convocation; and a house of laity elected every five years by the representative electors of the diocesan conferences. Its most important function was to prepare ecclesiastical measures to put before parliament, and these could be either accepted or rejected, but not amended.

The General Synod took over the powers of the Church Assembly together with some of the powers of Convocation. It is composed of the upper houses of the Convocations of Canterbury and York, a house of clergy consisting of the two lower houses of the Convocations, somewhat reduced in size, and a house of laity of not more than 250 elected members. Election is by members of the houses of laity of the deanery synods. The General Synod is required to meet at least twice a year. Matters concerning doctrine or church services can be approved only in terms proposed by the house of bishops. By the same measure, diocesan conferences were replaced by diocesan synods consisting of the bishop, the house of clergy, and the house of laity, members of the two latter houses being elected by the respective houses of the deanery synods. The base of the whole system remains the parochial church council.

Lambeth Conference 1930 defined the Anglican Communion as

'a fellowship, within the One Holy Catholic and Apostolic Church, of those duly constituted Dioceses, Provinces, or Regional Churches in communion with the See of Canterbury'. Lambeth Conference 1968 proposed the creation of the Anglican Consultative Council as a representative advisory body of approximately fifty bishops, clergy and lay people. Within the Anglican Communion, the Church of England consists of the province of Canterbury (including since 1980 the diocese of Europe) and the province of York. The Church in Wales has formed a separate province since 1920.

3 THE METHODIST CHURCH IN ENGLAND

In 1739 John Wesley started a society in London; in 1742 the first classes were formed; in 1743 the rules of the society were drawn up; and in 1744 six clergymen and four laymen assembled for the first Conference. From 1746 the societies were arranged in circuits, and, after Wesley's death, into districts.

The Wesleyan Connexion was first established by law in 1784 when Wesley lodged in the Court of Chancery a Deed of Declaration naming one hundred preachers as constituting the 'Conference of the people called Methodists' and defining the method of future appointments. Conference had power to appoint preachers to various preaching houses (later chapels), the ownership of which was vested in boards of trustees. In 1795 came the declaration that the admission of a preacher to 'full connexion with the Conference' conferred ministerial rights without any form of ordination, but the imposition of hands was nevertheless adopted by the Conference in 1836. On Wesley's death the membership of Conference was extended beyond the Legal Hundred to include all preachers in full connexion. Laymen were added in 1878 and laywomen in 1911.

The legal successor of the original Conference is regulated in statute law by The Methodist Church Union Act, 1929, and The Methodist Church Act, 1976. It consists of 288 ministers and 283 laypersons mostly elected by district synods; the ministers form the ministerial session and decide affairs concerning ministers, but decisions affecting the whole church are taken by the full Conference (representative session). It was in 1933 that the pastoral session became the ministerial session. In the Wesleyan tradition the pastoral session met after the representative session and had the right of reversing the vote of the former session in matters relating to the appointment of departmental ministers, and it had the last word on questions of doctrine. These are now the prerogative of the representative session. The only subjects exclusively within the province of the ministerial session concern the ministry (cf. pp. 64–5 above). Since 1963 the ministerial session has preceded the representative session. Conference annually elects a minister as president and, for the representative session, a layperson as vice-president. Conference delegates certain duties to the synods, held twice yearly in each district, of which there are 32 in Great Britain, containing about 20 or 30 circuits in each; it also appoints ministers to chair each district, and to superintend each circuit, the latter consisting of a number of local societies. Conference governs the selection, training and ordination of ministers and the appointment of those ordained. It also regulates the organisation of districts and circuits, sets up special initiatives such as the Anglican–Methodist conversations, and controls other central organisations and committees which are responsible to it.

NOTES

THE METHODIST CHURCH IN ENGLAND

1 Cragg (1970) 145.
2 Cragg (1970) 147.
3 Church (1949) 137.
4 Church (1949) 141.
5 Pyke (1941) 20–1.
6 Pyke (1941) 25.
7 Cf. the poster reproduced in Pyke (1915) facing p. 46.
8 Pyke (1941) 26–8.
9 Thorne (1865) 98, 99–100, 103–4, 106. O'Bryan went to Canada in 1831. Later he was reconciled to the Conference but he never rejoined it.
10 It has occasionally been necessary to go beyond official Conference documentation when considering women preachers in early Methodism. Dr Oliver A. Beckerlegge, who has been most helpful in directing me to Bible Christian sources, has drawn my attention to similar research in Swift (1951–2, 1953–4) and Beckerlegge (1955–6). For convenience I quote some of the data and conclusions. Any extended use of these helpful articles is acknowledged in the notes.
11 Taft (1828) 43.
12 Taft (1825) 23.
13 Taft (1825) 24. Also quoted with minor lexical variations in Taft (1828) 57–8.
14 Wesley (1931) 6: 290–1.
15 Wesley (1931) 7: 9.
16 Taft (1825) 84.
17 Taft (1825) 87.
18 Taft (1825) 27.
19 Taft (1825) 25.
20 Church (1949) 171–2.
21 Church (1949) 156.
22 See Taft (1828) 127.
23 Cf. Taft (1825) 178.

24 *Minutes of the Methodist Conferences*, 1803 (1862) 188–9.
25 Swift (1951–2) 91.
26 Church (1949) 137.
27 George Fox defended women's right to speak in public, as did women members of the Society of Friends. Margaret Fell wrote that those who denied it 'speak against Christ and his Church' in Fell (1710) 333. Although female members of the society had full right to such from the first, they too had a struggle to achieve equality within the organisation.
28 Swift (1951–2) 92.
29 Reprinted in Walford (1855) 172–7.
30 Walford (1855) 173.
31 *General Minutes of the Meeting held by the Primitive Methodist Connexion 1821* 13–14.
32 *Minutes of the First Conference of the Preachers in connexion with William O'Bryan. Held at Baddash in Launceston, begun Tuesday, the 17th, and ended Wednesday, the 25th August. 1819* (1825, Stoke-Damarel) 4–6.
33 An article on 1 Corinthians 14: 34, by 'Methodius', was printed in *Methodist Magazine* (1809) and it was presumably to this that the minute referred. It was a polemical rendering of a literal interpretation of the text, read in conjunction with 1 Timothy 2: 12. 'In short, to cut off every pretence for women's teaching in the Church, the Apostle asked them, "What? went the word of God forth into the world from you," women? Did Christ employ any of your sex as Apostles? "Or did the word only come to you" by the ministry of men? How, then, can ye pretend to teach men?' *Methodist Magazine for the Year 1809: Being a Continuation of the Arminian Magazine* vol. 32: 168–70 (1809, Popper).
34 Thorne (1865) 49, 52, 55, 62, 87, 95, 98, 99, 103, 106.
35 Beckerlegge (1955–6) 182.
36 Swift (1953–4) 76 notes a total of 'no fewer than' 71; 15 having reached double figures; 27 having travelled for three years or less. My list of names (Appendix B) derived from the *Minutes* is in agreement with Beckerlegge's listings (1968), who also uses other sources, with one year's difference in the entries for S. Baulch, E. Courtice, A. Tremelling, F. Tremain, M. Elson and S. de St Croix. A number of factors make certainty difficult: for example, the degree of accuracy of the original *Minutes*; the practice of changing the surname on marriage. When a name disappeared and reappeared after a brief interval I have assumed the same person was involved.
37 For a memoir of Jane Gardener (there are variant spellings of her name) see Sedwell (1841).
38 Swift (1953–4) 76–7.
39 The first three 'females on trial' were listed in *Minutes* 1828, 6.

40 See Beckerlegge (1955–6) 183–4, where he comments on Swift (1953–4) 82.
41 Swift (1953–4) 79.
42 Swift (1953–4) 80.
43 *Primitive Methodist Magazine* (1891) 564–5.
44 Swift (1953–4) 82.
45 For summary of key events see Appendix C.
46 Wesleyan Methodist Church, *Minutes* 1894, 320.
47 *Minutes* 1895, 323. For further historical details see summary of 1961 report on pp. 55–7.
48 *Minutes* 1901, 500–2; *Minutes* 1907, 523–5. Page references in the summary are to the 1901 entry.
49 *Minutes* 1909, 119; *Minutes* 1911, 389.
50 *Minutes* 1910, 365–6.
51 *Minutes* 1920, 263–4.
52 *Minutes* 1922, 272.
53 *Minutes* 1924, 94–6.
54 *MR* 24 July 1924, 16. The *Methodist Recorder* carried Conference debates verbatim, at least until 1948, when this period ends.
55 *Minutes* 1924, 301.
56 See *C.A.* 1925, 383–6.
57 *MR* 30 July 1925, 8.
58 *C.A.* 1926, 70–4. See also 469–72.
59 *C.A.* 22 July 1926, 13–14.
60 *Minutes* 1926, 144, 472.
61 *MR* 21 July 1927, 16.
62 As already noted, in 1907 their remaining itinerant woman had been required to resign in the interests of union (above, pp. 20–1).
63 *C.A.* 1928, 89–90.
64 *MR* 26 July 1928, 15, 16.
65 One deaconess remarked: 'A great many of us do not want to be ministers, and think we can do better work as Deaconesses, but we do want to back up any who seek an enlarged sphere of service.' A small committee was nominated to frame a resolution which 'should express deep gratitude for all that the Deaconesses are now enabled to do, but should urge that women should be given the liberty and scope that men now have, in order that they may do the work to which God calls them, whatever that work may be'. *MR* 7 June 1928, 5, and 14 June 1928, 4.
66 Chapter 1 of First & Scott's 'Early life on a Mission Station' (1980) makes interesting reading. In fiction, *The Jewel in the Crown* contains a telling example.
67 *Minutes* 1928, 254.
68 *MR* 25 July 1929, 18.

69 *C.A.* 1929, 83–4.
70 *Minutes* 1929, 71.
71 *C.A.* 1931, 431–2.
72 *MR* 27 July 1931, 11, 13.
73 *Minutes* 1931, 83, 261.
74 *C.A.* 1932, 317–19.
75 Uniting Conference took place on 20–3 September 1932 at the Royal Albert Hall, London. The Deed of Union was read and signed by representatives of the three uniting connexions. It was rendered possible and legal by the unanimous votes of the three contracting parties and by an act of parliament, the Methodist Church Union Act of 1929. The 1932 Deed of Union was superseded in 1976 by the Methodist Church Act.
76 *Minutes* 1933, 438–40.
77 *MR* 20 July 1933, 10.
78 *Minutes* 1933, 98, 287.
79 *C.A.* 1934, 563–4.
80 *MR* 26 July 1934, 14, 15, 21.
81 Agnes Maude Royden until 1914 edited *The Common Cause*, the publication of the National Union of Women's Suffrage Societies. In 1917 she became the assistant preacher at the City Temple, London, and thus the first woman in England officially to occupy the pulpit of a regular place of worship. See Fletcher (1989).
82 See *MR* 26 July 1934, 24.
83 *Minutes* 1934, 102, 249.
84 *MR* 22 July 1937, 21.
85 *C.A.* 1938, 489–90.
86 *Minutes* 1938, 80; *MR* 28 July 1938, 8.
87 *C.A.* 1939, 539–41.
88 *MR* 27 July 1939, 20, 21.
89 *Minutes* 1939, 96, 248.
90 *C.A.* 1944, 37–8.
91 *Minutes* 1944, 50, 153.
92 *C.A.* 1945, 315–16.
93 *MR* 26 July 1945, 12.
94 *Minutes* 1945, 50, 152.
95 *Daily Record* 1945, 46.
96 *C.A.* 1946, 325–8.
97 *MR* 25 July 1946, 11, 13.
98 *Minutes* 1946, 57.
99 *C.A.* 1948, 143–5.
100 *MR* 22 July 1948, 8.
101 *Minutes* 1948, 50, 162; *Daily Record* 1948, 76.

102 I am grateful to Pauline Webb for providing me with her private notes of this speech.

103 *C.A.* 1961, 13–29 – Committee on the Status of Deaconesses and the Admission of Women to the Ministry.

104 In the Methodist Church of the United States it was 1968 before women were guaranteed annual appointments following the uniting Conference of the Evangelical United Brethren and Methodist bodies that year. In 1979 sociologists collaborated in a survey featuring United Methodist clergywomen. I am grateful to Doris Moreland Jones for sending me a copy. Hale, King & Jones (1980).

105 For the Presbyterian Church of England, see my article in the *Heythrop Journal* 31: 2 (April 1990). For article on the subject, see *MR* 13 April 1961, 10, 11.

106 *MR* 13 July 1961, 15.

107 The matter was considered in a number of newspaper articles the following year. See Iva Wallis, 'Women in the Methodist Church', *Guardian* 10 January 1962; an analysis of the facts surrounding the discussion in *MR* 22 February 1962, 3; also Pauline Webb's reply to Clifford Lever (in which she found his arguments 'so illogical that they must surely defy even feminine methods of reasoning') in *MR* 19 April 1962, 7.

108 *Daily Record* 1961, 42.

109 *C.A.* 1963, 93–5.

110 (1) This resembled the mandate given to the archbishops' commission arising out of *Gender and Ministry* (above, p. 86) and resulting in *WHO* (1966) (above, pp. 89–97; see also note 114 below). (2) See the letter from Pauline Webb arguing against the postponement of the issue, *MR* 25 July 1963, 4.

111 *C.A.* 1964, 542.

112 *C.A.* 1965, 594.

113 *C.A.* 1966, 611–12.

114 A reference to *WHO* (1966), summarised above, pp. 89–97.

115 *MR* 14 July 1966, 8, 10.

116 See pp. 103–4 above.

117 *C.A.* 1970, 257–62.

118 *MR* 9 July 1970, 15, 16.

119 *Minutes* 1970, 78.

120 *C.A.* 1971, 23.

121 *Daily Record* 1971, 9.

122 *MR* 20 July 1972, 6.

123 *MR* 29 April 1971, 5.

124 *MR* 20 April 1972, 4; 27 April 1972, 9.

125 *MR* 3 May 1973, 6.

126 *Minutes* 1978, 29.

127 In *OWP(S)* 21. In 1978 research into the effect that women ministers were having on the Methodist Church was launched. In 1986 a woman minister, Ruth Davis, was granted study leave in order to work in this field, and in due course it is hoped that there will be some published result. Cf. Hale, King & Jones (1980) in the USA, note 104 above.

THE CHURCH OF ENGLAND

1 *CC(C)* 1859–61, 828–41.

2 *CC(C)* 1862–3, 910–23; 963–8.

3 *CC(C)* 1875, 286.

4 *CC(C)* 1878, 1–9.

5 *CC(C)* 1878, 238–67.

6 *CC(C)* 1883, 127–38.

7 *CC(C)* 1883, 168.

8 *CC(C)* 1885, 274–80.

9 *CC(C)* 1890, 111–24; 167–81.

10 *CC(C)* 1891, 42–6.

11 *LC* 1897, 35, res. 11.

12 *LC* 1897, 59.

13 *LC* 1908, 194.

14 See Morris (1973).

15 *CC(C)* 1919, 91.

16 *CC(C)* 1920, 30–2.

17 *CC(C)* 1919, 223. See also *LC* 1920, res. 47–52; pp. 102–5.

18 *CC(C)* 1921, 4–21; 21ff.

19 *CC(C&Y) 1921–70* (1971) 44–7. For return to the issue see *LC* 1930, res. 67–70; pp. 176–80.

20 *Women and Priesthood*, a 'private and confidential' edition, issued 'to members of the Lambeth Conference only' by the Anglican group formed to bring the subject of the ordination of women to the priesthood before the following Lambeth Conference. A shortened edition excluding a letter to the archbishop of Canterbury and two appendices was to be made generally available later. Three directions in which action was urged were: (1) 'a more explicit recognition that women Deacons form part of the threefold Ministry'; (2) 'that the functions of women Deacons should be made identical with those of men called to that Ministry'; (3) 'an authoritative statement that the exclusion of women hitherto from the office of priest has been a disciplinary rule of the Church, not the assertion of an incapacity inherent in womanhood' (18–19).

21 *CC(C&Y) 1921–70* (1971) 47–9. In 1966 Canon D1, printed in *WHO* 37, note 1, reads as follows:

Of the Order of Deaconesses

1. The Order of Deaconesses is the one Order of Ministry in the Church of England to which women are admitted by prayer and the laying on of hands by the Bishop.

2. It belongs to the office of a Deaconess, in the place where she is licensed to serve, to exercise a pastoral care especially over women, young people, and children, to visit the sick and the whole, to instruct the people in the faith, and to prepare them for the reception of the sacraments.

3. The Bishop may permit a Deaconess in any Church or Chapel within his jurisdiction at the invitation of the Minister thereof: (a) To read in case of need the services of Morning and Evening Prayer and the Litany, except those portions reserved to the Priest, and to lead in prayer. (b) To instruct and preach except during the service of Holy Communion.

4. The Order of Deaconess is not one of the Holy Orders of the Church of England, and accordingly Deaconesses may accept membership of any Lay Assembly of the Church of England without prejudice to the standing of their Order.

A revised form of canon D1 was presented for royal assent in 1972.

22 An alternative version of events with regard to the letter was offered by Canon A. C. Hall during a 1975 debate (above, pp. 134–5) where he stated that it did not reflect William Temple's own view and that (by implication) he therefore did not prepare it and that it was the work of Archbishop Garbett (*GS* 1975, 601).

23 During the Japanese occupation of Hong Kong, Deaconess Florence Li Tim Oi was in charge of the Anglican congregation at Macao. Eventually clergy were refused the monthly permit to visit Macao in order to celebrate communion. Bishop R. O. Hall decided in 1944 to ordain Deaconess Li to the priesthood to ensure that the Macanese community had the sacraments. At the first post-war meeting of the house of bishops of the Holy Catholic Church in China in 1946 a resolution was passed regretting the 'uncanonical action' of Bishop Hall. Deaconess Li offered her resignation from the priestly ministry to the bishop, which he accepted at the request of the house of bishops, for the sake of church harmony (*OWP* 55).

24 *CC(C&Y) 1921–70* (1971) 49–50.

25 The Church Assembly was brought into existence by the Enabling Act of 1919 and included a house of laity. It was superseded by the General Synod at the beginning of the 1970s.

26 *CA* 1962, 681–714.

27 See *Journal of the General Convention of the Protestant Episcopal Church in the USA* 9 September 1965, A.23, special meeting of the house of bishops.

28 This line of argument is to be found in the articles by Bouyer (1977) and Ratzinger (1977).

29 For the text of canon D1 see note 21 above.

30 *CA* 1967, 190–220.

31 *CA* 1967, 279–318.

32 *LC* 1968, 39–40.

33 *LC* 1968, 105–8.

34 Four days after Lambeth Conference 1968 ended, the bishop of Gloucester, the Right Reverend Basil Guy, discussed his opposition to the ordination of women with a *Citizen* reporter in episcopal terms: 'You can't have a Father in God in a skirt!' The reporter concluded that the setting up of the ACC was a progressive move which could affect policy – a reflection which was to prove correct. *Citizen* 5 September 1968, 8.

35 Stephenson (1978) 263; *GS* 1972, 298.

36 *CA* 1969, 556–84.

37 Its report was *The Time is Now* (1971, SPCK).

38 Joyce Bennett was at the centre of controversy in the summer of 1986 as a result of having presided over an extempore communion service at Church House, Westminster, following the AGM of the Movement for the Ordination of Women (MOW).

39 Her argument is developed in Kroll (1975).

40 *GS* 1972, 685–720. Where office-holders are named in *GS* alongside their speeches, I have included this information.

41 *CC(C)* 1973, 22–62. Preceding the Convocation of Canterbury debate Clifford Longley considered the most recent edition of *Veritas*, which had devoted most of its space to the case against the ordination of women, which was depicted as 'unnatural'. In conclusion Longley pointed to the lack of a theology of women's liberation and of sex itself (*The Times*, 14 May 1973, 14). But cf. his later article, 'Sexual Symbolism at the Altar' (*The Times*, 7 July 1986).

42 *York Journal of Convocation* 1973, 32–70.

43 *GS* 1973, 534–50.

44 See the report, *Partners in Mission* (1973), 37–42.

45 *GS* 1975, 542. For the memorandum from the standing committee to the dioceses, see GS Misc. 26, and for the standing committee report, GS 252. The summary of results is from *OWP(S)* 4.

46 *GS* 1975, 542–73.

47 Cf. Descamps (1977), who takes a similar line.

48 *GS* 1975, 573–614.

49 For a summary of the PBC's report, see Part One, Section Three.

50 Temple's biographer, F. A. Iremonger, in *William Temple, Archbishop of Canterbury* (1948), accredits him with the words, 'Personally I want (as

at present advised) to see women ordained to the priesthood' (452). Quoted in Hewitt & Hiatt (1973) 108.

51 *ACC 3 – Trinidad* (1976) 44–7.

52 For exchange and correspondence, see GS Misc. 53.

53 See Part One, Section Three.

54 *GS* 1978, 8–9. See letter in response in *Catholic Herald* 10 February 1978.

55 GS Misc. 85A.

56 GS Misc. 86.

57 *Pro and Con on Ordination of Women: Report and Papers from the Anglican–Roman Catholic Consultation in the USA* (1976). This 114-page document contains 10 papers by various authors.

58 *LC* 1978, 44–7. Appended to the report was an abbreviated version of Professor J. Macquarrie's introductory speech at the hearing on 31 July on the ordination of women to the priesthood (116–19).

59 Cf. summary of equivalent section of *WHO* (above, pp. 91–3).

60 Writing in 1970 about the response of the Presbyterian Church (USA) to women's rights, Clifford Earle concluded a study with the comments that (1) forty years after women had been given access to the office of ruling elder (in 1930), still one-third of the churches had none; (2) the average number of active women elders in churches with women on their sessions was less than three per church; and (3) 'The record of our church is very poor in its treatment of women in the ordained ministry' – since ordination had become available to women fourteen years previously hardly more than a hundred had been ordained, and he concluded, 'The church seems not to know what to do with them' Earle (1970).

61 *GS* 1978, 996–1070. Prior to this debate (and the Lambeth Conference that preceded it in August) two books from opposing perspectives were published: Montefiore's *Yes to Women Priests* and Moore's (ed.) *Man, Woman, and Priesthood.*

62 For an opposing play on these words, see the editorial gloss in *Theologia Cumbrensis: A Journal of Theology for the Church in Wales* (1988) 14.

63 *GS* 1979, 108–9; 135–6.

64 *GS* 1979, 2–3.

65 *ARCIC* (1982) 44.

66 *ARCIC* (1982) 44, para. 6.

67 *GS* 1980, 619–32.

68 *ACC 4 – Ontario* (1979) 4–15.

69 GS 415.

70 *GS* 1979, 842–79.

71 MOW was launched on 4 July. Addressing the inaugural meeting in the later autumn, Dr Runcie (then bishop of St Albans) said he happened to believe the movement to be 'mistaken in its particular

concentration but not in opening up the general debate about the place of women in the Church'.

72 *GS* 1982, 652–76.

73 *GS* 1983, 980–1007.

74 A (successful) petition that the measure should come under article 8 had been brought by thirty Synod members. *GS* 1983, 864.

75 *GS* 1984, 636–55. See also GS 598Y.

76 *GS* 1986, 61–9. For voting results see GS 716; for reporting of steering committee see GS 598Z.

77 *GS* 1986, 352–96; for the measure see GS 598B.

78 *GS* 1981, 1078–101.

79 GS 506.

80 *GS* 1981, 1101–16.

81 *GS* 1982, 919–51.

82 *GS* 1983, 620–43; 783–95; for the standing committee report see GS 580A.

83 *GS* 1984, 81–104.

84 *GS* 1985, 14–16. For draft measure see GS580C; for report see GS 580Z.

85 *GS* 1985, 435–8. For voting results see GS 688.

86 *GS* 1985, 439–63.

87 *GS* 1986, 396–401. See also GS 741; GS 742; GS 742A.

88 *GS* 1984, 1078–142. See also GS Misc. 198.

89 *GS* 1986, 632–82. For bishops' memorandum see GS Misc. 246.

90 *GS* 1987, 294–367. For the archbishop of Canterbury's correspondence with the Vatican, see GS Misc. 245, reprinted in GS 829, 125–37.

91 Promised in GS Misc. 269.

92 Print-out of debate kindly supplied by Miss Kerry Lewis of the GS office, Church House, prior to publication. See also GS 830; GS 830X; GS 831; GS 832; GS 833; GS 833X.

THE ROMAN CATHOLIC CHURCH

1 The decision to concentrate on official church documentation has resulted in an increasingly one-sided presentation of the argument in the move from Methodist, via Anglican, to Roman Catholic documentation. Responses to the Roman Catholic official position have been made by theologians: Stuhlmueller (1978) was a direct response to the Declaration; Schillebeeckx (1981 and 1985) considered the wider question of ministry; and Schüssler Fiorenza (1983) has produced the feminist theological reconstruction of Christian origins outlined in Part 2, Section 3.

2 'The Sociology of Roman Catholic Theology' in Martin *et al.*, eds. (1980) 120–35.

3 See Chardin (1965) 325.

4 Paul VI ignored the majority report on the issue on the basis that previous pronouncements could not have been in error. For discussion see Kung (1971) 42–3.

5 See Gheerbrant (1974) 121–263.

6 Martin *et al.*, eds. (1980) 133.

7 See *The Code of Canon Law in English Translation* (1983).

8 Ida Raming (1976) argues that the law limiting ordination to men was based on forgeries, mistaken identities and suppressions as well as on the assumption that women were inferior beings. For a critique of Raming, see Bonner (1978), where he argues that the fact alone that spurious texts were accepted into the *Decretum* does not necessarily vitiate their witness to a long-standing tradition; the fundamental question revolves around the value of that tradition.

9 See Brockett & Howard (1979).

10 For reference in Church of England debate, see *GS* 1975, 593 (above, pp. 133–4).

11 Report reprinted in English in Stuhlmueller (1978) 226–35.

12 See Trible (1979) 75, where she argues that 'helper' (*'ezer*) is a relational word denoting equality. For critique of Trible see Schüssler Fiorenza (1983) 19–21, where she argues that Trible's 'hermeneutic process', rooted in the structure of the biblical text, prevents her from relating it to liberating socio-cultural impulses.

13 For a collaborative statement on Mary by Roman Catholic, Anglican and Protestant scholars, see Brown *et al.*, eds. (1978); for a feminist perspective, Ruether (1977).

14 The commission assumed Pauline authorship.

15 *OWP(S)* 20 also translated διάκονος as 'deacon' (above, p. 109), whereas *MOW19* 4 preferred 'deaconess' (above, p. 73), as did the Methodist 'Committee [Report] on the Status of Deaconesses and the Admission of Women to the Ministry' (1961) 2 (above, pp. 51–2). In fact the term διακόνισσα did not appear until later. The first clearly accredited instance of διακόνισσα seems to be the nineteenth canon of the Council of Nicaea, and C. H. Turner notes (*MOW19* 93, note 3) that the earlier books of the *Apostolic Constitutions* used διάκονος but the author of the *Constitutions* preferred διάκονος, and the later, διακόνισσα, which suggests that the *Didascalia*, the third-century source of the first six books of the *Constitutions*, used διάκονος, but the author of the *Constitutions* preferred διακόνισσα. The (probably fourth-century) Latin translator of the *Didascalia* used 'diaconissa'.

16 For consideration of alternative forms of leadership in the early church, see Schillebeeckx (1981) 20–9, who relates his analysis to present-day grass-roots communities' ministerial practices and future perspectives; Brown (1979), noting 183–98 about women in the fourth gospel; Schüssler Fiorenza (1983) 315–33.

17 For discussion on the use of such language, see Stuhlmueller (1978) 10–11. This book was intended as 'a major contribution to the on-going discussion demanded by the viewpoints set forth in that document' (v), and consisted of contributions by thirteen faculty members of the Catholic Theological Union at Chicago.

18 For development of this view see Ware (1978); for an opposing view see Keifer (1978).

19 See also Bouyer's contribution in Moore, ed. (1978), 63–7.

20 This continued unabated in the wake of the Declaration. In 1978 the second Women's Ordination Conference (WOC) was held in Baltimore, Maryland, 10–12 November. The 2,000 delegates included English representatives from Roman Catholic Feminists (see note 23 below) and St Joan's International Alliance. (See 1978 articles by Carey; Hyer; Papa; Willoughby; and relevant issues of *New Women, New Church.*)

21 Von Allmen is also referred to in Church of England material (above, p. 114).

22 GS Misc. 245, reprinted in GS 829 125–37.

23 (1) Roman Catholic Feminists (RCF) was set up in 1977 'to unite and support women in their struggle to integrate feminism and Roman Catholicism'. RCF was invited to send a delegate to the National Pastoral Congress. (2) Fourteen months prior to publication of this report the ninth National Conference of Priests, meeting in Birmingham 4–8 September 1978, had rejected Fr M. Munnelly's motion: 'This conference calls for a wider participation of women at all levels of life and work within the Christian community', although it had been stressed that the intention was to demonstrate conference's sensitivity rather than to raise the issue of ordination. Opposing, Fr L. Hammond 'repeated that most people would interpret this as a plea for the ordination of women' (*Briefing* 8: 31 (1978) 39). According to Fr Munnelly the voting was 18: 45 with 8 abstentions. See also letter from RCF in *Catholic Herald* 29 September 1978. Eight months after the failure of this motion, and in the wake of the Women's Ordination Conference, USA, in 1978, a petition for the ordination of women was handed in at Archbishop's House, Westminster. See *Guardian* churches correspondent (1979 (Bibliography of references)).

24 The 2,000 delegates were divided into sectors A–G and each sector was subdivided into topic groups.

25 For text of sector reports, see *Universe* 9 May 1980, 3–4, 29–30.

26 See also Clifford Longley's article in *The Times*, 5 May 1980, 'Changing Attitudes on the Question of Women Priests', in which, having noted that the unity movement between the Church of England and the Free Churches was 'seriously at risk' because of 'the Church of England's reluctance to accept women priests very largely in the light of the

Roman Catholic Church's resistance to the idea', he saw the presence of Wijngaards (1977) on a congress reading list 'as a glimmer of hope for that vexed English ecumenical cause'.

27 *National Pastoral Congress: Topic Reports* 41.

28 'Archdiocese of Westminster: Report of the Follow-up Meeting of the JUSTICE SECTOR of the National Pastoral Congress (held on 21/3/81 in Islington Parish)' 4.

29 The International Commission on English in the Liturgy (ICEL) is a joint commission of Roman Catholic Bishops' Conferences. *Eucharistic Prayers* (1980), known also as the Green Book, contains a statement on discriminatory language on pp. 63–7. The American bishops approved the text in November 1980, and the Canadian bishops in 1981, and both revisions were sent to the Holy See for confirmation. (In 1988 the pope refused a request by the bishops of England and Wales to remove discriminatory language from Eucharistic Prayer 4.) ICEL has been actively concerned with the question since 1975 – see *ICEL Newsletter* 6: 4 (October-December 1979) 1–3. For a feminist critique of the Green Book see 'RCF Comments on ICEL's Green Book, *Eucharistic Prayers*, 1980' (20 August 1981).

30 See 'Council of Diocesan Affairs: Minutes of the Meeting held at Hare Street on Monday and Tuesday 11th and 12th May, 1981' 5.

31 See *Briefing* 13: 40 (1983) 3–7.

32 *The Review of Structures and Procedures* (1983) was the final report of the bishops' review committee set up to review the procedures of their own conference and the structures and work of their commissions.

UNDERCURRENTS

1 Thompson (1968) 100–2. He makes the point that, above all, Paine pointed to a theory of the state and of class power, albeit in a confused manner. Interestingly, Paine's rejection of the framework of constitutional government and his emphasis on the rights of the 'living' were written as a reply to Burke's *Reflections on the French Revolution* (1790), which strongly favoured reverence for tradition seen as a partnership between the living, the dead, and those awaiting birth. This ties in with my theory linking tradition, symbol, institution, and identity.

2 Wollstonecraft (1929) 12.

3 Goldmann (1967). I am indebted to this article as an important contribution towards my argument.

4 The example Goldmann gives is of National Socialism in Germany. The ideological nature of bourgeois morality has been considered by Denys Turner (1983). His hypothesis is that Marxism is an indispensable tool in the retrieval of moral language (i.e. truth) but it lacks a

symbol of 'absence' or 'possibility'. Christianity, itself freed from the accretions of bourgeois 'morality', could give credence to the possibility of a future state of affairs to shape our historical praxis.

5 (1) The relationship between law and equality for women can be shown to be economically determined; as women became more important to the economy, 'equal rights' legislation followed. Yet its non-essential character was underlined by the withdrawal of the female vote and the adoption of the '*Kinder, Küche, Kirche*' slogan in Nazi Germany. (2) According to Girard, the function of sacrifice in religion was to syphon off all unappeased violence. As the legal system took over, with the accompanying rationalisation of revenge, the 'transcendence' of religion was replaced by the ascendency of the Law – Girard (1977). Because of the link between sexuality and violence, this can be shown to have a bearing on the legal equality of women.

6 Wollstonecraft (1929) 15.

7 Wollstonecraft (1929), 44, note 1.

8 Wollstonecraft (1929) 62. This was tangentially the theme of *Vanity Fair*, which appeared in the 1840s. Moreover, the 'non'-heroine, Becky Sharp, had to be attributed with some 'vices' to accommodate the Victorian readership, and the choice significantly was prostitution. Thackeray (n.d.) cf. 98.

9 Italicised in Wollstonecraft (1929) 96.

10 Wollstonecraft (1929) 30, 31. This anachronistic (i.e. pre-Bultmann) use of the word 'mythologising' in relation to biblical criticism, which had yet to develop, is my own.

11 Wollstonecraft (1929) 101.

12 Wollstonecraft (1929) 33.

13 In Weber (1985).

14 Tawney (1938).

15 Thompson (1968) 404.

16 Valenze (1982).

17 Taft (1828) 146. In the Church of England 150 years later it was in the house of clergy that the vote to bring forward legislation for the ordination of women was lost.

18 Taft (1825) iii (cf. above, p. 13).

19 Taft (1828) 313. That women also had to contend with 'ignorance and inexperience' was noted by Mary Hewett (146). For another biographical sketch of Sarah Kirkland, see Herod (1854) 305–36.

20 Taft (1828) 256–7.

21 Taft (1825) 178.

22 Taft (1828) 144. The dreamer was Mary Hewett.

23 Thompson (1968) 427–8, where he disagrees with Hobsbawm's thesis that 'Methodism advanced when Radicalism advanced and not when it

grew weaker.' Hobsbawm makes the parallel point that the great religious revolutions did not really occur when economic conditions were coming to their worst. Hobsbawm (1957) 124.

24 Quoted in Thompson (1968) 419. For Thompson's 'spiritual graph' see p. 428.

25 Taylor (1978).

26 See Mack (1982) for the effect of contemporary symbols and stereotypes on the freedom of women prophets during the English Civil War. See also Thomas (1958).

27 Taylor (1978 and 1983).

28 The Owenites lacked the scientific social analysis Karl Marx was to provide. In the Communist *Manifesto* Marx and Friedrich Engels interpreted the Owenites' 'Utopian' vision as 'instinctive yearnings' for a 'reconstruction of society' – towards the realisation of which Marx was to indicate another path. Whereas Owenite women were accorded equality, Engels (1972) accorded priority to the overthrow of the class system with its attendant concern with inheritance. With the entry of women into production and its socialisation, the supremacy of man and the indissolubility of marriage would disappear, he argued, and 'individual sex love' would come into its own – although he stopped short of giving a blueprint of future marriage forms. See Delmar (1976) for a feminist critique of Engels' view.

29 Taylor (1978) 128.

30 George Eliot's aunt, Elizabeth Evans, was a Methodist preacher whose life was recounted in Taft (1825) 145–58. In Eliot's *Adam Bede*, she featured as the heroine, and a comparison of fact and fiction was made by Church (1949) 159–63. On p. 163 Church noted the fictional Dinah Morris' reply when asked whether the Methodist Church sanctioned women's preaching: 'It doesn't forbid them, sir,' she said, 'when they've a clear call to the work, and when their ministry is owned by the conversion of sinners, and the strengthening of God's people ... I understand there's been voices raised against it in the Society of late, but I cannot but think that their counsel will come to naught. It isn't for men to make channels of God's Spirit, as they make channels for the water-course, and say flow here but not flow there.' Church read this reply as representative of the life of Elizabeth Evans.

31 Taylor (1983) 138.

32 See Ruether, ed. (1974) 150–83.

33 For concise summary of legal and political changes, see Gavron (1968) 17–25.

34 Cf. Dr Maltby's comment that the worst obstruction was that which lay in the deep, subliminal parts of the mind. *MR* 23 July 1931, 13.

35 For concise history of the women's movement in Great Britain (to 1920s) see Strachey (1978).

36 This is an anachronistic use of the word 'feminism' since the word did not appear until towards the end of the century.

37 Vidler (1974) 48.

38 It is interesting to note that the feast of the Holy Family was granted to some dioceses by Leo XIII in 1893, and was inserted in the general calendar of the Roman rite by Benedict XV in 1921.

39 Significantly the feast of the Motherhood of the Blessed Virgin Mary was instituted by Pius XI in 1931.

40 See Joan K. Kinnaird, 'Mary Astell: Inspired by Ideas', in Spender, ed. (1983) 28–39.

41 Allchin (1958) 25.

42 Allchin (1958) 33.

43 Allchin (1958) 41. The attribution of madness to Joanna Southcott is not without interest. Not only is it hard to pinpoint 'madness' in the person (cf. Hamlet's madness and, for example, Ernest Jones' paper on the death of Hamlet's father (E. Jones (1947)), but the relationship between the labelling of madness and the social context has been raised by writers such as Thomas Szasz and R. D. Laing – an area I considered in my BA dissertation, 'R. D. Laing and the Social Context'. The move from burning witches (the 'devil-possessed') in a previous economy (which temporally overlapped with capitalism) and incarcerating the mad (the non-rational) in a bourgeois economy merits consideration.

44 Strachey (1978) 21.

45 'By marriage ... the very being or legal existence of a woman is suspended, or at least it is incorporated or consolidated into that of the husband, under whose wing, protection and cover she performs everything, and she is therefore called in our law a feme covert', in *Commentary on the Laws of England* (1765) by W. Blackstone, and quoted in Strachey (1978) 15.

46 Quoted in Strachey (1978) 190 from Lecky (1869). See (1877), vol. 2, 282–3.

47 Reprinted in Strachey (1978) 395–418.

48 For a discussion of neurasthenia in relation to women's social position, see Haller (1974), especially the introduction and Chapter 1. For an individual example, see Strousse (1981).

49 Strachey (1978) 414.

50 Walkowitz (1982b) 31.

51 Austen (1985) 51.

52 Austen (1942) 74–5. For contemporary writers, feminist George Eliot can be compared with anti-feminist Charlotte M. Yonge. The latter's books contain some of the earliest references to sisterhoods in English literature.

53 Allchin (1958) 103.

54 Allchin (1958) 83.

55 Allchin (1958) 214. See 205–16 for an account of the CEA, a charitable organisation founded in 1863 by Emily Ayckbown seven years prior to her foundation of the Community of the Sisters of the Church. The struggle related here has similarities with that of women with quasi-episcopal jurisdiction as recounted by Joan Morris (1973).

56 Allchin (1958) 82.

57 In Appendix IV (*MOW19*) Professor Robinson considered the varying treatment of the deaconess in the books of the *Apostolic Constitutions*. He showed how the third-century *Didascalia* revealed a 'lofty conception of the diaconate of women', which had 'dropped' by the time of the fourth-century writings. He concluded: 'It is plain that the deacon is rising and the deaconess is falling; her work among the sick and poor is passing out of sight, and so, too, is her direct relation to the bishop, as his servant in all matters where a woman's service is more suitable and more efficient than a man's' (71). Faced with the same evidence, Dr Turner (Appendix VI) came to an opposite conclusion: 'Speaking generally, the importance of the deaconess is still growing in the days of the *Constitutions*. It is true that we no longer hear of any teaching given by the deaconesses, and, of course, less is made of the difficulty of the clergy entering pagan households at a date when fewer households were pagan. But on the other side of the count a new function is attributed to the deaconess in the seating and supervision of the female part of the congregation' (97). However, Dr Collins (Appendix VII) expressed his agreement with Professor Robinson that a great change had come over the deaconess' position by quoting Professor Robinson's words: 'we feel instinctively that the deaconess has dropped. She is, indeed, first among the women of the Church, but Readers and Singers and Doorkeepers have got in front of her . . . The Deacon is the servant of the Bishop; the Deaconess is the servant of the Deacon' (quoted in *MOW19* 116 from Professor J. A. Robinson's appendix to *The Ministry of Deaconesses* by Deaconess Cecilia Robinson (1898, Methuen) 175).

58 See Walkowitz' article and book, and Taylor's review of the latter, Walkowitz (1982a), (1982b); Taylor (1981).

59 See Jenny Uglow, 'Josephine Butler: From Sympathy to Theory 1828–1906', in Spender, ed. (1983) 146–64.

60 Quoted by Uglow in Spender, ed. (1983) 154. Walkowitz (1982b) noted that unlike nonconformists and evangelicals, Anglican clergy could be counted on to lend their support to the regulationist cause rather than the repeal campaign (80, 162) and that George Butler was shouted down when he tried to read a paper critical of the acts at church congress in 1871. She concluded: 'by the 1880s most Protestant denominations, as well as the Catholic Church (in the person of

Cardinal Manning), had sided with repealers. In contrast, no official body of the Church of England formally opposed the acts' (278, note 56).

61 Following W. T. Stead's revelations on child prostitution in the *Pall Mall Gazette*, for a brief period in 1885 all groups combined – Anglican clergy, repealers, nonconformists, feminists, socialists – to demand the raising of the age of consent for girls from thirteen to sixteen. The result was the passing of the Criminal Law Amendment Act the same year. However, the act also gave power to suppress all houses 'in which women, whose relations with the other sex lack the sanction of priest or registrar, find shelter'. Walkowitz (1982b) 246–7.

62 Walkowitz (1982a) 89.

63 According to Sheila Jeffreys, some feminists were extending their critique of male sexual behaviour to proclaiming the virtue of remaining single and celibate, which generated anxiety among anti-feminists and some feminists. Their argument was that as the single woman improved her condition, she undermined the prestige of marriage and opened up a viable alternative for women. This was the position of many in the Women's Social and Political Union (WSPU) and was dubbed by one: 'The silent strike.' Opposition to this position was mounted by contributors to *The Freewoman* in such lines as: 'I write of the High Priestess of Society. Not of the mother of sons [*sic*], but of her barren sister, the withered tree, the acidulous vestal under whose pale shadow we chill and whiten, of the Spinster I write.' Quoted in Jeffreys (1982) 642. Interesting is the lack of argument, the emphasis on bodily function ('the mother of sons'), and above all, the level of anxiety raised – points that will be considered in the final section.

64 Weeks (1981) 126.

65 Margaret Llewelyn Davies, General Secretary of the Women's Co-operative Guild, collected the 160 letters. Written by members, they tell 'of childbirth and death, exhaustion and self-sacrifice, of totally inadequate pre-natal care, of poverty, abortion, sometimes despair'. From 'New Introduction' by Gloden Dallas to Davies (1978).

66 Weeks (1981) 195.

67 From letter to Carl Müller-Braunschweig, 1935, quoted in Mitchell & Rose (1982) 1.

68 Freud's name was not mentioned, and in the psychological section it is Havelock Ellis who is footnoted (*MOW 35* 79–87). For summary, see above, pp. 83–4, noting Grensted's refutation of the theory of the sexlessness of the male priest. The emergence of the argument in the documentation is interesting when viewed against the late- and post-Victorian background where the reverse was held, giving rise to a concern for 'denied' female sexuality in the post-war years.

69 Dinnerstein (1976) has moved from the violent pre-Oedipal relationship between mother and child in Klein to explain the theme of the hatred of women in public life, which she bases on the phantasy of the powerful mother. Chodorow (1978) takes up a similar theme, and attempts to explain how women learn to mother, but in so doing she refuses the distinction between social role and sphere of the unconscious. For feminist reactions, see Lorber, Coser, Rossi & Chodorow (1981); Sayers (1982).

70 Abbott (1966) 227–8.

71 Ratzinger (1977).

72 Cf. Vidler (1974) 262.

STRATEGIES

1 Radar interference system of pieces of metallic foil dropped by aircraft during the Second World War, code-named 'window'.

2 GS 764 16.

INTERPRETATIONS

1 *Letters of John Wesley* VI: 290–1, quoted in Church (1949) 139–40. Cf. Taft (1828) 58.

2 Taft (1825) vi.

3 *Minutes* 1819 (1825) 4–5.

4 *MR* 30 July 1925, 8.

5 *MR* 22 July 1948, 8.

6 *MR* 27 July 1939, 20.

7 Declaration (1976) Section 5.

8 Balthasar (1977) 7.

9 Martelet (1977) 7.

10 *CC(C)* 1862, 916.

11 *GS* 1972, 709. Cf. Descamps (1977).

12 *CA* February 1967, 211.

13 *CA* July 1967, 304.

14 *Partners in Mission* (1973) 37.

15 In Martin *et al.*, eds. (1980) 120–35.

16 See Emilio Betti, 'Hermeneutics as the General Methodology of the *Geisteswissenschaften*'; Hans-Georg Gadamer, 'The Universality of the Hermeneutical Problem'; Jürgen Habermas, 'The Hermeneutic Claim to Universality'; all printed in Bleicher (1980), 51–94; 128–40; 181–211 respectively. See also Habermas (1974). For the debate between Betti and Gadamer and also for the history of hermeneutics see Palmer (1969) and Bleicher (1980), both of which include sections on Schleier-

macher, Dilthey, and the theologians Bultmann, Fuchs and Ebeling. For the debate between Gadamer and Habermas see Bleicher (1980). Ashton (1975) considers the debate between Hirsch and Gadamer (as does Palmer), and between Gadamer and Habermas in relation to tradition and authority.

17 Stuhlmueller, ed. (1978) 95.

18 Reviews of Schüssler Fiorenza (1983) include the following (abbreviations given for journal titles are used in subsequent notes and in the text).

America [*Amer*] 149 (December 1983), 353–4, by Nancy C. Ring, Assistant Professor of Religious Studies at Le Moyne College, NY.

Anima [*Anima*] (Chambersberg, PA) 10 (2, 1984), 95–112 by Susan M. Setta (ed.) 96–8; Judith Plaskow 98–102; Susan Brooks Thistletwaite 102–5; Antoinette Clark Wire 105–9; with reply by Elisabeth Schüssler Fiorenza 109–12.

Best Sellers 43 (8, 1983), 188, by M. Filey.

Catholic Biblical Quarterly [*CathBibQuart*] 46 (7, 1984), 567–8, by Rose H. Arthur of Meadville/Lombard Theological School, Chicago.

Commonweal 110 (7 Oct. 1983), 537, by A. Swidler.

Cross Currents [*CrossC*] 33 (winter 1983–4), 455–61, by Mary Jo Weaver.

Doctrine and Life [*DocLi*] 34: 7 (9, 1984), 388–404 and 34: 9 (11, 1984), 495–9, by Jerome Murphy-O'Connor of the Ecole Biblique in Jerusalem.

East Asia Journal of Theology [*EAJT*] 3 (2, 1985), 147–53, by Kwok Pui Lan, who taught Religion and Society at Chung Chi Theology Division, the Chinese University of Hong Kong, and at the time of writing was studying at the Harvard Divinity School.

Ecumenist [*Ecumt*] 23: 6 (9–10, 1985), 86–9, by Mary Rose D'Angelo, Professor of New Testament, St Thomas Theological Seminary, Denver, CO.

Etudes 365 (7–8, 1986), 138, by René Marlé.

Furrow [*Fur*] 35 (3, 1984), 203–4, by Graine O'Flynn.

Horizons: Journal of the College Theology Society [*Horiz*] 11 (1, 1984), 142–57, by Pheme Perkins, Boston College, 142–4; John Koenig, The General Theological Seminary, 144–6; Rosemary Radford Ruether, Garrett Evangelical Theological Seminary, 146–50; Beverley W. Harrison, Union Theological Seminary, NY, 150–3; with reply by Elisabeth Schüssler Fiorenza, University of Notre Dame, 154–7.

Journal of Biblical Literature [*JouBibLit*] 104: 4 (1985), 722–5, by Ross S. Kraemer, Medical College of Pennsylvania, Philadelphia.

Journal of Religion [*JouRe*] 65 (1985) 83–8, by Robert M. Grant, University of Chicago.

Lexington Theological Quarterly (KY) [*LexTheolQuart*] 20 (2, 1985), 58–60, by Beverley R. Gaventa, Colgate Rochester Divinity School.

Louvain Studies [*LouSt*] 10 (spring 1984), 70, by R. Collins.

National Catholic Reporter 19: 41 (16 September 1983), 25, by Mary G. Durkin, pastoral theologian.

New Blackfriars 65 (3, 1984), 141–2, by Margaret Pamment.

New Catholic World 227 (9–10, 1984), 238, by J. Elliott.

Nouvelle Revue Théologique 108 (9–10, 1986), 759–60, by X. Jacques.

Religious Studies Review [*RelStRev*] 11: 1 (1, 1985), 1–4, by Cornel West of Yale Divinity School, New Haven, CT; and 6–9 by Ross S. Kraemer (see *JouBibLit*).

Revue Biblique [*RevBib*] 91: 2 (4, 1984), 287–94, by Jerome Murphy-O'Connor (see *DocLi*).

Revue Philosophique de Louvain [*RevPhLou*] 84 (5, 1986), 275–7, by Jean-Yves Lacoste.

Second Century [*SecCent*] 4 (3, 1984), 177–84, by William S. Babcock, Associate Professor of Church History at Perkins School of Theology, Southern Methodist University, Dallas, TX.

Sisters Today 55 (10, 1983), 144, by C. Litechy.

Spirituality Today 36 (spring 1984), 86, by Diana Culbertsen of Kent State University, Ohio.

Le Supplément (*Vie Spirituelle*) 157 (7, 1986), 145–9, by M. Morgan.

Theological Studies [*ThStu*] 45 (12, 1984), 729–31, by Robert Kress of the Catholic University of America.

A review of the collection of Schüssler Fiorenza's essays on biblical hermeneutics, *Bread Not Stone* (1984), is also included:

Theology [*Theol(BNS)*] XC (11, 481–4, by Marie E. Isaacs, Head of New Testament Studies, Heythrop College, University of London.

19 Schüssler Fiorenza draws on Chicago's work, which aims to reclaim the needlecraft heritage of women, which has not been recognised, as source of symbol and power. Schüssler Fiorenza (1983) xix.

20 See my article in *Modern Churchman* (1989) 30: 4, 35–41.

21 For discussion on Schüssler Fiorenza's methodology *vis-à-vis* other feminist theologians, together with author's reply, see *Anima* 102–5; 109–12. See also debate with Ruether (*Horiz* 146–50; 154–7).

22 Metz (1980) 112, quoted in Schüssler Fiorenza (1983) 32.

23 Cf *OWP(S)* 17. See Schüssler Fiorenza (1983) xix for western contextualisation.

24 Schüssler Fiorenza (1984) appears to move the criterion of revelatory authenticity from the community of disciples around Jesus, to the

contemporary experience of women struggling for liberation. For comment and review see *Theol(BNS)*.

25 Form and redaction criticism stress the aspect of community. See Perrin (1970) and Ashton (1972).

26 Differences of opinion over dating cannot be ignored. Henri-Charles Pugh writes, 'It is difficult to assign a very precise date to the *Gospel of Thomas*', and prefers AD 140, putting the last possible date at the beginning of the third century. The *Gospel According to Mary* he dates in the second century, and *Pistis Sophia* between 250 and 300. In Hennecke (1963) 305; 344 and 250 respectively. Babcock thinks that this is an example of Schüssler Fiorenza pushing her evidence; he would date the *Acts of Paul and Thecla* near the end of the second century (*SecCent* 182–3).

27 See R. Scroggs, 'The Earliest Christian Communities as Sectarian Movement', 2: 1–23, and Sheldon R. Isenberg, 'Power through Temple and Torah in Greco-Roman Palestine', 2: 24–52, both in Jacob Neusner (1975); S. R. Isenberg 'Millenarism in Greco-Roman Palestine' in *Religion* 4 (1974), 26–46; Gager (1975) and Theissen (1978).

28 Schüssler Fiorenza (1983) 84–92. She refers to Boulding (1976); Marilyn B. Arthur, 'Women in the Ancient World', in *Conceptual Frameworks for Studying Women's History* (1975, a Sarah Lawrence College Women's Studies Publication, NY) 1–15; and Sheila Ryan Johansson '"Herstory" as History: A New Field or Another Fad?' in Carroll (1976), 400–30.

29 But cf. the 1987 Roman Catholic Synod on the laity, where proposals to extend official ministries to women disappeared from the final proposals to be presented to the pope (see below, p. 347, note 3).

30 For consideration as part of the early Christian missionary movement, see Schüssler Fiorenza (1983) 168–75; for discussion on translation of the texts, 47–8. For a differing interpretation see Declaration (1976) Section 3.

31 Although I have linked the concept of equality with the eighteenth century, the early Christian community nevertheless aspired towards the implementation of Galatians 3: 28.

32 See Judge (1960), 60, and quoted in Schüssler Fiorenza (1983) 253.

33 Schüssler Fiorenza (1983) 262 refers to D. Balch, 'Let Wives Be Submissive: The Domestic Code in 1 Peter', in its dissertation form (1974, Ann Arbor: University Microfilms), 102.

34 In a variant reading of Luke 23: 1 attested for the first time by Marcion in the second century, Jesus is accused of leading astray both women and children, and the same accusation appears in the apocryphal Acts which was circulating in Asia Minor when 1 Peter and the pastorals were being written. Schüssler Fiorenza (1983) 265.

35 For this perspective, see Schillebeeckx (1981 (reviewed in Yarnold (1981)) and 1985).

36 Schüssler Fiorenza sites 'the *ekklesia* of women' at the centre, as 'the actual assembly of free citizens gathering for deciding their own spiritual-political affairs' (344). This does not imply a rejection of the institutional church, but an alternative perspective as a reversal of the marginalisation process. Kress finds this not to be on target (*ThStu* 730).

37 *MR* 23 July 1931, 13.

38 *MR* 22 July 1926, 13.

39 Cf. Freud's hypothesis of the way jokes are formed in the first person: '*a preconscious thought is given over for a moment to unconscious revision and the outcome of this is at once grasped by conscious perception*' (*PFL* 6: 223).

40 *PFL* 6: 237–8.

41 Bleicher (1980) 200.

42 Considering the rectification of prejudice required in the 'fusion of horizon', Bleicher writes: 'Critique, in the form of a cor(r)-ection, constitutes an integral element in the dialectical process of understanding' (1980) 153.

43 E. Jones (1953) 1: 247–8.

44 See 'The Question of the Subject: The Challenge of Semiology' in Ricoeur (1974) 236–66.

45 See 'Fatherhood: From Phantasm to Symbol' in Ricoeur (1974) 468–97. An earlier appearance of this interpretation occurs in Ricoeur (1970) 344–551.

46 Cf. Marx's economic analysis of society.

47 Schüssler Fiorenza (1983). Spender (1983) 1–7 has described a similar blocking process with regard to the theories of women.

48 See Ruether (1974) 150–83.

49 Disclosures surrounding Childline would lend further support to the argument that Freud's first interpretation was a more accurate perception of reality.

50 For case history see *PFL* 3: 73–102.

51 Meltzer (1978) 1: 18–19.

52 Her method here predates the case of Little Hans, to which both Habermas and Lorenzer refer.

53 The first appearance of the word – *PFL* 3: 100, note 1.

54 Van der Kleij notes that Freud, in *Aphasia* (1891), refuted the theory of localisation basing almost all his arguments on the English biologist Hughlings Jackson. As early as 1866 Jackson had argued against the atomistic approach which located speech defects in corresponding lesions of the brain. Van der Kleij (1982) 225.

55 *PFL* 4: 56.

56 Quoted in Laplanche & Pontalis (1983) 452.
57 For case history see *PFL* 8: 31–164.
58 *PFL* 8: 32.
59 Freud's use of the concepts of 'masculinity' and 'femininity' was ultimately conventional, linking the former with 'activity' (and hence with libido) and the latter with 'passivity'. He often stressed the varying usages of the concepts, and emphasised that mixtures of both appeared in the gendered human being as a result of 'bi-sexuality'. But in the wake of Darwin, and because of the close link between instinct, source and representation, ultimately he described specific character traits as 'belonging to' a specific sex. I suggest he did not notice the slippage between description and prescription because of his unconscious adoption of the androcentric paradigm as 'reality', and his consequent assumptions of which character traits biological gender 'normally' brought in its train, bi-sexuality being used as a 'screen concept'.
60 'Fragment of an Analysis of a Case of Hysteria' (1905[1901]) in *PFL* 8: 31–164.
61 Cf. *PFL* 8: 287 – the phantasy in which Little Hans bought a ride on a truck, which was interpreted to mean buying his mother from his father, and thus indicating a desire for his father's wealth/power (I would add: over women).
62 Cf. Geoffrey Gorer (1962) concerning Jane Austen's treatment of the father figure.
63 While pointing out that the concept of counter-transference had not yet evolved, Meltzer nevertheless appears to absolve Freud from such in the Dora case. Meltzer (1978) 1: 54–5.
64 *PFL* 5: 302.
65 *PFL* 7: 33–169.
66 'Analysis of a Phobia in a Five-Year-Old Boy' in *PFL* 8: 167–305.
67 *PFL* 8: 175–6, note 2.
68 Meltzer (1978) 1: 46–53.
69 Chasseguet-Smirgel (1976) was originally presented as part of a dialogue on 'Freud and Female Sexuality' at the 29th Congress of the International Psychoanalysis Association (IPA), London, July 1975. The congress was reviewed in Fuller (1975).
70 *PFL* 13: 43–224; *SE* 13: 1–161.
71 *PFL* 13: 203; *SE* 13: 142.
72 See Girard (1977) 193–222.
73 This can be compared with the perspective underlying Gregory van der Kleij's paper, 'Symbol and Horizon' (1980), unpublished manuscript, Turvey Abbey Library. I am grateful to him for drawing my attention to the work of Girard.

74 *PFL* 12: 93–178.
75 *PFL* 12: 134.
76 *PFL* 12: 147.
77 *PFL* 11: 341–407.
78 See Girard (1977) 169–92.
79 *PFL* 7: 325–43.
80 *PFL* 7: 337.
81 For a contemporary Lacanian feminist approach, see Mitchell & Rose (1982). This was reviewed by Ann Scott (1983), who raised the question of the linguistic categories used in the book and our conscious experience; psychical reality, she argued, remains unexplained.
82 *PFL* 2: 145–69.
83 *PFL* 2: 149.
84 In *Modern Churchman* 31: 2 (1989), 5–9.
85 Ricoeur (1974) 468–97.
86 Girard traces a link between the taboos surrounding menstruation and violence, arguing that menstrual blood symbolises sexual violence. He asks whether 'this process of symbolization does not respond to some half-suppressed desire to place the blame for all forms of violence on women'. However, his argument still leaves women as objects. Girard (1977) 33–6.
87 The plea to detach personality from sexuality recurs in the documentation. Cf. *C.A.* 1926, 73–4, in the Methodist Church; *C.A.* 1967, 291, referring to 279–82, in the Church of England.

THE US CONNECTION

1 Brailsford (1915) 13.
2 Fell (1710) 331–50.
3 Isichei (1970) 94; Leach (1979) 3–4.
4 Between 1667 and 1671 Fox and other Friends established a series of meetings. The central focus was the monthly meeting, responsible for membership and pastoral care, and matters of discipline. County quarterly meetings were established with a Yearly Meeting in London for the whole country. By the end of the seventeenth century there were six Yearly Meetings in the world, each autonomous, but often exchanging letters. The London Yearly Meeting of 1675 established a meeting for sufferings (persecution). The society recognises 'elders' responsible for the conduct of meetings for worship.
5 Brailsford (1915) 283; Braithwaite (1961) 274.
6 Braithwaite (1961) 287 quoting from J. S. Rowntree, *Meetings on Ministry and Oversight* no. 2, 16.
7 R. M. Jones (1921) 114–16.

8 Phinney (1969) 5.
9 *Journal of the General Conference (GC)* 1880, 353.
10 *Judicial Decisions of the General Conference*, 1903, 149–51.
11 *GC* 1924, 284, 317, 1697–98.
12 *Minutes*, New York Annual Conference, 1880, 4. See also Burke (1964) 2: 406.
13 Noll (1977) 120
14 Noll (1977) 120.
15 *Doctrines and Discipline of the Methodist Church*, 1956, 115, para. 303; 165, para. 562; *Daily Christian Advocate*, 25 April 1956, 3; *Decisions of the Judicial Council*, 1968, 365.
16 *Journal of General Convention (JGC)* 1889, 108–9, 134.
17 *JGC* 1919, 139.
18 *JGC* 1922, 155, 674–82.
19 *JGC* 1925, 600. See also 335, 599–605.
20 *JGC* 1934, 482–6. See also 199.
21 *JGC* 1949, 234.
22 *JGC* 1964, 247.
23 From xerox of pamplet, *Women in Priesthood*, p. 17, issued by the National Committee of Episcopal Clergy and Laity for the Ordination of Women to the Priesthood prior to the 1976 General Convention. I am grateful to Avis E. Harvey of the Sherrill Resource Center for her helpful references in connection with events in the Protestant Episcopal Church in the USA.
24 *JGC* 1970, 270–1.
25 *JGC* 1966, Appendix 35.4–35.12.
26 *JGC* 1970, 159. See also 60, 800.
27 *JGC* 1972, 1114–32.
28 *JGC* 1976, B–120–24, B–130.
29 From letter and xerox of 'The Affirmation of St Louis', sent by Dorothy A. Faber, ed., *Christian Challenge*.
30 *The Times*, 28 October 1977. See also letters to the editor.
31 *The Times*, 13 January 1982 (Clifford Longley). See also 18 January (Clifford Longley) and 25 January (Caroline Moorehead). I am grateful to Patience O'Leary for sending me these cuttings. For further details see my article, 'From Deaconess to Bishop: The Vicissitudes of Woman's Ministry in the Protestant Episcopal Church in the USA', *Heythrop Journal*, Oct. 1991/Jan. 1992.

STRUCTURES OF THREE INSTITUTIONALISED CHURCHES

1 Further information can be found in the following books from which this appendix has been assembled: primary source: Cross & Livingstone, eds. (1978); supplemented by Crockford (1985–6); Douglas, ed. (1974); Foy (1979); *New Catholic Encyclopedia* (1967) & (1974). I am grateful to Allison Palmer, Methodist Church Archivist at Rylands Library, for some helpful material on Methodist Conferences.

2 *Tablet* (2 March 1968) 212.

3 The 1987 Synod of Bishops discussed the role of the laity. There was a news blackout prior to the publication of the propositions to be presented to the pope. This was directed not only against the press. Lay representatives, who had no voting rights, were not allowed to see the list, and bishops were informed that it would be *gravely sinful* to show it to anyone or to photocopy it. The most striking discrepancy between the list drawn up by the small groups (*circuli minores*) and the definitive draft concerned lay ministries, particularly the proposal that these should be open to women and men equally – the entire section was deleted in the final list. *Tablet* (31 October 1987) 1189. For a brief summary of the propositions approved by the synod and presented to the pope see *Tablet* (14 November 1987) 1250–1.

4 Hornsby-Smith & Cordingly (1983) 5.

BIBLIOGRAPHY OF DOCUMENTS

Subsections within the bibliography of documents are in alphabetical order as follows: **Anglican-related material**: *Anglican Consultative Council, Anglican–Roman Catholic Consultation, Anglican–Roman Catholic International Commission, Church Assembly and related reports, Convocations, General Synod, Lambeth Conference;* **The Methodist Church in England**: *the Bible Christians, the Primitive Methodists, the Wesleyan Methodists, the Methodist Church (from 1932);* **Roman Catholic material**: *centralised documentation, English documentation, International Commission on English in the Liturgy, Women's Ordination Conference related material;* **World Council of Churches material**. *The schematic supplementary* **US material** *is ordered as follows: Anglican Catholic Church, USA; Protestant Episcopal Church in the USA; the Methodist Church in the USA: Methodist Episcopal Church, Methodist Protestant Church, Methodist Church (from 1940), United Methodist Church (from 1968). Sequences of documents under the subsection headings are arranged chronologically.*

ANGLICAN-RELATED MATERIAL

Anglican Consultative Council (ACC)

The Time is Now ACC 1 – Limuru (1971, Society for the Propagation of Christian Knowledge (SPCK), London) 34–9.

Partners in Mission ACC 2 – Dublin (1973, SPCK, London) 37–42.

ACC 3 – Trinidad (1976, ACC, London) 44–7.

ACC 4 – Ontario (1979, ACC, London) 4, 9, 14–16.

ACC 5 – Newcastle-upon-Tyne (1981, ACC, London).

ACC 6– Badagry, Nigeria (1984, ACC, London).

Many Gifts, One Spirit. Report of ACC 7 Singapore: 1987 (1987, Church House Publishing, London).

Anglican–Roman Catholic Consultation

Pro and Con on Ordination of Women: Report and papers from the Anglican–Roman Catholic Consultation in the USA (1976; Seabury Professional Services, 815 Second Ave, New York).

Anglican–Roman Catholic International Commission (ARCIC)

The Three Agreed Statements: Eucharistic Doctrine 1971; Ministry and Ordination 1973; Authority in the Church 1976 (1977, Catholic Truth Society (CTS) & SPCK, London).

The Anglican–Roman Catholic International Commission: The Final Report, Windsor, September 1981 (1982, CTS & SPCK, London).

Church Assembly and related reports

Church Assembly: Report of Proceedings (Church Information Office (CIO) & SPCK, London) 1962/681–714; 1967/190–220, 279–318; 1969/556–84.

The Ministry of Women: Report by a Committee appointed by the Archbishop of Canterbury (1919; SPCK, London, & Macmillan, New York).

Women and Priesthood (1929) Memorandum of Anglican Group for bringing the subject of the admission of women to the priesthood before the next [1930] Lambeth Conference (Rydal Press, Keighley).

The Ministry of Women: Report of the Archbishops' Commission (1935; Press and Publications Board of the Church Assembly, London).

Gender and Ministry: Report of the Central Advisory Council for the Ministry (1962; CIO, London).

Women and Holy Orders: Report of the Archbishops' Commission (1966; CIO, London).

Women and the Ordained Ministry: Report of an Anglican–Methodist Commission on Women and Holy Orders (1968; Epworth & SPCK, London).

Women in Ministry: A Study: Report on the Working Party set up jointly by the Ministry Committee of the Advisory Council for the Church's Ministry and the Council for Women's Ministry in the Church (1968; CIO, London).

Lambeth Essays on Ministry (1969) Archbishop of Canterbury, ed. (SPCK, London).

Convocations

The Chronicle of Convocation, being a Record of the Proceedings of the Convocation of Canterbury. 1861/828–41; 1862/910–68 (London). 1875/286, 338; 1878/1–9, 238–67 (Rivingtons, London). 1883/127–38, 168; 1885/274–80; 1890/111–24, 167–81; 1891/42–6 (National Society's Depository, London) 1919/82–, 223–; 1920/27; 1921/4–21; 1973/22–62 (SPCK, London).

The York Journal of Convocation Containing the Acts and Debates of the Convocation of the Province of York 1973/32–70 (CIO, London).

Acts of the Convocations of Canterbury and York (originally edited for the years 1921 to 1947 by A. F. Smethurst and H. R. Wilson extended to cover the years 1921 to 1970) (1971) H. Riley & R. J. Graham, eds. (SPCK, London) 43–50.

General Synod

General Synod: Report of proceedings (CIO, London).

GS. *Draft Canon D1. (As revised by the Committee appointed at the Autumn Group of Sessions 1970.) Of the Order of Deaconesses* (1971) GS 5A.

GS. *Petition to the Crown* (1972) GS 5B.

GS. *The Ordination of Women to the Priesthood* (1972). A consultative document presented by ACCM and compiled by Christian Howard (also known as the 'Howard Report') GS 104.

GS. *The Ordination of Women to the Priesthood* (1973) A summary of the consultative document presented by ACCM. GS 104A.

GS. *The Ordination of Women to the Priesthood: Reference to the Dioceses* (1973) Memorandum from the standing committee. GS Misc. 26.

GS. *Supplementary Report on: The Ordination of Women* (1975) GS 104B.

GS. *The Ordination of Women to the Priesthood: Report of the Standing Committee on Reference to the Dioceses* (1975) GS 252.

GS. *The Archbishop of Canterbury's Correspondence with Leaders of Other Churches on the Ordination of Women* (1976) GS Misc. 53.

GS. *The Ministry of Deacons and Deaconesses: ACCM Report* (1977) GS 344.

GS. *The House of Bishops – Minutes* (1978) HB(78)(M)M2.

GS. *The Ordination of Women: Anglican–Roman Catholic International Consultation* (1978) GS Misc. 85.

GS. *Anglican–Roman Catholic Consultation on the Ordination of Women to the Priesthood* (1978) GS Misc. 85A.

GS. *The Ordination of Women: Report of the Anglican/Orthodox Joint Doctrinal Commission* (1978) GS Misc. 86.

GS. *The Ordination of Women: Arrangements for the November Debate* (1978) GS Misc. 87.

GS. *The Ordination of Women: A Supplement to the Consultative Document GS 104* (1978) Prepared at the request of the standing committee by Miss Christian Howard. GS Misc. 88.

GS. *Woman [*sic*] Lawfully Ordained Abroad: Report of a Working Group appointed by the Standing Committee* (1979) GS 415.

GS. *Special Agenda: Private Members' Motions* (1979) GS 420.

GS. *Guidelines Concerning Women Priests Who Visit Other Provinces* (1980) GS Misc. 127.

GS. *The Deaconess Order and the Diaconate: Report by the House of Bishops* (1981) GS 506.

GS. *Ordination of Deaconesses to the Diaconate: Report by the Standing Committee* (1982) GS 549.

GS. *Draft The Ordination of Women as Deacons Measure* (1983) GS 580.

GS. *The Ordination of Women as Deacons: Report by the Standing Committee* (1983) GS 580A.

GS. *Draft Women Ordained Abroad Measure* (1983) GS 598.

GS. *Draft Women Ordained Abroad Measure: Explanatory Memorandum* (1983) GS 598X.

GS. *Draft Women Ordained Abroad Measure: Report of the Revision Committee* (1984) GS 598Y.

GS. *The Ordination of Women to the Priesthood: Further Report* (1984) Compiled by Christian Howard. GS Misc. 198.

GS. *Draft Women Ordained Abroad Measure: Draft Amending Canon No. 13: Reference Under Article 8: Memorandum of the Standing Committee* (1984) GS Misc. 208.

GS. *Draft Deacons (The Ordination of Women) Measure: Report of the Revision Committee* (1984) GS 580Y.

GS. *Draft Deacons (The Ordination of Women) Measure: Report of the Steering Committee* (1985) GS 580Z.

GS. *Draft Deacons (The Ordination of Women) Measure* (1985) GS 580C.

GS. *Draft Deacons (The Ordination of Women) Measure and Draft Canon C 4A – Of Women Deacons* (1985) GS 688.

Gs. *Draft Women Ordained Abroad Measure: Draft Amending Canon No. 13: Report by the Steering Committee* (1986) GS 598Z.

GS. *Draft Women Ordained Abroad Measure and Draft Amending Canon No. 13* (1986) GS 716.

GS. *The Ordination of Women: The Archbishop of Canterbury's Correspondence with the Vatican* (1986) GS Misc. 245.

GS. *The Ordination of Women to the Priesthood: The Scope of the Legislation* (1986) GS 738.

Gs. *Draft Canon C 4A (Of Women Deacons): A Report by the Standing Committee* (1986) GS 741.

GS. *Canon C 4A: Of Women Deacons* (1986) GS 742.

General Synod of the Church of England: Petition to the Crown (1986) GS 742A.

GS. *The Ordination of Women to the Priesthood: The Scope of the Legislation (GS 738): Memorandum by the House of Bishops* (1986) GS Misc. 246.

GS. *The Ordination of Women to the Priesthood: A Report by the House of Bishops* (1987) GS 764.

GS. *The Ordination of Women to the Priesthood: A Report by the House of Bishops (Memorandum by Chairman)* (1987) GS Misc. 269.

GS. *Women in Professional Ministry in the Church 1987* (1987) GS Misc. 273.

GS. *The Ordination of Women to the Priesthood: A Second Report by the House of Bishops of the General Synod of the Church of England* (1988) GS 829.

GS. *Draft Priests (The Ordination of Women) Measure* (1988) GS 830.

GS. *Draft Priests (The Ordination of Women) Measure: Draft Canon C 4B: Draft Amending Canon No. 13: Explanatory Memorandum* (1988) GS 830X.

GS. *Draft Canon C 4B (of Women Priests)* (1988) GS 831.

GS. *Draft Amending Canon No. 13* (1988) GS 832.

GS. Draft The Ordination of Women (Financial Provisions) Measure (1988) GS 833.

GS. Draft The Ordination of Women (Financial Provisions) Measure: Explanatory Memorandum (1988) GS 833X.

Making Women Visible: The Use of Inclusive Language with the ASB. A Report by the Liturgical Commission of the General Synod of the Church of England (1989), 1st edn 1988, for GS members GS 859 (Church House Publishing, London).

Lambeth Conference (LC)

Conference of Bishops of the Anglican Communion. Holden at Lambeth Palace, in July, 1897. Encyclical Letter from the Bishops, with the Resolutions and Reports (1897, SPCK, London & Brighton).

Conference of Bishops of the Anglican Communion. Holden at Lambeth Palace, July 5 to August 7, 1920. Encyclical Letter from the Bishops, with the Resolutions and Reports (1920, SPCK, London, & Macmillan, New York).

The Lambeth Conference 1930: Encyclical Letter from the Bishops with Resolutions and Reports (1930, SPCK, London, & Macmillan, New York).

The Lambeth Conference 1948: The Encyclical Letter from the Bishops; together with Resolutions and Reports (1948, SPCK, London).

The Lambeth Conference 1968: Resolutions and Reports (1968, SPCK, London, & Seabury Press, New York).

The Report of the Lambeth Conference, 1978 (1978, CIO, London).

The Truth Shall Make You Free: The Lambeth Conference 1988 (1988, Church House Publishing, London).

Women and the Episcopate: Report of the Primates' Working Party (also known as the Grindrod report) for Lambeth 1988.

THE METHODIST CHURCH IN ENGLAND

The Bible Christians

Minutes of the First Conference of the Preachers in Connexion with William O'Bryan. 1819 (1925, J. Thorne, at the office of the Arminian Bible Christians, Stoke-Damarel).

Minutes (Extracts from the Minutes) of the Second (-Ninth) Annual Conference between William O'Brian and the Preachers in Connexion with him. 1820 (-1827) (1825–27, Stoke-Damarel) 1820/4, 12–13; 1821/Q6; 1822/3–7; 1823/4–5; 1824/Q5; 1825/5, 7; 1826/5; 1827/5, 11.

Extracts from the Minutes of the Tenth (-Eighty-Eighth) Annual Conference of the Ministers and Representatives of the People denominated Bible Christians (1828–1907, Stoke-Damarel) 1828/5, 6; 1829/7; 1830/5, 13; 1831/4;

1832/4, 8; 1833/5; 1834/5; 1835/5; 1836/5; 1837/5; 1838/5; 1839/5; 1840/5; 1841/5, 7–8; 1842/5; 1843/6; 1844/6; 1845/5; 1846/5; 1847–74/list of female itinerants (FI); 1890–1904/FI; 1905/FI, 55–6; 1906/FI; 1907/6.

A Digest of Rules and Regulations and Usages of the People denominated Bible Christians (1838) compiled by order of the Annual Conference (J. Thorne, Shebbear, Devon).

The Bible Christians: Rules and Regulations Canadian Version. (1876, Bible Christian Book Room) 15.

The Magazine of the Bible Christian (1823–7).

The Bible Christian Magazine ... being a continuation of the Arminian Magazine 11–86 (1832–1907, Shebbear, Devon).

The Primitive Methodists

Primitive Methodist Minutes (James Bourne, Bemersley. After 1851, by Thomas Holliday, Primitive Methodist Conference Office and Book Room, London) 1819–1860.

Consolidated Minutes (1949).

Primitive Methodist Leader (1907).

Primitive Methodist Magazine (Bemersley. Vol. 25, etc., London) 1820–3; 1837; 1801; 1907.

The Wesleyan Methodists

Conference Agenda (Wesleyan Conference Office, City Road, London) 1923/79; 1924/401–2; 1925/383–6; 1926/70–4, 469–72; 1927/395–7; 1928/89–90; 1929/83–5; 1931/431–2; 1932/317–18.

Minutes of the Methodist Conferences, from the First, held in London, by the Late Rev. John Wesley, AM, in the Year 1744 (Conference Office, 14 City Road, London).

The Methodist Recorder (now at 122 Golden Lane, London EC1).

24 July 1924, 16, 'Women and the Ministry'.

30 July 1925, 8, 'Women and the Ministry'.

22 July 1926, 13, 14, 'Women and the Ministry'.

21 July 1927, 16, 'Women and the Ministry'.

7 June 1928, 5, 'At Ilkley – Without a Hat. The Deaconesses in Conference'.

14 June 1928, 4, 'Women's Work and the Deaconess Order'.

26 July 1928, 15, 16, 'Women and the Ministry'.

25 July 1929, 18, 'Women and the Ministry'.

23 July 1931, 11, 13, 'Women and the Ministry'.

Methodist Magazine (Methodist Publishing House, City Road, London) 1809; 1819.

(From 1932 Uniting Conference) The Methodist Church

Conference Agenda (CA.) 1933/541–3; 1934/563–4; 1938/489–90; 1939/85–8, 539–42; 1940/14; 1944/37–8; 1945/122, 315–16; 1946/73–6, 325–8; 1947/7, 156; 1948/9, 143; 1960/302–11; 1961/13–29; 1962/132; 1963/93–5, 563; 1964/542, 604; 1965/594; 1966/611–12; 1970/257–62; 1971/23, 87; 1972/'Provisional Legislation', 'General Purposes Committee'; 1973/13 (Methodist Publishing House, London)

Minutes of the Annual Conference of the Methodist Church held in London July 1933, 98–9, 287, 438–40; 1934/102, 249; 1937/82; 1938/80; 1939/96, 248; 1940/205; 1944/50, 153; 1945/50, 152; 1946/57, 163; 1947/54, 164; 1948/50, 162; 1970/78; 1971/11; 1973/12; 1978/29 (Methodist Publishing House, London).

Minutes of the Uniting Conference held in London, September 20th-23rd, 1932 (1932, London).

The Daily Record 1933/15; 1939/81; 1945/46; 1946/62; 1948/76; 1961/42; 1962/44; 1963/47; 1964/56; 1965/66; 1970/33; 1971/9 (Methodist Publishing House).

The Methodist Recorder (London).

20 July 1933, 10, 'Women and the Ministry'.

26 July 1934, 14, 15, 21, 'Women and the Ministry'; 24, Editorial – 'Women and the Ministry'.

22 July 1937, 21, 'Women and the Ministry'.

26 July 1938, 8, 'Women and the Ministry'.

27 July 1939, 20, 21, 'Women and the Ministry'.

26 July 1945, 12, 'Women and the Ministry'.

25 July 1946, 11, 13, 'Women and the Ministry'.

22 July 1948, 8, 9, 'Women and the Ministry'.

13 April 1961, 10, 11, 'A Woman's Place – the Changing Pattern'.

13 July 1961, 15, 'Ministry of Women'; 'Women in the Ministry'; 'Varied Nature of Deaconess Service'.

22 February 1962, 3, 'Women for the Ministry'.

19 April 1962, 7, '"Illogical" on Women in the Ministry'.

25 July 1963, 4, '"Women": The Debate Must Go On'.

14 July 1966, 8, 'Decisive Vote on Women and the Ministry: Pauline Webb's Amendment Wins the Day'; 10, 11, 'Women and the Ministry'.

9 July 1970, 15, 16, '"Yes" to Women in Ministry'.

29 April 1971, 5, 'They Want to be "the Rev. Sister"'.

17 June 1971, 12 'Women in the Ministry'.

20 April 1972, 4, 'Deaconesses Challenged by Implications of Ministry'; 9; 'More from the Deaconesses'.

29 June 1972, 11, 'Church Ready for Women Priests'.

20 July 1972, 6, 'Practical Problems of Women in the Ministry'.
3 May 1973, 6, 'Deaconesses Offer for the Ministry'.
Wesley Deaconess Order: 'Report of the Working Party on the Nature of the W.D.O., Recruitment, Training and Ordination' (Oct. 1976) xerox of internal document.
'Report of the Committee on Lay Orders in the Methodist Church' (1980) xerox of internal document.
Doers of the Word (magazine of the Wesley Deaconess Order) Dec. 1966; Autumn 1972.
A Way of Serving (magazine of the Wesley Deaconess Order) Autumn 1973–8.

ROMAN CATHOLIC MATERIAL

Centralised Documentation

Casti Connubii, signed by Leo XIII on 31 December 1930 (1931); Catholic Truth Society (Pamphlet Do 113), London).
The Documents of Vatican II See Abbott (1966).
'Report of Pontifical Biblical Commission'. (1976) In *Origins* 6 (1 July), 92–6. Reprinted in Stuhlmueller (1978) 226–35.
'Declaration on the Question of the Admission of Women to the Ministerial Priesthood' (1977) 1st edn 1976. *Briefing* 7: 5 (29 January).
L'Osservatore Romano (see also under authors in Bibliography of References): 20 January 1977, 5, 10; 10 February 1977, 6, 7; 17 February 1977, 6, 7; 24 February 1977, 6, 7; 3 March 1977, 3, 4; 10 March 1977, 6, 7; 17 March 1977, 6, 7; 12 May 1977, 6, 7; 2 March 1978, 5–8, 12.
Mulieris Dignitatem (1988, Catholic Truth Society, London).

English Documentation

'Ninth National Conference of Priests. Newman College, Birmingham. 4–8 September 1978' (1978). Being *Briefing* 8: 31 (22 September), 39 (now at Gabriel Publications, 33–9 Bowling Green Lane, London EC1R 0AB).
Congress Contact (1980) Newspaper for delegates to the National Pastoral Congress, 1–6 (Feb.; April; 3, 4, 5, 6 May).
Diocese of Westminster: Report to the National Pastoral Congress: Liverpool, May 1980 (1979).
'Pastoral Congress Statement on Sex Teaching' (1980) in *The Times* (6 May) 14.
'Sector G – Topics 1–5' (1980) In *National Pastoral Congress Topic Reports* 36–43 (xerox).
'Congress Reports' (1980) In *Universe* (9 May) 3–4, 29–30.

The Easter People (1980) A message from the Roman Catholic bishops of England and Wales in the light of the National Pastoral Congress, Liverpool 1980 (St Paul Publications, Slough).

'Archdiocese of Westminster: Report of the Follow-up Meeting of the National Pastoral Congress (held on 21.3.81 in Islington parish)' (1981) (xerox).

'Council of Diocesan Affairs: Minutes of the Meeting held at Hare Street on Monday and Tuesday 11th and 12th May, 1981' (1981) (xerox of extract 2.2: Decisions 1–23).

'Why Can't a Woman be More Like a Man?' (1983) A document prepared by a working party of the Laity Commission. Published to accompany *Briefing* 13: 1 (14 Jan) (Catholic Information Office).

'Laity Commission's Final Report' (1983) Accompanied *Briefing* 13: 40 (16 Dec.) (Catholic Information Office).

International Commission on English in the Liturgy (ICEL)

'Minutes of Discriminatory Language Subcommittee Meeting. March 5–6, 1977' (1977) (xerox from ICEL, 1275 K Street NW, Suite 1202, Washington DC 20005–4097).

'Discriminatory (Sexist) Language: A Summary of ICEL's Response to this question' (1979) in *ICEL Newsletter* 6: 4 (Oct.–Dec.).

'Ordination of Priests' (1980) Being *ICEL Newsletter* 7: 1 (Jan.–March).

Eucharistic Prayers (1980) For study and comment by the bishops of the member and associate countries of ICEL. (Also known as 'Green Book'.)

The Language of the Liturgy: Some Theoretical and Practical Implications (1984) Occasional paper (ICEL).

Women's Ordination Conference related material

Priests for Equality Charter (1975, PFE, PO Box 5243 West Hyattsville, MD 20782).

National Catholic Reporter 10 and 17 November 1978.

New Women, New Church (from July to Sept. 1978) 1: 3, *passim*. Newspaper of Women's Ordination Conference (WOC), PO Box 2693, Fairfax, VA 22031.

WORLD COUNCIL OF CHURCHES MATERIAL

Concerning the Ordination of Women. (1964) WCC Studies No. 7 (WCC, Geneva).

The Deaconess: A Service of Women in the World of Today (1966) WCC Studies No. 4 (WCC, Geneva).

What is Ordination Coming to? (1971, WCC, Geneva).

Study on the Community of Women and Men in the Church (1978) A joint program of The Faith and Order Commission and The Sub-Unit on Women in Church and Society (WCC, PO Box 66, 150 route de Ferney, 1211 Geneva 20, Switzerland).

ANGLICAN CATHOLIC CHURCH, USA

The Affirmation of St Louis (1977) (xerox sent by Dorothy A. Faber of Foundation for Christian Theology and *The Christian Challenge*).

The Christian Challenge Nov. 1976 (PO Box 9871, Austin, TX 78766).

PROTESTANT EPISCOPAL CHURCH IN THE USA

'Church and Minorities – Women' (n.d.) Being pp. 261–76 of *Church and Society*, produced by the Episcopal Church, 815 Second Ave, New York, NY 10017 (xerox sent by A. E. Harvey of the Sherrill Resource Center).

Journal of the General Convention of the Protestant Episcopal Church in the USA (General Convention) 1889/108–9, 134; 1892/242, 287, 379; 1901/47–9; 1904/64; 1919/139; 1922/91, 155, 674–82; 1925/335, 599–605; 1928/41; 1931/64, 227; 1934/199, 482–6; 1937/228, 423; 1940/270, 422–3; 1943/363; 1946/394; 1949/129–33, 234, 389–91; 1955/207; 1964/247–8; 1965/B7–8; 1967/26–9, 74, 265, 406, 519, A23–5, B50 35.4–35.12; 1970/60, 102, 158–9, 175, 249, 270–1, 532–9, 769–70, 800; 1973/101–2, 125, 216, 1064, 1108, 1114–32; 1974/B192–209; 1976/69, B54–8, B120–4, B130, B145–8, C50, D66–8, D132.

The Witness 25 Aug. 1974; Nov. 1976; July 1979 (see also under authors in Bibliography of references).

Women in Priesthood (1976) A pamphlet issued by the National Committee of the Episcopal Clergy and Laity for the Ordination of Women to the Priesthood (xerox of extract – two lists outlining events prior to the General Convention of 1976, from Sherrill Resource Center).

THE METHODIST CHURCH IN THE USA

Methodist Episcopal Church

The Doctrines and Discipline of the Methodist Episcopal Church (1888) 207–12.

General Minutes and Year Book for 1939–40. Minutes of the Annual Conference of the Methodist Episcopal Church, South, for 1939, 353.

Judicial Decisions of the General Conference of the Methodist Episcopal Church (1903), ed. R.J. Cooke (Jennings & Graham, Cincinnati, OH) 149–51.

Journal of the General Conference of the Methodist Episcopal Church 1872/391; 1876/252, 279; 1880/262, 264, 102, 353–4; 1924/284, 317, 1697–8.

Methodist Protestant Church

I am most grateful to Ronald E. Kircher, Director, and Susan May, Historical Records Librarian, of the Library of Wesley Theological Seminary, 4400 Massachusetts Ave, Washington DC 20016, for the helpful xeroxes sent:

Constitution and Discipline of the Methodist Protestant Church (1876) 3rd edn (Wm J. C. Dalany & Co. Baltimore) 28–9.

Constitution and Discipline of the Methodist Protestant Church: Revised by the General Conference of 1880 (1880, Board of Publication of the Methodist Protestant Church, Pittsburgh, PA) 22–5, 30–1, 70–1.

Journal of the Proceedings of the General Convention of the Methodist Protestant Church held at Baltimore, May 16, 1884 (1884) 22, 43–5.

Journal of the Fifteenth Quadrennial Session of the General Conference of the Methodist Protestant Church held in Adrian, Mich., May 18–28, 1888 (1888, Board of Publication of the Methodist Protestant Church, Pittsburgh, PA) 20–1.

Journal of the Sixteenth Quadrennial Session of the General Conference of the Methodist Protestant Church, held at Westminster, MD, May 20–31, 1892 (1892, Board of Publication of the Protestant Methodist Church, Pittsburgh, PA) 20, 26, 29–32, 63–4, 113–34.

Journal of the Twentieth Quadrennial Session of the General Conference of the Methodist Protestant Church, held in the City of Pittsburgh, Pennsylvania, May 15–23, 1908 (1908, Board of Publication of the Protestant Methodist Church, Pittsburgh, PA) 35–8, 100–4.

Minutes of the Fifty-First Session of the New York Annual Conference of the Methodist Protestant Church, held at Tarrytown, New York, October 6–13, 1880 (1880, Sunnyside Printing Company, Scarborough, NY) 4–6.

Minutes of the New York Conference of the Methodist Protestant Church (fifty-fifth session) held in the Canarsie M.P. Church, October 3rd to 9th, 1884 (1884, F. P. Cosper, Pittston, PA) 6–7, 17, 19, 20.

Methodist Church

Daily Christian Advocate (DCA) 1 May 1940/219; 6 May 1948/252, 299; 29 April 1952/220; 25 April 1956/3; 3 May 1960/246 (Methodist Publishing House, various locations).

Discipline of the Methodist Church 1940/para. 292; 1944/318; 1956/303, 562.

Decisions of the Judicial Council of the Methodist Church. Nos 1–255, Years 1940–68 (1968, Methodist Publishing House, Nashville, TN) 276, 277, 365.

Doctrines and Discipline of the Methodist Church (1956, Methodist Publishing House, Nashville, TN) 114–17, 165.

Journal of the Uniting Conference of the Methodist Episcopal Church, the Methodist Episcopal Church, South, and the Methodist Protestant Church. 26.4–10.5.1939 (1939) 266, 509.

Journal of the First (1944, 1952) General Conference of the Methodist Church 1940/330–1, 592; 1944/670; 1952/783.

United Methodist Church

Journal of the 1968 (1970, 1976) General Conference of the United Methodist Church 1968/1430–4; 1970/652, 586; 1976/257–8, 332.

'Proposed Legislation to 1980 General Conference from Committee to Study Diaconal Ministry' (internal document sent by Rosalie Betzinger of the Board of Higher Education and Ministry, United Methodist Church, PO Box 871, 1001 19th Ave, South Nashville, TN 37202).

'Proposed Legislation to 1980 General Conference from Division of Diaconal Ministry, Board of Higher Education and Ministry' (Internal document from the Board of Higher Education and Ministry).

Proposed Legislation: 'Diaconal Ministry Proposals to the 1980 General Conference'. A parallel illustration of the two entries immediately above (internal document from the Board of Higher Education and Ministry).

'A Theological Interpretation of Diaconal Ministry for the United Methodist Church' by the Committee to Study Diaconal Ministry (internal document from the Board of Higher Education and Ministry).

BIBLIOGRAPHY OF REFERENCES

Abbott, Walter M., ed. (1966) *The Documents of Vatican II* translation ed. Joseph Gallagher (Geoffrey Chapman, Corpus Books, New York).

Allchin, A. M. (1958) *The Silent Rebellion: Anglican Religious Communities 1845–1900* (SCM, London).

Ashton, John (1972) *Why Were the Gospels Written?* (Mercier Press, Cork & Dublin).

(1975) 'Tradition and Authority in Hermeneutical Theory' (xerox of article subsequently published in *Semeia* 4).

Austen, Jane (1942) *Emma*, 1st edn 1815 (Macmillan, London).

(1985) *Pride and Prejudice*, 1st edn 1813 (Penguin, Harmondworth).

Balthasar, Hans Urs von (1977) 'The Uninterrupted Tradition of the Church', 3rd in series in *L'Osservatore Romano* (24 Feb.) 6, 7.

Beckerlegge, Oliver A. (1955–6) 'Women Itinerant Preachers', with reply by Wesley F. Swift, in *Proceedings of the Wesley Historical Society* 30, 182–4.

(1968) *United Methodist Ministers and their Circuits, being an Arrangement in Alphabetical Order of the Stations of Ministers of the Methodist New Connexion, Bible Christians, Arminian Methodists, Protestant Methodists, Wesleyan Methodist Association, Wesleyan Reformers, United Methodist Free Churches and the Methodist Church 1797–1932* (Epworth, London).

Bernardin, Joseph L. (1977) 'The Ministerial Priesthood and the Advancement of Women', 4th in series in *L'Osservatore Romano* (3 March) 3, 4.

Bleicher, Josef (1980) *Contemporary Hermeneutics: Hermeneutics as Method, Philosophy and Critique* (Routledge & Kegan Paul, London).

Bonner, Dismas (1978) 'Church Law and the Prohibition to Ordain Women', in Stuhlmueller 71–83.

Boulding, Elise (1976) *The Underside of History: A View of Women Through Time* (Westview Press, CO).

Bourne, F. W. (1905) *The Bible Christians: Their Origin and History 1815–1900* (Bible Christian Book Room, 26 Paternoster Row, London EC).

Bourne, Hugh (1808) 'Remarks on the Ministry of Women', reprinted in Walford (1855) 172–7.

Bouyer, Louis (1977) 'Women Priests', in *L'Osservatore Romano* (20 Jan.) 5, 10.

Brailsford, Mabel Richmond (1915) *Quaker Women 1650–1690* (Duckworth).

Braithwaite, William C. (1955) *The Beginnings of Quakerism* 2nd edn (Cambridge University Press).

(1961) *Second Period of Quakerism* 2nd edn (Cambridge University Press).

Breuer, Josef (1974) 'Fraulein Anna O.' 1st edn 1895, *PFL* 3, 73–102.

Brockett, Lorna, & Howard, Christian (1979) 'The Ordination of Women', in *One in Christ* 15:1, 40–56.

Brown, Raymond E. (1979) *The Community of the Beloved Disciple* (Geoffrey Chapman, London).

Brown, Raymond E., *et al.*, eds. (1978) *Mary in the New Testament* (Fortress Press, Philadelphia, & Paulist Press, New York).

Burke, Emery Stevens, ed. (1964) *The History of American Methodism* vol. 2 (Abingdon Press, New York).

Cady Stanton, Elizabeth (1985) *The Woman's Bible*, 1st edn 1895, 1898 (Polygon Books, Edinburgh).

Carey, John (1978) 'American Women Threaten Mass Ban', in *Catholic Herald* (17 Nov.).

Carroll, Berenice A., ed. (1976) *Liberating Women's History: Theoretical and Critical Essays* (University of Illinois Press, Urbana).

Chadwick, Henry (1967) *The Early Church* (Penguin, Harmondsworth).

Chardin, Teilhard de (1965) *The Phenomenon of Man* (Fontana, London).

Chasseguet-Smirgel, Janine (1976) 'Freud and Female Sexuality. The Consideration of some Blind Spots in the Exploration of the "Dark Continent"' in *IJPA* 57, 275–86.

Chicago, Judy (1980) *Embroidering Our Heritage: The Dinner Party* (Anchor, Doubleday, Garden City, New York).

(1980) *Embroidery Our Heritage: The Dinner Party Needlework* (Anchor, Doubleday, Garden City, New York).

Chodorow, Nancy (1978) *The Reproduction of Mothering: Psychoanalysis and the Sociology of Gender* (University of California Press).

Christ, Carol P., & Plaskow, Judith, eds. (1979) *Womanspirit Rising: A Feminist Reader in Religion* (Harper & Row, New York).

Church, Leslie F. (1949) *More about the Early Methodist People* (Epworth Press, London).

Code of Canon Law in English Translation (1983, Collins, London).

Coward, Rosalind (1980) 'On the Universality of the Oedipus Complex: Debates on Sexual Divisions in Psychoanalysis and Anthropology', in *Critique of Anthropology* 15: 4, 5–28.

Cragg, Gerald R. (1970) *The Church and the Age of Reason 1648–1789* (Penguin, Harmondsworth).

Crockford's Clerical Directory 1985/6 (1985), 1st edn. 1858 (Church Publishing House, London).

Cross, F. L., & Livingstone, E. A., eds. (1978 (1974 edn reprinted with corrections)) *The Oxford Dictionary of the Christian Church* (Oxford University Press).

Cupitt, Don (1985) *Crisis of Moral Authority* (SCM, London).

Davies, Margaret Llewelyn (1978) *Maternity Letters from Working Women* (Virago, London).

Delmar, Rosalind (1976) 'Looking again at Engels' *Origin of the Family, Private Property and the State*', in Anne Oakley and Juliet Mitchell, eds. *The Rights and Wrongs of Women* (Penguin, Harmondsworth).

Descamps, Albert (1977) 'Significance for us Today of Christ's Attitude and of the Practice of the Apostles', 2nd in series in *L'Osservatore Romano* (17 Feb.) 6, 7.

Dinnerstein, Dorothy (1976) *The Rocking of the Cradle, and the Ruling of the World* (Souvenir Press, London).

Douglas, J. D. ed. (1974) *The New International Dictionary of the Christian Church* (Paternoster Press, Exeter).

Earle, Clifford (1970) 'The Response of the Church to the Movement for Women's Rights', unpublished study paper held at Presbyterian historical society, 425 Lombard Street, Philadelphia, PA 19147.

Engels, Frederick (1972) *The Origin of the Family, Private Property and the State* (Lawrence & Wishart, London).

Fell, Margaret (1710) 'Women's Speaking Justified, Proved and Allowed of by the Scriptures, All such as speak by the Spirit and Power of the Lord Jesus. And how Women were the first that Preached the Tidings of the Resurrection of Jesus, and were Sent by Christ's own Command, before he Ascended to the Father, John 20.17.' , in *A Brief Collection of the Remarkable Passages and Occurrences relating to the Birth, Education, Life, Conversion, Travels, Services and deep Sufferings of that Ancient, Eminent and Faithful Servant of the Lord Margaret Fell But by her Second Marriage Margaret Fox* (J. Sowle) 331–50.

Field-Bibb, Jacqueline (1989) 'From *The Church* to *Wickedary*: The Theology and Philosophy of Mary Daly', in *Modern Churchman* 30: 4, 35–41.

(1989) 'By Any Other Name: The Issue of Inclusive Language', in *Modern Churchman* 31: 2, 5–9.

(1990) 'Women and Ministry: The Presbyterian Church of England', in *Heythrop Journal* 31: 2, 150–64.

First, Ruth & Scott, Ann (1980) *Olive Schreiner* (Deutsch, London).

Fletcher, Sheila (1989) *Maude Royden* (Basil Blackwell, Oxford).

Foucault, Michel (1978) *The History of Sexuality. Volume 1: An Introduction* (Penguin, Harmondsworth).

Foy, Felician A., ed. (1979) *1980 Catholic Almanack* (Our Sunday Visitor Inc., IN).

Freud, Sigmund (1973–), *PFL* 15 vols., Penguin, Harmondsworth. 1953 *SE* 24 vols., Hogarth Press and the Institute of Psychoanalysis, London).

(1895) with Brewer, J. *Studies in Hysteria* (*PFL*3; *SE* 2).

(1900) *The Interpretation of Dreams* (*PFL* 4; *SE* 4–5).

(1901) *The Psychopathology of Everyday Life* (*PFL* 5; *SE* 6).

(1905c) *Jokes and their Relation to the Unconscious* (*PFL* 6; *SE* 8).

(1905d) *Three Essays on the Theory of Sexuality (PFL* 7, 33–169; *SE* 7).

(1905e (1901)) 'Fragment of an Analysis of a Case of Hysteria' (*PFL* 8, 29–164: *SE* 7).

(1907) 'The Sexual Enlightenment of Children' (PFL 7, 171–81; *SE* 9).

(1908) 'On the Sexual Theories of Children' (*PFL* 7, 183–204; *SE* 9).

(1909) 'Analysis of a Phobia in a Five-Year-Old Boy' (*PFL* 8 165–305; *SE* 10).

(1910) 'A Special Type of Choice of Object made by Men' (*PFL* 7, 227–42; *SE* 11).

(1912–13) *Totem and Taboo* (*PFL* 13, 43–224; *SE* 13).

(1915e) 'The Unconscious' (*PFL* 11, 159–222; *SE* 14).

(1915f) 'A Case of Paranoia Running Counter to the Psycho-Analytic Theory of the Disease' (*PFL* 10, 145–58; *SE* 14).

(1918) 'The Taboo of Virginity' (*PFL* 7, 261–83; *SE* 11).

(1920) 'The Psychogenesis of a Case of Female Homosexuality in a Woman' (*PFL* 9, 367–400; *SE* 18).

(1921) *Group Psychology and the Analysis of the Ego* (*PFL* 12, 91–178; *SE* 18).

(1923b) *The Ego and the Id* (*PFL* 11, 339–407; *SE* 19).

(1923e) 'The Infantile Genital Organisation' (*PFL* 7, 303–12; *SE* 19).

(1925) 'Some Psychical Consequences of the Anatomical Distinction between the Sexes' (*PFL* 7, 323–43; *SE* 19).

(1927) *The Future of an Illusion* (*PFL* 12, 179–243; *SE* 21).

(1930) *Civilization and its Discontents* (*PFL* 12, 243–340; *SE* 21).

(1931) 'Female Sexuality' (*PFL* 7, 367–92; *SE* 21).

(1933) 'Femininity', in *New Introductory Lectures on Psycho-Analysis* (*PFL* 2, 145–69; *SE* 22).

(1939) *Moses and Monotheism* (*PFL* 13, 237–386; *SE* 23).

Fuller, Peter (1975) 'A Chat of Analysts', in *New Society* (31 July) 237–8.

Gager, G. (1975) *Kingdom and Community: The Social World of Early Christianity* (Prentice Hall, NJ).

Garlick's Methodist Registry (1983, Edsall, London).

Gavron, Hannah (1968) *The Captive Wife: Conflicts of Housebound Mothers* (Penguin, Harmondsworth).

Gheerbrant, Alain (1974) *The Rebel Church in Latin America* (Penguin, Harmondsworth).

Girard, René (1977) *Violence and the Sacred*, trans. Patrick Gregory (Johns Hopkins University Press, Baltimore & London).

Goldmann, Lucien (1967) 'The Thought of the Enlightenment', in *Annales* 22: 4 (July/Aug.) 752–9.

Gorer, Geoffrey (1962) 'The Myth in Jane Austen', in Wilbur S. Scott, ed. *Five Approaches of Literary Criticism* (Collier Macmillan, New York & London).

Guardian Churches Correspondent (1979) 'Catholic Women who want Female Priests', in *Guardian* (1 May) 3.

Habermas, Jürgen (1974) *Theory and Practice*, trans. John Viertel (Heinemann, London).

Hale, Harry, King, Morton & Jones, Doris Moreland (1980) *New Witnesses: United Methodist Clergywomen* (Board of Higher Education and Ministry, Nashville, TN).

Haller, J. S. & R. M. (1974) *The Physician and Sexuality in Victorian America* (University of Illinois Press).

Hasler, August Bernard (1981) *How the Pope Became Infallible: Pius IX and the Politics of Persuasion*, trans. Peter Heinegg (Doubleday, Garden City, New York).

Hennecke, E. (1963, Vol. 1; 1965, vol. 2.) *New Testament Apocrypha*, ed. W. Schneemelcher, English trans. and ed. R. McL. Wilson (Lutterworth Press, London).

Herod, George (1854) *Biographical Sketches of some of those Preachers of the Primitive Methodist Connexion* (T. King, London).

Hewitt, Emily C., & Hiatt, Suzanne R. (1973) *Women Priests – Yes or No* (Seabury, New York).

Hirsch, Eric Donald (1967) *Validity in Interpretation* (Yale University Press, New Haven and London).

Hobsbawm, E. J. (1957) 'Methodism and the Threat of Revolution', in *History Today* (Feb.) 115–24.

Hornsby-Smith, Michael P., & Cordingley, Elizabeth S. (1983) *Catholic Elites: A Study of the Delegates to the National Pastoral Congress*, Studies in English Catholicism No. 1 (Department of Sociology, University of Surrey).

Hyer, Marjorie (1978) 'Catholic Women's Move for Reform goes beyond Ordination', in *Washington Post* (13 Nov.).

Isichei, Elizabeth (1970) *Victorian Quakers* (Oxford University Press).

Jeffreys, Sheila (1982) '"Free from all Uninvited Touch of Man": Women's Campaigns around Sexuality, 1880–1914', in *Women's Studies International Forum* 5: 6, 629–45.

Jones, Ernest (1947) 'The Problem of Hamlet and the Oedipus Complex', in *Hamlet. With a Psycho-Analytical Study* (Vision Press, London).

(1953) *Sigmund Freud: Life and Work*, 3 vols. (Hogarth Press, London).

Jones, Rufus M. (1921) *The Later Periods of Quakerism*, Vol. 1 (Macmillan, London).

Judge, E. A. (1960) *The Social Pattern of the Christian Groups in the First*

Century: Some Prolegomena to the Study of New Testament Ideas of Social Obligation (Tyndale Press, London).

Keifer, Ralph A. (1978) 'The Priest as "Another Christ" in Liturgical Prayer', in Stuhlmueller (1978) 103–10.

Kroll, Una (1975) *Flesh of My Flesh* (Darton, Longman & Todd, London).

Kung, Hans (1971) *Infallible? An Enquiry*, trans. Eric Mosbacher (Fount/ Collins, London).

Laplanche, Jean, & Pontalis, J.-B. (1983) *The Language of Psycho-Analysis*, trans. Donald Nicholson-Smith (Hogarth Press and Institute of Psycho-Analysis, London).

Leach, Robert J. (1979) *Women Ministers: A Quaker Contribution*, ed. Ruth Blattenberger. No. 227 of Pendle Hill Publications, Wallingford, PA, 19086.

Lecky, William Edward Hartpole (1869) *History of European Morals from Augustus to Charlemagne*, 2 vols. (London).

Ligier, Louis (1978) 'The Question of Admitting Women to the Ministerial Priesthood', in *L'Osservatore Romano* (2 March) 5–8, 12.

Lorber, Judith, Coser, Rose Laub, Rossi, Alice S., & Chodorow, Nancy (1981) 'On *Reproduction of Mothering*: A Methodological Debate', in *Signs* 6: 3, 482–514.

Mack, Phyllis (1982) 'Women as Prophets during the English Civil War', in *Feminist Studies* 8: 1 (spring 1982), 19–45.

Martelet, Gustave (1977) 'The Mystery of the Covenant and its Connections with the Nature of the Ministerial Priesthood', 5th in series in *L'Osservatore Romano* (17 March) 6, 7.

Martimort, A. G. (1977) 'The Value of a Theological Formula "*in Persona Christi*"', in *L'Osservatore Romano* (10 March) 6, 7.

Martin, David, Mills, John Orme, & Pickering, W. S. F., eds. (1980) *Sociology and Theology: Alliance and Conflict* (Harvester Press, Brighton).

Marx, Karl, & Engels, Frederick (1969) *The Manifesto of the Communist Party*, 1st edn 1848 (Progress Publishers, Moscow).

Mascall, Eric Lionel (1958) *Women and the Priesthood of the Church* (Church Union, London).

Meltzer, Donald (1978) *The Kleinian Development*, 3 vols. (Clunie Press, Perthshire).

Metz, Johann Baptist (1980) *Faith in History and Society: Toward a Practical Fundamental Theology*, trans. David Smith (Burns & Oates, London).

Mill, John Stuart (1929) *The Subjection of Women* in Wollstonecraft (1929).

Mitchell, Juliet, & Rose, Jacqueline, eds. (1982) *Feminine Sexuality: Jacques Lacan and the Ecole Freudienne* (Macmillan, London).

Moltmann, Jürgen (1976) *The Crucified God: The Cross of Christ as the Foundation and Criticism of Christian Theology*, trans. from German by R. A. Wilson and John Bowden (SCM, London).

Montefiore, Bishop Hugh (1978) *Yes to Women Priests* (Mayhew-McCrimmon, Essex, & Mowbray, Oxford).

Moore, Peter, ed. (1978) *Man, Woman, and Priesthood* (SPCK, London).

Morris, Joan (1973) *Against Nature and God: The History of Women with Clerical Ordination and the Jurisdiction of Bishops* (Mowbrays, London).

Müller, Josine (1932) 'A Contribution to the Problem of the Libidinal Development of the Genital Phase in Girls', in *IJPA* 13, 361–8.

Neusner, Jacob, ed. (1975) *Christianity, Judaism and Other Greco-Roman Cults: Studies for Morton Smith at Sixty*, 4 vols. (Brill, Leiden).

New Catholic Encyclopedia (1967, vols. 1–15; 1974, Supplement vol. 16) (McGraw Hill, NY, & Publishers Guild Inc., in association with McGraw Hill, Washington & NY).

Noll, William T. (1977) 'Women as Clergy and Laity', in *Methodist History* (Jan.) 107–17. USA publication.

Palmer, Richard E. (1969) *Hermeneutics: Interpretation Theory in Schleiermacher, Dilthey, Heidegger, and Gadamer* (Northwestern University Press, Evanston).

Papa, Mary (1978) 'Women Set Siege on Male Bastions', in *National Catholic Reporter* (10 Nov.).

(1978) 'Bishops Shun Women's Ordination Conference', in *National Catholic Reporter* (17 Nov.).

Perrin, Norman (1970) *What is Redaction Criticism?* (Fortress Press, Philadelphia).

Phinney, William R. (1969) *Maggie Newton Van Cott: First Woman Licensed to Preach in the Methodist Episcopal Church* (Commission on Archives and History, New York Annual Conference, United Methodist Church).

Pius XI, Pope (1931) *Christian Marriage – Casti Connubii* (Catholic Truth Society Pamphlet D.113, 38–40 Eccleston Square, London SW1).

Pyke, Richard (1915) *The Golden Chain: The Story of the Bible Christian Methodists . . . from 1815 to . . . 1907 . . .* (Farring Library).

(1941) *The Early Bible Christians*, Wesley Historical Society Lectures 7 (Epworth, London).

Raming, Ida (1976) *The Exclusion of Women from the Priesthood: Divine Law or Sex Discrimination?*, trans. Norman R. Adams (Scarecrow Press, Metuchen, NJ).

Ratzinger, Joseph (1977) 'The Male Priesthood: A Violation of Women's Rights?', 7th in series in *L'Osservatore Romano* (12 May) 6, 7.

Ricoeur, Paul (1970) *Freud and Philosophy: An Essay on Interpretation*, trans. Denis Savage (Yale University Press, New Haven & London).

(1974) *The Conflict of Interpretations: Essays in Hermeneutics*, ed. Don Inde (Northwestern University Press, Evanston).

Ruether, Rosemary Radford, ed. (1974) *Religion and Sexism: Images of Women in the Jewish and Christian Traditions* (Simon & Schuster, New York).

(1977) *Mary – The Feminine Face of the Church* (Westminster Press, Philadelphia).

Sayers, Janet (1982) 'Psychoanalysis and Personal Politics', in *Feminist Review* 10, 91–5.

Schillebeeckx, Edward (1981) *Ministry: A Case for Change*, trans. John Bowden (SCM, London).

(1985) *The Church with a Human Face: A New and Expanded Theology of Ministry* (SCM, London).

Schüssler Fiorenza, Elisabeth (1963) 'Grundlagen, Tatsachen und Möglichkeiten der beruflichen Mitarbeit der Frau in der Heilssorge der Kirche', Licentiate thesis; published as *Der vergessene Partner* (Patmos, Düsseldorf, 1964).

(1972) *Priester für Gott, Studien zum Herrschafts- und Priester motiv in der Apokalypse* (NTA NF 71; Aschendorff, Münster).

(1983) *In Memory of Her: A Feminist Theological Reconstruction of Christian Origins* (SCM, London).

(1984) *Bread Not Stone: The Challenge of Feminist Biblical Interpretation* (Beacon Press, Boston).

Scott, Ann (1983) 'Who's a Freud of Virginia Woolf?', in *Health Services* (3 June) 16.

Sedwell, Richard (1841) 'Memoir of Jane Gardener', in *Bible Christian Magazine*, 227–59.

Seymour, Alice (1909) *The Express ('My Express Must Fly'. The Spirit of Truth). As foretold one hundred years ago, to be published by the hand of a woman in the tenth year of the century; and containing the Life and Divine Writings of the late Joanna Southcott*, 2 vols. (Simpkin, Marshall, Hamilton, Kent & Co. Ltd., London).

Southcott, Joanna (1804) *Copies and Parts of Copies of Letters and Communications, Written from Joanna Southcott and Transmitted by Miss Towney to Mr W. Sharp in London* (printed by S. Rousseau).

Spender, Dale, ed. (1983) *Feminist Theorists: Three Centuries of Women's Intellectual Traditions* (Women's Press, London).

Spiazzi, Raimondo (1977) 'The Advancement of Women according to the Church', 1st in series in *L'Osservatore Romano* (10 Feb.) 6, 7.

Stephenson, Alan M. G. (1978) *Anglicanism and the Lambeth Conferences* (SPCK, London).

Strachey, Ray (1978) *The Cause: A Short History of the Women's Movement in Great Britain* (Virago, London).

Strousse, Jean (1981) *Alice James* (Jonathan Cape, London).

Stuhlmueller, Carroll, ed. (1978) *Women and Priesthood: Future Directions* (Liturgical Press, Collegeville, MN).

Swift, Wesley F. (1951–2) 'The Women Itinerant Preachers of Early Methodism', in *Proceedings of the Wesley Historical Society* 28, 89–94.

(1953–4) 'The Women Itinerant Preachers of Early Methodism' (ctd) in *Proceedings* 29, 76–83.

Sykes, Stephen Whitefield (1978) *The Integrity of Anglicanism* (Mowbrays, London).

Szasz, Thomas (1973) *The Manufacture of Madness: A Comparative Study of the Inquisition and the Mental Health Movement* (Paladin, Frogmore).

Taft, Zachariah (1825, vol. 1; 1828, vol. 2) *Biographical Sketches of the Lives and Public Ministry of Various Holy Women, whose eminent usefulness and successful labours in the Church of Christ Have entitled them to be enrolled among the great benefactors of mankind; in which are included several Letters from the Rev. J. Wesley, never before published* (H. Cullingworth, Leeds).

Tawney, Richard Henry (1938) *Religion and the Rise of Capitalism* (Penguin, West Drayton).

Taylor, Barbara (1978) 'The Woman-Power: Religious Heresy and Feminism in Early English Socialism', in Susan Lipshitz, ed. *Tearing the Veil: Essays on Femininity* (Routledge & Kegan Paul, London).

(1981) 'Female Vice and Feminist Virtue', in *New Statesman* (23 Jan.).

(1983) *Eve and the New Jerusalem: Socialism and Feminism in the Nineteenth Century* (Virago, London).

Thackeray, William Makepeace (n.d.) *Vanity Fair: A Novel Without a Hero*, ed. George Saintsbury. 1st edn in book-form 1848 (Oxford University Press).

Theissen, Gerd (1978) *The First Followers of Jesus* (SCM, London).

Thomas, Keith (1958) 'Women in the Civil War Sects', in *Past and Present* 13, 42–62.

Thompson, E. P. (1968) *The Making of the English Working Class* (Penguin, Harmondsworth).

Thorne, J. (1865) *A Jubilee Memorial of the Incidents in the Rise and Progress of the Bible Christian Connexion* (Shebbear, Devon).

Trible, Phyllis (1979) 'Eve and Adam: Genesis 2–3 Reread', in Christ & Plaskow (1979).

Turner, Denys (1983) *Marxism and Christianity* (Basil Blackwell, Oxford).

Valenze, Deborah (1982) 'Pilgrims and Progress in Nineteenth-Century England', in Raphael Samuel & Gareth Stedman Jones, eds. *Culture, Ideology and Politics* (Routledge & Kegan Paul, London).

Van der Kleij, Gregory (1980) 'Symbol and Horizon', unpublished manuscript, Turvey Abbey Library, Bedfordshire.

(1982) 'About the Matrix', in *Group Analysis* 15: 3 (Dec.), 219–34.

Vidler, Alec R. (1974) *The Church in an Age of Revolution: 1789 to the Present Day* (Penguin, Harmondsworth).

Walford, John (1855) *Memoirs of the Life and Labours of the Late Venerable Hugh Bourne*, Vol. 1 (T. King, London).

Walkowitz, Judith R. (1982a) 'Male Vice and Feminist Virtue: Feminism and the Politics of Prostitution in Nineteenth-Century Britain', in *History Workshop Journal* 13, 79–93.

(1982b) *Prostitution and Victorian Society: Women, Class, and the State* (Cambridge University Press).

Ware, Kallistos (1978) 'Man, Woman, and the Priesthood of Christ', in Moore, ed. (1978).

Weber, Max (1985) *The Protestant Ethic and the Spirit of Capitalism*, trans. Talcott Parsons (Unwin Paperbacks, London).

Weeks, Jeffrey (1981) *Sex, Politics and Society: The Regulation of Sexuality since 1800* (Longman, London).

Wesley, John (1931) *The Letters of the Rev. John Wesley, A. M.*, ed. John Telford. Standard Edition, 8 vols. (Epworth Press, London).

Whitehorn, Constance M. (1958) *Women's Share in the Life and Work of the Church with special reference to English Presbyterianism* (Presbyterian Historical Society, 86 Tavistock Place, London).

Wijngaards, John (1977) *Did Christ Rule Out Women Priests?* (Mayhew-McCrimmon, Great Wakering).

Willoughby, William F. (1978) 'New Pressure on US Catholic Bishops', in *Washington Post* (13 Nov.).

Winter, Michael M. (1985) *Whatever Happened to Vatican II?* (Sheed & Ward, London).

Wollstonecraft, Mary (1929) *A Vindication of the Rights of Woman*, 1st edn 1792 (Dent, London) (contains Mill (1929)).

Yarnold, Edward (1981) Review of *Ministry* by Edward Schillebeeckx, in *Tablet* (18/25 April).

INDEX

[b]	Bible Christian	[r]	Roman Catholic
[e]	Church of England	[w]	Wesleyan
[m]	Methodist (from 1932)	[date]	of first speech in this book

Indexing of people by name or/and title follows usage in the relevant debate or document. Titles alone are followed by (date) of reference.